D1090836

TURNING POINTS
IN ENDING

THE COLD WAR

2/19/08

For Dr. & Mrs. Charpie —
With best regards

TURNING POINTS
IN ENDING

THE COLD WAR

Kiron K. Skinner

Edited by **Kiron K. Skinner**

Forewords by **Pavel Palazhchenko**
and **George P. Shultz**

HOOVER INSTITUTION PRESS
Stanford University
Stanford California

The Hoover Institution on War, Revolution and Peace, founded at Stanford University in 1919 by Herbert Hoover, who went on to become the thirty-first president of the United States, is an interdisciplinary research center for advanced study on domestic and international affairs. The views expressed in its publications are entirely those of the authors and do not necessarily reflect the views of the staff, officers, or Board of Overseers of the Hoover Institution.

www.hoover.org

Hoover Institution Press Publication No. 538

First printing, 2008
14 13 12 11 10 09 08   9 8 7 6 5 4 3 2 1

Manufactured in the United States of America

The paper used in this publication meets the minimum requirements
of the American National Standard for Information Sciences—
Permanence of Paper for Printed Library Materials, ANSI Z39.48-1992.

Library of Congress Cataloging-in-Publication Data

Turning points in ending the Cold War / edited by Kiron K. Skinner.
        p.   cm. — (Hoover Institution Press publication ; no. 538)
    Includes bibliographical references and index.
    ISBN-13: 978-0-8179-4631-9 (cloth: alk. paper)
    ISBN-13: 978-0-8179-4632-6 (pbk.: alk. paper)
    1. Cold War.   2. Soviet Union—Foreign relations—United States.
3. United States—Foreign relations—Soviet Union.   4. Soviet Union—
Foreign relations—1975–1985.   5. Soviet Union—Foreign relations—
1985–1991.   6. United States—Foreign relations—1981–1989.
I. Skinner, Kiron K.   II. Series: Hoover Institution Press publication ; 538.
D849.T893 2008
327.4707309′048—dc22   2006008247

CONTENTS

Forewords

Pavel Palazhchenko   *A Perspective from Moscow*   vii

George P. Shultz   *A Perspective from Washington*   xix

Introductory Essay

Kiron K. Skinner   *Talking Across the Cold War Divide*   1

Chapter 1

Jack F. Matlock Jr.   *The End of Détente and the Reformulation of American Strategy: 1980–1983*   11

Commentary

Alexei Arbatov   *What Lessons Learned?*   40

Chapter 2

Oleg Grinevsky   *The Crisis that Didn't Erupt: The Soviet-American Relationship, 1980–1983*   63

Commentary

Kiron K. Skinner   *An Alternative Conception of Mutual Cooperation*   93

Chapter 3

Anatoli Cherniaev   *Gorbachev's Foreign Policy: The Concept*   111

Commentary

David Holloway   *Moving to Globalization*   141

Chapter 4

Georgi I. Mirski   *Soviet-American Relations in the
                            Third World*   149

Commentary

Peter W. Rodman   *Reversal of Fortune?*   182

Chapter 5

Robert L. Hutchings   *Europe Between the Superpowers*   191

Commentary

Karen Brutents   *Europe Between the Superpowers:
                            A Soviet Perspective*   218

Chapter 6

Philip Zelikow and
    Condoleezza Rice   *German Unification*   229

Commentary

Vladislav Zubok   *German Unification from the Soviet
                            (Russian) Perspective*   255

Chapter 7

Michael McFaul   *Boris Yeltsin: Catalyst for the Cold
                            War's End*   273

Commentary

Nikolai Petrov   *Boris Yeltsin: Catalyst for the
                            Cold War's End?*   306

Contributors   327

Acknowledgments   333

Index   335

FOREWORD

Pavel Palazhchenko : *A Perspective*
: *from Moscow*

THERE IS LITTLE DOUBT that the
period we call the cold war, including the way it was waged and the
manner in which it ended, will attract the keen interest of historians for many decades to come. It was a unique and unprecedented
era in that the threat of a major conflict, very likely involving the
use of nuclear weapons, was real, or was at least clear and present
in the minds of those who ducked under tables during civil defense
alerts and lived through the terror of the Cuban missile crisis.
There is much that needs to be clarified and understood about the
cold war's origins and causes. For example, a question that deserves
serious consideration is whether the cold war was inevitable because of the nature of the Soviet regime or whether it could have
been avoided with a different interpretation of the doctrine of containment. Perhaps of even greater interest is the question of why
the cold war ended and whether other scenarios of its end were
possible. Though the unique circumstances that brought about the
cold war are unlikely to be repeated, it would be hard to deny the
importance of considering such questions and thereby learning lessons for the future.

Debates about the cold war and the way it ended are inevitably
clouded by the politics of the day. In Russia, the collapse of the
hopes of the intelligentsia, who had expected radical changes following the breakup of the Soviet Union to result in almost over-
night prosperity and a major role for Russia in a new world order,
has led many to question the disengagement from the cold war.
The Russian press is rife with writings accusing Mikhail Gorbachev

and his foreign minister, Eduard Shevardnadze, of having betrayed Russia's national interests, even though Russia as a separate entity under international law did not exist on their watch. In the United States during the administration of the first President Bush, the general consensus of welcoming the peaceful end of the cold war was soon replaced by the celebration of the West's—and most particularly America's—victory in the cold war. This, in turn, reinforced the feelings of inferiority and injury felt by many members of the Russian establishment, feelings that are not conducive to a sensible debate either about the past or about Russia's present foreign policy.

Depoliticizing the study of the cold war would only benefit the discussion, and although it may not be possible in current media debates, one would hope that historians would at least strive for this goal. Something else would also help: we should bear in mind that the notion of the cold war is, after all, a metaphor that captures the confrontational aspect of that period but is not, and cannot be, its full and accurate description. Much of the inaccurate and unhelpful loose talk about the cold war and its end is, in fact, the result of either unfamiliarity with the facts and the documentary record or taking the metaphor too literally. It was not, after all, a war. In fact, preventing war was perhaps the essence of that period and was of greater importance and concern to its protagonists than preparing for war or winning the various battles or skirmishes, whether in propaganda or geopolitics, that occupied so much space in the press of that time. War prevention as a substantive aspect of the cold war has only recently begun to receive sufficient attention from historians.

Contributions to the cold war's historical record by former Soviet and U.S. officials who were active during the various phases of that era are invaluable. Much credit is due to the conferences, books, and oral history interviews that aim to develop the factual basis for further study and debate. An example is the recent Cuban missile crisis conference held in Havana and attended by former U.S., Soviet, and Cuban political and military officials. We can be grateful for the efforts to make available documents from the cold war years from both the U.S. and the Russian sides, yet it is unlikely that a large body of such material will soon become accessible to historians. A more realistic possibility is that participants in the making and implementation of policies on both sides will speak and write about their recollections, as some of them do in the present book. As a Russian, I only regret that such literature is being published more in the United States than in my own country, but in any case, the fact that a significant body of evidence is gradually emerging is positive and welcome. Much of what follows in this foreword is based on my recollections of the events that I witnessed and participated in from 1985 to 1991 and then recorded in *My Years with Gorbachev and Shevardnadze*, published in the United States in 1997.

The phrase "turning points," as used in the title of this book, is another metaphor. Though it has often served to describe the events surrounding the end of the cold war, perhaps an even better metaphor would be "going forward," for it is this relentless movement away from the past that stands out as we recall that era. There was not so much a turn in a particular direction, for the direction stayed basically the same, as a refusal to go back despite frequent temptations to do so.

Since it is often asserted, particularly in Russia, that the West alone benefited from the end of the cold war, it would be useful to consider the benefits that accrued to the Soviet Union and its successor states by first taking a look at the international position that Gorbachev inherited from his predecessors. In the early 1980s, the Soviet Union was saddled with an astounding range of foreign policy problems. It found itself in a situation that could almost be described as "us against the world." Its relations were confrontational with the United States; tense, at best, with Europe; and downright hostile with China. The unsuccessful war in Afghanistan was having a destructive effect on both the domestic situation and relations with the West and much of the rest of the world. The country was bogged down in several regional conflicts in third world nations with little hope of extricating itself from them. The USSR had no real friends, and the Soviet elite knew only too well that the Warsaw Pact countries could not be regarded as reliable allies. The Soviet Union's negotiating position in arms control talks reflected a sense of isolation, insecurity, and pervasive hostility. In the INF talks, for example, the Soviet delegation initially asked to be allowed the same number of weapons as all its potential adversaries put together.

By mid-1991, the Soviet Union had worked out its relations with both the West and China. The arms buildup had been stopped, and two treaties, INF and START, calling for real and deep cuts in nuclear weapons had been signed. Steps had been taken toward the Soviet Union's acceptance by and eventual admission to the Group of Seven industrialized nations. The Charter of Paris proclaimed a Europe without dividing lines. Gorbachev's visit to China, in the words of Deng Xiaoping, closed the book on the past and opened the future. Soviet troops had left Afghanistan, and conflicts in Cambodia, Central America, and Angola were being defused. Iraq's invasion of Kuwait had been rejected and reversed, with the United States and the Soviet Union taking a stand against the aggression and working through the United Nations to put an end to it. Finally, and perhaps most importantly, the changes in Central and Eastern Europe benefited the Soviet Union by ending an unsustainable relationship in a peaceful manner without the burden of long-term bad blood.

As Henry Kissinger said to Gorbachev in Moscow in February 1992, "As a result of your policies, Russia is more secure than ever before." This is important to bear in mind since Gorbachev's critics assumed that his policies had the opposite effect.

The years from 1985 to 1991 can be divided into two distinct periods in international politics. Each period saw changes in the direction of ending the ideological, political, and military confrontations between East and West and the Soviet Union's reintegration into the world community, but the pace of this process was relatively slow during the first period and extremely fast during the second, which began in early 1989. The quickening of the pace was the result of internal developments in the Soviet Union and Central Europe that could be controlled, in my view, only by sacrificing the process of change itself and turning back. Gorbachev bore the brunt of decision making at that time; had he yielded to the temptation to reverse course, history would have taken a different and, most likely, a much more dangerous path.

Working with Gorbachev and Shevardnadze during those years, I recall the difference in the psychological makeup and the political agendas of the two periods. During the first three years (1985–1988), there was a feeling that history had given us sufficient time to disengage from confrontation and build a sound basis for new international relations. This was a time when Gorbachev engaged the West on arms reduction and proposed the adoption of "the new thinking," a set of non-ideological, commonsense, international law–based principles in which he profoundly believed. During the second period, there was a feeling that events were running ahead of the Soviet Union and, increasingly, that the best thing to do was manage change and assure its peaceful character without prejudging the outcome. It was a humbling experience, but I believe that the new thinking greatly facilitated the Soviet Union's adaptation to and acceptance of both the pace of change and its eventual outcome.

The new thinking was based, above all, on the understanding that much of the old, ideology-driven agenda of international relations had become obsolete. The words "the new thinking" had been used before, of course, and the substance of the concept was not totally new. Indeed, in the early 1980s, the Palme Commission had presaged many tenets of the new thinking such as, for example, the concept of common security as opposed to security at the expense of others. And in his essay, Oleg Grinevsky reviews Kremlin decisions and events in the early 1980s that provided background conditions for the new thinking in the Gorbachev era. Nevertheless, the Soviet Union under Gorbachev was the first state to declare and elaborate these principles, setting in motion a major revision of, and shift in, the international agenda. As David Holloway points out in his perceptive essay, the new thinking "provided a vision of the Soviet Union's place in the world that reassured the Soviet public as well as foreign leaders and publics. It thereby exercised a calming influence on the process of change."

In addition to the influence of the new thinking in facilitating change in the nature of international relations was the conscious application of the human factor by the leading protagonists of the end of the cold war. While recognizing the role of Margaret Thatcher, François Mitterrand, and Helmut Kohl, I believe most of the credit should go to Mikhail Gorbachev and Ronald Reagan. During their interaction from 1985 to 1989, I could see them persevere to build a personal rapport. They regarded this rapport as an important political goal despite Gorbachev's "dogmatic Communist heritage," as noted in Anatoli Cherniaev's essay, and Reagan's strong ideological views about the Soviet Union as an evil empire.

Unlike their predecessors, Reagan and Gorbachev did not allow inevitable setbacks, such as the death of U.S. Army Major Arthur Nicholson, killed by a sentry at a Soviet military base in the GDR, or the arrest of U.S. reporter Nicholas Daniloff in response to the arrest of Soviet UN official Gennadi Zakharov in New York, to distract them from the pursuit of their goal. Many fascinating details of the relationship between the two leaders, and much of what was happening behind the scenes, are described by Ambassador Jack Matlock both in this book and in his other writings.

To add to the recollections and accounts contained in this volume, I first saw Ronald Reagan in person in September 1985 when I was interpreting at his White House meeting with Eduard Shevardnadze. From that first encounter, he struck me as a warm and forthcoming person anxious to engage and even please his guest. The reason, in retrospect, seems to be that Reagan, though deeply conservative, was not dogmatic or aggressive. The view of Ronald Reagan presented in Kiron Skinner's essay is consistent with my impression. This is what Gorbachev has often emphasized in his recollections of Reagan, including his interesting letter on the occasion of the ceremony at which Ronald Reagan was awarded the Congressional Medal of Honor. He wrote, "While adhering to his convictions, with which one might agree or disagree, Ronald Reagan was not dogmatic. He was ready to negotiate and cooperate. That is what enabled us together to take the first steps toward ending the Cold War."

For both Reagan and Gorbachev, intuition played an important role in shaping their attitudes and actions. Of particular interest in this regard is the remark Mitterrand made to Gorbachev in the summer of 1986, quoted by Cherniaev: "Reagan is among those leaders who intuitively want to put an end to the existing status quo." I think intuition made Reagan support the inclusion, in the final communiqué of the Geneva summit in 1985, of the phrase, "Nuclear war cannot be won and must never be fought," although at least the first part of it contradicted the views of some of his advisers. Gorbachev is usually regarded as a politician for whom instincts were less important, but I believe that without trusting his instincts he would not have been able to accomplish as much as he did.

Another important factor in building his rapport with Reagan and other Western leaders was Gorbachev's healthy respect for people elected through a democratic process. I remember how, in Geneva, when one of his advisers began to over-eagerly criticize Reagan, Gorbachev said rather curtly that Reagan was the elected president of the United States and we had to deal with him.

The relationship between the two men was, of course, often bumpy, but it was always respectful and equal. I must disagree with the assertion by some Russian scholars, such as Dr. Anatoli Utkin of the Institute of U.S. and Canada Studies, and Vladislav Zubok, in this book, that Soviet leaders developed some kind of psychological dependence on their U.S. counterparts and therefore became almost subservient to them. My view is also held by my U.S. Department of State colleagues with whom I shared interpretation duties.

Trust was the product of both human rapport and the new political direction, and it gradually became a significant factor in U.S.-Soviet relations. Surprisingly to some observers, the idea of trust has now been revived in the relationship between George W. Bush and Vladimir Putin, and both presidents have encountered some criticism for being naïve in this regard. But trust is not the same as blind faith. While the latter is something no statesman can afford, the former is indispensable to relations between civilized nations.

The new thinking in the Soviet Union, reciprocated by the West's willingness to engage and negotiate, and the gradually emerging trust in relations between the leaders of the great powers, set the stage for a new relationship between the world's major power centers. In this new context, many of the things that seemed all-important at the height of the cold war gradually lost their value. This devaluation was related to the importance of ideology in international relations, third world alliances, and the value of the nuclear arsenals conceived and built in a confrontational environment.

In his essay, Professor Georgi Mirski recalls a conference at the Soviet Ministry of Foreign Affairs in 1987, convened at Shevardnadze's initiative in order to hear from non-MFA thinkers on foreign policy issues. It was an eye-opener for many in the ministry and was one of the first times that the concept of de-ideologizing international relations was discussed openly and favorably. In such a context, the struggle for influence in the third world no longer appeared to many in the Soviet foreign policy establishment as the "moral as well as . . . strategic opportunity" that it was for much of the cold war, as Peter Rodman writes in his essay. Working in the Soviet foreign ministry, I witnessed this "third world fatigue" and the declining interest in third world influence among officials at all levels in the second half of the 1980s. The Soviet Union made a serious effort to resolve or disengage from the conflicts in the third world, and, as Rodman points out, the Reagan and Bush administrations accepted Gorbachev's good faith and sought negotiated outcomes to the conflicts then raging in various parts of the world.

It is clear that no country, and certainly not the Soviet Union, could bear indefinitely the burden of the geopolitical obligations assumed under Stalin, Khrushchev, and Brezhnev. The Soviet Union's withdrawal from Afghanistan may be seen as a good, though by no means perfect, example of the art of letting go with dignity. In hindsight, a more cooperative attitude on the part of the United States both in the negotiating process and in the post-withdrawal period would have served the best interests of everyone. When the United States showed little interest in such cooperation, Gorbachev suggested to Secretary of State James Baker in May 1989, "Perhaps we should let the Afghans stew in their own juices for some time." Later, however, Afghanistan's fate was left largely in the hands of Pakistan's military intelligence service, a course chosen by two U.S. administrations with well-known consequences. The lesson to be learned from this is that neglecting the third world agenda may be dangerous.

Of even greater importance than the disengagement from regional conflicts was the decline in the importance of the superpowers' nuclear arsenals. Indeed, as Robert Hutchings observes in his essay, "The vast U.S. and Soviet nuclear arsenals" were becoming "increasingly irrelevant" even "to the realities of the late cold war," and certainly, one might add, to the post–cold war environment that both sides were looking forward to at that time. The negotiations on arms control produced two seminal agreements that are still in effect: the INF and START treaties. Even this achievement, however, is often disputed today in Russia, for reasons that are described cogently by Alexei Arbatov in his commentary on Jack Matlock's essay. In fact, however, the two treaties constitute a legacy that Russia has found to be fully consistent with its best interests; it successfully insisted on the reaffirmation of the START I treaty in the nuclear disarmament agreements concluded by Presidents George W. Bush and Vladimir Putin in May 2002.

The story of the arms control negotiations has been told many times, with little disagreement among serious scholars as to its main turning points and achievements. I would note in this regard a statement by George Shultz that has received far less attention than it deserves. At a conference at Princeton University in 1993, Shultz expressed regret that, mostly because of the resistance of hard-liners within the U.S. administration, it had proved impossible to sign the START treaty in 1988. The fact remains that the agreements achieved by Gorbachev, Reagan, and Bush, including the unprecedented exchange of letters between Presidents Bush and Gorbachev on the elimination of many of the two countries' shorter-range nuclear weapons, were equitable and beneficial.

It may be argued that Europe was the centerpiece and the focus of the process that led to the end of the cold war. The most dramatic and potentially the most explosive developments in Europe at the time were taking place in Germany. The leaders who had to manage that process are often accused of lacking foresight and failing to anticipate events. It is questionable whether the kind of prescience that the critics seem to call for was possible. The essay by Philip Zelikow and Condoleezza Rice contains numerous excerpts from statements by Soviet, U.S., and European leaders that make it clear that no one expected German unification to happen as fast as it did. This includes the amazing comment made in December 1989 by Helmut Kohl on Henry Kissinger's supposition that East and West Germany might unite within two years: "This [is] obviously impossible." In any case, it is doubtful that a better forecast would have done much good. What mattered more was the attitude of the main players toward the prospect of German unification. The material provided by Zelikow and Rice is consistent with my own impressions at the time based on what I heard during talks on the issue and discussions among Soviet leaders.

Margaret Thatcher manifested herself as most suspicious of a unified Germany and she was viscerally antagonistic to the prospect of unification. During a meeting with Shevardnadze in London in November 1989, she did not bother to disguise that antagonism. I recall her expression of barely suppressed fury combined with resignation. Certainly neither during that meeting nor, to my knowledge, in subsequent discussions and communications with Soviet leaders did she propose any measures capable of slowing down the process. Rather, she seemed to be trying to probe the depth of the Soviet leaders' apprehensions about German unity and their willingness and ability to act against it. It appears from what we know now that Mitterrand's attitude was similar to Thatcher's, though perhaps less furious. Yet my conversations with French diplomats in Moscow and my familiarity with diplomatic cables from Paris suggest that, having no plan to counteract the process, Mitterrand rather quickly resigned himself to the outcome.

The pivotal factor in speeding up German unification was the explosive expression of the Germans' desire for it. Zelikow and Rice emphasize the "judicious splashes of gasoline" applied by Kohl and Bush "instead of . . . a fire extinguisher." Yet the breakdown of public order in the GDR began in December 1989 when Bush's position, as expressed at a NATO meeting, still left open the possibility of a slow process with an uncertain outcome: "We should not at this time endorse nor exclude any particular vision of unity." My impression, from some of Bush's remarks made at Malta and even later, was that he might have preferred a slower process. Yet, once the people of East Germany began to show their ability to impose their will, all leaders had to adjust, and a more welcoming attitude was only natural for Kohl and for Bush, as the Western world's leader.

As for the attitude of the Soviet leaders, I recall no expressions of panic, either about the prospect of German unification itself or about the domestic consequences of it in the Soviet Union. It is notable that although experts on German affairs in the foreign ministry and the Communist Party Central Committee called for maximum possible resistance to unification, a poll commissioned by the Ministry of Foreign Affairs in 1990 indicated a generally positive attitude toward a united Germany among all strata of the population including, surprisingly, the military. Credit for the general acceptance of unification should be given to the Russian people, who both then and later showed themselves to be much more level-headed and realistic than many members of the Russian elite, and to Gorbachev, whose calming influence played an important role. In subsequent conversations, Gorbachev confirmed to me that at no point in the process was the use of force to prevent unification proposed as a possible course of action either by himself, by other members of the Soviet leadership, or by the military.

The study of the history of the cold war and the events that brought it to a peaceful end will continue to produce new factual material and new interpretations of the actions and motives of the main players. In order to better understand what happened and why, historians may both question the wisdom of the decisions taken by the leaders and speculate on various "what if" and "what might have been" scenarios. In fairness, however, they should try to put themselves in the shoes of the decision makers who had to contend with forces often beyond their control in an environment changing at a breathtaking pace. The counterfactual points proposed for consideration mean little if they reflect policy options not even contemplated at the time. Contributors to this volume give priority to the deep mining of facts, thus making this book a valuable resource for readers and historians alike.

George P. Shultz : *A Perspective*
from Washington

THE COLD WAR had many turning
points, none more compelling than those of the 1980s. The decade
started with the war as cold as it could be and ended with the cold
war over. These essays illuminate the process, and the authors have
the advantage of experience, depth of observation, and historical
perspective. They confirm that no one factor can explain what took
place.

The essays offer stimulating viewpoints, and, although they differ in many respects, they are similar in one interesting way. All are
rich in ideas and full of references to key individuals. The predominant names are Ronald Reagan and Mikhail Gorbachev, but the
roles of other prominent individuals in ending the cold war are also
discussed. Philip Zelikow and Condoleezza Rice examine the policies of George H. W. Bush, Helmut Kohl, François Mitterrand, and
Margaret Thatcher. Oleg Grinevsky investigates Yuri Andropov's
contribution to the transformation of Soviet foreign policy in the
early 1980s. Nikolai Petrov analyzes Boris Yeltsin's rise to power,
and, in another essay on Yeltsin, Michael McFaul begins with a concisely stated key point: "Individuals matter."

My perspective is dominated by my experiences in the 1980s,
particularly my close association with President Ronald Reagan
and my frequent meetings with General Secretary Gorbachev and
his foreign minister, Eduard Shevardnadze. I had the advantage of
having met with top Soviet leaders relatively often in the 1970s, including encounters with General Secretary Leonid Brezhnev and
Premier Alexei Kosygin, and I had many meetings with Foreign

Minister Andrei Gromyko when I was secretary of state. These contacts gave me the perspective that comes from contrast.

So I will talk about a few ideas as they relate to my time as secretary of state and to the people I knew best. In doing so, I endorse another statement in McFaul's essay: Ideas also matter. This premise is at the heart of the essays by Anatoli Cherniaev and David Holloway, both of whom examine how Gorbachev's embrace of the ideas of human dignity and universal values influenced the Soviet system and, in turn, the whole world.

One powerful but too often overlooked idea is that strength and diplomacy go together. They are not alternatives, as is often implied. Rather, when done right, they are complementary. President Reagan believed in the importance of being strong, not only in military terms but also in our economy and self-confidence. He nourished strength but he never forgot about diplomacy. He loved negotiations, and he and I would exchange stories drawn from our common experiences in the arena of labor relations.

Many of President Reagan's supporters were all for strength but they distrusted any effort to negotiate with leaders of the Soviet Union. By contrast, I found that Ronald Reagan was self-confident and ready to negotiate whenever appropriate. I also recalled a statement made to me as I entered office by my good friend Helmut Schmidt, who was then chancellor of West Germany. He said, "The situation is dangerous; there is no human contact." I resolved to do something about the problem and started weekly meetings with Soviet ambassador Anatoli Dobrynin.

In early 1983, the U.S. economy was recovering, with inflation coming under control, and our military capacity was on the rise, although neither was at a satisfactory level. By chance, a snowstorm kept the Reagans in Washington one winter weekend and my wife and I were invited to supper with the president and Nancy. As our conversation unfolded, I could see how ready the president was to talk with Soviet leaders, so I suggested that I bring Ambassador Dobrynin over to see him the following Tuesday, February 15, when the ambassador was to arrive at my office for our regular weekly meeting. The president welcomed the idea and said the meeting would be short because all he wanted to say was, "If your new leader [Andropov] is ready for a constructive dialogue, so am I."

The meeting lasted much longer than expected and touched all the bases. I could see that Dobrynin was surprised that President Reagan was so well informed and so strong in his convictions. The president dwelt on human rights and identified the two Pentecostal families who had been living in our embassy in Moscow for several years as a virtual statement of the problem. His message was that if the Soviet Union allowed these families to emigrate and worship as they chose, he would not say a word. As Dobrynin and I rode back to my office, he suggested that we make that a project. A statement emerged with language that was far looser than we had wanted, but Dobrynin well understood our full intent. In the end, we persuaded the Pentecostals to leave the embassy, and they were allowed to emigrate with all their family members about three months later. The agreement was: We'll let them out if you don't crow. President Reagan never crowed. I had to believe that the Soviet leaders were impressed that President Reagan was a man of his word, able to resist the political temptation to crow, and he was therefore a good person with whom to negotiate. So President Reagan's first deal with the Soviets was a human rights agreement realized against the background of improving strength.

President Reagan inherited the idea of linkage; that is, what happens on one front affects what happens on other fronts. The idea of linkage was vividly on display when President Jimmy Carter cut nearly all relations with the Soviets after they invaded Afghanistan. He was surprised, and he reacted: the United States boycotted the Moscow Olympics, withdrew the second strategic arms control treaty from consideration by Congress, and canceled Foreign Minister Gromyko's annual visit to Washington, D.C., during the UN General Assembly meeting, among other actions.

President Reagan would not be constrained by linkage. Dramatically, in the wake of the brutal shoot-down of a Korean airliner by

a Soviet fighter pilot on September 1, 1983, and the resulting turmoil, President Reagan sent me, against a lot of linkage-type advice, to what turned out to be a stormy meeting with Gromyko.
But we met, and I let him know how deeply we detested their
deadly strike against a 747 aircraft that was clearly a passenger
plane. Even more dramatically, the president sent our arms negotiators back to Geneva.

So linkage is a powerful idea, but a president need not be its
slave. And President Reagan knew that strength and diplomacy in
tandem is a better idea. He used his diplomacy—consulting with
allies, bargaining skillfully and visibly with the Soviets—at a time
when clear resolve was necessary to gain the deployment of U.S.
nuclear missiles in England, Italy, and especially in West Germany
in late 1983. That deployment, in turn, showed the strength and
cohesion of the NATO countries, a strength that would soon lead
to the series of negotiations that changed the world scene dramatically. Jack F. Matlock Jr. and Kiron Skinner investigate the Reagan
administration's deliberations and policies that made the strategy
of strength possible. Alexei Arbatov and Oleg Grinevsky provide
insightful analyses of both the Soviet response to that strategy and
the evolution of Soviet foreign policy during those years.

I was part of the U.S. delegation attending the funeral of General
Secretary Konstantin Chernenko in March of 1985. Our delegation
had a long meeting with Chernenko's successor, Mikhail Gorbachev, whom none of us had met before. Because Vice President
Bush served as the head of our delegation, I had the luxury of making limited comments and observing Gorbachev carefully. In front
of him was a pile of notes. He shuffled them around but never
bothered to look at them. He was in complete intellectual control
of a wide range of issues. He enjoyed the give-and-take. You could
feel his energy and intensity even at the end of what must have been
an exhausting period for him. Having observed other Soviet leaders, I could say with confidence that this new leader would be a
formidable adversary, but he clearly liked ideas and was ready for
vigorous conversation. This individual would matter.

The first meeting between Ronald Reagan and Mikhail Gorbachev took place in Geneva in November 1985. Early on, Ambassador Dobrynin came to my office ready to start negotiations on a communiqué that would emerge from the meeting. I had unexpected news for him: President Reagan looked forward to meeting General Secretary Gorbachev, and he thought that whatever was reported afterward should reflect what they had talked about, not what the staff agreed upon in advance. Dobrynin was baffled and uneasy, but I told him that, based on my exposure to Gorbachev, I thought he might like this approach. This unscripted meeting turned out to be extraordinarily productive. The two leaders were in charge of the meeting, and the joint statement issued afterward was a good one, although we struggled all night to produce it. The big fact was that two individuals who mattered had talked to each other at length—by themselves and in large groups. They had taken each other's measure and decided that progress could be made.

I recall meeting with Gorbachev after we both had left office. He came to my house on the Stanford campus and we sat in the backyard talking over what had taken place and where the world was going. I said to him, "When you and I entered office, the cold war was about as cold as it could get, and when we left, it was basically over. What do you think was the turning point?" He did not hesitate. "Reykjavik," he said. My mind went back to that little room in Hofdi House where Ronald Reagan and I sat for two days with Mikhail Gorbachev and Eduard Shevardnadze. We talked about every conceivable aspect of our relationship, including crises in the third world, many of which Georgi Mirski and Peter Rodman thoughtfully analyze in their essays.

The basic agreement to eliminate intermediate-range nuclear weapons took place at Reykjavik, as did the agreement to reduce strategic arms by half to equal levels with a satisfactory counting rule for bombers, and a formal agreement that human rights would be a recognized part of our agenda. I also remember how it all broke up. The Soviet proposal to, in effect, stop the effort to develop a strategic missile defense system was not acceptable to

President Reagan, who had my strong support. Nevertheless, the bottom lines were on the table and would materialize. With all this in mind, I asked former president Gorbachev why he thought Reykjavik was the turning point. "Because," he said, "the leaders talked about all the important issues over an extended period." The results could not have been achieved in any other way, and in the end they led to a deepening of the personal relationship.

Then Gorbachev asked me what I thought the turning point was, and I said, "The deployment on German soil of Pershing missiles that you thought could reach Moscow." That deployment took place at the end of 1983 after intense negotiations and a bruising propaganda battle in Europe. Beyond the missiles themselves, intended to counter the threat from deployed Soviet SS-20 missiles, was the demonstration of the strength and cohesion of the NATO countries. The resolution of the issues that divided Europe for many decades, as discussed in the essays by Karen Brutents, Robert Hutchings, Condoleezza Rice, Philip Zelikow, and Vladislav Zubok, are the defining results of policies of the early 1980s that explicitly combined strength and diplomacy.

As Gorbachev and I reminisced, I thought: Strength and diplomacy go together. Gorbachev has a point and so do I, but we would not have reached the endgame without the power of sound ideas and two individuals who could act on them.

Kiron K. Skinner : *Talking Across the Cold War Divide*

THERE WERE SOUND REASONS for the apocalyptic predictions that abounded after the Soviet Union invaded Afghanistan in December 1979. In retaliation for its aggression, President Jimmy Carter imposed economic and political sanctions on the Soviet Union, increased defense spending, began a covert assistance program for Afghanistan's mujahedeen, and tabled the second Strategic Arms Limitation Treaty (SALT II), which both sides had signed after seven years of negotiations. However rocky, superpower détente had provided a respite during the cold war. Now it was over.

By 1983, U.S.-Soviet relations appeared to be in an uncontrollable free fall. That year, President Ronald Reagan dubbed the Soviet Union an "evil empire"; he announced the Strategic Defense Initiative (SDI), a massive military research and development program; and he succeeded in obtaining permission from the governments of Western European nations to deploy intermediate-range nuclear forces (INF) on their soil. The Soviet government, which had been supporting the "peace offensive" to undermine the defense policies of governments in the West, retaliated by walking out of the INF and Strategic Arms Reductions Talks. *Time* declared: "The suspensions left the superpowers for the first time in 14 years with no arms-control talks of any kind in progress and with even regular diplomatic contacts frosty."[1]

Yet, as these events were unfolding, "the first successful negotia-

---

1. "Men of the Year," *Time*, January 2, 1984.

tion with the Soviets in the Reagan administration" was taking place.[2] Throughout the first half of 1983, Reagan and General Secretary Yuri Andropov privately negotiated the release of two Soviet Pentecostal families who had taken refuge in the U.S. embassy in Moscow four years earlier. The families had sought asylum from religious persecution as well as safe transport out of the Soviet Union in order to practice their faith freely. The release of the Pentecostals served to encourage bilateral contact on other issues, as reflected in the correspondence between Reagan and Andropov in the summer of 1983 about their mutual desire to eliminate the nuclear threat and advance the cause of peace.[3]

Unprecedented improvements in bilateral relations took place in the years that followed. In 1985, Reagan and Mikhail Gorbachev, the new Soviet leader, held their first summit and jointly declared, "The sides, having discussed key security issues, and conscious of the special responsibility of the USSR and the U.S. for maintaining peace, have agreed that a nuclear war cannot be won and must never be fought." While in Moscow three years later, Reagan was asked whether he still considered the Soviet Union an evil empire. He replied, "I was talking about another time, another era." A few months later, Prime Minister Margaret Thatcher proclaimed, "We're not in a Cold War now."[4] Between 1988 and 1991, revolutions spread throughout Eastern Europe as the Warsaw Pact nations embraced democracy. And at the conclusion of the December 1989 shipboard summit at Malta between President George H. W.

---

2. George P. Shultz, *Turmoil and Triumph: My Years as Secretary of State* (New York: Charles Scribner's Sons, 1993), 171.

3. Reagan's July 1983 letter to Andropov, which he wrote by hand, is reproduced in Kiron K. Skinner, Annelise Anderson, and Martin Anderson, eds., *Reagan, A Life in Letters* (New York: Free Press, 2003), 742–743.

4. The U.S.-Soviet communiqué covering the Reagan-Gorbachev summit of November 19–21, 1985, is reprinted in the *New York Times*, November 22, 1985. For Reagan's statement, see Russell Watson with Thomas M. DeFrank, John Barry, Robert B. Cullen, Joyce Barnathan, and Steve Strasser, "Reagan's 'Moscow Spring,'" *Newsweek*, June 13, 1988, 16. Thatcher's statement is found in Don Oberdorfer, "Thatcher Says Cold War Has Come to an End; Briton Calls for Support of Gorbachev," *Washington Post*, November 18, 1988, A1.

Bush and General Secretary Gorbachev, the Soviet leader declared that "many things that were characteristic of the cold war should be abandoned, also the stake on force, the arms race, mistrust, psychological and ideological struggle, and all that. All that should be things of the past."[5] In response to Saddam Hussein's invasion of Kuwait, the Soviet Union joined an international coalition that quickly forced Hussein to retreat in January 1991. On December 25 of the same year, the Union of Soviet Socialist Republics was dissolved, and the newly constituted Russian Soviet Federative Socialist Republic was renamed the Russian Federation.

These historic events defied widespread expectations. The renewed cold war briefly turned colder, but it did not produce a freeze. In fact, bipolarity gave way to a most interesting transformation of the international system; one side abandoned its adversarial role and joined the other in a broad community of free states. Why and how did this happen? Many experts expected the cold war to end with a nuclear war. Why were they proved wrong? And, what, exactly, defines the end of the cold war?

Scholars and statesmen have debated these questions for many years and will undoubtedly continue to do so for decades to come, but most agree on two main points: (1) there is no one answer as to why or how the cold war ended; and (2) the end of the U.S.-Soviet era was very much a process, and understanding that process is as important as the specific event that one favors. These general points of agreement provide the catalyst for this book.

In the late 1990s, Condoleezza Rice and I invited American and Russian scholars, statesmen, and policymakers to engage in candid discussions across the cold war divide about the turning points they considered central to ending the cold war. We instructed them to identify and analyze pivotal decisions, events, or policies of the final decades of the cold war, from the 1970s through the early 1990s. Those who served in government during this period were

---

5. Quoted in "Transcript of the Bush-Gorbachev News Conference in Malta," *New York Times*, December 4, 1989, A12.

asked to consult and make reference to their private records. We asked that all assessments be based on arguments and evidence rather than polemics or ideology. To encourage this type of conversation, we asked several scholars and statesmen to submit short commentaries on essays by authors from the other side of the cold war divide.

Numerous scholarly conferences have focused on emerging evidence that sheds light on what brought the cold war to a close. Transcripts of some of these meetings have been published and erudite treatises have been written about the implications of the end of the cold war for international relations theory and international history.[6] We sought to build on these studies to produce a scholarly work that systematically addresses and analyzes the end of the cold war from a comparative perspective.

Contributors to this study were interested primarily in elucidating turning points, but some included analyses of events they considered to be the most causative moments in the final years of the cold war. For instance, Philip Zelikow and Condoleezza Rice, White House officials during the administration of President George H. W. Bush, contend that German unification signified the end. Alexei Arbatov, a specialist in U.S.-Soviet relations and member of the Russian parliament (State Duma) from 1994 to 2003, maintains that it was Gorbachev's rise to power in March 1985 that triggered the end of the cold war. He asserts that the new Soviet leader and his colleagues initiated a revolution from above that was based on discarding old Communist concepts and policies. An-

---

6. For a few studies on the end of the cold war see Richard K. Herrmann, *Ending the Cold War: Interpretations, Causation, and the Study of International Relations* (New York: Palgrave Macmillan, 2004); Richard Ned Lebow, *International Relations Theory and the End of the Cold War* (New York: Columbia University Press, 1995); Gabriel Partos, *The World that Came in from the Cold* (London: Royal Institute of International Affairs, 1993); Silvio Pons and Federico Romero, *Reinterpreting the End of the Cold War: Issues, Interpretations, Periodizations* (London: Frank Cass, 2005); William C. Wohlforth, *Witness to the End of the Cold War* (Baltimore, MD: Johns Hopkins University Press, 1996); and William C. Wohlforth, ed., *Cold War Endgame: Oral History, Analysis, Debates* (University Park, PA: Pennsylvania State University Press, 2003).

other Russian specialist in U.S.-Soviet relations, Georgi Mirski, considers Gorbachev's rise to power as the general secretary of the Communist Party of the Soviet Union (CPSU) to be a watershed event. He points out that the Soviet Union's decision to withdraw from Afghanistan was initially made in a Politburo meeting during Gorbachev's first year in office. Gorbachev's genuine desire to humanize the Soviet system provided strong reinforcement for that decision.

The dynamic nature of international diplomacy is demonstrated as the authors identify unanticipated turning points on the road to the end of the cold war. Robert Hutchings, former special adviser to Secretary of State James Baker and director of European affairs at the National Security Council, contends that the Conference on Security and Cooperation in Europe process, which many American conservatives regarded with great skepticism, opened the door for trans-European social and political interaction as well as arms control proposals that undermined bipolarity.

Oleg Grinevsky, director of the Soviet foreign ministry's Middle East department in the early 1980s, provides a vivid account of the dilemmas and vulnerabilities of maintaining an extended empire in the third world, especially in the Middle East. He reveals how these challenges influenced the Soviet government to reassess its long-standing foreign policy based on expansionism.

Other contributors submit that perestroika, or economic restructuring, and the new political attitude toward foreign policy were turning points. These policies unleashed forces, unanticipated by Gorbachev, that fundamentally undermined the system that the Soviet leader had sought to reform. According to Michael McFaul, professor of Russian politics at Stanford University, a decisive moment in the unraveling of the cold war was Gorbachev's realization that political reform was necessary to break the bonds of the CPSU's *nomenklatura*, who were blocking economic reform measures. The reforms instituted by the Soviet general secretary opened the door for political contenders such as Boris Yeltsin, who eventually advanced political liberalization far beyond anything

Gorbachev had envisioned. The Soviet leader wanted to reform, not end, socialism, but McFaul notes that Yeltsin's campaign to give birth to an independent Russia raced on at an astonishing pace. In McFaul's opinion, the transformation of the international system was not fully evident until the Soviet Union ceased to exist at the end of 1991.

Karen Brutents, deputy head of the International Department of the Central Committee of the CPSU during the 1980s, holds that the false political premises about the Warsaw Pact were readily exposed when the movement toward political liberalization began within the Soviet Union. While Gorbachev presumed that such liberalization throughout the Soviet bloc would remain within acceptable boundaries, member states were moving toward a break with Communist rule.

German unification is another example of how the Soviet leader's authority was being overtaken by the very events he helped initiate. Zelikow and Rice report that Gorbachev expected change in the German Democratic Republic to occur gradually. He was thus unprepared for the onslaught of diplomatic activity that ultimately led to a unified Germany becoming a member of the North Atlantic Treaty Organization.

Yet the Soviet leader is hardly portrayed as a helpless bystander who witnessed history unfold. Anatoli Cherniaev, senior foreign policy adviser to the Soviet general secretary from 1986 to 1991, calls attention to Gorbachev's December 7, 1988, speech at the United Nations in which he deliberately renounced the international class struggle.[7] The speech represented a point of no return

---

7. In his speech before the General Assembly of the United Nations, Gorbachev said, "The new phase [of Soviet foreign policy] also requires de-ideologizing relations among states. We are not abandoning our convictions, our philosophy or traditions, nor do we urge anyone to abandon theirs. But neither do we have any intention to be hemmed in by our values. That would result in intellectual impoverishment, for it would mean rejecting a powerful source of development—the exchange of everything original that each nation has independently created. In the course of such exchange, let everyone show the advantages of their social system, way of life or values—and not just by words or propaganda, but by real deeds. That would be a fair rivalry of ideologies. But it should not be extended to

for Gorbachev. The Soviet Union had embraced a policy of mutual cooperation with the West that was far more sweeping than anything it had previously advocated, and the cold war, already in demise, would never regain its former dominance over international relations.

Gorbachev was not alone in playing a causative role in ending the cold war, according to the authors. Oleg Grinevsky and I posit that the judicious diplomacy practiced by both Andropov and Reagan prevented the dangerous course of U.S.-Soviet relations from sliding toward Armageddon in the early 1980s. And Nikolai Petrov, a Russian presidential adviser in the mid-1990s, concurs with McFaul that Boris Yeltsin was a central figure in the end of the cold war. But Petrov states that Yeltsin used democratic processes not to promote political reform but to advance his own electoral ambitions. Once in control, he turned against the very ideals that had elevated him to power.

Debate about which leader was most responsible for the cold war's end is often overshadowed by the authors' acknowledgments that many key actors took part in the strategic interactions that precipitated its conclusion. For instance, Peter Rodman, director of the Policy Planning Staff at the State Department in the mid-1980s, notes the influence of General Secretary Leonid Brezhnev. He states that the Soviet reappraisal of its expansion into the third world under the Brezhnev Doctrine stemmed from an awareness of the West's unrelenting military and political pressure, especially during the Reagan administration.

Most of those who assign great responsibility to Ronald Reagan and his presidency repudiate the victory, or cold war triumphalism, perspective frequently proffered by conservative writers.[8] Jack Matlock, U.S. ambassador to the Soviet Union from 1987 to 1991,

---

relations among states." See "Excerpts From Speech to U.N. on Major Soviet Military Cuts," *New York Times*, December 8, 1988, A16.

8. For an important challenge to cold war triumphalism, see Ellen Schrecker, ed., *Cold War Triumphalism: The Misuse of History After the Fall of Communism* (New York: New Press, 2004).

contends that Reagan had no master plan when he assumed the presidency. Instead, claims Jack Matlock, he embraced a set of axioms that guided his Soviet policy. Yet, I have unearthed original writings by Reagan that suggest that he did formulate what was, in effect, a grand strategy before taking office. These ideas and strategies were directly reflected in the core national security directives of his presidential administration. Matlock and I agree that Reagan's policies of realism, strength, and negotiation served to hasten, rather than prolong, the end of the cold war. But neither of us seeks to deny the important endgame contributions made by Soviet leaders of the 1980s and 1990s.

Alexei Arbatov offers a different appraisal. He contends that by early 1986, less than a year after he assumed the post of general secretary of the CPSU, Gorbachev was prepared for genuine improvement in bilateral relations. But Reagan's arms buildup, among other stringent policies directed at the Soviet Union, hardened the Soviet position for a final round of cold war competition.

Arbatov also presents hard-hitting analysis of recent complications in U.S.-Russia relations, placing blame on leaders and policies on both sides for what appears to be a move to reprise old cold war differences on arms control, security threats in the Middle East, and economic policy. On a related point, the analysis provided throughout this volume on the difficulty of finding a way toward mutual cooperation sometimes bears chilling resemblance to great power rivalry in the twenty-first century. Consequently, these essays offer lessons of historical caution for those studying and engaging in contemporary international relations.

Anatoli Cherniaev, who discusses how Western leaders affected General Secretary Gorbachev's policies, reinforces the view that deep interaction between the Soviet Union and the United States in the 1980s contributed to the transformation of Soviet strategy. He writes:

> Gorbachev's talks with President Reagan in Reykjavik also gave him impetus to add the issue of human rights to the new political thinking. He could feel the importance of this problem for global politics

not only at the summit meetings; it also was often raised during his numerous contacts with representatives of the Western scientific and cultural elite. Gorbachev was becoming increasingly convinced that unless changes took place in this area, it was hopeless to expect significant improvement in relations with the West and progress on the issue of disarmament. As a result, the problem of human rights soon appeared on the domestic agenda as an indispensable component of perestroika.

Thus the new level of strategic interaction between the Soviet Union and the United States initiated by Gorbachev not only led to considerable improvement of the international political climate but also brought about radical political changes within the Soviet system.

Robert Hutchings adds complexity to the political leadership narrative by analyzing Europe as the international system was changing in the 1980s. He observes that Prime Minister Thatcher desired internal political change both within the Soviet Union and throughout its bloc. But she was skeptical about the likelihood of such change, and she was concerned about its implications for the cohesiveness of the Western alliance. Her strategic analysis emboldened her to encourage the administration of President Bush to join in a coordinated Western effort to bolster Gorbachev's political initiatives. Like Britain, France was apprehensive about Gorbachev's overtures, but President François Mitterrand emerged as an important leader in the construction of a new Europe. West German officials such as Foreign Minister Hans-Dietrich Genscher moved forward with Gorbachev's policies of political openness, which were central to unifying Germany.

Analyzing German unification and its implications for the West, Zelikow and Rice portray President Bush and Secretary of State Baker as wise statesmen. On one hand, the American president's decision to support Germany's desire for unification, and especially the efforts of Prime Minister Helmut Kohl in December 1989, made it difficult for the British and French to launch a counteroffensive. On the other hand, the U.S. leaders worked to ensure that the unified German state would be a democracy and a member of NATO, thus making it a strong bulwark against the Soviet Union.

David Holloway asserts that Gorbachev's new political thinking not only liberalized Soviet foreign policy but turned international attention to the Soviet leader's precepts of universal human values. These precepts form the basis for current discussions about globalization policies. According to Holloway, this unintended consequence continues to make Gorbachev relevant in international politics.

The stimulating analyses in this volume are accompanied by the authors' recognition that, despite the significance of individual events, the end of the cold war was produced by a series of turning points, each building upon and reinforced by its predecessor. The authors further acknowledge that future historians, who will benefit from additional evidence and a broader perspective gained through time, may arrive at quite different conclusions.

. . . .

I invited George P. Shultz, U.S. secretary of state from 1982 to 1989, and Pavel Palazhchenko, Gorbachev's interpreter and one of his closest advisers, to contribute to this volume. Drawing upon recollections of their first-hand involvement in the diplomacy and negotiations that helped transform the international system, Shultz and Palazhchenko have written forewords that offer revealing glimpses across the cold war divide.

CHAPTER 1

Jack F. Matlock Jr. · *The End of Détente and the Reformulation of American Strategy: 1980–1983*

ON DECEMBER 26, 1979, a special unit controlled by the Soviet Committee on State Security, the KGB, stormed the presidential palace in Kabul, killing Prime Minister Hafizullah Amin, his family, and all who happened to be in the building at the time. It was an act of treachery as the forces were in Kabul ostensibly to protect Amin. The next day, large numbers of Soviet regular troops rolled into the country to make sure an Afghan exile under their control, Babrak Karmal, could seize the reins of the Afghan government and the ruling political party.[1] With this act, Soviet leaders plunged their country into a hopeless war and swept away the last remnants of the fraying détente that had been inaugurated with great fanfare during Richard Nixon's meeting with Leonid Brezhnev in 1972.

President Jimmy Carter reacted to the Soviet invasion of Afghanistan with a fury that at times failed to take into account the ultimate effect of his actions. He prohibited or severely limited most commercial ties with the Soviet Union. He appealed to athletes throughout the world to boycott the summer Olympic Games scheduled for Moscow in 1980. He closed the small U.S. consulate

---

1. Many accounts of what happened have been distorted by deliberate Soviet falsification. The most concise and accurate description, based on documents released after the Soviet collapse, can be found in Dmitri Volkogonov, *Sem' Vozhdei: galereia liderov SSSR* (Moscow: Novosti, 1996), 2:54–63.

in Kiev and required the USSR to withdraw its consular officers from New York. He limited educational and cultural exchanges and allowed the bilateral agreement that provided for them, which had been in force since 1956, to expire. His representatives sponsored condemnatory resolutions in the United Nations. He requested the U.S. Senate to suspend consideration of the SALT II agreement that had been submitted for ratification a few months earlier. Senior U.S. officials let journalists know that the United States would be willing to provide small arms to Afghan forces that resisted the Soviet incursion.

All of these moves were damaging to Soviet prestige, but they were not sufficient to convince the Soviet leaders that they had anything to gain from withdrawing from Afghanistan before they had accomplished their purpose. Except for the UN resolutions, none of these measures received full support from U.S. allies, who for the most part had not been consulted before the moves were announced. Most embargoes of exports simply shifted Soviet procurement to other sources. The Soviet Union needed to import large quantities of grain, and other countries were pleased to sell their products to Moscow when Washington placed limits on U.S. exports. Meanwhile, American farmers chafed at the loss of their largest foreign market.

Some sanctions, such as the attempt to boycott the Olympic Games, were one-time gestures that could have no positive effect after the event had passed. Others, such as the closure of consulates and the suspension of exchanges, were actually contrary to U.S. interests. When the handful of Soviet consular officials left New York, over 700 Soviet officials remained in that city under the auspices of the United Nations. When U.S. officials left Kiev, no resident Americans were left to observe events and maintain contacts with the Ukrainian people. Cultural and educational exchanges had been one of the few avenues open to the United States to communicate with Soviet intellectuals; by suspending them, the United States became an active partner in maintaining the iron curtain.

Any U.S. administration would have reacted vigorously to an

outrage such as the invasion of Afghanistan, but one not taken by surprise might have been more judicious in selecting the most effective means to counter it. One that paid more attention to the implications of Soviet military activities in Africa, the Near East, and the Western Hemisphere, and was willing to make clear that arms control agreements would be impossible if these activities continued, might possibly have deterred it. As it was, however, the Soviet action made Carter look both naïve (by his own admission, it was "the greatest surprise" of his life) and ineffectual, since his response did nothing to reverse, or even moderate, Soviet military action in Afghanistan or elsewhere. Following the prolonged hostage crisis in Iran, the Soviet invasion suggested a shocking loss of U.S. power.

This perception inevitably provided the Republicans with powerful ammunition during the presidential campaign. Their candidate, Ronald Reagan, long a proponent of more vigorous resistance to the Soviet threat, charged that Carter had allowed U.S. strength to decline and had failed to contain Soviet aggression. Carter countered with charges that Reagan's policies would risk war.[2] Many Americans found Reagan's arguments the more persuasive. The feeling that Carter had poorly managed U.S. relations with the Soviet Union, a feeling bolstered by the administration's inability to resolve the hostage crisis in Iran, doubtless played a role in Carter's electoral defeat.

For their part, the Soviet leaders were oblivious to the reasons for the U.S. reaction to their invasion of Afghanistan. They considered ratification of the SALT II treaty the ultimate test of U.S. intentions. When opposition developed in the U.S. Senate, it was thought to be the result of a die-hard anti-Soviet sentiment rather

---

2. For example, on September 22, 1980, Carter told an AFL-CIO convention in Los Angeles that the election "will determine . . . whether we have peace or war." Subsequently, the White House press secretary acknowledged that the charge was "obviously an overstatement," but Carter continued to suggest that the sort of policies Reagan had proposed would risk war even if this were not Reagan's intent. See *Facts on File*, September 26, 1980.

than genuine doubts about some features of the treaty. In Moscow's cynical interpretation, fumbling by the Carter administration while the treaty was before the Senate was evidence of a deliberate attempt to sabotage ratification. For example, Moscow considered the public clamor over the Soviet brigade in Cuba to be a calculated provocation to undermine ratification of the SALT II treaty.[3]

The Soviet leaders did not consult their experts on the United States before they made their decision to send troops to Afghanistan. Even if they had, it is unlikely that Soviet diplomats would have predicted the vehemence of the U.S. reaction. Senior officials such as First Deputy Foreign Minister Georgi Kornienko and Brezhnev's foreign policy aide Andrei Aleksandrov-Agentov have since written that, although they considered the invasion of Afghanistan to be a grave mistake, they doubted that the SALT II treaty would have been ratified even if the invasion had not occurred.[4] Equally pertinent, by not repeatedly warning against direct Soviet military intervention as the Soviet stake in Afghanistan grew, the Carter administration left the erroneous impression that what happened in Afghanistan was of no great importance to the United States. Therefore, the Soviet leaders considered Carter's reaction to the event both unexpected and inexplicable except in terms of a general desire to disrupt U.S.-Soviet relations.

A sharp divergence in each country's understanding of détente lay behind the emotions unleashed by the Soviet invasion of Af-

---

3. In response to an inquiry from Senator Frank Church about the presence of a Soviet brigade in Cuba, Secretary of State Cyrus Vance unwisely informed him that reports to that effect had no foundation. Subsequent examination of overhead photography, however, revealed that there was, in fact, a Soviet brigade in Cuba. U.S. intelligence agencies had not been tasked with looking for it and therefore had not reported it, but it had been there for years without U.S. objection. When Vance notified the senator of the error, the matter became a public issue because the initial assumption was that the Soviets had recently introduced these troops.

4. See Georgi Kornienko, *Kholodnaia voina: svidetel'stvo ee uchastnika* (Moscow: Mezhdunarodnye otnoshenia, 1994); and Andrei Aleksandrov-Agentov, *Ot Kollontai do Gorbacheva* (Moscow: Mezhdunarodnye otnoshenia, 1994).

ghanistan. To the Soviet leaders, détente, or *razriadka* (relaxation), was a strictly limited concept. It meant controlling the U.S.-Soviet arms race (if possible to the Soviet advantage) and not much else. It specifically excluded relaxation in the sphere of ideology, limits on the Soviet "right" to fulfill its "international duty" (supporting pro-Communist insurrections or Socialist regimes), and any "intrusion" in Soviet internal affairs, such as political pressure on behalf of human rights.

The American view was much broader. Most Americans thought that any détente worthy of the name meant relaxation across the board. President Nixon and General Secretary Brezhnev had signed a declaration of principles in 1972 that committed both sides to refrain from seeking "unilateral advantage." In American eyes, the appearance of Soviet arms, advisers, and Soviet-financed Cuban troops in hot spots in Africa and Latin America violated this agreement. Furthermore, Americans thought that the Helsinki Final Act, signed in 1975, obligated the Soviet Union to alter its practices to permit greater openness and respect for human rights. The invasion of Afghanistan seemed to be the culmination of increasingly assertive Soviet policies on taking advantage of U.S. restraint following its defeat in Vietnam. Therefore, to much of the American public, the promise of détente seemed to have been betrayed even before December 26, 1979. Reagan's charge that détente had been a "one-way street" was taken as an obvious truth.

The Soviet leaders seemed incapable of understanding the reasons for American disquiet, but, dissatisfied as they may have been with Carter's policies, they preferred him to Reagan, whom they considered a reckless right-wing ideologue. There was a general expectation in Moscow that Carter would win the 1980 election, and Reagan's victory came as a shock.

Exit Carter; Enter Reagan

Ronald Reagan's charge during his campaign that President Carter had allowed U.S. defenses to deteriorate was not mere campaign rhetoric. He genuinely believed that the United States had become too weak to negotiate effectively. Therefore, when he took office he set as his first priority a restoration of U.S. military strength. He sought an even larger defense budget than the one Carter had requested,[5] and he set about trying to improve the country's economic performance and shore up its political will.

Reagan considered the negotiating climate to be unfavorable during his first two years in office, and he took his time spelling out in detail his policies toward the Soviet Union. From the very beginning of his administration, however, he set forth several key themes that were to persist throughout his eight years in office. During his first press conference, on January 29, 1981, Reagan stated that he was in favor of negotiations to achieve "an actual reduction in the numbers of nuclear weapons" on a basis that would be verifiable. He also declared that during any negotiation one had to take into account "other things that are going on," and for that reason he believed in "linkage." He also referred to détente as having worked to the Soviets' advantage.

These themes, limited as they were, represented a departure from President Carter's approach. In proposing an actual reduction in nuclear weapons, Reagan was implicitly critical of the SALT II treaty that Carter had signed and the Vladivostok Agreement concluded by President Ford, both of which would have placed limits on the number of weapons without requiring a substantial reduction of existing arsenals. The condition that any agreement be verifiable was also intended to differentiate Reagan's approach from Carter's since Reagan had charged that the verification provi-

---

5. Carter's final defense budget request, submitted to Congress after his electoral defeat, called for a 14.2 percent increase in authorized expenditures for fiscal 1982, equivalent to an increase of 4.4 percent after allowing for inflation. He also projected annual increases of about 5 percent in subsequent years. Reagan subsequently called for an increase in the fiscal 1981 year and an inflation-adjusted increase of 7.3 percent for fiscal 1983. He projected additional increases of about 7 percent annually in subsequent years. See *Facts on File*, January 16, 1981, and March 6, 1981.

sions of SALT II were inadequate.[6] Reagan's endorsement of linkage was also an about-face in U.S. policy, for the Carter administration had considered arms control too important to be influenced by other issues.

Initially, Reagan's policy neither required nor assumed a fundamental change in the internal power structure in the Soviet Union. Secretary of State Alexander Haig, who spoke in greater detail than Reagan on U.S.-Soviet relations, emphasized that it was not necessary for the Soviet Union to change internally "for East and West to manage their affairs in more constructive ways."[7] He stressed that the U.S. goal was "to demonstrate to the Soviet Union that aggressive and violent behavior will threaten Moscow's own interests" and added that "only the U.S. has the power to persuade the Soviet leaders that improved relations with us serve Soviet as well as American interests."[8]

Both Reagan and Haig spoke of the Soviet Union as a failed system facing increasing difficulties, and both felt that the growing Soviet reliance on military power abroad, while a danger to the peace, was also a source of weakness at home. They believed that the Soviet leaders would have no choice but to seek accommodation with the West if the United States could demonstrate that the USSR could not save their faltering system with military victories abroad and could not win an arms race with the United States. Haig put it most clearly in an address to the U.S. Chamber of Commerce in April 1982 when he remarked, "We must place our policy in the context of important changes that are taking place in the world and in the Soviet empire that may make Moscow more amenable to the virtues of restraint. The Soviet attempt to change

---

6. The treaty permitted encryption of telemetry from Soviet weapon tests, which would have made accurate verification of some of the treaty commitments exceedingly difficult, if not impossible.

7. Statement to French television network Antenne 2 on February 23, 1981; text in *Department of State Bulletin* (April 1981), 15.

8. Speech of April 24, 1981, to the American Society of Newspaper Editors; text in *Department of State Bulletin* (June 1981), 6.

the balance of power has produced a backlash of increasing international resistance. . . . As a consequence, the Soviet leaders may find it increasingly difficult to sustain the status quo at home while exporting a failed ideology abroad."[9]

Reagan sounded the same theme, but with a more positive tilt, in his first speech on U.S.-Soviet relations, delivered in May 1982 at Eureka College, where he said: "I'm optimistic that we can build a more constructive relationship with the Soviet Union. . . . The Soviet empire is faltering because it is rigid. . . . In the end, this course will undermine the foundations of the Soviet system. [A] Soviet leadership devoted to improving its people's lives, rather than expanding its armed conquests, will find a sympathetic partner in the West."[10]

The American news media paid scant attention to statements reflecting Reagan's negotiating stance but concentrated instead on comments he made, usually in response to questions, about the nature of communism and Marxist doctrine. For example, during the same press conference at which he called for negotiations to reduce the number of nuclear weapons, he was asked about Soviet intentions and specifically whether he thought "the Kremlin is bent on world domination." Reagan replied that the Soviet leaders had consistently said that "their goal must be the promotion of world revolution" and that "the only morality they recognize is what will further their cause, meaning they reserve unto themselves the right to commit any crime, to lie, to cheat, in order to attain that. . . . I think when you do business with them, even at a détente, you keep that in mind."[11]

Journalists and news analysts repeated this statement out of context for years, as if it had been meant to preclude negotiation rather than to pledge appropriate caution when dealing with people hold-

---

9. Speech of April 27, 1982; text in *Department of State Bulletin* (June 1982), 43.

10. Speech at Eureka College, May 9, 1982; *Weekly Compilation of Presidential Documents* 18, no. 19: 599ff.

11. *Weekly Compilation of Presidential Documents* 17, no. 5:66–67.

ing different ideological and ethical standards. Few critics were naïve or dishonest enough to deny that what Reagan said was true; rather, they claimed that "excoriating" the Soviet leaders would make it impossible to deal with them.

Soviet Reaction

Reagan's frank assessment of the Communist system and its ideology doubtless reinforced the Soviet leaders' conviction that he would be a difficult and perhaps impossible negotiating partner. However, this was not the cause of the heightened tensions that marked U.S.-Soviet relations from 1980 until at least November 1985. Those tensions were the result of the incompatibility of Soviet and Western concepts of an acceptable relationship. They would have existed, in much the same form, even if the U.S. president had been more restrained in his public comments on Soviet policy.

Fighting intensified in Afghanistan during Reagan's first years in office. As the free trade union Solidarity gained adherents and influence in Poland, Soviet criticism of the Polish government seemed an ominous prelude to direct intervention; General Wojciech Jaruzelski's declaration of martial law in December 1981 was obviously in response to intense Soviet pressure. The Soviet leaders continued to deploy a new generation of intermediate-range missiles in Europe and refused to consider either removing them to make NATO deployments unnecessary or limiting them to a small number that would apply to both sides. Arms supplies to insurgents in Latin America increased, as did military support for parties in local wars in several parts of Africa. Jamming of Western radios was intensified. Political arrests and expulsions of dissidents continued; Andrei Sakharov languished in internal exile in a city closed to visits by foreigners. Jewish emigration dropped from tens of thousands a year to a few hundred.

The Soviet message seemed to be: Ratify SALT II or nothing else will work in the relationship. Accordingly, the Soviet leaders refused any meaningful discussion of other issues raised by the United States, and they initiated a propaganda battle designed to convince U.S. allies in Europe—and, if possible, the American public as well—that Reagan was threatening a nuclear war.

Defense Minister Dmitri Ustinov's November 1981 speech on the anniversary of the Bolshevik Revolution summed up the Soviet reaction to the early Reagan administration. Ustinov accused the United States of "undermining the military-strategic balance" by seeking military superiority, attempting to stop "forces of national and social liberation," and "besieging" the Socialist countries. Ignoring evidence that some terrorist groups were receiving support from the Soviet Union, Ustinov charged that the United States and NATO were employing "the methods of international terrorism." The United States, he charged, had called into question "all that had been jointly achieved" (during détente) and had become an "uncontrolled military threat." The Soviet Union, he asserted, "has never embarked and will never embark on the road of aggression."[12]

This, of course, was public rhetoric, designed for a celebratory occasion normally marked by braggadocio and self-congratulation. However, it was also a direct and frank expression of the Soviet leaders' attitude at the time. Their positions in private coincided with those Ustinov expressed in public on behalf of the Politburo. The Soviet leaders were oblivious to the irony implicit in their accusations that the United States sought superiority by planning to do what the Soviet Union was already doing and in their assurances that the Soviet Union was incapable of aggression because it had never indulged in it. Whatever the Politburo had declared to be the truth was, in their minds, the truth, and anyone who questioned it was an enemy.

During Reagan's first year in office, negotiations began with the

---

12. The Russian text of Ustinov's speech can be found in *Pravda* (November 7, 1981); comments on it by the U.S. embassy in Moscow are in 81 Moscow 13344 (November 6, 1981).

Soviet Union on only one important issue: intermediate-range nuclear forces (INF) in Europe.[13] From 1976 the Soviet Union had begun replacing its nuclear missiles targeted on NATO countries with a much more capable weapon, the SS-20. It was more accurate than its predecessors, had a significantly greater range, was mobile (therefore less vulnerable), and carried three independently targeted warheads. It could strike most NATO capitals in Europe in minutes. NATO countries viewed it as altering the nuclear balance in Europe and, in 1979, decided to deploy a smaller number of U.S. missiles in Europe to counter the threat unless negotiations with the Soviet Union made the deployments unnecessary.[14]

The negotiations, which began in November 1981, turned out to be futile, but not because the United States—as some of Reagan's critics charged at the time—negotiated in bad faith. The initial U.S. proposal to eliminate INF weapons altogether was neither self-serving nor a propaganda gesture. It was actually in the strategic interest of the Soviet Union not to have any nuclear missiles of this type deployed in Europe. Such U.S. missiles on European soil could reach the Soviet Union, but comparable Soviet missiles could not reach the United States. Nor was the proposal offered on a take-it-or-leave-it basis; both Reagan and Haig described it from the outset as an optimum goal that could be reached in steps.

The Soviets, however, refused to negotiate on any basis that would have been acceptable to NATO. By the summer of 1982 it became clear to the Soviet negotiator, Yuli Kvitsinski, that the Soviet leaders had decided that any concession to the U.S. position

---

13. Initially, the sides could not even agree on a name for the talks—a dispute based on differing views as to which weapons systems should be covered. The United States at various times called them theater nuclear forces (TNF), long-range theater nuclear forces (LRTNF), and long-range intermediate nuclear forces (LRINF). The Soviets generally preferred medium-range nuclear forces (MRF, MNF, or MRNF). Eventually, both sides accepted the INF acronym.

14. The decision, taken formally on December 12, 1979, was to deploy 108 Pershing II ballistic missiles and 464 ground-launched cruise missiles (GLCMs). All were replacements for less capable weapons that would be removed from Europe, and both types of missiles together had only a fraction of the destructive power of the SS-20s that were eventually deployed by the USSR.

would undermine the "peace movements" in Europe that were attempting to block INF deployments. Thus, the repeated efforts of the U.S. negotiator, Paul Nitze, to find a compromise solution came to naught, even though Kvitsinski had initially tried to interest his government in them.[15] Fundamentally, the Soviet military, which still determined the Soviet position on arms control issues, was unwilling to trade weapons at hand for weapons that were not yet in place. As a consequence, the Soviet position not only doomed the negotiations but also facilitated public approval in Europe for the U.S. deployments.

Negotiations on strategic arms, delayed both by disputes within the U.S. administration and by Reagan's sense that the time was not opportune for successful negotiation, were not resumed until Reagan's second year in office. As was the case in the INF forum, the U.S. proposals differed radically from the Soviet approach, which had evolved only slightly in the decade since the ABM Treaty and Interim Agreement had been concluded in 1972. The U.S. proposals aimed for major reductions in the quantity of weapons, particularly heavy MIRVed ICBMs, suitable for a disarming first strike. The Soviet arsenal was tilted sharply in favor of such weapons; the U.S. nuclear arsenal was more balanced among the legs of the triad of land-based missiles, sea-based missiles, and aircraft, and was designed for deterrence or, failing that, retaliation.

The United States sought deep reductions in Soviet land-based heavy missiles and increased reliance on sea-based systems in order to create a more stable, and thus safer, balance. This approach ran counter to entrenched Soviet doctrine and would have required a major Soviet effort and no little expense to implement, but it was not inherently one-sided or a blatant effort to secure U.S. superiority, as its critics charged. The Soviet Union had proved its ability to

---

15. Their accounts of these negotiations can be found in Paul H. Nitze, *From Hiroshima to Glasnost: At the Center of Decision—A Memoir* (New York: Grove Weidenfeld, 1989), 366–398; and in Julij A. Kwizinskij, *Vor dem Sturm: Erinnerungen eines Diplomaten* (Berlin: Siedler Verlag, 1993), 291–351.

rapidly match U.S. technological advantages, and the Soviets would have had a decade or more to make the adjustments. Nevertheless, given the Soviet mind-set of the early 1980s, it was no surprise that the U.S. proposal was dismissed out of hand.

Reagan added an additional major element to the U.S. position on strategic weapons in March 1983 when he announced "a comprehensive and intensive effort to define a long-term research and development program to begin to achieve our ultimate goal of eliminating the threat posed by strategic nuclear missiles."[16] He called this program the Strategic Defense Initiative (SDI); his critics dubbed it "Star Wars."

Reagan had several motives for promoting strategic defenses. Most fundamentally, he was uncomfortable with the prevailing doctrine of Mutual Assured Destruction, which would require him to respond to a nuclear attack on the United States with a nuclear strike against the population of the attacking country. Also, he was devoted to the idea of eliminating nuclear weapons but feared that this would never be feasible unless there was a defense against them. Furthermore, the Soviets were resisting deep cuts in their heavy ICBMs, and the U.S. Congress had refused to authorize deployment of the mobile MX, a tradable counterpart to the Soviet heavy missiles. If the Soviet leaders could be convinced that the United States was capable of building a defense against such missiles, it might make it easier to persuade Moscow to reduce their numbers. And, finally, the Soviet Union had active research programs in many of the areas critical to developing a strategic defense system. In Reagan's view, it would be foolhardy for the United States to leave the field to them entirely.

The Soviet leaders immediately condemned SDI as an American attempt to "militarize space" and establish military superiority. Initially, however, SDI was not the problem for negotiators that it was to become later.

---

16. The text of the speech is in *Weekly Compilation of Presidential Documents* 19, no. 12:442–448.

Causes of the U.S.-Soviet Stalemate

The Soviet leaders of the early 1980s considered arms control the central issue of U.S.-Soviet relations. President Reagan, however, was convinced that the arms race was the result of political hostility rather than its cause. One of his favorite aphorisms was, "Nations don't fear each other because they are armed; they arm because they fear each other." He believed that the U.S.-Soviet relationship had to improve before the arms race could end. That is why he believed that arms reduction, to which he was genuinely devoted, should be viewed in the context of the overall relationship. The use made of arms, the record of compliance with past agreements, and the adversary's doctrine and nature of its rule at home were all relevant issues, and all were discouraging when he took office. The Soviet leaders were insisting on a limited form of arms control without changing anything else in the relationship.

Reagan's goal was to shift the U.S. strategy from reacting to events and limiting damage to a concerted effort to change Soviet behavior. His approach constituted a direct challenge to the Soviet leadership because it explicitly denied fundamental tenets of Communist ideology and required a Soviet about-face on many issues under negotiation. It was a challenge to think differently about Soviet security, the place of the Soviet Union in the world, and the nature of Soviet society. It altered both the substance of negotiations and the way the dialogue was conducted, but it did not require the Soviet Union to compromise its own security. Soviet claims to the contrary, Reagan never threatened military action against the Soviet Union itself.

Reagan was aware that the Soviet leaders would initially reject his approach. But he was confident that the United States had a long-term strategic advantage: a healthier economy, more solid alliances, and most of all a political system that could adapt to change and stimulate the creativity of a free people. He could wait.

While waiting, however, there were things that needed to be

done to prepare for the day when some Soviet leader would recognize that things could not go on as they had. Aside from improving America's capacity to deter war and negotiate a real peace, it was important to define the issues, to establish a pattern of equality and reciprocity in the bilateral relationship, and to improve communication with both the Soviet leaders and their people.

Reagan had no master plan, just a congeries of impulses and general judgments. During the early years of his presidency, policy was made on the fly in the maelstrom of heated disputes within his administration, disputes that sometimes produced exaggerated or inconsistent statements by senior officials. With rare exceptions (which were always given heavy play in the press), Reagan's own statements, as well as those by his two secretaries of state, were consistent in regard to the fundamental issues.

Preparing for Gorbachev

No one, of course, could have been sure in 1981 or 1982 that Mikhail Gorbachev would become general secretary of the Communist Party of the Soviet Union in March 1985. It was clear, however, that as the youngest member of the Politburo to hold simultaneously a seat on the Secretariat, he was in the best position to succeed members of the old guard when they finally allowed power to pass to a new political generation.

It was also impossible to be certain what sort of policies Gorbachev or one of his contemporaries would follow when they succeeded to power. It was, however, reasonable to assume that a younger leader might be more willing than the older leaders to look at Soviet interests from a more realistic perspective. Gradually, after George Shultz replaced Alexander Haig as secretary of state and Reagan became more confident of his negotiating strength, the United States articulated a policy that aimed to reduce, and, if possible, eliminate, the grounds for antagonism and confrontation in U.S.-Soviet relations. Simultaneously, the administration concentrated on efforts to improve the channels of communication with the Soviet leadership and the Soviet public and to inject a greater measure of reciprocity in their use.

Brezhnev died in November 1982 and Reagan made the unexpected gesture of going to the Soviet embassy in Washington, D.C., to sign the official condolence book. It was intended as a signal to Brezhnev's successor that he desired to initiate a more fruitful dialogue than had been possible with Brezhnev. This elicited no greater response than had earlier efforts to communicate,[17] but, from early 1983, Reagan began to press his staff to prepare for serious business with Moscow. He approved policy guidance, previously delayed by bureaucratic disputes, that summarized U.S. goals as follows: "U.S. policy toward the Soviet Union will consist of three elements: external resistance to Soviet imperialism; internal pressure on the USSR to weaken the sources of Soviet imperialism; and negotiations to eliminate, on the basis of strict reciprocity, outstanding disagreements."[18]

After describing these three elements in greater detail, the directive stated explicitly that "the U.S. must make clear to the Soviets that genuine restraint in their behavior would create the possibility of an East-West relationship that might bring important benefits to the Soviet Union." The U.S. goal, therefore, as stated in its most sensitive and authoritative internal policy directive, was to bring the Soviet Union to the negotiating table to conclude agreements that would be, in its words, "consistent with the principle of strict reciprocity and mutual interest." It also set a goal of promoting "the process of change in the Soviet Union toward a more pluralistic political and economic system" in order to reduce Soviet aggressive tendencies.

From early 1983, Reagan began thinking about a possible meeting with Yuri Andropov, who had succeeded Brezhnev as general

17. Reagan, for example, had penned a personal message to Brezhnev while still in the hospital recovering from an assassination attempt. He received only a cold formal reply.

18. From NSDD-75, signed on January 17, 1983. Originally classified Secret/Sensitive, it has been declassified and was published in facsimile in Robert C. McFarlane, *Special Trust* (New York: Cadell and Davies, 1994), 372–380.

secretary. In February, Secretary of State Shultz arranged for Reagan to see Anatoli Dobrynin, the Soviet ambassador, privately in order to make it clear that he wished to improve relations. At that meeting, Reagan requested the Soviet government to allow the emigration of the seven Pentecostal Christians who had taken refuge in the U.S. embassy in Moscow five years earlier. Within a few months they were allowed to depart along with members of their families who had remained in Siberia. Reagan took this as a signal that Andropov might be prepared for more substantial negotiations, and he instructed the White House staff to work with the State Department to develop a negotiating agenda. He approved without cavil a forward-looking statement Secretary of State Shultz made to the Senate Foreign Relations Committee on June 15, 1983, that went beyond criticism of Soviet actions to stress the need for accommodation. In Shultz's words, "Strength and realism can deter war, but only direct dialogue and negotiation can open the path toward lasting peace."[19] From that point, "realism, strength, and dialogue" became a catchphrase to describe the Reagan administration's approach to the Soviet Union.

Contingent preparations for a meeting with Andropov continued through the summer at the White House. The idea was controversial within the administration. Some senior officials, both in the White House and in the Department of Defense, were opposed to the idea, fearing that the president would be under pressure to conclude a faulty arms control agreement to avoid accusations of failure. Secretary of State Shultz, in contrast, favored a meeting to establish direct communication with the Soviet leadership. Reagan was eager to deal directly with Andropov but was not certain that he should propose meeting unless there was some indication that it would bring tangible progress toward some important U.S. objectives.[20]

---

19. *Department of State Bulletin* (July 1983), 69.

20. As Special Assistant to the President for National Security, responsible for Europe and the USSR, I was instructed in June 1983 to prepare a paper giving the pros and cons of a near-term meeting with the Soviet leader. It was clear from Reagan's comments on the paper that he favored preparing for such a meeting as long as he would not be seen as the *demandeur*.

If the Soviets had shown any inclination to reach an INF settlement along the lines negotiator Paul Nitze had proposed the year before, Reagan most likely would have approved a meeting to conclude an agreement on that basis. The Soviets, however, had rejected Nitze's compromise proposal out of hand, and there seemed little prospect that agreement could be reached before the INF deployments scheduled for November. Therefore, it was necessary to devise an agenda that did not center on arms control and to prepare the public for a "get acquainted" meeting that might not produce a breakthrough in arms control. Accordingly, the NSC staff at the White House and the European Bureau in the State Department worked on an agenda that would broaden ties and revive some cooperative projects. They included an expanded program of cultural and educational exchanges, a new agreement for grain sales that would assure American farmers of larger Soviet purchases, improvements in the hot line and other confidence-building measures, and the expansion of air service between the United States and the USSR.

Few in the administration opposed these measures in principle, but some objected that restoring and expanding such agreements would signal an acceptance of the Soviet invasion of Afghanistan. Most of these ties had been broken as a result of the Soviet invasion. The prevailing view in both the White House and the State Department, however, was that many of these "sanctions" had been unwise and had damaged the United States more than the Soviet Union. A way needed to be found to keep pressure on the Soviet Union to leave Afghanistan while restoring channels of communication and increasing interaction with the Soviet leadership and the Soviet public.[21] Without better communication, improvement in the relationship over the long term would be impossible.

---

21. This logic led to a series of decisions to reverse many of the Carter-era sanctions that were considered self-defeating and simultaneously to increase aid to the resistance forces in Afghanistan.

These preparations came to an abrupt halt in September, when a Soviet fighter shot down a Korean civilian airliner that had blundered into Soviet airspace, plunging 269 persons, including a U.S. congressman, to their death. Though nothing could have diminished the tragedy for the victims and their relatives, the Soviet leaders' response to the action of its air defense forces turned it into a major international issue. Instead of apologizing, attributing the action to human error, offering to pay damages and to take steps to avoid such incidents in the future, the Soviet leaders first denied what had happened and then fabricated accusations that the United States was to blame because it had tried to use the plane to spy. There was no evidence supporting the latter charge, and the Soviet government, having recovered the plane's black box and much of the debris, knew very well that there was none.

Both Reagan and Shultz were outraged. Reagan personally drafted a speech to the American public and delivered it with passion. If he had been primarily a propagandist at heart, he might have welcomed the opportunity to cite the Soviet reaction as the latest proof of his contention that the Soviet leaders were capable of lying and cheating to further their cause. In fact, he did not welcome the incident, not only because he genuinely deplored the loss of life but also because he had been seeking ways to ease tensions with the Soviet Union. This latest demonstration of Soviet mendacity could only impede that process.

Nevertheless, Reagan considered a vigorous U.S. reaction indispensable. The Soviet leaders had to learn that misrepresentation of facts, and military rules of engagement that permitted, even encouraged, destruction of civilian aircraft, were harmful to their own interests. Much of the world community agreed. Resolutions condemning the Soviet action passed with overwhelming margins in the United Nations and in the International Civil Aeronautics Organization (ICAO). NATO allies and others applied temporary sanctions against the Soviet airline.

The Soviet reaction to the KAL shoot-down precipitated a telling confrontation within the Reagan administration. At issue was whether the United States should show its indignation by postponing planned negotiations and canceling meetings with senior Soviet officials. A meeting of foreign ministers had been scheduled in Madrid on September 6 to conclude the CSCE review session, and Secretary Shultz had agreed to meet Foreign Minister Gromyko while they both were there. Negotiations on INF and START were also scheduled to resume. Some in the Reagan administration, notably Secretary of Defense Weinberger, urged Reagan to cancel the meeting with Gromyko and postpone the negotiations on nuclear arms. Shultz argued that these meetings should go forward as planned because the United States could achieve more by talking than by refusing to talk to the Soviet leaders. Reagan agreed with Shultz's position (though he instructed Shultz to discuss only the KAL shoot-down with Gromyko), and the meetings went forward as scheduled. The meeting with Gromyko resulted in little more than a shouting match, but at least the two were still talking in each other's presence.

In deciding to proceed with planned meetings and negotiations despite the destruction of the Korean airliner and the Soviet refusal to take responsibility, Reagan set an important precedent. Subsequently, he always ruled in favor of keeping the U.S.-Soviet dialogue on track rather than using some unacceptable Soviet action as a pretext to shut it down.

Soviet Intransigence

Aside from the release of the Pentecostals and a few other small concessions made to secure U.S. consent to bring the CSCE review conference in Madrid to a close, there was no positive response from Moscow to the feelers Reagan put out periodically in 1983. The Soviet leaders still were insisting on arms control on their terms before any other questions could be usefully addressed. Indeed, Gromyko stated repeatedly that most of the issues the Americans raised had no place in the U.S.-Soviet dialogue at all. In their attempt to avert NATO's INF deployments by supporting the "peace movement" in Europe, Soviet officials maintained a drumbeat of accusations that the United States was planning nuclear war. To intensify a general feeling that East-West tensions were dangerously high, Andropov threatened to terminate arms control negotiations if the INF deployments went forward.

On September 29, 1983, Andropov issued a statement bordering on the hysterical. It accused the United States of a "sophisticated provocation" that resulted in the loss of life on the downed Korean plane and it misrepresented statistical measures in an attempt to demonstrate that the United States, not the USSR, had been driving the arms race in the 1970s. (Actually, the United States had reduced its armed forces and arsenals following the war in Vietnam, while the Soviets were steadily expanding theirs.) As if to justify in advance the subsequent Soviet action in ending arms control negotiations, Andropov stated flatly, "If anyone had any illusions about the possibility of an evolution for the better in the policy of the current American administration, events of recent times have thoroughly dispelled them."[22]

The Reagan administration ignored Andropov's charges, which in fact had become surreal in their absurdity. But in its response, the administration noted that Andropov had failed "to address concrete steps to reduce tensions," reminded him that "peace is imperative to mankind if it is to survive," and invited him to "get down to the task at hand."

This, however, was not to happen in Andropov's lifetime. On November 22, 1983, the German Bundestag voted to proceed with the deployment of Pershing IIs, and the missiles began to arrive in Germany within hours. On November 24, Moscow announced that its negotiators would not return to either the INF or START negotiations.

A few weeks earlier, on October 25, 1983, U.S. forces had invaded Grenada to depose a cabal of hoodlums, who had murdered Prime Minister Maurice Bishop, and to evacuate U.S. citizens, most

---

22. Statement published in *Pravda* and *Izvestia* on September 29, 1983.

of whom were students at a medical college. Although the island's governor general and the Organization of Eastern Caribbean States had asked the United States to intervene, the U.S. action was criticized severely not only by the Soviet Union (the news agency TASS called it "an act of undisguised banditry and international terrorism") but also by many U.S. allies. Criticism quickly subsided in the United States when television broadcasts showed the evacuated students kissing the ground upon their arrival in the United States and carried interviews with students who described their fear of being taken hostage. Criticism elsewhere subsided when it became obvious that the overwhelming majority of Grenadians welcomed their liberation from the thugs who had seized power with Cuban military support and Soviet blessing.

The United States had not invaded Grenada primarily to impress the Soviet Union with its resolve—the decisive motivations were fear of a hostage situation and a desire to protect the region from Cuban military interference—but many in the Reagan administration thought that the action sent a beneficial message to Moscow. If the Soviet leaders imagined that they could support violent revolutions with impunity, they would now be on notice that the United States had emerged from its post-Vietnam passivity and would oppose such efforts whenever it was practical to do so. The Soviet leaders probably needed no such reminder. They had entered no new theaters of conflict since Reagan took office, though they continued to support parties to conflicts that had begun earlier.

Moscow, of course, added the "crime" of invading Grenada to their bill of particulars against Reagan. But their propaganda machine, including extensive clandestine "assets," had been focused for months on selling the slogan "Reagan means War."[23] The sei-

---

23. Oleg Gordievsky, who worked on behalf of British intelligence in the KGB from 1974 until his defection in 1985, described this campaign in the book he coauthored with Christopher Andrew, *KGB, The Inside Story of Its Foreign Operations from Lenin to Gorbachev* (London: Hodder & Stoughton, 1990), 494.

zure of Grenada added little to the extravagant charges already being made.

The Soviet propaganda campaign failed to persuade the West Germans to refuse the Pershing II missiles (although it came close to succeeding), but it had the unintended effect of frightening the Soviet public. Traditionally, the Soviet government had avoided publicizing the dangers of nuclear war because it did not want to deal with an aroused public that might demand an end to testing or more restraint in military activities abroad. Now, however, there was so much talk of the nuclear threat that the Soviet public became sensitized to the importance of the issue. For decades Soviet citizens had been told that they need not worry about nuclear war; their government was powerful enough to protect them. Now they were being told that they were vulnerable.

The propaganda, contrived as much of it was, also may have had an effect on the thinking of the Soviet leaders themselves, for they began to fear that the United States was, in fact, preparing a nuclear first strike. There was no evidence to support this thought and much circumstantial evidence tending to disprove it.[24] Therefore, the reasons for their alarm remain obscure. We may speculate, however, that it stemmed from a combination of three factors: autosuggestion (a tendency to believe one's own propaganda if it is repeated enough), mirror imaging (they would cloak aggressive intent in peaceful-sounding rhetoric, and therefore believed others were capable of doing the same), and the reluctance of intelligence organizations to contradict fixed ideas held by their political leadership. In this case, KGB operatives in the field found no evidence to substantiate the fear and considered the tasks demanded by

---

24. For example, if Reagan had indeed contemplated a nuclear strike against the Soviet Union, he would hardly have said repeatedly that he believed the Soviet leaders did not want war. Instead, he would have tried to whip up hysteria that they were planning an attack on the United States. For a description of the absurd lengths the KGB in Moscow went to in order to secure information on a possible nuclear strike (an operation code-named RYAN), see Andrew and Gordievsky, *KGB,* 488–508, 524, 525.

Moscow a waste of time, but they prudently refrained from questioning the basis of their leaders' fear.

As 1983 drew to a close, U.S.-Soviet polemics were at a peak, and it appeared to those with short memories that the cold war had reached unprecedented intensity. The fear of war that infected a vocal segment of the public posed a political problem for the Reagan administration, but the president and his closest advisers were confident that the world was in fact safer than it had been in 1981 when Reagan took office. The strident Soviet propaganda casting Reagan as a warmonger was taken to be the impotent raving of politicians who suddenly saw the tide of history turning against them.

However shrill the Soviet rhetoric, it was clear to U.S. policymakers that the Soviet government could not easily sustain its intransigence beyond the U.S. election year of 1984. Some senior Soviet officials also must have understood this because the Reagan White House began to receive informal messages, apparently authorized in Moscow, suggesting that the Soviet leaders would have to sulk for a few months but would be willing to resume serious business in the fall of 1984.[25] Therefore, even as hopes faded for any short-term breakthrough in relations with the Soviet Union, attention in Washington turned to working out more details of a negotiating approach and conveying it to the public.

Secretary of State Shultz was distressed by disputes within the administration over policy toward the Soviet Union, and he undertook further efforts to build a consensus. To do so, he hosted a series of unpublicized meetings over breakfast on Saturdays with senior White House, defense, and intelligence officials, including Vice President Bush, Defense Secretary Weinberger, and Director of Central Intelligence Casey. Although these gatherings did not bring about a complete meeting of minds, a general consensus on

---

25. The author described one of these in Matlock, *Autopsy on an Empire*, 83. At the same time the KGB was acting under instructions issued in February to plan "active measures" to prevent Reagan's reelection. See Andrew and Gordievsky, *KGB*, 494.

U.S. goals emerged: reduction in the use or threat of force in international disputes, smaller arsenals (particularly of weapons of mass destruction), and a gradual opening of the Soviet Union by increasing bilateral ties and supporting human rights. There remained disagreement on the specific terms of acceptable agreements to reduce arms, but there was strong support for a policy that linked arms reduction with the use made of arms, and recognized that more openness and pluralism within the Soviet Union would facilitate Soviet acceptance of these goals.

In November, as the Soviet Union withdrew from negotiations on nuclear arms, President Reagan decided that he needed to clarify his position on the entire range of U.S.-Soviet issues, and he instructed his staff to work on a speech on the topic. Reagan personally read and commented on several drafts, discussed them in meetings with senior advisers, and finally added several paragraphs in his own hand. The result was his considered view of the U.S.-Soviet relationship and an outline for diplomatic interaction throughout the rest of his presidency. Specific policies were subsequently elaborated, but the basic reformulation of a U.S. policy to replace détente was complete when Reagan delivered the speech in the East Room of the White House on January 16, 1984.

After explaining why he had considered it necessary to strengthen defenses and the U.S. economy when he came to office, Reagan made it clear that this was the means to an end and not the end itself: "Deterrence is not the beginning and end of our policy toward the Soviet Union. We must and will engage the Soviets in a dialogue as serious and constructive as possible, a dialogue that will serve to promote peace in the troubled regions of the world, reduce the level of arms, and build a constructive working relationship."

He pointed out that, with all our differences, "We do have common interests. And the foremost among them is to avoid war and reduce the level of arms." He went on to formulate U.S. goals as common problems and common tasks, not as U.S. demands:

First, we need to find ways to reduce—and eventually to eliminate—the threat and use of force in solving international disputes. . . . As a first step, our governments should jointly examine concrete actions we both can take to reduce the risk of U.S.-Soviet confrontation in these areas. And if we succeed, we should be able to move beyond this immediate objective.

Our second task should be to find ways to reduce the vast stockpiles of armaments in the world. . . . We must accelerate our efforts to reach agreements that will greatly reduce nuclear arsenals, provide greater stability, and build confidence.

Our third task is to establish a better working relationship with each other, one marked by greater cooperation and understanding. . . . Complying with agreements helps; violating them hurts. Respecting the rights of individual citizens bolsters the relationship; denying these rights harms it. Expanding contacts across borders and permitting a free interchange of information and ideas increase confidence; sealing off one's people from the rest of the world reduces it. Peaceful trade helps, while organized theft of industrial secrets certainly hurts.

He then explained in nonconfrontational terms the meaning of the watchwords "realism, strength, and dialogue." Realism: "We must be frank in acknowledging our differences and unafraid to promote our values." Strength: "Soviet leaders know it makes sense to compromise only if they can get something in return. America can now offer something in return." Dialogue: "We're prepared to discuss the problems that divide us and to work for practical, fair solutions on the basis of mutual compromise."

Throughout the speech, Reagan emphasized the need for cooperation and the U.S. willingness to compromise. He also suggested interconnections among the various problems, pointing out that "greater respect for human rights can contribute to progress in other areas of the Soviet-American relationship."

For most Americans, the most memorable part of the speech was the portion Reagan wrote himself, the "Ivan and Anya" story, which imagined a Soviet couple and an American couple meeting by chance and finding that they have much in common and wish to be friends. It demonstrated Reagan's respect for the Soviet people, whom he always distinguished from the government that had been imposed upon them, and illustrated one of his fundamental tenets: "People don't make wars, governments do." He then ended the speech with a statement of assurance and a direct appeal: "If the Soviet Government wants peace, then there will be peace. Together we can strengthen peace, reduce the level of arms, and know in doing so we have helped fulfill the hopes and dreams of those we represent and, indeed, of people everywhere. Let us begin now."

Subsequently, the three "problem areas" Reagan cited in the speech became four when Secretary Shultz decided that the human rights issue was so important that it should be singled out for separate treatment. Thus was born the "four-part agenda" that provided a framework for the negotiations that brought the cold war to an end.

. . . .

The four-year interval between the Soviet invasion of Afghanistan and Reagan's speech in January 1984 is one of the most misunderstood periods of the entire cold war. Reagan's political opponents in the United States charged him with reckless brinkmanship, risking a nuclear war in pursuit of some ideological Holy Grail.[26] Many of his supporters, following the Soviet collapse in 1991, credited him with a grand design to bring down the evil empire.[27] Other commentators have assumed that he reversed his policy toward the

---

26. Such charges were made during both the 1980 and 1984 presidential campaigns, when they might have been dismissed as campaign hyperbole. Some prominent politicians repeated them, however, even when they were not on a political stump. For example, Soviet ambassador Dobrynin wrote that Speaker Thomas J. (Tip) O'Neill told him in 1983 that if Reagan were reelected he would "give vent to his primitive instincts and give us a lot of trouble, probably, put us on the verge of a major armed conflict. He is a dangerous man." Anatoli Dobrynin, *In Confidence: Moscow's Ambassador to America's Six Cold War Presidents* (New York: Random House, 1995), 548.

27. See, for example, Peter Schweizer, *Victory: The Reagan Administration's Secret Strategy that Hastened the Collapse of the Soviet Union* (New York: Atlantic Monthly Press, 1994).

end of his first term.[28] Some have even argued that Reagan's policy prolonged, rather than hastened, the end of the cold war.[29]

None of these interpretations will withstand an objective examination of the facts. Reagan's policies never brought the United States to the brink of military conflict with the Soviet Union, as, for example, Kennedy's policies did during the Cuban missile crisis, and Nixon's arguably did during the Yom Kippur War of 1973. He did not seek to destroy the Soviet Union but rather offered cooperation if it abandoned its militaristic and expansionist course. Reagan delayed serious negotiation as long as he felt too weak to negotiate effectively, and subsequently refined his policies in the light of experience, but his strategy when he left office was precisely what he had in mind when he took office.

As evidence now available proves beyond reasonable doubt, the Soviet leaders who preceded Gorbachev were unwilling to make the changes in their policies and practices that could have brought the cold war to a close. They wanted a limited arms control skewed in their favor and a free hand to pursue their traditional goals in every other sphere. They believed implicitly in the international class struggle and the eventual final victory of socialism as Lenin and Stalin had defined it. It was this belief that lay at the root of the cold war from its very beginning. Until it was abandoned, the cold war persisted.

By January 1984, Reagan had placed the United States in a position to deal with Mikhail Gorbachev, the first Soviet leader pragmatic enough to grasp that the cold war was not in the Soviet Union's interest, and the only one to realize that the cold war could not end unless the Soviet Union itself changed. The positions

---

28. The most detailed exposition of this point of view can be found in Beth A. Fischer, *The Reagan Reversal: Foreign Policy and the End of the Cold War* (Columbia, MO: University of Missouri Press, 1997).

29. Argued explicitly in Richard Ned Lebow and Janice Gross Stein, *We All Lost the Cold War* (Princeton, NJ: Princeton University Press, 1994), 369–376; and implicitly in Raymond L. Garthoff, *The Great Transition: American-Soviet Relations and the End of the Cold War* (Washington, DC: Brookings Institution, 1994).

Reagan staked out more than a year before Gorbachev came to power anticipated Gorbachev's "new thinking" and were totally compatible with it. Perhaps this is why Gorbachev and his associates have not joined Reagan's critics in their assessment of his policy toward the Soviet Union or of him as a statesman.

Anatoli Dobrynin, the former Soviet ambassador, has written, "The Reagan I observed . . . had a clear sense of what he wanted and was deeply involved in diplomatic events. He became a principal protagonist in ending the cold war."[30] And Gorbachev stated in his *Memoirs*, "In my view, the 40th President of the United States will go down in history for his rare perception."[31]

---

30. Dobrynin, *In Confidence*, 477.
31. Mikhail Gorbachev, *Memoirs* (New York: Doubleday, 1996), 457.

Alexei Arbatov : *What Lessons Learned?*

LOOKING BACK at the recent history of Soviet-U.S. relations is not only fascinating but instructive when coping with current and future issues. Ambassador Jack Matlock's chapter on the last, but crucial, turning point of the cold war in 1980–1983 is written with impressive knowledge, thoughtfulness, and a subtle touch of personal experience and involvement.

In the early 1980s, as the two superpowers and their allies were sliding into yet another round of dangerous confrontation, no one could imagine that only a decade later the cold war would be over and communism would collapse, while Russia and the West would embark on an unprecedented course of economic, political, and military cooperation with the goal of becoming strategic partners and even allies. Likewise, very few in the early 1990s would have predicted that ten years later Moscow and Washington would again enter a state of high tension and bitter controversy across a broad range of issues, treating each other with distrust, misunderstanding, and revived stereotypes of the cold war.

Understanding the domestic and external driving forces of these inexorable dynamics and learning what is good or bad for Soviet-U.S. relations is a great challenge for thinkers in both countries. Jack Matlock's essay is a valuable contribution to this endeavor.

Why did the détente of the first half of the 1970s collapse and give way to a new phase of the cold war in the first half of the 1980s? Matlock quite correctly points to the 1979 Soviet intervention in Afghanistan and the U.S. reaction to it, as well as the U.S. failure to ratify SALT II, which shocked the Soviets. Furthermore, he rightly explains that Americans reacted vehemently because they viewed the invasion of Afghanistan as final proof of the deep and unacceptable divergence between U.S. and Russian definitions of détente.

The United States considered that détente implied a broad cooperation on economic and security issues, restraint in arms buildup and intervention abroad, and Soviet softening on human rights and freedom of immigration. In contrast, Moscow believed détente meant U.S. credits and economic assistance unlinked from Soviet domestic affairs, security cooperation in Europe, final legalization of U.S.-Soviet strategic parity through SALT II, and unrestricted expansion of Soviet influence in the third world through "support for the national liberation movements." Each side's understanding and conduct of détente gravely disappointed the other; hence their return to a new round of confrontations between President Ronald Reagan during his first term and Leonid Brezhnev, Yuri Andropov, and Konstantin Chernenko on the Soviet side. But there was much more to the U.S.-Soviet rift of the early 1980s.

The beginning of the last two decades of the cold war saw an unprecedented U.S. military decline following its crushing defeat in Vietnam. The U.S. defense budget was cut by 35 percent between 1968 and 1976, U.S. armed forces were reduced from 3.6 million to 2.1 million, and nuclear and conventional modernization programs were curtailed. In 1976, the U.S. military had 400,000 troops in the Asia-Pacific and other regions, a reduction of 65 percent from its 1968 level. There were growing controversies with NATO allies in Europe over such issues as the neutron bomb and the Persian Gulf. The post–Vietnam War syndrome against military intervention abroad, the failing economy and high inflation at home, and the widening split between public opinion and the administration over foreign policy and arms control culminated in the humiliation of U.S. diplomats taken hostage in Iran and the failure of the U.S. rescue operation in April 1980. Ronald Reagan entered the White House with a clear mandate to restore American prestige and power abroad as well as self-respect, prosperity, and unity at home.

In stark contrast, during these decades the Soviet Union was experiencing the peak of its power and foreign expansion not just since World War II but even as far back as the 1917 Bolshevik Revolution. By the early 1980s the Kremlin had seemingly fulfilled Lenin's goal of making the backward rural country in the eastern backyard of Europe one of the world's two superpowers. Having built the second largest highly centralized and militarized economy in the world with a GNP equal to 60 percent of U.S. GNP, the USSR surpassed the United States in military expenditures and possessed the most powerful army in the world, numbering 3.9 million troops and exceeding the U.S. nuclear arsenal by 40 percent (45,000 versus 24,000 nuclear weapons, respectively). The Soviet foreign military presence of 800,000 personnel in Eastern and Central Europe, Mongolia, Afghanistan, North Korea, Vietnam, Aden, Syria, Libya, Iraq, Ethiopia, Mozambique, Angola, Cuba, and Nicaragua, as well as naval and air force deployments in the Mediterranean, Atlantic, Pacific, and Indian oceans, expanded its reach across the globe.

The Soviet defense industry was turning out massive quantities of weapons and equipment, lagging behind the United States only in the construction of aircraft carriers, heavy bombers, and nuclear-powered cruisers. In Europe, the Warsaw Pact had tripled Soviet superiority over NATO in conventional arms. The USSR had more weapons in certain categories than the rest of the world put together, including strategic and tactical nuclear munitions, surface-to-surface ballistic missiles of all ranges, surface-to-air missiles, tanks, nuclear-powered submarines, and military space launchers. The Soviet Union led the world in foreign arms sales ($30 billion) and was the only country in the world that had active ABM and ASAT systems, a permanent space station in orbit, two nuclear test sites, and three missile space ranges.

Yet beneath the surface of this impressive military power and foreign influence were serious signs of the deep internal deterioration of the Communist empire. In fact, just as Soviet power reached its pinnacle, it began its decline toward eventual collapse one decade later. Besides the USSR's wide rift with China and instability in the occupied countries of Eastern Europe, which led to a Polish crisis in 1980, the deepening inefficiency of the Soviet economy undercut the foundations of the Communist regime and its huge defense establishment. But the sheer magnitude of Soviet Union resources dedicated to defense (approximately 12 percent of GNP and 40 to 50 percent of the state budget, compared with 5 percent and 20 percent, respectively, in the United States) was not the whole problem. As a matter of fact, the radical 90 percent reduction in Soviet defense expenditures from 1992 to 1998 did not lead to economic growth, but further exacerbated the country's economic crisis.

The crisis grew out of the organization of the Soviet economy. Massive military production, which relied on centralized planned allocation of material and human resources and strict control over prices and incomes, had become inefficient by the late 1960s. The extra revenue from foreign oil sales following the 1973 OPEC embargo had disappeared by the late 1970s. There were no sources of intensive growth through efficient capital investment or the introduction of high technology because there was no self-generating consumer market economy. The state-owned and state-planned economy could achieve efficiency only through meticulous regulation.

Growing shortages of consumer goods and services, the rapidly declining quality of state social safety nets (communal services, housing, health care, and education), the falling standard of living of the general population, cultural stagnation, and massive legal emigration from the Soviet Union were irreversibly eroding the ideological foundations and political dominance of the regime. The system was collapsing because of the widening gap between its outdated economic, political, and ideological mechanisms, and the demands and expectations of its urban educated populace.

During the 1970s, the liberalization of Soviet society, if not the Soviet state, became intertwined with détente in foreign affairs and the avalanche of contacts, goods, and information coming from abroad. In another unique development of the late 1970s, the

Kremlin's foreign policy and defense programs were challenged from inside for the first time. Some departments of the foreign ministry, the academic community (the Institute of U.S. Studies, IMEMO, and the Institute of Europe), professional journals, public organizations such as the Committee of Scientists for Peace, and even members of the CPSU Central Committee began to doubt the wisdom of the intervention in Afghanistan, the massive military buildup and deployment of SS-20 medium-range missiles, the official stance on Reagan's SDI, START and INF talks, and the reduction of conventional arms in Europe in the early 1980s.

Public challenges would not arise until the Gorbachev era, but in closed sessions and in the Aesopian language used by the mass media, it was apparent that a pluralism of opinion on the most important issues of national security was developing. These alternative assessments undermined the traditional monopoly of the military establishment and the aging Communist leadership.

Whereas formerly the Central Committee of the CPSU, the Council of Ministers, and Gosplan (the State Planning Committee) had ruled with a Stalinist iron fist, by the 1980s they had been transformed into a forum of competing lobbying groups and vested interests. The entire ruling class of *nomenklatura* had split into numerous central and regional clans and groups of corporate interests, such as the KGB "firm," military top brass, nuclear complex, energy elite, and agricultural "mafia." The elite establishment was losing its former homogeneity, discipline, and stringent organization. Deeply plagued by corruption, cynicism, and materialism, and stagnant from inbreeding and nepotism, it was rotting from the inside. A decade later, most of the *nomenklatura* were so demoralized and cowardly that they did not put up any serious resistance when the rule of the CPSU, the USSR, and the Communist system was collapsing in 1991. Instead, they waited passively for the outcome of the infighting in Moscow.

After 1991, the *nomenklatura* adapted quickly to the new Russian system of quasi-market economy and quasi-democracy by moving en masse into new semi-criminal businesses and leftist, nationalist, and power-state (*derzhavnye*) political parties. Eventually, most of them, having easily shed Communist ideology, joined the new *nomenklatura* and concentrated around the ruling party, United Russia, which formed the political base of President Vladimir Putin's regime.

Ambassador Matlock's assessment of the ideological motivation of the Kremlin gerontocracy is only partially correct. No doubt the old party and state leaders referred to Marxist-Leninist teachings to justify their decisions and policies. Moreover, sometimes their ideological cover had its own momentum, committing Moscow to actions that it would not have taken otherwise, such as overextending itself in Africa in the 1970s. However, with few exceptions, the men in the Kremlin did not really believe in Marxist or Leninist ideologies (which, perhaps with the exception of Mikhail Suslov, they understood only superficially and mostly through popular quotations), or in class struggle or the eventual victory of communism in the cold war. They were merely operating within an established, convenient, and utopian ideology, ironclad since Stalin's times, while in fact they were cautious, pragmatic, and conservative imperial rulers whose primary concern was preservation of the Soviet empire.

All of their domestic and external actions may be explained as the behavioral patterns of an imperial, nationalistic, statist, totalitarian, corporate establishment. The Soviet Union in the 1980s was like medieval Europe, when Christian dogmas and disputes framed and masked politics that were driven by materialistic motives. A widely circulated joke in the 1980s was that the best deterrent to a possible Soviet attack was not U.S. strategic force but the fact that the children and grandchildren of the Soviet elites were serving in diplomatic missions and other sinecures in the West.

The Soviet Union's moves to expand its influence in the third world were not motivated by a desire to compensate for the liabilities of the system at home by pointing to its growing power abroad, even if only indirectly and remotely. In contrast to the romantic periods of the 1920s, the 1950s, and the 1960s, by the 1980s

Moscow's costly support of the national liberation movements abroad, poised against the background of economic decline and ideological disillusionment at home, caused universal irritation among the public and diminished the appeal of the Soviet Communist regime. The December 1979 intervention in Afghanistan was met with resentment and even horror by the majority of the population despite a massive official propaganda campaign. The people's sober assessment that Afghanistan was the "Soviet Vietnam" proved to be correct. Totalitarian empires cannot afford defeat, even in a remote war. The debacle in Afghanistan was not only a turning point in the Soviet expansion of the 1970s and 1980s but also a crushing blow to the empire, accelerating its demise. The Soviet withdrawal from Afghanistan was followed by its retreat from Germany, most of the third world countries, Eastern and Central Europe, and finally by the collapse of the USSR itself.

Soviet interventions in Asia, Africa, and Latin America were driven by the bureaucratic momentum of the International Department of the CPSU Central Committee, the foreign ministry, the KGB, the ministry of defense, and the GKES (State Committee on Foreign Economic Cooperation dealing with military assistance and arms transfers). The strategy was to seek low-risk tactical gains and self-promotion in a never-ending geostrategic competition with the West and China. Similarly, the massive and persistent arms buildup was seldom motivated internally (and then, mostly at tactical and operational levels) or justified by the overt goal of achieving strategic superiority over the United States and its allies, regardless of how it may have seemed to foreign observers. For instance, the Soviet Union justified its obvious superiority in tanks by the prospect of heavy losses in armor due to enemy air strikes and the use of tactical nuclear weapons, areas in which NATO countries allegedly dominated.

With the monopoly of the ministry of defense and the KGB over all relevant intelligence and military assessments, presentations made to the Kremlin always aimed at negating real or projected Western strategic advantages and emphasizing parity and the defensive capability of the Socialist camp. Anyone on the inside who challenged those assessments and proposals would immediately forfeit his career. The traditionally paranoid Kremlin gerontocracy, who retained a vivid memory of the disaster of June 22, 1941, generally accepted such proposals at face value. Thus the Soviet elites overburdened the economic resources of their empire while fortifying the rigidity of the system at a time when reforms were urgently needed to prevent revolution and make the transition less tumultuous and devastating.

Paul Kennedy has precisely described the dialectics of external decline and domestic erosion in his book *The Rise and Fall of the Great Powers*:

> Wealth is usually needed to underpin military power, and military power is usually needed to acquire and protect wealth. If, however, too large a portion of the state's resources is diverted from wealth creation and allocated instead to military purposes, then that is likely to lead to a weakening of national power over the longer term. In the same way, if a state overextends itself strategically—by, say, the conquest of extensive territories or the waging of costly wars—it runs the risk that the potential benefits from external expansion may be outweighed by the great expense of it all—a dilemma which becomes acute if the nation concerned has entered a period of relative economic decline.[1]

Kennedy's description accurately fits what was happening in the Soviet Union at the beginning of the 1980s.

Such was the setting in the international arena and within the USSR when President Reagan came to power. Without a proper assessment of these circumstances, it is impossible to understand the effects of Reagan's policies on U.S.-Soviet relations and the causes of the final spasm of the cold war at the beginning of the

---

1. Paul Kennedy, *The Rise and Fall of the Great Powers: Economic Change and Military Conflict from 1500 to 2000* (New York: Random House, 1987), xvi.

1980s. Jack Matlock addresses some very important points, but it is worthwhile to add a few other observations.

First, the Reagan administration's national security personnel, selected by the president's "kitchen cabinet," ensured that Reagan's policies would be very tough. Many of these individuals came from the Committee on the Present Danger and the notorious Group B, which included 50 posts altogether from conservative business circles, defense industries, and the anti-SALT II press. The most prominent among them were Alexander Haig, Caspar Weinberger, Richard Allen, William Casey, Richard Pipes, Richard Burt, Fred Ikle, Richard Perle, Richard DeLauer, John Lehman, Eugene Rostow, Edward Rowny, Paul Nitze, and T. Harding Jones, all of whom were either staunchly conservative or outright hawkish.

During 1981 and 1982, public declarations by these officials on the possibility of conducting and winning a protracted nuclear war, on strategic superiority, on the arms race, and on arms control were overtly provocative, causing panic not only in Moscow but also in the United States and Western Europe. Statements of this kind could fill an anthology, but it will suffice to present two of them. The first is by President Reagan, who formulated in his distinctive way a clear readiness to sanction a preemptive nuclear strike: "Suppose you're the President, and suppose you have on unassailable authority that as of a certain hour the enemy is going to launch those missiles at your country—you mean to tell me that a President should sit there and let that happen. . . ?"[2] The second is a statement on the possibility of nuclear victory by Vice President George Bush, who was certainly not the most hawkish member of the administration and who had a more statesmanlike outlook on strategic affairs: "You have a survivability of command and control, survivability of industrial potential, protection of a percentage of your citizens, and you have a capability that inflicts more damage

---

2. Robert Scheer, *With Enough Shovels: Reagan, Bush, and Nuclear War* (New York: Random House, 1982), 240–241.

on the opposition than it can inflict upon you. That's the way you can be a winner."[3]

These and numerous other similar statements may be dismissed as flamboyant rhetoric, which stemmed from lack of knowledge or was geared for domestic consumption and did not reflect U.S. strategic policy or planning. However, it goes without saying that official declarations made by such high-level officials are in and of themselves part of practical policy and may affect relations with other states more than secret concepts and plans for actual deployment of military weapons. The "peace-loving" propagandistic declarations of Soviet leaders certainly contradicted their actions in the arms race and in foreign interventions, but had they instead mirrored U.S. rhetoric, tensions and the threat of war would have risen still higher.

In contrast to Matlock's arguments, the practical policies of Reagan's administration mainly conformed to the tough and aggressive rhetoric used by its representatives from 1981 to 1982. Its overall defense program envisioned a crash buildup of all armed services and a large-scale procurement of a panoply of ground-, air-, sea-, and space-based weapons, equipment, and systems. The defense budget was immediately increased by $32 billion in the 1981–1982 fiscal years and cumulatively reached almost $1.8 trillion for the 1984 through 1988 fiscal years.

In the area of strategic nuclear forces, the expenditure of $180 billion for the 1983 through 1987 fiscal years included the restoration of the B-1B bomber procurement program (100 airplanes), deployment of 100 MX ICBMs and 1,000 Midgetman light mobile ICBMs, expansion of the construction of Trident SSBNs from 13 to 18 boats, accelerated deployment of Trident-2 SLBMs, and expansion of the procurement programs from 3,400 to 4,300 ALCM and 700 SLCM missiles. Altogether, the envisioned buildup of strategic power by number of warheads was only about 10 percent, but

---

3. Ibid., 261.

conceived qualitative shifts were much more significant. The plan was to increase by the mid-1990s: counterforce-capable warheads by a factor of 4.5; counterforce-capable warheads on survivable platforms by a factor of 4; and survivable counterforce capability on "fast-flyers" (ballistic delivery vehicles) by a factor of 20. In Europe, the new administration was determined to proceed with the planned deployment of 572 Pershing II and GLCM missiles.

In March 1983, Reagan announced the SDI program to create a space-based antimissile defense, which was to violate the ABM treaty of 1972 and undercut Soviet strategic deterrence. The scale of the arms race was so unprecedented that before long it stirred opposition in the U.S. Congress and the academic community and provoked a popular antimissile movement in Western Europe. Although Matlock describes the SDI program as unrealistic in its ambitions, the Pentagon, the research-industrial complex, and the conservative community conceived of it as a major strategic breakthrough toward U.S. superiority. They clearly understood all the destabilizing and provocative implications for the military balance of power and arms control. The USSR maintained an inefficient operational ABM system around the city of Moscow. It was conducting various research programs on space arms and directed energy weapons, but in most cases the Soviet Union lagged far behind the United States in SDI programs, and in many areas the USSR had nothing analogous to U.S. technical developments.

With respect to arms control, the administration maintained its pre-election position. In particular, SALT II, the subject of six years of exhausting negotiations, was declared "dead as a coffin nail" and in 1986 it was violated by the United States. In fact, its numerical limitations were rather moderate in terms of actual required reductions. SALT II was much more impressive, however, in its qualitative limitations, transparency, and cooperative measures, which had a greater limiting effect than numerical ceilings. After a failure to prohibit the introduction of any new type of ICBM (proposed by Moscow in May 1978), the parties agreed to confine themselves to only one new light type of ICBM each. This limit on new weapon types was an unprecedented achievement in restraining the qualitative arms race, which was unfortunately abandoned in later disarmament treaties. Another breakthrough was the limit on increasing the number of warheads on existing MIRVed missiles. New ICBM and SLBM types could not carry more than the maximum number on existing missiles (10 and 14, respectively). By the same logic, no more than an average of 28 ALCMs could be placed on heavy bombers and no more than 20 on existing types. Other cruise missile types were covered by a treaty that prohibited their deployment until the end of 1981. The treaty itself was to continue through 1985.

In order for the parties to similarly interpret and verify these limitations, they undertook an unprecedented effort in transparency and cooperation. Meticulous definitions were given to each term used in the treaty, including classes and types of weapon systems, MIRV systems, and missile launch-weights and through-weights. Direct figures were exchanged on the existing numbers of various classes of strategic arms and all types of missile warheads. New type limits dictated strict rules governing permitted modernization or modification of existing ICBM types as to their number of stages, length, diameter, launch-weight and through-weight, weight of warheads, and type of propellant in each stage. There were also flight-test rules including, in particular, dispensing MIRV warheads from the "bus." In order to facilitate verification, concealment measures, including telemetry encryption during flight tests, were prohibited. The "rule of type" and the requirement that treaty-limited systems have "functionally related observable differences" restricted the technological freedom of each side by putting a price tag on noncompliance.

The Soviet Union cancelled its SS-16 mobile ICBM system and made a promise not to extend the range of the Tu-22M bomber, provide it with air-refueling capacity, or increase the production rate of Backfires. Both sides had to modify their strategic modernization plans (in particular, the MIRVed missile and ALCM deployment programs) in technical characteristics, scale, and rate of

introduction and withdrawal of strategic weapons. All in all, with
its rather high aggregate ceilings and marginal enhancement of strategic stability, SALT II would have gone far toward placing qualitative restrictions, establishing the "book of rules" and "dictionary" of arms control, and initiating transparency and cooperative verification measures.

It was undoubtedly a misfortune of historic proportions that the superpowers failed to separate their strategic nuclear relationship and SALT II from foreign policy tensions over the 1979 Soviet intervention in Afghanistan, in contrast to their success in doing so with SALT I and the war in Vietnam in 1972. Almost 20 years later, a similar situation would arise in connection with START II, which Russia failed to ratify in late 1998 and early 1999 because of U.S. strikes against Iraq and NATO aggression toward former Yugoslavia. If SALT II had been ratified and implemented in the 1980s, it would certainly have taken far less than 12 years to take the next step with the START I treaty in 1991. Matlock seems to underestimate the strategic liabilities related to the loss of SALT II.

Under Reagan, U.S. arms control proposals were not designed to reach an agreement with the USSR. In fact, they were formulated in such a way that they would never be accepted by Moscow, as was vividly described later by Strobe Talbott, a high official in successive Democratic administrations.[4] The INF "zero option" advanced by President Reagan in November 1981 was designed to cool the popular European antimissile movement, and the START proposal of May 1992 was aimed primarily at pacifying a disturbed U.S. Congress and calming proponents of the American antinuclear movement. On this topic, it is impossible to agree with Matlock's benign assessment of the Reagan administration's motives.

Moscow later accepted the INF "zero option" in an even more radical version of "double zero" that included tactical missiles (INF-SRF). By contrast, START I, signed in 1991, was very different from Reagan's START proposal of May 1982, which did not

---

4. See Strobe Talbott, *Deadly Gambits* (New York: Alfred A. Knopf, 1984).

include any limits on bombers and called for the virtual elimination of heavy ICBMs and put severe limits on other MIRVed ICBMs. With medium-range missiles, Mikhail Gorbachev was determined to make a real breakthrough and demonstrate new political thinking. Thus, he went even further than realistic compromise, such as that agreed upon during the famous "walk in the woods" might suggest. Besides, it had been broadly recognized since the early 1980s that the USSR itself had created the problem by starting an unprovoked massive deployment of SS-20 missiles. But in the early 1980s, in the environment of a resumed cold war, an accelerated arms race, and heated anti-Soviet rhetoric from Washington, Reagan's arms control initiatives could not be, and were not meant to be, a serious proposition for a disarmament deal.

The eventual fate of these proposals, particularly the INF treaty, was not the result of Reagan's prophetic insight but rather a historic coincidence caused by social and political transformations of a very different nature. INF-SRF, CFE, START I, and other historic achievements in Soviet-Western relations occurred during a distinctly different stage in world politics associated with Gorbachev's rise to power and the second term of Reagan's presidency, which began in 1985. No doubt the changes in Soviet policy were much greater than those in U.S. rhetoric and actions, but contrary to Matlock's contention, Reagan's second term was quite different from his first.

After 1984, the United States softened its stance due to broad opposition to its strategic policy in Western Europe, escalation of tensions with the USSR, and the breakdown of negotiations on nuclear arms in 1983 and 1984. In addition, there were setbacks to U.S. interventions, such as that in Lebanon in 1983. Congressional cuts in unrealistic defense budget requests, which led to a curtailment of weapons programs, including SDI, Reagan's favorite; rising domestic opposition to the administration's defense policy; the Senate's rejection of the broad interpretation of the ABM treaty; disputes within the administration over policies toward the USSR; and changes in its personnel, such as the appointment of George

Shultz as secretary of state: all led to a tangible softening of U.S. policy in 1984.

President Reagan, advancing in years and holding rather simplistic views on foreign relations, may have sincerely believed that his policies from 1985 to 1988 were consistent with those he had espoused from 1981 to 1984. Similarly, Soviet elders might have thought that their policies of the early and late 1970s were basically the same. But in both cases, policies differed distinctly between the first and second halves of the decades, and they were reflected in changing U.S.-Soviet relations.

What impact did Reagan's policies have on the Soviet Union's international conduct and domestic evolution? In politics, it is often difficult to link outcomes to specific causative factors; therefore all the conclusions presented here are highly speculative. However, in contrast to Matlock's arguments, it seems that the effects of Reagan's influence were quite controversial.

It was not the first time that the Kremlin had met with an aggressive White House; in the early 1960s, there was the case of Nikita Khrushchev and John Kennedy. But it certainly was the first time in the history of U.S.-Soviet relations since 1933 that top Soviet leaders found themselves facing an opponent who was more inexperienced and naïve in terms of world affairs, more blinded by ideological dogma, more nationalistic and self-righteous, more blunt in his rhetoric, and more devoted to simplistic fixes of complex problems than they themselves were. The Soviet leaders saw their own image reflected in Reagan's posturing, and it was a frightening phenomenon. Apparently there was a widespread visceral feeling in the Kremlin that, when dealing with Reagan, Moscow could not afford any miscalculations or sharp turns, because they could no longer count on wise and safe conduct by the other side. They believed there was an even more reckless driver at the helm in Washington than there was in Moscow. Hence, the practical policies of Moscow were twice as cautious from 1981 to 1984, with the exception of the KAL shooting, which was unintentional. For all the renewed hostility and threatening posturing by both sides, there were no serious confrontations comparable to the crises of 1956, 1962, or 1973. Whether that achievement was attributable to Reagan's administration or to sheer luck is an issue of great contention.

Soviet leaders were also seriously frightened by the U.S. arms buildup, especially the intention to deploy Pershing II and GLCM systems in Europe and proceed with the SDI program. Their fear was largely caused by their ignorance in strategic matters and their isolation from alternative views at home and from foreign information and analysis. They fully relied on one-sided assessments from the Soviet military and the KGB, both of which had vested interests in inflating the U.S. threat in order to obtain still greater resources for their own programs and to toughen positions in arms control talks. For instance, the commonly accepted view was that U.S. missiles in Europe could reach Moscow in five minutes, thus effectively launching a decapitating strike against the USSR that would deprive it of its retaliatory capability. Soviet gerontocrats were unaware that Pershing II ballistic missiles lacked the range to reach Moscow, whereas GLCMs had sufficient range but, being subsonic, had a two-hour flight time and, in a massive strike, could not penetrate Soviet airspace unnoticed by the multilayered Soviet air defense. They were also led to believe that the Soviet launch-on-warning system could be undercut by U.S. INF deployments. Ironically, under Gorbachev this self-generated fear was used by the proponents of INF to justify the "double-zero" element of the treaty that envisioned eliminating three times more Soviet missiles than U.S. missiles. Such an idea would never have been accepted by the United States had the tables been turned.

The situation was similar with respect to SDI. Uninformed of the basic Kepler-Newton laws of astrodynamics, Kremlin autocrats believed that laser space battle stations would permanently hang over their heads, threatening instant annihilation by scorching beams. As Matlock correctly points out, the reasons for Moscow's alarm were autosuggestion, mirror imaging, and the subservience of intelligence institutions. But the net effect was not a softening of

Moscow's posture but, on the contrary, tougher and more unrealistic propositions by the USSR for INF counting and limits, and proposals for a treaty to ban arms in outer space. In addition, under pressure from the military, the Soviets approved an "asymmetric response" to SDI. It envisioned unprecedented weapons programs to develop a variety of antimissile systems analogous to SDI, SDI-killers (mostly of the antisatellite type) intended to directly counter space-based SDI platforms, and a huge offensive arms modernization effort to enhance missile-penetration capabilities against all layers of U.S. defenses.

Was this program responsible for the economic collapse of the USSR? No, without any doubt, it was not. Beyond the complicated interaction between the Soviet economy and defense industries, or the allocation of resources for strategic and conventional forces, there are more simple and direct arguments to prove this point. In a normal cycle of development and deployment of major weapons programs, the asymmetric response and its economic burden would not have begun to take effect until the late 1990s, at the earliest. The present Topol-M ICBM system is one of the very few leftovers from this program.

But the Soviet Union collapsed a decade earlier for reasons of a very different nature. President Reagan's policies did not hasten this collapse. On the contrary, they made the Soviet system toughen, for the last time, when its foundations were already melting down. This melting process was triggered most of all by a generational turnover in Soviet leadership beginning in 1985 that matched new leadership with a deeply transformed society ready to discard the outdated Communist ideology, economy, and political regime.

Gorbachev was deeply and negatively impressed by the last spasm of the cold war from 1980 to 1984, and he came to power determined to finish it once and for all. He certainly realized that the USSR bore a large part of the responsibility for this confrontation and had to take the first step to change this pattern. Hence the new political thinking and a long sequence of unilateral concessions by Moscow beginning in 1987, which led to a series of break-throughs in disarmament and the end of cold war. Quite unexpectedly for Gorbachev and his supporters, this also quickly brought about the reunification of Germany, the disbanding of the Warsaw Pact, and, finally, the collapse of the USSR as well as the global Communist economic and political system. But SDI had nothing to do with these grandiose historic events; actually, the "Star Wars" program had been largely curtailed by that time.

Reagan's course in the early 1980s sent a clear signal to Gorbachev and his associates of the dangerous and counterproductive nature of the Soviet Union's further expansion, which was over-stretching its resources, aggravating tensions, and provoking hostile reactions across the globe. However, Reagan obviously overreacted, and the momentum of U.S. foreign policy and arms buildup, as well as the toughening posture and accelerating arms buildup by Moscow, complicated and delayed genuine improvement in U.S.-Soviet relations until the late 1980s, although Gorbachev was ready for it as early as the 1986 Reykjavik summit. In this sense, it may well be argued that Reagan's policies prolonged the cold war. Besides SDI and Soviet countermeasures, huge resources were wasted on the last round of the arms race in the second half of the 1980s that certainly could have been used for better purposes.

Eventually, the end of the cold war coincided with the disintegration of the USSR and certainly, in some respects, encouraged it, since the system had been built unequivocally for war and confrontation, not for transparency and cooperation. At first, this disintegration led to an unprecedented improvement in U.S.-Russian relations and a degree of multifaceted cooperation that would have been unthinkable even by the most optimistic experts in 1981, only a decade earlier. But further trends in Russian domestic evolution, as well as changes in the international environment, including U.S. and NATO conduct, led to new U.S.-Russian controversies and tensions at the turn of the century.

Which of Reagan's beliefs proved to be correct? The historic record is mixed indeed. He believed that nuclear weapons could be abolished only if overall relations between the two countries improved, leading to increased confidence and less suspicion, but marginal limitations created more problems than they resolved. However, in an era of unprecedented cooperation and trust between the United States and Russia during most of the 1990s, strategic forces were actually decreased from about 10,000 warheads for each side to around 5,000. Further reductions now envisioned by Russia are the result of economic limitations and have nothing to do with trust in the United States, which at present is probably as low as it was in the early 1980s. (One noteworthy difference is that in the past this mistrust was imposed on the people by official propaganda but it was never really accepted, whereas now it reflects the genuine mood of a majority of the public.)

Besides, START I, START II, START III, and the 2002 Moscow SORT were nothing but partial cuts and limitations, and the abolition of nuclear arms is now as unlikely as ever; even the most radical version of SORT would leave both sides with nuclear forces at levels of the late 1960s. Moreover, during the 1990s, NATO failed to completely withdraw tactical nuclear weapons from Europe, failed to cut conventional forces seriously below CFE levels, as negotiated in the 1980s, and refused to abandon the first-nuclear-use doctrine. Russia followed suit and readopted this doctrine in 1993 and later expanded such strategies from 2001 to 2003 under President Putin's leadership.

These points make Reagan's belief seem quite detached from complicated political-military realities. No doubt, improvement of political relations and increased trust among nations are essential for the progress of nuclear disarmament. However, as the experiences of the 1990s demonstrated, these are not sufficient to achieve nuclear disarmament. Persistent and complicated negotiations and treaties are necessary, and they must be developed in gradual steps. It is precisely such steps that improve political relations, enhance trust and confidence, and make this process less prone to setbacks. Good political relations are not a substitute for technical arms control negotiations, but they are a necessary condition for facilitating such talks and creating stronger treaties. Without them, nuclear proliferation would continue its self-generating momentum and eventually undercut political relations among nations. Apparently, this dialectic was not understood by either President Reagan or U.S. and Russian leaders during the 1990s and the first half of the current decade, and the ensuing deterioration of both military and political relations between the two nations is evident today.

Reagan was convinced that a democratic Soviet Union would not be a threat to the United States or its neighbors. Again, as correct as such a maxim looks on the surface, it is unrelated to political reality. The development of democracy based on a civilized market economy is a long, complicated, controversial, and sometimes painful process, especially for a nation such as Russia, which was under Communist rule for so many years. It would be naïve to expect that one day Russia would become a full-fledged democracy and then the West would open its doors to a new member of the club. Russia's domestic evolution is deeply intertwined with the dynamics of its international relations. For Russia, foreign policy is not just a matter of relations with other countries; it is largely a matter of choosing a model for its own economic and political development. Hence, all actions by the West that estrange Russia internationally or provide negative examples to follow are highly detrimental to Russia's democratic development since they undermine positions of liberal pro-Western political parties and movements inside the country.

NATO military action against Yugoslavia in 1999 and unjustified extension to the east (including the planned expansion into post-Soviet space, right up to Russian borders); the United States' arbitrary use of force in Iraq in 2003; its failure to ratify CTBT and its withdrawal from the ABM treaty against Russian objections; its rejection of Moscow's proposals to cut nuclear arms deeper than SORT envisions (down to between 1,000 and 1,500 warheads); and its foot-dragging at negotiations on Russia's acceptance to WTO and reluctance to cancel the 1972 Jackson-Vanik Amendment: these are just a few of the most conspicuous examples of policies that have been deleterious to Russia's democratic evolution.

Moreover, owing to failures of a joint Western-Russian reform program implemented in Russia during the 1990s, a large number of Russians presently—and certainly wrongly—believe what Soviet leaders before Gorbachev believed: that a planned egalitarian economy and a stringent political regime, as well as constant vigilance against the evil intentions of the West, are in the interest of the people. And Mikhail Gorbachev's popularity rating, even after all the disenchantment with his opponent Boris Yeltsin in the 1990s, undeservedly never rises above one percent.

All historic analogies are distorting, but in some respects the situation in the first years of the twenty-first century was reminiscent of that in the early 1980s, but with the sides reversing their respective positions. The United States was self-assured, prosperous, building up its military power, expanding its influence, and intervening around the globe on its own and with its allies, even without UN approval. Russia was in deep economic crisis, politically split at home, and suffering from an inferiority complex, with liberals and democrats in full retreat and populist and nationalist leaders rising to take over the government. The state was challenged by armed Muslim fundamentalists but the West provided no real support and condemned Moscow's "excessive use of force," just as the USSR condemned "state terrorism" in the early 1980s. Russia was (and still is) militarily vulnerable and faced the superior conventional and nuclear power of foreign states and alliances. The Kremlin was engaging in irresponsible nuclear rhetoric, parliament and the general public were dissatisfied with arms control and hostile to the United States, and Russia as a whole was keen to reassert its international status and regain its self-respect.

In relative and absolute terms, Russia is now much weaker internally and externally than the United States was 20 years ago. The West has much stronger leverage to influence Russia's conduct at home and abroad. But is the United States capable, willing, and interested in using this leverage wisely and with full understanding of its implications? Is it more sensitive than the USSR was two decades ago, and farsighted enough to take seriously Russia's deep feeling of humiliation, which is fueling nationalism and revanchism and precipitating a new round of confrontation abroad? Is the West sufficiently flexible and stable to check some of its own aggressive trends, including the first-nuclear-use doctrine, the buildup of military power, unilateral military interventions abroad, and the application of double standards to foreign arms transfers and nuclear technology sales, while preserving cooperation in other areas to avoid provoking confrontation across the board? Will the United States be too conservative (as the USSR was in the early 1980s) to use opportunities for fast, radical arms control endeavors and security cooperation? Apart from the economic advantages, these opportunities include deep cuts in strategic nuclear weapons beyond the SORT framework, radical reduction and restructuring of conventional arms in Europe, development of joint missile early-warning and antimissile-defense systems, common nuclear nonproliferation strategies, and genuine peacekeeping cooperation with the full involvement of Russia in NATO's decision-making process.

Sadly, it seems that yet another turning point occurred between 2001 and 2003. After the tragedy of 9/11, President Putin, acting in opposition to the majority of the Russian political community, offered full support to the United States for the operation of the antiterrorist coalition in Afghanistan. In contrast to Putin's possible expectations, Washington responded to this support by withdrawing from the ABM Treaty; expressing unwillingness to create, with a two-page SORT, a substantive arms reduction agreement (with appropriate counting rules, weapons-dismantling procedures, and a verification system); pushing forward the next phase of NATO expansion; and launching a unilateral military intervention in Iraq in 2003.

Since then, the United States has sunk deeper into the Iraqi quagmire and soaring oil prices have increased Russia's self-confidence.

Despite changing circumstances, Americans are finding it hard to abandon the model of relations with Russia that evolved during the 1990s, while Russians regard it with a "never again" attitude. As a result, the two nations face growing controversies over developments in Iran, post-Soviet space and energy export issues, Russian domestic politics, Moscow's relations with China, and general nuclear balance and nonproliferation issues. In a more general sense, the two nations are once again in a widening disagreement on their respective international roles and on the long-term prospects of their relationship. Their cooperation has neither a solid economic foundation nor influential domestic lobbying groups, while the regime of arms control treaties is quickly disintegrating.

How will the United States and Russia overcome another forthcoming tense and difficult period in their relations? What positive and negative lessons, if any, they will draw from the history of the 1980s remains to be seen. Unfortunately, many current examples confirm the statement by Vasili Kliuchevski, a great Russian historian of the nineteenth century, that "History does not teach anybody anything—it only punishes for not learning its lessons."

CHAPTER 2

Oleg Grinevsky *The Crisis that Didn't Erupt: The Soviet-American Relationship, 1980–1983*

THE EARLY 1980s were among the most volatile years in Soviet-U.S. relations. They might be equated with the early 1960s, the era of the Berlin and Cuban missile crises. There was no direct U.S.–Soviet confrontation in the 1980s, but international tensions were greatly intensifying, and once again the world could have come to the brink of war. The situation in the Middle East in 1983 almost erupted into a crisis that would have been more difficult to resolve than the crises in either Berlin or Cuba. This occurred not because war was desired and prepared for by the leaders of both superpowers, but because, not knowing and understanding one another, they suspected the worst of each other's intentions. In a fit of temper, Yuri Andropov called the events that led to the Cuban missile crisis a "war of the blind." Then history repeated itself.

Ronald Reagan's landslide victory in the presidential election of November 1980 did not come as a surprise to Moscow. Under the Carter administration, Soviet-U.S. relations went steadily downhill, and Moscow was prepared for the return to the White House of conservatives who would take a firm stand on foreign policies. The Republican Party defined its goal as achieving military superiority over the Soviet Union so that the United States would be ready for military action in areas of Soviet vulnerability and able to destroy Soviet military targets.[1] Therefore, the Kremlin prepared for serious complications in its relations with the United States and for a drastic increase in international tension and a growing threat of war.

The Soviet leadership was not particularly interested in Reagan's personality. They thought the new president was merely a provincial actor, a puppet manipulated from behind the scenes by U.S. monopolies and the military-industrial complex. Besides, he was behaving as a "zoological anti-Communist." But that was not their major concern. Sometimes it was rather handy for the Soviet leaders to do business with anti-Communists who took a clear and stable stance. Such was the case with President Richard Nixon, for example.

Uncertainty worried them. What would the policies of the new U.S. administration be like? Would there be a dramatic change of course? Or would the rhetoric of the election campaign be followed by a return to normalcy?

On November 17, 1980, Yuri Andropov and Andrei Gromyko dispatched a report to the Central Committee of the Communist Party in which they proposed contacting Reagan's closest circle of advisers through the Soviet embassy in Washington, D.C. They intended to question those who would assume key positions in the administration to learn about their foreign policy views, especially toward the Soviet Union.

It was not difficult to identify members of Reagan's closest circle and learn about their viewpoints. U.S. newspapers were filled with this information, and staff reshuffles in the White House gave rise to heated discussions in the U.S. capital. Therefore, officials of the Soviet embassy in Washington, D.C., needed only to read the newspapers and attend receptions to keep informed.

And that is what they did. Moscow started receiving informa-

---

1. Proceedings and Debates of the 96th Cong., 2nd sess., *Congressional Record*, s10445–s10470.

tion that the key figures in the new administration were Richard Allen, Caspar Weinberger, William Casey, and Alexander Haig. The second and third ranks were filled with members of the four U.S. organizations considered to represent the stronghold of conservatism: the Hoover Institution at Stanford University, the Center for Strategic and International Studies at Georgetown University, the American Enterprise Institute in Washington, D.C., and the Committee on the Present Danger.[2] These organizations provided the White House not only with people but also with ideas. Sarcastic clerks at the Soviet Union's Ministry of Foreign Affairs and the KGB would sometimes refer to them as "brains with [the] screeching of a hawk." Andropov used to define them as ardent anti-Communists and anti-Soviets. Moscow did not expect to have a good rapport with the new team in Washington, and first contacts with the new administration seemed to confirm their expectations.

On January 24, 1981, Secretary of State Alexander Haig dispatched a message to his colleague Andrei Gromyko. It contained tough warnings relating to Soviet policies toward Poland, Afghanistan, and Africa, but problems of Soviet-U.S. negotiations on disarmament and bilateral relations were not even mentioned. Gromyko's immediate response to Haig was cold and instructive. "In our relations, indeed there are many problems, which in fact deserve to be paid foremost attention. One may only regret that these problems, judging by your message, have escaped the new Administration's attention," wrote Gromyko. Then, his response outlined the Soviet position on disarmament.

This exchange coincided with the first press conference given by Haig and Reagan. On January 28, the secretary of state accused the

---

2. Later, Moscow received information that the Hoover Institution provided the Reagan administration and the U.S. government with 40 people; Georgetown University provided 40; and the American Enterprise Institute and the Committee on the Present Danger provided 32 each. The most famous of them were Richard Pipes (National Security Council), Richard Perle, Fred Ikle, John Lehman (Department of Defense), and Eugene Rostow (Arms Control and Disarmament Agency). Edward Rowny, Paul Nitze, and Richard Staar headed the disarmament negotiations.

Soviet Union of "training, financing, and arming international terrorism," which implied supporting national liberation movements in Asia, Africa, and Latin America.[3] The next day the president went even further. He called détente "a one-way street that the Soviet Union has used to purpose its own aims." Then he went on to say that Soviet leaders kept declaring at their Communist Party conventions that their ultimate goal was the promotion of world revolution and a global Communist state. They "reserve unto themselves the right to commit any crime, to lie and to cheat in order to achieve this goal."[4]

Moscow was shocked. In addition, Ambassador Anatoli Dobrynin reported from Washington, D.C., that Haig told him confidentially that Reagan was "unconditionally committed to [a] sharp increase in military expenditures" to liquidate the "gap between the USA" and the USSR in this area.[5] Defense Secretary Weinberger said that his mission was "to re-arm America." More importantly, he declared publicly that the United States would start deploying neutron warheads on their missiles.

The situation sounded serious, and on February 11 the Politburo again discussed relations with the United States. The discussion was surprisingly heated, and everyone reproached Reagan. They concluded that his election meant that the most unbridled forces of imperialism had come to power in the United States.

Dmitri Ustinov and Yuri Andropov raised the alarm. In their public speeches and private communications, they warned that basic U.S. politics were poised for dramatic revision. The warlike statements made by the new president about crusades against communism and accusations of the Soviet Union's guilt of all the deadly sins were merely a propagandistic background that shielded the development of an aggressive military and strategic course, the essence of which was the new role nuclear weapons were to play.

---

3. *New York Times*, January 28, 1981.

4. "The President's News Conference of January 29, 1981," *Weekly Compilation of Presidential Documents* 17 (February 2, 1981), 66.

5. Anatoli Dobrynin, *Sugubo Doveritel'no: posol v Washyngtone pri shesti prezidentakh SshA, 1962–1986* (Moscow: Avtor, 1996), 504–505.

Even under Nixon, the United States and the Soviet Union had worked out a clear understanding of mutual containment by each side's ability to inflict unacceptable damage upon the other. The understanding that nuclear war was meaningless because no victory was possible was secured by two treaties finalized in Moscow in May 1972. The SALT I and ABM treaties were the foundation of strategic stability in the world for the next dozen years.

By 1980, what had changed? The concept of a limited war, inherited from Carter's presidency, had been updated by Reagan's National Security Decision Directive (NSDD) 32, which was based on the possibility of waging a protracted nuclear war with the Soviet Union in which the United States would prevail. The assumption that a nuclear war was not only possible but that the United States would win it laid the foundation for new U.S. defense policies. Huge military budgets and the development of modern weapons were essential elements of these new policies.

This conclusion was supported by the fact that two weeks after Reagan arrived at the White House, he requested Congress to increase the defense budget by $32.6 billion. Congress readily approved the request, and the new administration launched a program to develop new intercontinental ballistic MX missiles, each equipped with ten multiple warheads, and Trident ballistic missiles based on submarines and also equipped with MIRV warheads. In addition, heavy B-1 bombers and long-range sea- and air-launched cruise missiles were quickly developed.

Minister of Defense Dmitri Fedorovich Ustinov commented on the Pentagon's plans by saying, "This is a rather dangerous turn in the arms race. 100 MX ICBMs is one thousand highly accurate nuclear warheads with 600 kilotons each. This means that the capacity of each warhead is thirty times higher than the one dropped onto Hiroshima." Even more anxiety was raised by Ustinov in connection with U.S. plans to deploy intermediate-range Pershing missiles in Europe:

These American missiles with the range of 2500 km are the first strike weapons. . . . As stated in the Pentagon Directive Order on

Building of the Military Forces of the U.S.A., those are targeted at state and military authorities of the USSR first of all, as well as our intercontinental ballistic missiles and other strategic installations. The flying time of a Pershing II is about 6 minutes, which as the aggressor thinks makes it difficult to prepare for any counter measures. This means we are not talking about a simple arithmetic addition of 600 missiles to the strategic potential of the U.S.A., but about a qualitative change in the overall strategic situation in favor of the United States.[6]

At the time, the Soviet Union did not possess similar weapons. According to intelligence data, Moscow alone was the target of 200 warheads. All of this led to the conclusion that Washington was determined to break the parity and achieve military superiority. Ustinov estimated that by 1990 the United States would have 20,000 warheads.

In this context, it is interesting to compare Ustinov's worries with the concerns of his U.S. colleagues, Secretary of Defense Caspar Weinberger and CIA Director William Casey. Strangely enough, they were focused on the same issue, but as a mirrored reflection. This is quite eloquently explained in the CIA Estimate of February 15, 1983, "Soviet Capabilities for Strategic Nuclear Conflict, 1982–1992," which was declassified in the mid-1990s. It states that the Soviet leaders "seek through strategic and other military programs to continue shifting the military component of the correlation of forces in favor of the USSR and its allies." They "regard . . . nuclear war as a continuing possibility . . . and seek superior capability to fight and win the nuclear war."

Then, using the same phrases employed by the Soviets, the CIA Estimate states that the Soviet Union continued to modernize and deploy highly accurate SS ICBMs (SS-18s and SS-19s with multiple warheads), submarine-launched ballistic missiles (with MIRVs), and long-range Backfire bombers, as well as intermediate-range SS-20 missiles in Europe. In addition, the document contends that

---

6. *Pravda*, December 7, 1982.

Moscow was active in the development and testing of a new generation of SS-24 and SS-25 missiles, Typhoon-class submarines, and Blackjack and Bear bombers. By the end of 1982, according to U.S. intelligence, the Soviet Union possessed 2,300 ICBMs and SLBMs with 7,300 warheads. By 1990, the number of missiles would increase by 10 to 15 percent, but the number of warheads on them would reach 21,000.[7]

By and large, U.S. and Soviet intelligence arrived at similar estimates. It is regrettable that the leaders of both nations could not peek into one another's intelligence reports, for their anxieties might have been calmed. Why try in vain to destroy parity and unbalance the forces when the ratio would remain the same? By simple arithmetic, the USSR and the United States would each have 20,000 warheads by 1990, so why make a fuss?

There was one difference between Moscow and Washington in their evaluations of the strategic situation. According to recently published documents, the intelligence community of the United States did not have a unified view of the Soviet Union's perspective on waging a nuclear war. Official CIA statements indicated that the USSR sought superior capabilities "to fight and win a nuclear war with the United States." However, the Bureau of Intelligence and Research of the Department of State assumed that "the Soviets recognize that nuclear war is so destructive, and its course so uncertain, that they could not expect an outcome that was 'favorable' in any meaningful sense."[8]

But Moscow did not have any doubts. It had concluded that Washington sought to shift the balance of forces in its favor so as to perform a surprise nuclear attack first and to reduce the responsive strike from the Soviet Union. The Soviet leadership was serious about preparing for such an inevitable war. Then, as if to play up the fears behind the Kremlin walls, Reagan delivered two con-

---

7. *Witnesses to the End of the Cold War,* ed. William C. Wohlforth (Baltimore, MD: Johns Hopkins University Press, 1996), 26–27, 306.
   8. Ibid., 28, 309.

secutive speeches. In the first, given on March 8, 1983, he declared the Soviet Union the evil empire. Two weeks later, he announced the development of an antimissile shield over America to protect it from this evil empire.

Moscow was racking its brains over why Reagan was making such provocative pronouncements. Not long before, on February 15, the president had invited Soviet ambassador Dobrynin to the White House where they talked for over two hours (an unusually long time for Reagan), proposing to establish good working relations with Moscow. How could one take that proposal seriously when simultaneously Reagan called the Soviet Union the evil empire? How could one accept his proposal to start negotiations on arms reduction when he had announced the necessity of developing new technologies that would ruin the foundation of Soviet military power?

On Andropov's instructions, his aide Andrei Aleksandrov and I had to urgently prepare a reply to Reagan that was published in *Pravda* on March 27. Andropov was in Kuntsevo Hospital at the time, and his first question to us was: "What's . . . Reagan's trick all about? He might be a sincere believer in all those fairy tales about [a] nuclear-free world. But Reagan is an actor, not a politician. But whose scenario is he performing? Who is the scriptwriter? Reagan just could not invent that SDI scheme!" We could not answer those questions, and Andropov was displeased.[9] He argued:

> When the Americans create their anti-missile defense system, the Soviet nuclear weapons will prove outdated. But the American nuclear power will still be up-to-date and efficient. That means the USA is getting an opportunity to get away with the first nuclear strike. The entire geopolitical military stability system, which was

---

9. The quotes from private conversations throughout this essay are from the author's personal notes and some of them appear in his book *Scenario for World War Three*.

created within the last decades, will be destroyed. The USSR will just stop being a superpower.

The question, however, is whether it is possible, given today's technological know-how, to create a reliable anti-missile defense system, which would shield the whole country. . . . I talked to Ustinov asking him to have a word with his scientific research specialists. According to him they are not sure. It looks like it can't be done now as such a system can be broken by various means. However, in 10–15 years' time the situation might change. But what if not in 10–15 years, but in 5 years? One can't set hopes upon the forecasted time.

Let's sum up. What do we have? The Americans know, and they can't fail to know, that a reliable anti-missile defense system cannot be created now. However, they publicize their plans to create such a system, though in practice it would be neither efficient nor reliable. Why all that masquerade then?

- To intimidate us and use us as a pressing tool?
- To pay out a large sum of money to its military industrial complex and to draw us into the arms race in areas where the U.S. enjoys a considerable technological advantage?
- Or else, according to Ustinov, in order to destabilize the strategic situation, so as to dramatically decrease the Soviet retaliatory strike consequences? Let's imagine the following scenario: the USA delivers a first nuclear strike to the Soviet intercontinental ballistic missile sites. That will weaken our retaliatory strike, which, in its turn, will be partially repulsed by the anti-missile defense system.

The situation is too serious, and I am not going to disregard both of the possible scenarios, even the possibility to create an efficient anti-missile defense system. Irrespective of the fact [of] whether the system is practicable or not, it is a real factor in . . . today's U.S. policies. And we can't ignore it.[10]

The discussion had further consequences. Deep in the military-industrial complex, the "adequate responsive measures" were being

---

10. Oleg Grinevsky, "Spektakl pod nazvaniem Zvezdnye voiny" [The Star Wars Show], *Dipkurier, Nezavisimaia Gazeta*, May 18, 2000.

worked out, and Andropov warned about their importance. Naturally, he did not mention what kind of measures were being readied, to avoid frightening everybody still more, but Andropov demonstrated his concern with gestures: "Creating their anti-missile defense system, Americans will await a strike from . . . outer space [and he waved his hand in a zigzag pattern, showing how missiles will fly from outer space], and we'll deliver a strike from here [and his hand showed a missile flying from below, evidently from under the water]."

But apparently the Soviet military system did not pin any special hopes on underwater missiles. Therefore, among other "adequate measures," they were developing the Dead Grip system. If the Americans delivered a surprise first nuclear strike on Moscow, destroying the Soviet capital and killing all the Soviet leaders, what then? The Dead Grip system would provide for an automatic full-power nuclear strike on the United States in the case of even one nuclear explosion in Soviet territory.

Boris Stroganov, head of the Missile and Outer Space Problems Sector at the CPSU Central Committee Defense Department, closely monitored top-secret research. A trial system for early detection and an automatic retaliatory strike was deployed at one of the proving grounds, but luckily the project did not go beyond the development stage. Meanwhile, a secret operation coded RYAN— Nuclear Missile Attack was already in full swing.

In the spring of 1981, on Ustinov and Andropov's joint initiative, the CPSU Politburo approved a directive to both Soviet intelligence service branches, the KGB and GRU, to collect any evidence of U.S. and NATO plans to launch a surprise attack on the Soviet Union. It was the largest peacetime intelligence operation in Soviet history and it lasted until 1984.

In March 1981, Andropov spoke at the secret All-Union KGB meeting. According to General Viacheslav Sharonin, deputy head of the KGB Counterintelligence Service, special emphasis was put on the aggravation of the international situation and the increased threat of a new war. Andropov said, "The Soviet KGB officers should learn how to act more purposefully, accurately, and fast. The major objective is not to overlook the enemy's military preparations for a nuclear strike, not to overlook a real threat of a new war." KGB professionals, Sharonin continued, understood Andropov very well. "The main threat was a surprise first strike. To overlook it means to perish. That's why Andropov insisted: don't overlook, don't overlook."[11]

Special instructions were sent to all chiefs of intelligence stations in the West and some neutral countries directing careful monitoring of all political, military, and intelligence service activities that might indicate preparations for a surprise nuclear attack. Along with intelligence information, such evidence could include lights left on in government offices and military installations at night, mobility of important government officers at unusual times, a dramatic increase in blood donations, and an increase in anti-USSR propaganda. The foreign ministry was kept in the dark about this operation. No cables or directives on it were sent to Soviet ambassadors. It was believed that diplomats were not aware of it, but, in fact, they were. In foreign embassies, diplomats and intelligence service officers lived next door to each other, working on the same team for years, and now and then some of them would complain about needing to check to see if windows were lit up at night. It should be noted that they were skeptical about the operation.[12]

I witnessed a similar episode in London in the summer of 1983. Almost all of the Soviet diplomatic group had gathered at a diplomat's apartment to celebrate, merrily and noisily, someone's birthday. Naturally, alcohol was abundant. In the middle of the celebration, close to midnight, all the intelligence officers got to their feet to say good-bye. They were asked to stay on, but they refused, claiming some urgent task. After a couple of hours, some

---

11. Viacheslav Sharonin, *Pod kolpakom kontrrazvedki: tainaia podopleka perestroiki* (Moscow: Paleia, 1996), 328–329.

12. Dobrynin, *Sugubo Doveritel'no*, 550–552; Christopher Andrew and Oleg Gordievsky, *KGB: The Inside Story of Its Foreign Operations from Lenin to Gorbachev* (New York: HarperCollins Publishers, 1990), 586–597.

of them returned. They were met with sarcastic gibes: "Well, have you caught the enemy?" to which they merely shrugged their shoulders and said, "Goddamn'em. Went all over the city again and looked [to see] if the windows were lit up. If they are, there'll be a war!"

Meanwhile, both the NATO and the Warsaw Pact countries were carrying out maneuvers. Plans for using tactical nuclear weapons, largely in Germany, were being developed, but only on maps, for the time being.

In 1983, the United States carried out Global Shield maneuvers using two important U.S. strategic force components: intercontinental ballistic missiles (ICBMs) and strategic bombers. On a special signal from the command post, air forces set off to simulate conditional nuclear strikes on targets in the USSR and its allied territories.

Moscow anxiously noted that in scale, length, and volume of the performed operation, the maneuver exceeded all previous such actions. Over 1,000 aircraft and 100,000 military troops participated in it. As if in response, Soiuz-83 secret maneuvers were held in the Soviet Union. The maneuvers simulated delivery of over 100 nuclear strikes on West German territory, with the subsequent advance of the Soviet armed forces to the English Channel.

I then asked Nikolai Ogarkov, head of general staff, if he sincerely believed that such a war would not extend beyond Europe and develop into a global nuclear conflict. "I personally don't believe in it," the marshal replied, "but because the Americans speak about a possibility of a limited nuclear war in Europe, I should be ready for it."

The insanity reached a critical point. NATO nuclear launch maneuvers, or Able Archer maneuvers, as they were called, were held in November 1983. They involved simulated strikes, including nuclear strikes, on 50,000 targets in the Soviet Union. U.S. military bases located around the Soviet Union were put on alert. When Reagan was informed about the forthcoming maneuvers, he called the situation "a scenario for a sequence of events that could lead to the end of civilization." Nonetheless, he approved the maneuvers.[13]

Moscow detected the NATO maneuvers and determined that preparation for a nuclear strike was in progress. Soviet troops were also put on alert and strategic bombers carrying nuclear weapons were transferred to East Germany.[14] Several days later, Marshal Ustinov said that a dangerous set of maneuvers held in recent years by the United States and NATO was stirring anxiety. They were carried out on a grand scale and "it gets more and more difficult to differentiate them from real armed forces deployment for aggressive purposes."[15] In these circumstances, one wrong move was enough to cause a catastrophe.

Since the early 1980s, Soviet foreign policy had been deeply stuck in the quadrangle of Afghanistan, Poland, U.S. missiles in Europe, and Middle Eastern problems. It was already involved in the Afghan war, which would last for almost ten years. Brezhnev grumbled at the military: "What a mess they've got into! Can't cope with a bunch of ragamuffins!"

In Poland, a democratic fomentation was occurring. The Solidarity opposition was gaining more political influence and the Polish government was in panic. "Jaruzelski has become entirely apathetic, Kania drinks a lot," was Andropov's report to the Politburo. In short, he said, the Communist regime there is verging on collapse. What should be done?

To the east of the Polish borders, Warsaw Pact maneuvers were continuing, but just as a threat, for the time being. However, Erich Honecker, Todor Zhivkov, and other leaders of Socialist countries demanded that allied forces be sent into Poland, as had been done in Hungary and Czechoslovakia. In Moscow, there was ample sup-

---

13. Desmond Ball and Robert C. Toth, "Revising the SIOP," *International Security*, Spring 1990; and Ronald Reagan, *An American Life* (New York: Simon & Schuster, 1990), 585–586.

14. *Novosti Razvedki i Kontrrazvedki* 2: 1998, 14.

15. *Pravda*, November 19, 1983.

port for this scenario, including that of the powerful Andropov. But Ustinov and Gromyko were not prepared for such decisive action and they managed to convince Brezhnev that bringing in the troops was not yet necessary.

On September 15, 1981, the Politburo discussed an express-coded cable from Petr Abrasimov, the Soviet ambassador in Berlin, about Honecker's suggestion to summon immediately leaders of the "fraternal parties" for a meeting to decide on sending in the troops. However, the Politburo determined at that time not to bring the armed forces into Poland. Ustinov voted definitely against the proposal and argued that the Poles were not prepared to invite the Soviet troops.

Upon his return from meeting at the foreign ministry, Gromyko spent a long time silently pacing back and forth in his office. Then he enigmatically pronounced, "Afghanistan saved Poland. The Poles should thank Allah in their churches!"

The crisis had passed. The situation did not progress beyond the introduction of martial law, and the situation in Poland stabilized itself without the interference of Soviet armed forces, but tension remained.

The situation was much worse with medium-range missile deployment in Europe. In the mid-1970s, the Soviet Union started to replace the obsolete SS-4 and SS-5 missiles with new three-headed Pioneer missiles. In the West they were referred to with the impersonal label SS-20. However, replacement was not the only problem. The number of missiles grew from year to year, and Europeans, especially West Germans, were raising the alarm and asking what was happening and what the goal was for such a mass deployment of Soviet missiles in Europe.

Their nervousness was well founded. Sharp tongues in the foreign ministry told a story about Brezhnev and Ustinov personally crawling on all fours around a map of Western Europe that was spread out on the floor in the general secretary's office and measuring the areas of the prospective nuclear strikes with the help of a pair of compasses. Their conclusion was that it would take only 20 nuclear warheads to demolish human society there. In fact, there were already 360 Pioneer missiles with 1,080 nuclear warheads deployed in Europe by the end of 1983.[16]

Early in the 1980s, the Middle East became the center of the USSR-U.S. geostrategic competition. It had first surfaced during the U.S. election campaign in 1979. Reagan outlined his foreign policy objectives, saying that America's major concern was to prevent the Middle East from falling under Soviet domination. This was not just another fight for a piece of the globe. Had the Soviet Union managed to gain domination in the Middle East and consequently to control all of that area's oil resources, it would have been a threat to the economies of the major industrially developed countries. The ability of NATO and Japan to resist Soviet pressure would have been "seriously damaged," and almost surely that would have led to "Western Europe and Japan taking a neutral position." That would have meant a blow for the United States as well, as inevitably it would have been isolated. For greater emphasis, Reagan added, "The Soviet navy is currently furrowing the waters of the Mediterranean." In short, the United States was challenging the Soviet Union in the Middle East, and Moscow was prepared to meet the challenge.

In the middle of February 1981, a representative Soviet delegation headed by Admiral Nikolai Smirnov, first deputy of the commander-in-chief of the Soviet navy, arrived in Damascus. For many years, every time a new weapons contract was under negotiation with Syria, the Soviet military raised the issue of setting up a base in Syria. Syrians had deftly evaded the question and the decision was postponed, but during negotiations in Moscow on November 8, 1980, President Hafez al-Asad unexpectedly gave his consent. Consequently, Admiral Smirnov's delegation had to choose a location for the Soviet military base in Syria. They carefully explored the entire coastline and decided on a spacious area between Latakia

---

16. Yuli Kvitsinski, *Vremia i sluchai: zametki professionala* (Moscow: Olma-Press, 1999), 346.

and Tartus. The spot was perfect for a naval base, and it had an area behind it to build an airfield for base air cover. The admiral reported that construction would take only six months. In addition, deep in Syria to the west of Deir-Az-Zor, construction of another air base for Soviet long-range aircraft was being planned. Of course, it was the Soviets' understanding of the geostrategic situation, not Syria's security, that motivated them to build these military bases.

The Soviet Union was on the offense. But for the first time in Soviet—and possibly Russian—history, the enemy was across the ocean. That required a radical change in strategy, switching priorities from land forces to weapons that could defeat the enemy thousands of kilometers from Soviet borders. Hence, the navy took on a new role.

Obviously, the Soviet military could not compete with the United States in the number of bases in the Mediterranean. However, in their opinion, setting up a base with an airfield in Tartus would provide a number of strategic advantages to the Soviet Union, including the following:

1. It was in close proximity to both Bosporus and Gibraltar. The Soviet navy in the Mediterranean could control access to these straits of strategic importance.
2. It created a powerful counterbalance to U.S. bases and weapons, including nuclear missiles, in the Mediterranean and the Persian Gulf. The United States had expanded and modernized its military base at Diego Garcia Island in the Indian Ocean and had bases in Egypt, Oman, Somalia, and Kenya. The U.S. Sixth Fleet was there with its 20 warships, including two aircraft carriers and five submarines. In the Indian Ocean they had a group of rapid deployment forces consisting of an aircraft carrier, three submarines, and a dozen other ships constantly controlling the approach to the Persian Gulf.
3. The Soviets believed that their influence in the Middle East would increase. The oil factor was critical as the ability to

block oil deliveries from the region to the United States and Western Europe could seriously influence the entire situation in the West.

However, the Syrians had something different in mind. Their consent to the Soviet Union to set up military bases was not the result of their concern about Soviet geostrategic interests. Rather, they wanted to shield Syria with Soviet missiles in case of a war with Israel. Therefore, President Asad put forward the condition that the Soviet Union should deploy two regiments of their air defense missile systems along the Syrian-Israeli border and one regiment around Damascus to protect the Syrian capital. The missiles were to be serviced by the Soviet military.

The Soviet defense ministry supported the idea. However, Ustinov's optimism was met with an ambiguous reaction from other members of the Politburo. The potential for war in the Middle East was becoming stronger. Gromyko preferred to be cautious. Andropov held a more radical position, but he did not actively promote it. He said:

> USSR-USA strategic parity made any direct conflict between them pointless and absurd as both the parties will be simply annihilated in the nuclear war. As to the borders of confrontation they are strictly outlined in Europe and in the Far East—they must not be crossed. Therefore, the struggle takes place only when and where any direct conflict between them can be avoided. So it happens in the so-called "third world"—Asian, African and Middle East countries. People there are starting to oppose imperialism, and our duty is to help them. That's why we need bases and the fleet operating in the ocean, as our buttresses to provide that help.

However, Leonid Brezhnev was growing increasingly frail and he had little interest in bases. After the invasion of Afghanistan, he generally avoided radical changes in politics. The creation of Soviet military bases in Syria and Asad's provisions were not discussed at Politburo meetings, and the decision was simply postponed.

Everything changed in the summer of 1982 after the Israeli invasion of Lebanon. President Asad, frightened by the bloody assault on Beirut, paid two secret visits to Moscow. Now it was he who asked for the deployment of Soviet air defense missile systems and air forces in Syria. He assured the Soviet Union that he was ready to provide it with naval and air bases without any conditions. Defense Minister Ustinov held one-on-one talks with him, and on October 18 an agreement to deploy two Soviet air defense missile regiments along with Soviet military personnel was signed at the defense ministry on Frunze Street in Moscow. The foreign ministry was cut off from the negotiations, and even Gromyko was not informed about the contents of the agreement. However, Moscow's concerns lay elsewhere. Brezhnev's days were numbered, and the Kremlin was busy with a secret struggle for power.

Meanwhile, the Soviet missile deployment in Syria was in full swing. The first Soviet troop carrier arrived at the port of Latakia on January 10, 1983. The other five troop carriers arrived several days later. All the military troops wore civilian clothes and looked like tourists. Air Defense Regiment #231 with long-range anti-aircraft missiles was deployed near Dumeira, 40 kilometers west of Damascus. By February 1, Anti-aircraft Regiment #220 with long-range missiles was deployed 5 kilometers east of Homs. A technical support regiment arrived in one of Damascus's suburbs. Helicopter detachments for radio-electronic operations were deployed at a military aerodrome in the capital, and similar ground units were placed in the Golan Heights and the Bekaa Valley. S-200 (SAM-5) missiles, launched from Syria, could cover all of Lebanon and a major part of Israel, which made it possible to bring down Israeli aircraft there.

There were no regular Soviet units in Lebanon and Syria. However, there were numerous military advisers and specialists in Syrian military units and headquarters. They even participated personally in military operations, and their losses amounted to 200 injured and 13 killed. The total number of Soviet troops in Syria was now reaching the level of 8,000 servicemen.

However, disenchantment set in rapidly. Clouds were gathering on the international horizon, and the Kremlin feared that a storm might break out in the Middle East. Wars were amazingly regular there, erupting every eight or nine years (1948, 1956, 1964, and 1973), but the Soviet Union had not been directly involved in them. On the contrary, they allowed the USSR to consolidate its influence in the area. Now, however, not only Soviet missiles but also Soviet servicemen could be in danger. Those whose mission it was to protect Syria found themselves unprotected. Their special concern was not the prospect of an air strike on Soviet missiles but ground operations by the Israeli army. Those missiles were protected by a handful of Soviet soldiers and were, in fact, defenseless. Syrian or Palestinian units could not be relied upon. To prevent an attack on Soviet missiles and the capture of Soviet soldiers by Israel, many generals of the defense ministry and general staff, with Ustinov's support, suggested drastic plans ranging from making threatening statements and saber rattling to sending Soviet troops to Syria. However, Marshal Nikolai Ogarkov, head of general staff, bluntly discounted these ideas, saying:

> Under no circumstances can we provide communication lines and service support to that grouping. On the ground, they are cut off by Turkey—a member of NATO. It can immediately block the Bosporus and Dardanelles, and the U.S. Sixth Fleet will block the access to Lebanon and Syria in the Mediterranean Sea. What should we do then—should we try to break through Turkey causing the start of World War III? Or should we leave the Soviet troops there to be disgracefully defeated and taken prisoners?

Ogarkov managed to win the battle. Andropov and Gromyko supported him, and Ustinov chose not to protest. But the question about what should be done remained.

The possibility of delivering a nuclear strike to the Dimona Nuclear Research Center in Israel's Negev Desert was discussed at the general staff meeting early in June 1983. The meeting was presided over by General Sergei Akhromeev, who was then deputy head of general staff. He warned from the beginning that the discussion was one of an operational hypothesis with its advantages and disadvantages. Such a strike would not result in many victims, but Israeli nuclear power would be annihilated, and that would encourage the Arabs to consolidate and enter the war with a united front. Israel would be demoralized and deprived of its main weapon, which would predetermine its defeat. The negative aspects of the hypothesis, according to Akhromeev, included the risk of the Soviet Union's involvement in a nuclear world war, although he thought it very unlikely.

The foreign ministry strongly objected to the idea of striking Israel, arguing that the action would be very dangerous, especially for the Soviet Union. That operation would not rescue a handful of Soviet soldiers in Lebanon but rather would leave them to the mercy of fate. The use of nuclear weapons would lead to a disastrous conflict in the Middle East. The United States would support Israel and the Arabs would withdraw. Would the next step be confrontation with the United States? The Soviet Union would face an unacceptable dilemma: either to admit its defeat as the aggressor that had used a nuclear weapon first, or to launch a nuclear war and risk its consequences, including the annihilation of their country.

No decision was made, but Moscow received alarming information through KGB and GRU channels about possible provocation to directly involve the Soviet Union in the Middle East conflict. The provocation was expected from both Arabs and Israel, and there were serious grounds for such scenarios.

After the bloody developments in Beirut, Washington sent U.S. marines to Lebanon, where they, in alliance with French troops, acted as peacemakers. They were separated from the Soviet soldiers by only about 50 kilometers. At that time, Lebanon appeared to be a boiling pot of civil war where everyone was fighting. U.S. marines were also gradually dragged into the struggle. In mid-September, they delivered the first artillery strike on targets in Lebanese territory controlled by Syria. The Syrians warned that henceforth they would retaliate.

Things went from bad to worse. On October 23, 1983, a five-ton truck broke the barrier at the gates of the U.S. barracks in Beirut not far from the airport, and the driver blew himself up in the vehicle stuffed with 300 kilos of explosives. In the attack, 239 marines perished. Suspicion focused on Shia Muslims, who operated from the Lebanese territory controlled by Syria, and Washington threatened to retaliate. The U.S. media warned that new bombardment and shelling might lead to Soviet military deaths, "which in its turn might lead to serious U.S.-Soviet confrontation." Former deputy secretary of state James Ball warned that a strike on Soviet missiles in Syria might become a "scenario for Third World War."[17] Therefore it is not surprising that in the summer and fall of 1983, every Politburo meeting included discussions, in one form or another, of the issues connected with the Middle East situation.

A decision to transfer missiles to Syria and to withdraw Soviet military personnel by the summer of 1984 was taken in April 1983, but it failed to calm tensions. Troops and missiles were still there, and the information from the Middle East grew more and more alarming, so the Politburo kept discussing these uneasy issues.

Once again, at the Politburo meeting held on July 7, one of the major issues on the agenda was the situation in the Middle East. Andropov outlined it as follows:

> Some time ago we made an error, when we sent our air defense missile systems to Syria together with the military servicemen. We were caught in a trap. Irrespective of our supplies of the most modern weapons to Syria, it stands in fact no chance to defeat Israel. Therefore, whether our detachment commander there will carry out the Syrian order to launch missiles or not, Arabs will lay the whole blame of Syrian defeat on the Soviet Union. The situation might turn still worse for us, if we are drawn into the conflict directly. Then there might be far more serious consequences.
>
> Although on a small scale, today's situation in the Middle East looks like the 1962 Cuban missile crisis. Of course, both the scale

---

17. See, for example, *New York Times*, October 19, 1983.

and the enemy are different. But the danger of our being involved in a Syria-Israel armed conflict exists as not only our missiles are under a threat of being attacked, but our people, too.

I know that at working levels here, plans for possible military actions are being developed. Forget them. Some measures have already been taken to minimize the risk of our involvement in the conflict, and we were quite firm talking to Syrians that in the case of . . . war with Israel they should rely on themselves.

Now we need to define our strategies for the future. In short, I mean caution and restraint. The priority should be carrying out the Politburo decision to transfer the Soviet missiles to Syria and withdraw our military personnel from that country. The sooner, the better.

We have to be adamant in our policy to prevent an Israel-Syria military conflict, first of all, using political tools. In case of an Israeli attack, we should examine possibilities of some demonstrative actions to induce the USA and Israel to be reserved. But whatever the developments are, we should not overstep the limits of direct involvement in the military actions.

After Andropov's speech at the Politburo meeting, the decision was made to accept these considerations:

> In the case of the conflict extension to Syrian territory, to examine a possibility of using some demonstrative actions in order to induce the USA, and Israel through them, to be reserved. Our measures should not overstep the limits of direct involvement in the military actions.[18]

But along with direct involvement, there was always the risk of chance events, especially in an atmosphere fraught with suspicion and tense nerves.

On August 31, 1983, Korean airliner KAL-007 began its usual flight from New York to Seoul by way of Anchorage, Alaska. For reasons that are still unknown, it strayed 500 kilometers off course

---

18. Politburo Decision P115 /Y1, July 7, 1983.

and flew for several hours over Kamchatka and Sakhalin, penetrating Soviet airspace. Computer simulation of the flight performed by the International Civil Aviation Organization (ICAO) of the United Nations revealed that three minutes after the airliner took off from Anchorage, the automatic pilot was on. The airliner followed a straight course although, according to the flight plan, it should have changed course on nine occasions. The trig navigation system showed a side deviation to the right of the route, but the pilots took no measures to correct it. The only explanation, as expressed by the ICAO, was that the flight crew had flown a great deal in the previous weeks and had crossed many time zones, thus their attention, concentration, and judgment had suffered. The Korean pilots who were members of the ICAO commission acknowledged that pilots should not fly under such conditions.

However, on September 1, at 4:51 A.M., Kamchatka time, Soviet radar in Kamchatka spotted the Korean airliner and marked it as target 60–65. The target did not respond to queries but steadily headed toward the USSR's state borders. The anti-aircraft defense officers on duty identified it first as an American KC-135 tanker plane, and later as an RC-135 reconnaissance plane.

What is interesting is that one hour before, the same radar had identified and monitored target 60–64, which was maneuvering north of Karaginski Island and was also failing to answer queries. It was an American RC-135 reconnaissance plane. Later, the United States Department of Defense admitted that the plane was observing Soviet missile tests and anti-aircraft defense activities in Kamchatka as part of the Cobra Dane program.

At some point, the two airplanes were only 75 miles away from each other. As they approached each other, their tracking marks fully merged on Soviet radar screens, and they flew next to each other for about ten minutes. Then one of the planes turned around and set course for Alaska while the other kept flying toward Kamchatka.

At 5:30 A.M., that plane entered USSR territorial airspace. General Kamenski, the anti-aircraft defense commander in the Far East

Military District, reported to the general staff in Moscow that an American military reconnaissance plane had penetrated Soviet airspace. Moscow responded with instructions to try to force the plane to land, and, if that failed, to follow existing operational procedures.

Further decisions were taken by the local air command in the Far East. Fighter planes took off to intercept the airliner, but to no avail. The intruder simply did not react to their signals and warnings, and within half an hour left Soviet airspace. However, it was still heading directly to Sakhalin.

Then ten fighters took off. Soon Soviet fighter pilot Lieutenant Colonel Gennadi Osipovich got lucky. The target, a large aircraft with its lights and flashers on, was in front of him. Nonetheless, the pilot insisted that he "never thought for a moment" that he was following a civilian airliner. "The trouble for all Soviet pilots is that we do not study civilian aircraft belonging to foreign companies," said Osipovich many years later. He fired several warning shots in an attempt to force the plane to land. As the intruder did not react, he fired two missiles. One of them hit the target, and the Korean Boeing started a rapid descent. Within approximately 12 minutes, it crashed into the sea.[19]

On the morning of September 1, Secretary of State George Shultz made a harsh statement accusing Soviet authorities of a barbarous international assault on an unarmed civilian passenger plane. Pronouncing those words, the secretary of state was surely playing by cold war rules. He would later write in his memoirs that he had not realized that neither he nor the president had complete information. Only on the day after the event did the CIA and the NSA acknowledge that the Soviets may have believed the plane to be a reconnaissance intruder.[20]

---

19. The 1993 ICAO report confirmed that the decision to shoot was based on Soviet error in believing the aircraft to be a U.S. reconnaissance intruder, not willful or deliberate action against a civilian airliner. (*New York Times*, June 16, 1993, A7; *Izvestia*, October 9, 1993).

20. George P. Shultz, *Turmoil and Triumph: My Years as Secretary of State* (New York: Charles Scribner's Sons, 1993), 361–367.

This, however, was not the whole truth. In the famous speech in which he accused the Soviet Union of a "murderous attack," President Reagan, for greater impact, played part of the tape recording of intercepted communications in which the Soviet pilot pronounced those famous words: "The target is destroyed." But he did not play other parts of the tape in which the pilot repeatedly attempted to communicate with the airliner, including the use of signals with cannon fire. It was later revealed that President Reagan had been intentionally provided with an incomplete and partially edited recording of the Soviet pilot's intercepted communications.[21]

As Seymour Hersh, a journalist who conducted a thorough investigation of the incident, bitterly remarked, there was "a frightening irony in all this: the President of the United States, relying on information that was wholly inaccurate and misleading, was accusing the other side of telling lies and was perceived as being moderate in so doing."[22]

Another question is still unanswered. How could the U.S. antiaircraft defense have overlooked the Korean airliner's noticeable deviation from the international airway and failed to warn it? If they really did not notice anything that night, then, according to U.S. journalist David Pearson, it was "the worst failure of the American early warning and communications systems, command, management, and intelligence in the entire history of the United States."[23]

However, this explanation would not justify the Soviet Union's action resulting in the death of innocent passengers on the Korean airliner. Moscow was worried about whether or not to admit that the Soviet Union had shot down the civilian airliner. Ustinov

---

21. Raymond Garthoff, *The Great Transition* (Washington, DC: Brookings Institution, 1994), 118–121.

22. Seymour Hersh, *The Target Is Destroyed* (New York: Random House, 1986), 131.

23. David Pearson, "K.A.L. 007: What the U.S. Knew and When We Knew It," *The Nation*, August 18–25, 1984, 97.

sternly warned everyone: "Keep silent! The Americans can prove nothing." Andropov, who had just been admitted to Kuntsevo Hospital, washed his hands of it, saying, "Sort it out without me." Gromyko maintained his usual position of not sticking his neck out and did not argue with Ustinov.

As a result, an absurd TASS statement appeared on September 2 with the message that the Soviet Union was unaware that any aircraft had been shot down in its airspace. After that, unintelligible prattle continued for several more days. In the end, TASS admitted that an "unidentified plane" had been warned by Soviet fighters and had flown away in the direction of the sea. Obviously, that statement only added to the worldwide condemnation of the Soviet Union's actions.

The Korean airliner incident showed the deep distrust between the USSR and the United States. Each party was ready to think the worst of the other. For Washington, it was a vivid illustration of the Soviet Union as evil empire, and for Moscow, it was just more evidence of U.S. imperialistic policies, espionage, and exploitation of human emotions in conjunction with the tragic loss of life. Therefore, it is not at all surprising that Soviet-U.S. relations deteriorated further.

One week after the attack on the Korean airliner, Gromyko and Shultz met in Madrid. The meeting was timed to coincide with the end of the marathon Conference on Security and Cooperation in Europe (CSCE). As initially conceived, the meeting of the two ministers was intended to outline the first steps to improve Soviet-U.S. relations, most especially in their negotiations on intercontinental and medium-range missiles. If they were successful, then talks between Andropov and Reagan could be held late in the fall.

The disastrous incident with the Korean airliner halted all progress. At the National Security Council meeting of September 2, there was a lengthy discussion about whether the Madrid meeting was necessary at all. Secretary of Defense Caspar Weinberger and others suggested canceling it. However, Shultz insisted on the meeting and President Reagan supported him. They compromised, proposing that the meeting should be held but lunch would not be served, and the talks with Gromyko would be restricted to three topics: the Korean airliner, human rights, and the Soviet Union's default of its obligations on the disarmament agreements.

Moscow also questioned the necessity of the meeting. Those hesitations originated with Gromyko himself, who expected that the conversation with Shultz would be harsh and unpleasant with uncertain results. But Andropov said: "The meeting should be held. Let the Americans, if they wish, break the ties. Then it will be their entire fault. But you should take a firm stand in Madrid."

In his usual manner, Gromyko did not argue. As envisaged by the itinerary, he went to the U.S. ambassador's residence in Madrid, where over 200 reporters had gathered on the front lawn. However, breaking common protocol rules, Shultz did not meet his guest at the door. The negotiating table was empty, although earlier plans had called for lunch to be served. No cups of coffee, no glasses of water, not even paper or pencils were in sight. The Americans thereby showed their dissatisfaction with the Soviet position.

Gromyko did not blink an eye but simply set his jaw and frowned. Shultz coldly invited him into a small office, styled as a library, for a tête-à-tête. There he announced immediately and without diplomatic courtesy that he wanted to discuss the problems of the Korean airliner and the release of the Soviet dissident Anatoli Shcharansky. Gromyko balked and said that he would not discuss those issues as they concerned Soviet internal affairs. Shultz would not budge and announced that he only intended to discuss those two topics according to his president's instructions. Gromyko immediately countered, saying: "The commission given to you as the secretary of state does not oblige me as a representative of another state to follow the American president's instructions. Are you going to discuss those issues on your own?"

Several minutes later, their faces flushed with anger, Shultz and Gromyko left the embassy library and joined the advisers sitting at the empty dinner table, but the discussion continued in the same manner there. Gromyko said that he had already clearly explained in their private conversation that he did not intend to discuss the issues of the Korean airliner and Shcharansky, and if Shultz insisted, there was no point in continuing. As if to confirm his determination, the minister collected his papers and stood up to leave. Shultz also stood up abruptly and headed to the door. For a moment, it seemed that the imposing secretary of state intended to block Gromyko's way, but instead, Shultz threw the door open and said brusquely, "If you're going to leave, fine. Go."

However, Gromyko did not leave, but went on talking as he paced back and forth. For several minutes he and Shultz exchanged sharp verbal lunges. Each insisted on his own opinion and did not want to listen to the other. At last they agreed to let everyone discuss whatever they wanted. Gromyko sat down and started to explain the Soviet Union's position on the prevention of a nuclear war. Shultz sat silently with a gloomy expression on his face. When Gromyko finished, the U.S. secretary of state started to talk about the Soviet attack on the defenseless Korean airliner. Now it was Gromyko who kept silent. That game lasted for two hours. Gromyko commented later: "It was probably the most harsh of the talks I have held with the fourteen U.S. secretaries of state for many years."

Gromyko returned from Madrid in a gloomy mood. He paced the length of his enormous office for a long time and then said, "Something has to be undertaken. . . . Otherwise, everything will fall apart."

Relations between the two superpowers seriously deteriorated that uneasy September. Along with many other reasons discussed in this chapter was the collision of two stubborn idealists—the ardent anti-Communist Ronald Reagan and the no less ardent champion of Communist ideas, Yuri Andropov. Here were two outstanding personalities, two firm characters, two deep believers.

As a result, Soviet-U.S. relations were strained to the extreme. For the first time in his long career as foreign minister, Gromyko canceled his annual trip to New York to attend the UN General

Assembly session. On the same day, President Reagan made a series of harsh speeches condemning the Soviet Union.

Just a few days after the U.S. invasion of Grenada, Reagan remarked to the Heritage Foundation that containing Soviet expansion was not enough. He declared, "We must go on the offensive with a forward strategy for freedom. . . . The struggle now going on in the world is essentially the struggle between . . . what is right and what is wrong."[24] The measured policy framework of seeking a dialogue set forth by Shultz in June seemed to have disappeared.

For Moscow, this Reagan speech sounded like a declaration of war on the third world, at least. But Andropov was even harsher in his response. In his opinion, the United States had become a "country obsessed with . . . unprecedented militarist paranoia," and he accused Reagan of "extreme adventurism." This statement, made on September 28, represented the first authoritative overall evaluation of the Reagan administration's policy. Andropov stressed that this "militarist course represents a serious threat to peace. Its essence is to try to ensure a dominant position in the world." He concluded: "If anyone had any illusions about the possibility of an evolution for the better in the policy of the present American administration, recent events have dispelled them once and for all. . . . Reagan's administration goes so far in their imperialist ambitions that one starts to doubt if Washington has any brakes available and [is] able to keep them from crossing the line, at which any reasonable person will stop."[25]

Pope John Paul II commented on the situation by saying that the postwar era had entered "a new prewar phase."

Only one positive event occurred that autumn. An agreement was reached in Madrid to convene a conference on disarmament in Europe. Its first phase, devoted to the development of measures

---

24. Heritage Foundation, October 3, 1983, *Presidential Documents* 19 (October 10, 1983), 1383–84.

25. *Pravda*, September 28, 1983.

to create mutual trust and security in Europe, was to be held in Stockholm. And as history has shown, it was the first step in the right direction. Three years later, the agreement on security and confidence-building measures was reached in Stockholm. This agreement removed the veil of secrecy over the military activity of both NATO and the Warsaw Pact and, for the first time, put in place an on-site inspection regime. The improvements in mutual trust that grew out of this agreement paved the way for the conclusion of the INF treaty, under which all U.S. and Soviet intermediate-range nuclear forces were eliminated; the treaty on deep reduction of the conventional forces of both NATO and the Warsaw Pact (the CFE treaty); and the treaty on a 50 percent reduction of the strategic nuclear forces of the United States and the Soviet Union (START-1). With these agreements in place—as well as major changes in other aspects of U.S.-Soviet relations herein discussed—the cold war ended.

Kiron K. Skinner : *An Alternative Concept of Mutual Cooperation*

> The first part of the 1980s [was] the most dangerous period because the two sides mistrusted each other again as they did in the 1950s, but this time with much larger arsenals and weapons.[1]
>
> ALEKSANDR A. BESSMERTNYKH
> Soviet First Deputy Foreign Minister
> 1987–1989

IN HIS ESSAY, Oleg Grinevsky makes a persuasive case that judicious decision making by American and Russian leaders is the primary reason that the superpowers avoided a catastrophic clash in the early 1980s. He recalls, however, that Soviet officials questioned President Ronald Reagan's control of his country's foreign and defense policies. For instance, following Reagan's March 23, 1983, announcement that he was authorizing research and development of a missile defense system, the Strategic Defense Initiative (SDI), Grinevsky reports that Soviet General Secretary Yuri Andropov declared: "What's . . . Reagan's trick all about? He might be a sincere believer in all those fairy tales about [a] nuclear-free world. But Reagan is an actor, not a politician. But whose scenario is he performing? Who is the scriptwriter? Reagan just could not invent that SDI scheme!"

---

1. Quoted in William C. Wohlforth, ed., *Witness to the End of the Cold War* (Baltimore, MD: Johns Hopkins University Press, 1996), 11.

Grinevsky presents a detailed analysis of deliberations and decisions by Soviet leaders and interactions of Soviet and American officials during the early 1980s, but leaves it to his responder to answer Andropov's questions. The following review of speeches and statements made by President Reagan and members of his administration is presented in order to establish that, in the early 1980s, there was a well-defined American national strategy based on anti-classical thinking about nuclear weapons and grand strategy.

In other words, Reagan disagreed with some of the prevailing views about the strategic posture of the United States. He did not believe that unilateral restraint would eventually lead to similar behavior by the Soviet Union. Furthermore, he disagreed with the focus of the arms control community, as expressed by Secretary of State Cyrus Vance, that "if we make progress on SALT [the Strategic Arms Limitation Treaty], then a lot of things will fall into place that do not fall into place otherwise."[2] He disagreed with the view that "a nuclear order based on mutual deterrence should be . . . [the] highest priority" for statesmen.[3] Reagan also disagreed with the détente-era argument that the Soviet Union should be treated as a normal state in the international system. He was in accord, however, with the predominant view that the superpowers should consistently undertake negotiations on nuclear weapons and engage in extensive cultural and scientific exchanges. In terms of nuclear weapons, Reagan advocated negotiations that would reduce the number of weapons, not merely control the pace of the arms race.

---

2. The statement by Vance is found in the declassified minutes of the Special Coordinating Committee held at the White House on March 2, 1978. Reprinted in Odd Arne Westad, ed., *The Fall of Détente: Soviet-American Relations During the Carter Years* (Oslo, Norway: Scandinavian University Press, 1997), 267.

3. Robert Gilpin, "Theory of Hegemonic War," *Journal of Interdisciplinary History* (Spring 1988): 613. For social science research reflecting the view that unilateral restraint may reduce the likelihood of aggression, see Michael D. Wallace, "Old Nails in New Coffins: The Para Bellum Hypothesis Revisited," *Journal of Peace Research* 18, no. 1 (1981): 91–95.

Reagan's handwritten documents, which I discovered and subsequently reproduced in several co-authored books, show that even before he became president, Reagan had an abiding commitment to abolishing nuclear weapons and he forcefully opposed Mutual Assured Destruction (MAD), yet he was a strong advocate of U.S.-Soviet engagement on the full range of issues under dispute.[4] Scholars have been using recently released archival evidence, including the documents in my books, as they contribute to the evolving reassessment of Reagan's role in the development of U.S. national security policy during the final decades of the cold war.[5] In my view, this reassessment requires further grounding in Reagan's own writings and in an interpretation of his presidential security directives based on these documents.

My research suggests that Reagan's philosophical orientation, as expressed in his public and private writings before and during his presidency, was the intellectual bedrock of U.S. strategy in the 1980s. His deepest imprint is found in three elements of that strategy: (1) engage the Soviets in negotiations (considered as important as the military buildup); (2) eliminate nuclear weapons; and (3) seek the peaceful implosion of the Soviet system, followed by its units joining the community of free states. Each of these elements will be examined following a review of the development of U.S. grand strategy during the early 1980s.

American Grand Strategy During the 1980s

Grinevsky refers to National Security Decision Directive 32 (NSDD-32), the "U.S. National Security Strategy," as evidence

---

4. See Kiron K. Skinner, Annelise Anderson, and Martin Anderson, eds., *Reagan, In His Own Hand: The Writings of Ronald Reagan that Reveal His Revolutionary Vision for America* (New York: Free Press, 2001); Skinner, Anderson, and Anderson, eds., *Reagan, A Life in Letters* (New York: Free Press, 2003); and Skinner, Anderson, and Anderson, eds., *Reagan's Path to Victory: The Shaping of Ronald Reagan's Vision, Selected Writings* (New York: Free Press, 2004).

5. See John Lewis Gaddis, *Strategies of Containment: A Critical Appraisal of American National Security During the Cold War*. Revised and expanded edition.

that the Reagan administration assumed it could win a nuclear war with the Soviet Union and that this assumption "laid the foundation for new U.S. defense policies." He is correct in one sense but mistaken in another. Among the objectives of U.S. foreign policy listed in the May 20, 1982, White House document was the enhancement of the "strategic nuclear deterrent by developing a capability to sustain protracted nuclear conflict." The directive also stated: "Deterrence is dependent on both nuclear and conventional capabilities. Nuclear forces will not be viewed as a lower-cost alternative to conventional forces. At the same time, the possible use of nuclear weapons must remain an element of our overall strategy."

But NSDD-32 set out two other global goals and an overarching objective, which Grinevsky does not mention. One goal was "to strengthen the influence of the U.S. throughout the world by strengthening existing alliances." The other was "to contain and reverse the expansion of Soviet control and military presence throughout the world, and to increase the costs of Soviet support and use of proxy, terrorist, and subversive forces." The principal objective was to foster "long-term liberalizing and nationalist tendencies within the Soviet Union and allied countries." According to Thomas C. Reed, an adviser to President Reagan on security policy at the National Security Council and one of the drafters of the directive, NSDD-32 was a call for "the dissolution of the Soviet regime."[6] Thus, the directive was far more ambitious than President Dwight D. Eisenhower's advocacy of rolling back Soviet influence in Eastern Europe.

Though a secret document, the essence of NSDD-32 was made public soon after it was issued.[7] President Reagan discussed the

---

(New York: Oxford University Press, 2005). John Lewis Gaddis, *The Cold War: A New History* (New York: Penguin Press, 2005); and Paul Lettow, *Ronald Reagan and His Quest to Abolish Nuclear Weapons* (New York: Random House, 2005).

6. See Thomas Reed, *At the Abyss: An Insider's History of the Cold War* (New York: Random House, 2004), 236–237.

7. NSDD-32 was declassified on February 16, 1996. A copy of this document, NSDD-75, other directives, and National Security Study Directives, are located in

substance of the strategy document in an address to members of the British Parliament on June 8, 1982: "The objective I propose is quite simple to state: to foster the infrastructure of democracy, the system of a free press, unions, political parties, universities, which allows a people to choose their own way to develop their own culture, to reconcile their own differences through peaceful means. . . . What I am describing now is a plan and a hope for the long term—the march of freedom and democracy which will leave Marxism-Leninism on the ash-heap of history. . . ."[8]

As John Lewis Gaddis observes, "No American president had ever before talked like this, and the effects were profoundly unsettling in Moscow."[9] TASS declared, "[T]he American President slandered the Soviet Union and called for a crusade against communism."[10] The Soviet news agency had a point. President Reagan had just let the world know that he was marshalling the resources of the United States to work toward the *dissolution* of the Soviet Union. Reagan was making a radical break with the doctrine of containment that had guided the United States' Soviet policy since the 1940s. Under Reagan's plan, the United States would exert pressure from every direction on the Soviet Union in an unrelenting effort to push the Soviet regime toward extinction. The pressure would come from substantial increases in defense spending, ongoing high-level contacts, cultural and educational exchanges, and negotiations on the full range of bilateral issues, including nuclear weapons. NSDD-32 offered a plan to prevail if nuclear war

---

Records Declassified and Released by the National Security Council, Box 1, at the Ronald Reagan Presidential Library, Simi Valley, CA.

8. The perspective presented in NSDD-32 was reflected in other public statements. See Clarence A. Robinson Jr., "Strategy Keys Military Plans to Policies," *Aviation Week & Space Technology*, July 19, 1982. The article is based on an interview with Reed. See also a speech given by National Security Adviser William P. Clark at Georgetown University on May 21, 1982; Reed's speech to the Armed Forces Communications and Electronics Association on June 16; and *At the Abyss*, p. 237. Reagan's June 8, 1982, speech is found at http://www.presidency.ucsb.edu/ws/index.php?pid = 42614&st = &st1 = .

9. Gaddis, *Strategies of Containment*, 356.

10. "Further Reaction to Reagan UK Parliament Speech," *Foreign Broadcast Information Service, Soviet Union*, June 10, 1982, G1.

occurred, but nuclear confrontation was not seen as a means of achieving goals.

Grinevsky does not mention NSDD-75, to which NSDD-32 was a precursor, but that January 17, 1983, directive on "U.S. Relations with the USSR" was the grand strategy blueprint of the Reagan administration.[11] It listed three objectives: (1) resist and roll back Soviet imperialism; (2) pressure the internal political structure within the Soviet Union in order to weaken its capacity to pursue aggressive policies abroad; and (3) engage in negotiations with the Soviet government that are based on "strict reciprocity." The primary instruction of NSDD-75 was to foster "antitotalitarian changes within the USSR and refrain from assisting the Soviet regime to consolidate further its hold on the country," as National Security Adviser William P. Clark wrote in a December 16, 1982, memorandum to President Reagan.[12]

The directive "contained no suggestion of a desire to destroy the Soviet Union to establish U.S. military superiority, or to force the Soviet Union to jeopardize its own security," explains Jack F. Matlock Jr., a Soviet specialist on the NSC staff from 1983 to 1986 and U.S. ambassador to the Soviet Union from 1987 to 1991. "In fact," he continues, "it aimed for agreements that not only enhanced U.S. interests and were reciprocal, but also served a 'mutual interest.'"[13] In a meeting on May 21, 1983, Secretary of State George P. Shultz reminded the president that NSDD-75 called for cultural and sci-

---

11. NSDD-75 was declassified on July 16, 1994.

12. Clark's memorandum was a status report to the president on the interagency work being done on NSDD-75. Ten days before his memo was sent to the president, L. Paul Bremer III, the executive secretary of the State Department, transmitted an interagency paper to Clark. The paper cast NSDD-32 in a narrowly military context and referred to the forthcoming NSDD-75 as a political strategy: "U.S. military strategy for successfully contending with peacetime, crisis, and wartime contingencies involving the USSR on a global basis is detailed in NSDD 32. This military strategy must be combined with a political strategy. . . ." See Records Declassified and Released by the National Security Council, Box 1, Ronald Reagan Presidential Library, Simi Valley, CA.

13. See Jack F. Matlock Jr., *Reagan and Gorbachev: How the Cold War Ended* (New York: Oxford University Press, 2004), 53.

entific exchanges with the Soviets as a means of influencing people inside the Communist bloc. He also made the case that the "opening of U.S. and Soviet consulates in Kiev and New York would have the advantage of getting us onto new Soviet terrain." Shultz writes that he "ran into intense opposition from the NSC staff" and believed they were less inclined to put the cooperative elements of the new strategy into practice.[14]

Despite bureaucratic battles, by mid-1983 President Reagan had endorsed the four-part agenda as a means of activating NSDD-75. It was a rejection of the Nixon-era strategy of "linkage," or making superpower progress in one area dependent on progress in another. Instead, the four-part agenda called for simultaneous bilateral negotiations on arms control, human rights, regional issues, and bilateral exchanges. It became a central aspect of the Reagan administration's Soviet policy.[15]

Naturally, there were members of the Reagan administration who attempted to downplay the messages contained in the speeches and statements of the president and secretary of state by leaking to the press their view that the administration was not fully committed to negotiations with the Soviet Union.[16] As will be discussed in the next section, however, Reagan "stayed on message"

---

14. George Shultz, *Turmoil and Triumph: My Years as Secretary of State* (New York: Charles Scribner's Sons, 1993), 276.

15. Shultz presented an outline of the four-part agenda in a memorandum to the president in early March 1983. See Shultz, *Turmoil and Triumph*, 266. The ideas driving the four-part agenda were presented in Shultz's June 15, 1983, testimony before the Senate Foreign Relations Committee and Reagan's televised address to the nation on January 16, 1984. These statements and others by Reagan, Shultz, and Vice President George H. W. Bush are found in a State Department publication that categorizes speeches and statements in such a way that each dimension of the four-part agenda is emphasized. See *Realism, Strength, Negotiation: Key Foreign Policy Statements of the Reagan Administration* (Washington, DC: United States Department of State, Bureau of Public Affairs), May 1984. The most comprehensive statement about the four-part agenda was Shultz's speech in Los Angeles on October 18, 1984. See "Managing the U.S.-Soviet Relationship Over the Long Term," *Current Policy* No. 624, Department of State, Bureau of Public Affairs.

16. See Matlock, *Reagan and Gorbachev*, 85.

in his public and private statements and acted upon the strategy of cooperation presented in the directive, even when advisers disagreed. Furthermore, the objectives of NSDD-75 are fully consistent with the Soviet strategy that Reagan drafted in writings before and during his presidency.

The Strategic Defense Initiative was another component of the president's strategy. In his SDI speech, Reagan asked whether MAD was an ethical means of deterring nuclear war, and he authorized research and development on a future defensive shield that would "begin to achieve our ultimate goal of eliminating the threat posed by strategic nuclear missiles." He then added: "This could pave the way for arms control measures to eliminate the weapons themselves."[17]

Determined to move quickly, Reagan issued NSDD-85 on "Eliminating the Threat from Ballistic Missiles" two days after his SDI announcement. His newest directive was an unequivocal instruction to his national security team to abandon conventional deterrence, including MAD: "I would like to decrease our reliance on the threat of retaliation by offensive nuclear weapons and to increase the contribution of defensive systems to our security and that of our allies. To begin to move toward that goal, I have concluded that we should explore the possibility of using defensive capabilities to counter the threat posed by nuclear ballistic missiles." The president added that "these actions will be carried out in a manner consistent with our obligations under the ABM (Anti-Ballistic Missile) Treaty," but in two earlier directives, NSDD 59 and 61, tacit support was given to breaking out of the 1972 agreement with the Soviet Union.[18] In a private letter, President Reagan clarified his view on the constraints imposed on missile defense

---

17. Reagan's SDI speech may be found at http://www.presidency.ucsb.edu/ws/index.php?pid=41093&st=&st1=.

18. See Christopher Simpson, *National Security Directives of the Reagan and Bush Administrations: The Declassified History of U.S. Policy and Military Policy, 1981–1991* (Boulder, CO: Westview Press, 1995), 233. The quote from NSDD-85 is found on page 287.

under the ABM treaty: "I still . . . have problems with the ABM treaty. . . . I can tell you though I will not let the treaty or anything else hold us back. If we agree to any times for deploying etc. they will be based on our own knowledge of when we believe we'll be ready which is still down the road a way."[19]

Andropov was not alone in wondering who was responsible for the SDI concept. Arms controllers around the world were mystified. In rejecting MAD—the doctrine designed to prevent nuclear war by allowing populations in both the United States and the Soviet Union to be vulnerable to a nuclear attack—as the basis for the nation's national security policy, the U.S. president had jettisoned decades of theorizing about nuclear deterrence. His announcement was truly a bolt out of the blue. Did Reagan really mean that he wanted to eliminate nuclear weapons? If so, he was aligning himself with the nuclear freeze and peace movements.

Ronald Reagan and the Three Elements of American Strategy

Grinevsky concisely reviews many of the moves and countermoves by the superpowers in hot spots all over the world that constituted the crisis of the early 1980s. To understand the United States' contribution to preventing that crisis from erupting, national strategy is a necessary, but not sufficient, condition. The other condition has to do with political leadership. Was the strategy actually deployed? If so, what, if anything, did President Reagan do on behalf of the national strategy? These are, in effect, the questions Andropov asked.

Negotiating with the Soviet Union

Critics expected that Reagan's defense policies would ratchet up the nuclear arms race while further eroding bilateral contacts and

---

19. Reagan to William A. Rusher, April 1, 1987, in *Reagan, A Life in Letters*, ed. Skinner et al., 430.

negotiations, many of which had been cancelled or put on hold by President Jimmy Carter in response to the Soviet invasion of Afghanistan in December 1979. Reagan's critics either ignored or considered as election-year rhetoric his campaign pledge to engage the Soviets in negotiations and to develop closer ties. In a major campaign speech on August 18, 1980, Reagan declared: "I think continued negotiation with the Soviet Union is essential. We need never be afraid to negotiate as long as we keep our long term objectives (the pursuit of peace for one) clearly in mind and don't seek agreements just for the sake of having an agreement."[20] Reagan's commitment to bilateral negotiations, even in the face of opposition from conservatives, was particularly evident in the area of human rights.

Reagan discussed his commitment to U.S.-Soviet negotiations and his negotiating style in private correspondence written during his presidency. In a July 9, 1981, letter he wrote:

> I know I'm being criticized for not having made a great speech outlining what would be the Reagan foreign policy. I have a foreign policy; I'm working on it.
>
> I just don't happen to think that it's wise to always stand up and put in quotation marks in front of the world what your foreign policy is. I'm a believer in quiet diplomacy and so far we've had several quite triumphant experiences by using that method. The problem is, you can't talk about it afterward or then you can't do it again.[21]

The president's statement could be read as defensive posturing in a letter responding to a concerned American citizen, but a proposal he made to Soviet General Secretary Leonid Brezhnev was consistent with the message in that letter.

In March 1977, Anatoli Shcharansky, a Soviet dissident, was arrested. After 16 months in Lefortovo prison, he was exiled to Sibe-

---

20. Skinner et al., eds., *Reagan, In His Own Hand*, 484.
21. Reagan to John O. Koehler, July 9, 1981, in *Reagan, A Life in Letters*, ed. Skinner et al., 375.

ria in July 1978. In the same year, seven Soviet Pentecostals rushed past guards and entered the U.S. embassy in Moscow in protest against the Soviet government's policies that barred them from freely practicing their religion. Responding to a May 25, 1981, letter from Soviet General Secretary Leonid Brezhnev, Reagan requested that the Pentecostals and Shcharansky be allowed to leave the Soviet Union. The method Reagan suggested for their release was consistent with the quiet diplomacy he advocated. In the June 16 draft of his letter, Reagan wrote:

> If you could find it in your heart to do this [allow Shcharansky to emigrate to Israel] the matter would be strictly between us which is why I'm writing this letter by hand.
>
> While on this subject may I also enter a plea on behalf of the two families who have been living in most uncomfortable circumstances in our embassy in Moscow for three years. . . . Again as in the case of Shcharansky this is between the two of us and I will not reveal that I made any such request. I'm sure however you understand that such actions on your part would lessen my problems in future negotiations between our two countries.[22]

Reagan continued to make such pleas to Brezhnev's successors. Two months after declaring the Soviet Union an evil empire, he confided to a friend in a letter that his administration had "more contact with the Soviets than anyone is aware of and whether to have a meeting or not is on the agenda at both ends of the line."[23] The president was most likely referring to the discussions under way with Moscow on human rights issues such as the plight of the Pentecostals and Shcharansky.

By the summer of 1983, at the height of the cold war chill, Reagan and Andropov had privately worked out the details of the Pentecostals' release from the U.S. embassy in Moscow and the families were allowed to leave the country. As Secretary Shultz

---

22. Ibid., 741 and 742.
23. Reagan to Paul Trousdale, May 23, 1983, ibid., 409.

writes in his memoir, this "was the first successful negotiation with the Soviets in the Reagan administration." Shultz further notes, "The president's own role in it had been crucial."[24] On February 11, 1986, Shcharansky was allowed to leave the Soviet Union; he arrived in Israel that evening. On May 13, Reagan received Shcharansky at the White House, where the human rights leader thanked the president for working toward his release from the Soviet Union.

Most of the president's advisers were unaware of the fact that Reagan had persistently advocated the release of the Pentecostals and dissidents such as Shcharansky in his nationally syndicated radio program, which was heard by between 20 and 30 million people each week throughout the late 1970s.[25] In a private letter he wrote during this time, Reagan revealed that he was using the unique national platform that his radio program provided to address the plight of Soviet dissidents: "Thank you very much for your letter and the material on Ida Nudel [a Jewish Refusenik under confinement in the Soviet Union]. . . . I've already done some radio commentaries on this general subject and will continue to call attention to this continuing tragedy. I agree with you about the Soviet susceptibility to public opinion. Maybe I can be of help in arousing public opinion by calling attention to the situation of Mrs. Nudel."[26] In October 1987, Nudel was granted an exit visa and she relocated to Israel. President Reagan declared that the United States rejoiced over her release and that of other Soviet Jews.[27]

---

24. Shultz, *Turmoil and Triumph*, 171.

25. Shcharansky is mentioned in a radio broadcast taped on September 1978, and the Soviet Pentecostals are the subject of an October 2, 1979, radio commentary. See Skinner et al., eds., *Reagan, In His Own Hand*, 147–148 and 177–178. For a review of the statistics regarding the listening audience of Reagan's radio program, see Skinner et al., eds., *Reagan's Path to Victory*, xiv.

26. Reagan to Mrs. Alvin Turken, circa November 1976, in *Reagan, A Life in Letters*, ed. Skinner et al., 374. A November 30, 1976, radio commentary was devoted to Nudel's plight. Skinner et al., eds., *Reagan, In His Own Hand*, 144–145.

27. See "Remarks at the Welcoming Ceremony for President Chaim Herzog of Israel," November 10, 1987. *Public Papers of the Presidents of the United States: Ronald Reagan* (Washington, DC: U.S. Government Printing Office, 1987), 1309.

Working toward the liberation of those seeking religious freedom was one of the American president's primary agenda items when he interacted with Soviet officials.

Eliminating Nuclear Weapons

In a major speech on the second strategic arms control treaty (SALT II) on September 15, 1979, Reagan argued that the main reason he opposed the treaty was that "SALT II is not a strategic arms limitation; it is a strategic arms buildup."[28] He repeated his position throughout this period in private letters, writing in April 1980 that he wanted to see the superpowers "negotiate a legitimate reduction of nuclear weapons on both sides to the point that neither country represented a threat to the other." Three years later, he made a similar entreaty in a letter to Andropov, which he wrote by hand: "If we can agree on mutual, verifiable reductions in the number of nuclear weapons we both hold could this not be a first step toward the elimination of all such weapons. What a blessing this would be for the people we both represent. You and I have the ability to bring this about through our negotiations in the arms reduction talks."[29]

Reagan also kept a conversation going with those in the peace and nuclear freeze movements. He typically reminded them, as he did in a letter to a Catholic bishop in April 1983, that "we have no disagreement about the absolute necessity of achieving peace in the world. Possibly we only differ with regard to the path we take to reach our goal." He was more explicit in his disagreement with the freeze movement in his SDI speech: "A freeze now would make us less, not more, secure and would raise, not reduce, the risks of war. It would be largely unverifiable and would seriously undercut our

---

28. Reagan delivered this speech before the San Diego convention of the Republican State Central Committee of California. A copy of the speech is found in Ronald Reagan Subject Collection, Box 3 Folder RR Speeches 1979. Hoover Institution Archives, Stanford, CA.

29. Reagan to Charles Burton Marshall, April 8, 1980, and Reagan to Andropov, draft circa July 8, 1983, in *Reagan, A Life in Letters*, ed. Skinner et al., 399 and 742–743.

negotiations on arms reduction. It would reward the Soviets for their massive military buildup while preventing us from moderniz-ing our aging and increasingly vulnerable forces. With their present margin of superiority, why should they agree to arms reductions knowing that we were prohibited from catching up?"

Following the Reykjavik summit where he met with Gorbachev for the second time, Reagan wrote to a friend: "I have never enter-tained a thought that SDI could be a bargaining chip. I did tell Gor-bachev that if and when we had such a system they would join us in eliminating nuclear missiles; we'd share such a defense with them. I don't think he believes me." In a letter to William Buckley Jr. on May 5, 1987, Reagan reminded the conservative writer that "when I announced SDI I made it plain it should be based on the elimina-tion of ballistic missiles and that I favored sharing it with everyone."[30]

Reagan considered SDI a potential escape route from MAD. He had a long-standing concern about the moral implications of mak-ing civilian populations vulnerable to a nuclear attack as a means of preventing nuclear war under MAD. It is well known that in the fall of 1967 Governor Reagan attended a briefing on the testing of the ballistic missile defense system under way at Lawrence Liver-more Laboratory. It is also well known that Reagan's speech at the Republican convention on August 19, 1976, was a veiled statement against MAD and nuclear weapons: "We live in a world in which the great powers have poised and aimed at each other horrible mis-siles of destruction, nuclear weapons that can in a matter of minutes arrive at each other's country and destroy, virtually, the civilized world we live in." Reflecting Reagan's policy positions, the Repub-lican platform of 1980 advocated the development of a program of "strategic and civil defense which would protect the American peo-ple against nuclear war at least as well as the Soviet population is

---

30. Reagan to Bishop Mark J. Hurley, April 19, 1983; Reagan to Laurence W. Beilenson, October 16, 1986; and Reagan to William Buckley Jr., ibid., 393, 419, 429. For Reagan's SDI speech see http://www.presidency.ucsb.edu/ws/index. php?pid = 41093&st = &st1 = .

protected."[31] During his presidency, Reagan publicly revealed that SDI was his idea and he reported that before announcing SDI he met with the Joint Chiefs of Staff and asked whether "it would be worthwhile to see if we could not develop a weapon that could perhaps take out, as they left their silos, those nuclear weapons. . . . [W]hen they did not look aghast at the idea and instead said yes, they believed that such a thing offered a possibility and should be researched, I said, 'Go.'" In private correspondence, Reagan wrote, "[SDI] was my idea to begin with and we will deploy when it is ready."[32]

Until recently, few were aware that Reagan crystallized his ideas on domestic and foreign policy during the late 1970s. And although he was ignored by many elites and scholars, Reagan formulated his policy positions in full view of the public. In January 1975, he began broadcasting a nationally syndicated radio program, writing a nationally syndicated newspaper column, and giving numerous speeches around the country on behalf of conservative causes. Eliminating nuclear weapons, challenging the limits set by the ABM treaty of 1972, and thinking through the problems of MAD were the subjects of numerous radio commentaries that Reagan wrote himself.[33] For instance, in a radio commentary taped on March 23, 1977, Reagan stated: "They [the Soviets] have developed 6 new strategic nuclear systems and apparently are engaged in a

31. For a review of Reagan's briefing at Lawrence Livermore Laboratory, see Edward Teller, *Memoirs: A Twentieth-Century Journey in Science and Politics* (Cambridge, MA: Perseus Publishing, 2001), 509. Reagan's speech at the 1976 convention is found in Ronald Reagan Subject Collection, Box 1, Hoover Institution Archives, Stanford, CA. The statement from the 1980 Republican platform is found in George Thomas Kurian, ed., *The Encyclopedia of the Republican Party*, vol. 2 (New York: M. E. Sharpe, 1997), 692.

32. "The President's View: Reagan discusses Star Wars, MX and the Arms Talks," *Newsweek*, March 18, 1985, 21. The meeting with the JCS that Reagan is referring to was held on December 22, 1983, three months before he publicly announced SDI. For confirmation of the meeting, see The President's Daily Diary, Box 8, Ronald Reagan Presidential Library, Simi Valley, CA. For the private correspondence about SDI, see Reagan to Robert Dick, July 7, 1988, in *Reagan, A Life in Letters*, ed. Skinner et al., 431.

33. See Skinner et al., eds., *Reagan, In His Own Hand*, 64–128.

crash program to develop an effective anti-ballistic missile system. You'll remember we bargained away our right to have such a weapon for the protection of our cities. That was one of our contributions to détente."[34]

During the late 1970s, after he had substantial national political experience behind him—having served two terms as governor of California and having made four trips abroad on behalf of the Nixon administration—Reagan began to ground his anticlassical ideas about defense policy and deterrence with more extensive evidence. It is worth noting that NSC-68, the containment-strategy document written under the direction of Paul Nitze while he was director of the State Department's Policy Planning Staff from 1949 to 1950, was the subject of two of Reagan's radio commentaries in May 1977, two years after the document was declassified.[35] Reagan's advocacy of missile defense and his criticism of MAD were not based on a script he was given but on an analysis he developed as he read some of the most important strategic documents of the cold war era.

One of the most important findings in my co-edited volumes of these radio essays is Reagan's extensive use of sources and expert testimony as he developed arguments about defense policy for his listening audience. His sources included basic conservative fare such as *Human Events* and *National Review*, but he also cited the contemporary writings and statements of Nitze and other defense experts and referred to numerous government documents as he presented his defense policy views, which were at odds with prevailing perspectives favoring arms control, détente, and MAD.[36]

---

34. Ibid., 119.

35. Ibid., 109–113. In the years following its declassification, NSC-68 became the subject of numerous scholarly analyses. See Samuel F. Wells Jr., "Sounding the Tocsin: NSC 68 and the Soviet Threat," *International Security* 4 (Autumn 1979): 116–158; and John Lewis Gaddis and Paul Nitze, "NSC 68 and the Soviet Threat Reconsidered," *International Security* 4 (Spring 1980): 164–176.

36. The section on defense policy, for example, in *Reagan, In His Own Hand* is replete with references to defense experts, articles, and books. See pages 64–128. In October 1978, Reagan devoted more than a week's worth of radio commentaries to the views on the second strategic arms control treaty (SALT II) of Eugene

Dissolving the Soviet Union and Ending the Cold War

Reagan's national security directives reviewed in this essay were a major departure from the containment doctrine that had guided the United States' Soviet policy earlier in the cold war. Some interpreted these directives as war plans, but they called for bilateral negotiations, and especially for reducing, instead of controlling, nuclear weapons. As Richard Pipes, a Soviet specialist at the National Security Council during the early 1980s, writes, NSDD-75 ". . . contained clauses that ran counter to all the policy statements that had previously guided American policy toward Moscow in that it called for not merely punishing unacceptable Soviet behavior but for doing all in our power to avert such behavior by inducing changes in the nature of the Soviet regime on the premise that it was the source of Soviet behavior." Pipes continues, "Without taking undue credit, I believe I can claim this idea as my main contribution to the Reagan administration's foreign policy."[37]

As with the other dimensions of his national security policy, Reagan was actually the architect of the concept to which Pipes refers. In a speech he appears to have delivered around 1963, which I located in the Hoover Institution Archives and which my coauthors and I reproduced in *Reagan, In His Own Hand*, Reagan expressed his vision about how the cold war should end: "If we truly believe that our way of life is best aren't the Russians more likely to recognize that fact and modify their stand if we let their economy come unhinged so that the contrast is apparent? . . . [I]n an all out race our system is stronger, and eventually the enemy gives up the race as a hopeless cause. Then a noble nation believing in peace extends the hand of friendship and says there is room in the world for both of us."[38]

Rostow, a Yale professor who became the first director of the Arms Control and Disarmament Agency during Reagan's presidency. See pages 92–99.

37. Richard Pipes, *Vixi: Memoirs of a Non-Belonger* (New Haven, CT: Yale University Press, 2003), 188.

38. Skinner et al., eds., *Reagan, In His Own Hand*, 442.

In a January 1977 meeting with Richard V. Allen, a foreign policy expert who would become President Reagan's first national security adviser, Reagan presented his blunt assessment of what should happen in the cold war: "My view is that we win and they lose." Allen later recalled, "I was flabbergasted. I'd worked for Nixon and Goldwater and many others, and I'd heard a lot about Kissinger's policy of détente and about the need to 'manage the Cold War,' but never did I hear a leading politician put the goal so starkly."

Back in 1977, Reagan "was able to *see* a post-Soviet world."[39] He envisioned that world coming about not through nuclear war but through the Soviet side joining the community of free states. Reagan authorized and signed directives such as NSDD-75 because they represented his views, most of which he had worked out years before he had any advisers.

As Grinevsky aptly demonstrates, Ronald Reagan and U.S. policy during his presidency were essential elements in preventing an escalation of the crisis in superpower relations in the early 1980s.

39. Peter Robinson, *How Ronald Reagan Changed My Life* (New York: HarperCollins, 2003), 72. The meeting between Reagan and Allen is recounted on pages 71 and 72 of Robinson's book and in Richard V. Allen, "Peace Through Strength: Reagan's Early Call: Win Cold War," *Human Events* (online), October 24, 2003.

CHAPTER 3

Anatoli Cherniaev : *Gorbachev's Foreign Policy: The Concept*

MIKHAIL GORBACHEV'S APPROACH to foreign policy was based on his political philosophy, which became widely known as "new political thinking." He professed it throughout his tenure as the leader of the Soviet Union. However, Gorbachev used this term even before he became the head of the Communist Party and the country. During a visit of Soviet officials to Great Britain in December 1984, Politburo member Gorbachev had a private talk with Prime Minister Margaret Thatcher. In the course of that meeting, Gorbachev first announced that "the nuclear age made new political thinking an imperative." At the time, this denoted a need for a constructive dialogue, a quest for areas of agreement, and the ability to live together in accordance with the realities of a new, rapidly changing world. Although hardly an elaborate concept, this idea was still unusual for a high-ranking Soviet statesman. It shows that Gorbachev, not yet burdened with the brunt of responsibility for his country, was already aware of the abnormal situation in the world and saw the worrisome proximity to the dangerous brink, which was the result of decades of confrontation.

It took Gorbachev several more years to conceptualize his idea about this new political thinking and make it known to the world community. It was the dominant theme of his speech at the United Nations in December of 1988 and was a philosophical underpinning of his breakthrough policy proposals. Gorbachev's speech signified the turning point, not only in the Soviet Union's changing attitude toward the West but also in the country's new understanding of its overarching purpose in the world. There was, however, nothing inevitable about the choice to which Gorbachev publicly committed himself during that speech. The road to the UN podium had taken four hard years, during which the last leader of the Soviet Union overcame the ideological truisms of the Brezhnev era, the initial distrust of his Western partners, the growing resistance of rigid conservatives in his inner circle, and his own dogmatic Communist heritage. This chapter outlines the central principles of new political thinking and contrasts Gorbachev's outlook with that of his predecessors. The events leading to this turning point helped Gorbachev shape his ideas and, by doing so, to transform the whole world. Gorbachev's new thinking in Soviet foreign policy made possible such historic events as the unification of Germany, the democratization of Eastern Europe, and the creation of a new transatlantic partnership.

New Political Thinking: Its Essence and Origins

The following principles constitute the basis of Gorbachev's new political thinking:

- The world is becoming more interdependent. As a result, relations among the states have a great impact on their policies and on the world's development.
- Nuclear weapons and an endless conflict between man and nature, exacerbated by the scientific and technological revolutions, have threatened mankind. Therefore, humanity must strive for survival.
- Under these conditions, sharp confrontation in the form of the cold war leads to catastrophe. To prevent it, the arms race should be halted and the number of nuclear weapons should be reduced and gradually eliminated.
- International security is indivisible and can be effective only

as a project in which all states participate. Therefore, no single state can achieve security at the expense of others.

- The class approach to national and international security is unacceptable because it presumes victory of one side over the other and creates permanent tension, which might result in war.

- In the new de-ideologized Soviet foreign policy, priority should be given to basic human values, democracy, and human rights.

- National interests should not be sought at the expense of the interests of other states. International relations of the new epoch should be based on the principle of the balance of interests. Their standard source is international law, and international organizations should be responsible for their regulation.

- The concept of new political thinking rejects reliance on force, or threats of using force, in achieving foreign policy goals. Priority in solving international problems and conflicts should be given to political methods, which enable the search for wise compromises.

- Dialogue should become the permanent means of communication among state leaders, as it promotes mutual understanding and trust among countries.

- All people should have freedom to choose their way of life and their political and socioeconomic system. Thus tolerance, nonintervention in other states' internal affairs, and respect for the world's diversity should become the guiding principles of international relations.

- The moral component in domestic and foreign policy should be acknowledged and respected. This morality, in the Christian understanding of the term, is different from the meaning of morality commonly accepted in the USSR, which corresponds to Marxist-Leninist ideology and benefits communism.

The introduction of these principles to the decision-making process signified the dismantling of everything that for decades had formed the basis of the Soviet state and society. This dismantling was an attempt to include the country in the modern world as an honest partner and an equal participant. It also signaled the Soviet Union's desire to stop playing the role of an alternate system in the world community, an antagonist with the ambitions of an ideological superpower.

All of Gorbachev's predecessors after Joseph Stalin more or less understood the imperatives for a new approach to dealing with the West. However, they were not capable of advancing a new well-grounded concept that would make some of the traditional Communist postulates obsolete. Nikita Khrushchev, during the Twentieth Congress of the CPSU in 1956, declared an era of peaceful coexistence and stated that world war, despite the predictions of Leninist-Stalinist theory, was avoidable. However, he is remembered with a shoe in his hand threatening capitalists in the United Nations. He also sent missiles to Cuba and promised to "bury American capitalism." This was not mere rhetoric but was an expression of his approach to world politics.

Some of the elements in Leonid Brezhnev and Alexei Kosygin's foreign policy were based on common sense. Brezhnev readily hugged Richard Nixon and signed a treaty on the limitation of strategic arms. During his rule, the Soviet Union also initiated the all-European Helsinki Process in 1975, which led to the signing of an agreement on three groups of issues ("three baskets"), one of which required the USSR to respect human rights. In other words, there was a common understanding within the Soviet leadership that in the nuclear age one should be more cautious with the class struggle on the world scale.

Nevertheless, before Gorbachev came to power, peaceful coexistence remained just "a form of the class struggle on the world arena between socialism and capitalism," as described in the 1961 program of the CPSU. It aimed at increasing Soviet military power, subjecting the whole economy to the interests of the military-industrial complex, and militarizing the societal consciousness against the enemy of imperialism. The psychology of the "fortress under siege" preserved in public memory the "complex of 1941" to persuade the people to tolerate enormous defense expenditures, which exhausted the material and intellectual resources of the nation. The policies of the Soviet Union toward its Socialist allies, the third world, the national-liberation movements, and the international Communist movement were also subject to the goal of victory in world struggle. Gorbachev put an end to this way of thinking.

There were two motives behind Gorbachev's initiative: pragmatism and morality. They were both linked to his understanding of the Soviet national interest. His pragmatic motive was the result of objective analysis of the situation in the country and in the world. This analysis showed that the previous policy was obsolete, was damaging the Soviet people, and had brought the world to the verge of nuclear disaster.

The moral motive was an essential component of Gorbachev's actions. Both Konstantin Chernenko and Yuri Andropov knew about the critical situation in their country and saw how the Soviet position in the world had deteriorated from year to year. Nevertheless, they followed the course set by Stalin and Brezhnev. They did not feel the pain of the people or understand the national interest. They were not ashamed of their people's poverty and suffering. Why did Gorbachev feel "pain and shame" for the people and follow the call of conscience, which would not allow him to ignore their pitiful existence? The answer lies in his human qualities, in his peasant upbringing, traditionally based on common sense and simple norms of morality, and in the education he received at Moscow State University. This education brought to his lively and talented mind the first doubts about the absolute goodness of the Soviet system. Gorbachev describes this realization in his memoirs.

In short, new thinking is not just a theory in the commonly accepted sense of the word, but is a combination of political will and humanitarian ideas that have been known since Kant, Montesquieu, Tolstoy, and Solov'ev, among others. In this respect, attempts to portray the Soviet *institutchiki* from academic centers like IMEMO or ISKAN as authors of Gorbachev's politics misrepresent the driving force of the new thinking. This concept came about as a result of Gorbachev's understanding of the necessity to reject the traditional Soviet confrontational course coupled with a moral impulse. Some of the elements of the new thinking, such as indivisibility of security or interdependence of the world were suggested by academicians only later, when Soviet society was in the process of implementing Gorbachev's political will. At the same time, it would be wrong to suggest that new thinking had at some point been born whole in Gorbachev's mind and then applied in the foreign and domestic arenas, for his ideas developed as a result of his work as a leader of the Soviet state.

The Making of New Political Thinking

Immediately after Gorbachev acceded to supreme political power in March of 1985, he emphasized the urgent need for adopting new approaches in the conduct of Soviet foreign policy. He made this clear during the very first meeting of the Central Committee of the CPSU held under his chairmanship. Gorbachev argued that it was impossible to initiate far-reaching internal transformations while preserving traditional foreign policy. Rejecting the idea that confrontation between the Soviet Union and the United States was foreordained, he pointed to an opportunity for improved Soviet-U.S. relations. In Gorbachev's view, only through disarmament in nuclear and other areas could the Soviet Union secure sufficient resources to rebuild the economy.

Gorbachev's initial actions indicated that he was willing to act in accordance with his new principles. He enthusiastically accepted the offer to meet with President Reagan, which was conveyed to him by Vice President Bush and Secretary of State Shultz during their visit to Moscow for Chernenko's funeral. In various public statements that preceded the meeting, including his noteworthy interview for *Time* in September of 1985, Gorbachev demonstrated a positive attitude toward the prospects of Soviet-U.S. cooperation. It was clear that he wanted to create the most favorable atmosphere for the forthcoming meeting with President Reagan. However, a Geneva meeting on November 19–21, 1985, between the two leaders failed to change Gorbachev's ideologically biased view about Reagan's "evil" intentions. He still saw Reagan as the leader of a "hostile imperialist world." Nevertheless, there was some sort of human rapport between the two leaders that gave hope for change. It was underscored by the famous formula from the final communiqué, which stated, "The parties, being aware of a particular responsibility of the USSR and the USA in maintaining peace, announced that a nuclear war must never be unleashed for it could not be won."

In keeping with the spirit of the Geneva meeting, Gorbachev made a statement on January 15, 1986, proposing the elimination of nuclear weapons by the year 2000. The draft of the document was thoroughly scrutinized by scientists and experts from the ministries of defense and foreign affairs. However, the final statement was not taken seriously in the West, which viewed it as one more political move on the Kremlin's part. Even many Soviet officials, including several of Gorbachev's colleagues, were skeptical or even cynical about it. The new general secretary, in their view, wanted to make a show of himself and stun the world with a smashing idea. Time proved that neither of them was right. It was an effective step toward preventing a nuclear showdown at a time when the arms race was already out of control, and it led to future agreements on arms control and disarmament.

Gorbachev's vision of a nuclear-free world was still, however, bound by traditional Communist dogma, reflected in his report to the Twenty-sixth Congress of the CPSU in February 1986. His analysis of the political situation in the world was based on class conflict and the opposition between capitalism and socialism. Nevertheless, striking a note of controversy, Gorbachev introduced the idea of kinship between all parts and the interdependence of processes in today's world, a new and unusual attitude for the Soviet mentality. Such interdependence, according to Gorbachev, enabled constructive interaction between opposing social systems. Among its chief priorities was "to stop the material preparation for a nuclear war," to put an end to the arms race, and to work toward "general security." Thus, Gorbachev did not allow the ideological component, still evident in his views, to dominate his thinking about foreign policy. With this speech, he started the gradual de-ideologization of Soviet foreign policy, which corresponded to the vital interests of the country. The ambiguous foreign policy of the Communist Party congress made it easier for Gorbachev to implement his reformist ideas and, in fact, it even legitimized them. That is how the first brick was put into the foundation of the new political thinking.

De-ideologization of Soviet foreign policy meant denying the Marxist-Leninist postulate about the eventual withering away of the capitalist system. It necessitated admitting the absurdity of spending almost 80 percent of the nation's material, scientific, political, and informational resources on confrontation with the West. Finally, it made ordinary common sense a fundamental source of policymaking. At the same time, however, reform was made under the cover of Communist rhetoric and in accordance with the proper ideological ritual. This explains the initial Western disbelief about the sincerity of Gorbachev's foreign policy initiatives. Despite Western doubts and even explicit U.S. sabotage, Gorbachev was resolute in pursuing the line that he had adopted in his statement on the elimination of nuclear weapons. The following account, made privately by Gorbachev in the spring of 1986, helps to reveal his mind-set at the time:

> We have gotten no response [from the U.S.] to our proposal on the elimination of nuclear weapons, although the things we are offering could be quite feasible. We do want to achieve disarmament and we are not deceiving anyone. But what do we hear in return? As it turns out, they [the United States] now want to have more Pershings. Moreover, they are explicitly provoking us. The U.S. naval vessels near the Crimean coast, the expulsion of the Soviet staff from the UN, and the new anti-Soviet propaganda campaigns. This is how

they want to provoke and embitter the USSR. But we remain hopeful, and we are waiting.

In another private conversation, Gorbachev shared his concerns about the obstacles that hindered the improvement of U.S.-Soviet relations:

> The question is whether or not we should go ahead with the Geneva process. It is not only in our interests, but also in everyone's interests. This is the right time for new thinking. It is imperative, it is knocking on the door, because we have reached a point beyond which—as we keep saying—the process will go out of hand. Naturally, we are concerned with SDI, but I considered this matter and discussed it with experts: perhaps, we should stop being afraid of SDI?! They count on the fact that the USSR is afraid of SDI morally, economically, politically, and militarily. They are going ahead with it in order to wear us out.

Gorbachev repeated his views about SDI publicly during his speech in Toliatti. The most effective Soviet response to this program, in his view, would be to start the development of a system similar to SDI on a much smaller scale: "Ten percent of the SDI cost would be sufficient to render SDI ineffective." Nevertheless, Gorbachev recognized in his speech that the Soviet Union was "being tested as to the sincerity of its peaceful intentions." Therefore, in his view, such a Soviet defense initiative would be counterproductive for the objective of easing tensions between the USSR and the United States.

In addition to tolerating foreign provocation, Gorbachev also had to show persistence and courage in overcoming internal resistance to his reformist ideas. Introduction of new thinking in Soviet foreign policy was seriously hampered by the well-established Gromyko tradition of confrontational diplomacy. Gorbachev once raised this problem at a Politburo session:

> I can see a gap between our political declarations and the actions of our negotiating teams. Once political decision is there, we must act

accordingly. Our negotiators, however, are sluggish and tied up to old approaches. This undermines all our political statements. Why is there such a gap? Most likely, it is the result of inertia. If this, however, is due to conscious obstruction we cannot work with these comrades. The world is now scrutinizing us. Unless we really change our behavior, they will accuse us of bluffing. The news reports show nothing but deadlocks. Our stubbornness discredits everything. Any bargaining should be reasonable and priority in the negotiation process should be given to the political solution.

After Shevardnadze replaced Gromyko as the minister of foreign affairs and appointed new deputies, there was no resistance or sabotage of new thinking from diplomatic circles. This was not only because diplomats sincerely accepted the new course but also because within the diplomatic environment there was a strict discipline that made instances of sabotage very rare. However, some still preserved their old behavioral manners and job habits, which were inadequate for effective implementation of the new course. As a result, there were instances of dogmatism, aggressiveness, and lack of flexibility, which Gorbachev could not tolerate. As to the military, dissatisfaction among the generals and within the Soviet defense ministry coincided with the downsizing of the military budget in 1986. However, open resistance to Gorbachev's foreign policy and public criticism of his course occurred only in 1989, when withdrawal of Soviet troops from Eastern Europe was being discussed. During the first four years of perestroika, the generals maintained strict discipline in the presence of the general secretary of the Central Committee and could complain only among themselves. Real attempts of sabotage occurred only at the end of Gorbachev's rule, when his authority was already challenged. The following example illustrates this point.

Secretary of State James Baker, in his conversation with Gorbachev on March 15, 1991, raised the issue of Soviet violation of the treaty on conventional arms in Europe, which was signed at the

Paris conference of the CSCE. The problem first erupted in late October 1990. Chief Soviet negotiator Oleg Grinevsky informed from Vienna that negotiations on conventional arms were on the verge of a breakdown, which meant that the signing of the document adopted at the Paris meeting of the CSCE was also doomed. Generals in Moscow gave special orders to their representatives in the Soviet delegation, and they tied Grinevsky's hands despite his position as the head of the delegation. Gorbachev asked Defense Minister Dmitri Yazov and Foreign Minister Eduard Shevardnadze to solve the problem in two days. However, there was no progress even after three months. Shevardnadze could do nothing since he resigned soon afterward. President George Bush sent a letter to Gorbachev in which he called this episode a "central problem of our relations." Then the embassies of the main countries of the CSCE joined in discussing this episode. The issue consisted of three components, and the main component dealt with "the naval infantry." The Soviet generals argued that naval infantry and coastal defense were not ground forces, and therefore Soviet military equipment should not be accounted for under the terms of the treaty. All other participants at the Paris meeting argued that it could not be excluded from the treaty. Although the amount of armaments at stake was relatively small, the important question was: If the Soviet delegation could, at its convenience, interpret certain articles of the treaty, even after it had been signed by the country's leader, then how could they be trusted?

The problem was solved only after eight months of protracted discussions. Chief of General Staff Mikhail Moiseev went to Washington, D.C., in May of 1991 and yielded to the U.S. demands while acting as if nothing could have been achieved without his personal involvement. In reality, the officials from the general staff together with Sergei Akhromeev tried to discredit Gorbachev. This example characterizes the atmosphere in which Gorbachev had to act. He could not discount experts from the defense ministry, and they used this situation to put bureaucratic sticks into the wheels of big politics. Although they did not succeed in reversing the treaty (and not all of them were in favor of reversal), they managed to slow the process.

Gorbachev's own initial skepticism about the U.S. imperialists started eroding even before his decisive meeting with President Reagan in Reykjavik. Through conversations with various world leaders he developed a different perspective on the objectives of the United States and of its leader. His meetings with President François Mitterrand and former President Richard Nixon in the summer of 1986 were especially important in this regard. During a lengthy conversation, President Mitterrand emphasized several times that the intentions of the U.S. military-industrial complex should be dissociated from the policies of the Reagan administration and the objectives of President Reagan. The French leader told Gorbachev that "despite his political past, Reagan is among those leaders who intuitively want to put an end to the existing status quo and in contrast to other American politicians he is not a machine, but a human being." Nixon conveyed a similar message to Gorbachev about Reagan's intentions: "I [have] know[n] President Reagan for more than thirty years now. I am firmly convinced that he has a personal stake in Soviet-American relations. He was greatly impressed with the substance of your proposals and with your personal devotion to the cause of peace between our two countries. President Reagan shares this devotion with you." The words of these two statesmen not only changed Gorbachev's perception of Reagan but also strengthened his determination to stand behind a new foreign policy course. The Reykjavik meeting was its logical continuation.

Gorbachev wanted to make this meeting serve his principal aim: to start the process of nuclear disarmament and thus remove the threat of nuclear war. On September 22, 1986, he had a meeting with the Politburo members and his assistants. This is how he presented his approach: "The first draft of our response to Reagan's letter is good for nothing. It does not meet our objective of achieving a shift in relations with the U.S. That's why I disagreed. I want it to be presented in more dramatic terms. Whether Reagan will reciprocate or not is quite another matter. But we cannot offer Americans something they are sure to reject."

Two weeks later, during a meeting with his assistants who were responsible for preparing the summit documents, Gorbachev further deliberated about the objectives of the summit and the means to achieve them:

> Our fundamental objective is to foil the arms race. Unless we do this, the threat will certainly grow. We will be drawn into an arms race we cannot afford, and we are sure to be defeated in it because we are exhausted to the very uttermost. Therefore, the prevalent approach must be political, not arithmetic. We should negotiate on the assumption that [n]either side is going to wage war on the other. All of us—myself, the Politburo, defense and foreign ministries—should understand that [even] if our proposals might lead to weakening of U.S. security, we are bound to fail. Americans will never agree to this. So we should follow the principle of greater security for all through equal reductions in armament levels. Our proposal is to have a 50 percent reduction in all types of nuclear weapons during the first stage. As for the INF, all intermediate nuclear forces will have to be withdrawn from Europe. The Soviet Union also wants to work toward an agreement on a nuclear test ban and to prevent militarization of outer space. If these proposals fail we would still be able to show what we were ready to accept!

The Reykjavik summit did not yield the results Gorbachev had hoped for. After he bid a sad farewell to President Reagan, the failure seemed obvious. In 20 minutes, however, he astonished reporters and even members of his delegation by saying, "This is not a failure, but a breakthrough!" His audience, expecting to hear the worst, burst into applause. Gorbachev's words were not demagoguery or sheer propaganda but reflected his genuine feelings after his conversation with Reagan. The turning point of their meeting was Reagan's reaction to the Soviet proposal for a 50 percent reduction of all types of strategic weapons. Gorbachev's proposal was the result of his political and ideological evolution during the time he occupied the office of general secretary. If accepted, the proposal would have led to a dramatic shift in politics as usual between the two superpowers. Reagan, for his part, intuitively sensed something natural and humane in Gorbachev's unexpected initiative. The president's immediate positive response to the Soviet offer revealed the great wisdom of this outstanding statesman. Although later in the talks the U.S. negotiating team convinced Reagan that the Soviet proposal required more detailed consideration, Gorbachev was impressed with Reagan's initial reaction. Moreover, that episode convinced the Soviet leader that he would be able to cooperate successfully with the U.S. president, who had a sincere and deep-seated conviction of the need to relieve the world of the nuclear threat. It was the first time that Gorbachev perceived Reagan not as a "representative of U.S. imperialism," but as a trustworthy partner who shared similar hopes and ideas. Mutual trust between the two leaders was another touchstone of the new political thinking that was crucial in bringing the cold war to an end.

One week after Gorbachev's return from Reykjavik, in a discussion with foreign policy advisers, he gave the following analysis of the significance and results of his second meeting with the U.S. president:

> During the summit we had no major difficulty in coming to an agreement on strategic weapons and intermediate nuclear forces. We can understand the president's difficulties in making the final decision on these issues and one more attempt might be needed to get over things that still divide us. But the Reykjavik experience indicated that the need for a dialogue had increased. That is why I am even more optimistic after this summit.

Gorbachev's talks with President Reagan in Reykjavik also gave him impetus to add the issue of human rights to the new political thinking. He could feel the importance of this problem for global politics not only at the summit meetings; it also was often raised during his numerous contacts with representatives of the Western scientific and cultural elite. Gorbachev was becoming increasingly convinced that unless changes took place in this area, it was hopeless to expect significant improvement in relations with the West and progress on the issue of disarmament. As a result, the problem of human rights soon appeared on the domestic agenda as an indispensable component of perestroika.

Thus the new level of strategic interaction between the Soviet Union and the United States initiated by Gorbachev not only led to considerable improvement of the international political climate but also brought about radical political changes within the Soviet system. As Gorbachev came to power, he comprehended the urgent need for reforming the failing Soviet economy, which was overburdened by military expenditures. His groundbreaking foreign policy proposals, designed to curb the arms race and stabilize relations with the West, especially the United States, also served his aim of taking the excessive military burden off the Soviet economy. However, after four bitter decades of the cold war, the spirit of distrust toward the Soviet Union was so deep among the U.S. political elite that a breakthrough in Soviet-U.S. relations could have been achieved only if the Soviet leadership adequately addressed internal political issues. The constant focus of Reagan administration officials on the issues of human rights and political freedoms in the USSR to a certain extent facilitated the growing understanding by Gorbachev (under the influence of the mounting difficulties of economic reform) that the success of this reform demanded the wider political liberalization of Soviet society.

Glasnost helped to build momentum for the success of the new Soviet foreign policy. The Politburo agreed to single out the issue of the SS-20 missiles from the general strategic nuclear weapons package and discuss it separately. On February 28, 1987, Gorbachev announced this decision on Soviet television and proposed to "conclude urgently a separate agreement on this issue." The groundwork for the agreement was prepared in the ensuing negotiations with Secretary of State Shultz, who visited Moscow twice in

1987. His second meeting with the Soviet leader, on October 23, 1987, became a breakthrough for the real disarmament process between the two countries. First, the agreement on intermediate-range nuclear missiles in Europe was finalized. Second, the two sides created an unofficial and practical negotiating mechanism on the issues of arms control and disarmament. Finally, on a personal level, Shultz played an outstanding, even historic, role in changing the character of Soviet-U.S. interaction. As a result of his meetings with Gorbachev in 1987, mutual trust became the centerpiece of their relationship. Although exchanges of sarcastic remarks during the negotiation sessions were commonplace, they only facilitated political and human interaction and increased the mutual understanding between the two statesmen. The resoluteness of Gorbachev and Shultz in serving a common cause was not limited to the defense of their national interests but was aimed at benefiting the interests of the whole world.

The Soviet-U.S. agreement on short-range and medium-range missiles (INF) was signed during Gorbachev's first official visit to the United States in December of 1987. This agreement included measures that would not just halt the arms race but would lead to the substantive reduction of Soviet missile arsenals. As Gorbachev emphasized at the Politburo meeting after his return from the United States: "The signing of [the] INF Treaty was a critical point in our relationship with the Americans. Progress on this issue opened the way toward other areas of disarmament—in nuclear, chemical, and conventional weapons. It set the background for equally businesslike approaches to solving regional problems and developing . . . our bilateral ties." The numerous unofficial contacts between Gorbachev and American students, intellectuals, newsmen, the business community, and the political and cultural elite were other high points of the visit. As he acknowledged during the same Politburo meeting:

> In Washington we have for the first time clearly felt the importance of [the] human factor in international politics. Initially we viewed

Reagan just as a representative of the most conservative part of the American capitalist system. After our visit to Washington we understood that . . . responsible politicians also embody purely human qualities, as well as interests and hopes of millions of common people, who elected them. In our age this has a great significance for political decision-making. . . . My visit would not have yielded any results without the state wisdom exemplified by President Reagan and Secretary Shultz in their determination to prevent a nuclear war.

Gorbachev's successful visit to the United States and the signing of the INF treaty were the first real major achievements of new thinking, and Reagan's visit to Moscow in the summer of 1988 contributed to greater openness in Soviet society. Reagan welcomed the profound changes that were taking place in the Soviet Union and was moved by the sympathetic attitude of the Soviet people. Having declared that he no longer viewed the USSR as an evil empire, the U.S. president proved that the ideological wall around the Soviet Union was temporary.

The culmination of four years of Gorbachev's energetic activities in the world arena was his speech at the United Nations General Assembly on December 7, 1988. He asked his assistants in Moscow who were preparing a draft of the speech to make it "anti-Fulton" in substance with an emphasis on demilitarization and humanization of Soviet thinking. He said, "We have to acknowledge that the Soviet Union has more troops in the center of Europe than NATO. If we continue our military presence at that level it would be hard to get support for our policies from the Western public opinion. Therefore, having one [of] our soldier[s] against every NATO soldier is an unacceptable approach."

These instructions were reflected in the final text of the speech with a public commitment to reduce unilaterally Soviet armed forces by 500,000 men, to withdraw armored divisions from the German Democratic Republic, Czechoslovakia, and Hungary by 1991, and to withdraw airborne assault units from those countries. This was impressive material proof of the Soviet Union's new approach to foreign policy, which was widely reported by the international media.

Few, however, took note of another aspect of Gorbachev's speech at the United Nations. In contrast to his earlier public addresses at the party congress or on other official occasions, his UN speech did not contain the slightest trace of Marxist-Leninist philosophy. Gorbachev appraised current events realistically, objectively, and without any ideological clichés. Thus his speech signified an open break with the class approach to world politics. Such an honest and unprejudiced position devoid of Communist dogmatism was a result of the gradual transformation of Gorbachev's views and ideas, partially due to the influence of his numerous contacts on the other side of the iron curtain. The philosophical ground for such cooperation became Gorbachev's new political thinking, outlined by the Soviet leader during his speech at the UN. This was his public commitment to the international community symbolizing a point of no return for the bitter antagonisms of the preceding cold war period. Gorbachev stood resolutely behind this commitment, which led to the historical transformations in Europe in the following two years.

The Achievements of New Political Thinking

The first serious trial of Gorbachev's concept of new political thinking was the problem of the Soviet military intervention in Afghanistan. When Gorbachev came to power, Soviet armed forces had been fighting in Afghanistan for five years. As soon as Gorbachev was elected general secretary, he defined the Afghanistan problem as his top priority. On May 5, 1986, he presented to the Politburo the following assessment of the situation:

> It is clear that a military victory is impossible, no matter how many troops we have there. It is clear that we have not carried out a social revolution for the Afghans—this intention was doomed to failure from the very outset and "by definition." It is also clear that instead

of building up our "southern underbelly," we have gotten for our-selves a zone of instability and internal conflict. We have provoked a much larger U.S. presence in the region than before. We have in-cited the Muslim world against ourselves and pushed Pakistan into open hostility. In a word, this is a total defeat.

The Politburo members did not question the need to relieve Russia of the Afghan burden, but this proved to be a difficult task. According to my notes, from 1985 to 1988 the Politburo discussed this issue more than two dozen times.

The Soviet leadership wanted to avoid the kind of hasty and in-glorious withdrawal the Americans had experienced in Vietnam. Many third world countries also voiced their concerns about the possibility of such an outcome since they were interested in pre-serving the image of the USSR as a great power. Moreover, the So-viet Union wanted to leave Afghanistan with a stable political arrangement that would be more or less acceptable to the rival par-ties. Military analysts predicted that withdrawing troops might turn out to be more dangerous and result in far more casualties than bringing them in. For all these reasons, the Soviet armies did not withdraw from Afghanistan until four years after the beginning of perestroika.

On May 5, 1986, the Politburo decided to start with the with-drawal of five regiments from Afghanistan. At that meeting, Gor-bachev said: "We were demonstrating that the USSR did not intend to stay in Afghanistan and obtain 'an access to the warm seas.' This indicated that our words were followed by relevant actions. And the Afghan leaders, too, must understand we were serious about what we were doing. So let them take everything in their hands. Let them take care of their country themselves."

In February 1987, Gorbachev said at a Politburo meeting: "Do not let us exclude America from agreements on Afghanistan until we have done something really serious. We have to establish con-tacts with Pakistan. Perhaps, we should invite President Zia-ul-Haq to meet me in Tashkent. And even do something to 'pay' him.

In short, we need flexibility and speed, otherwise there will be a massacre."

At a March 3, 1988, Politburo meeting, Gorbachev said, "We have firmly decided that we will start the withdrawal in May: 50 percent we must withdraw now, while all the remaining troops at the second stage." Then on April 18, 1988, Gorbachev said at a Politburo meeting:

> It is our moral and political duty to our people, the international community, and the Afghans to do everything in our power to alleviate negative consequences of the decision, which had been made before us and had proven to run counter [to] the principles of perestroika and new thinking. In our view the Afghan problem stopped being just our problem and a problem in our bilateral relations long ago. It is an international issue of principle, which is directly linked to the topical problems arising at a new stage in the world's development. . . . An important element was the beginning of our cooperation with the Americans in achieving the Geneva Accords and the involvement of the United Nations as well as our regular contacts with the Indian leadership, the governments of certain Muslim states and, later, a direct contact with mujahedeens.

Gorbachev met with newspaper editors, writers, and the ideological staff of the Central Committee on May 7, 1988, and said:

> We are being told that we have lost Afghanistan as if we had conquered it before. They say we have suffered fewer losses in comparison with the Great Patriotic War. This is a disgraceful line of reasoning! Every human life is valuable. Is it really an insignificant loss to have 13,000 killed and 43,000 wounded? Over one million people have lived through a nightmare. Not to mention the economy: we spent 5 billion a year. We should get out of that country from any point of view, human or economic. Just think of whom we have been fighting. The people! The solution of the problem of Afghanistan is an important and, in some degree, a key point in bringing about the new thinking. We made no mistake in this. And

this has influenced not only the settlement of other regional conflicts, but also the entire international situation.

This is the way Gorbachev characterized his actions on February 15, 1989, the day the Soviet troops completely withdrew from Afghanistan. However, even before this day, a changing Soviet attitude toward Afghanistan was perceived in the world as the decisive proof of radical changes in the entire Soviet foreign policy. It also became a symbol of the new thinking and an important factor contributing to the success of Soviet foreign policy in other areas.

From the outset, Gorbachev's greatest expectations were associated with the progress of Soviet relations with Western Europe. On the one hand, he wanted to relieve Europe of the formidable arms arsenals accumulated on its territory. On the other hand, European economic potential could be helpful in transforming the Soviet economy and making it more effective. Finally, Russia remained part of Europe historically, anthropologically, and culturally. Gorbachev's perestroika was aimed at returning Russia to the mainstream of modern civilization by assimilating European political, economic, scientific, and technological values. It also meant opening Russia to humanitarian and cultural communication with Europe. The idea of a "common European home," which Gorbachev declared during his visit to Prague in April of 1987 and vigorously promoted in his numerous contacts with Europeans, helped him develop a democratic European mentality and initiate a sharp turn in Soviet relations with Europe. He advocated the new approach to Europe during a Politburo meeting on March 26, 1988:

> I might be wrong, but I think we have badly studied Europe and our knowledge of it is insufficient. . . . It is clear that nowadays no issue can be settled without Europe. We should also remember that Europe is our major partner. We need it even for our internal transformations, for perestroika. On the foreign policy level, there is no replacement for Europe. We have major interests in Europe and therefore we should not be afraid of reducing military confrontation to a minimum.

To achieve this goal, Gorbachev asked to revise the military doctrine and consider reduction of the Soviet military presence in Eastern Europe. He also called for a thorough plan of Soviet relations with Western European countries and proposed to set up the Institute of Europe, a center for European studies. In addition, he wanted the leading research institutions, headed by Evgeni Primakov and Yuri (Georgi) Arbatov, to provide an objective, candid, and detailed analysis of European affairs on a quarterly basis.

Out of the three largest countries in Europe, Great Britain was traditionally viewed as being of secondary importance to the Soviet Union. As a result, throughout the cold war period, Soviet-British relations were full of animosity and tension. Paradoxically, in the second half of the 1980s Britain became the chief promoter of the Soviet Union's positive image in Western Europe. Margaret Thatcher was impressed with Gorbachev's reformist views as early as 1984, even before he became the leader of the Soviet Union. Although she never spared sharp criticism of the Communist system and the Soviet military-industrial complex in later meetings, Thatcher trusted Gorbachev's commitment to transform the country internally as well as to change its role in the world. Advocating the credibility of the Soviet new thinking, she led the way to its recognition by the Western world and opened a new arena of European politics for the Soviet leader. Gorbachev did not let Thatcher down and proved his commitment to the new philosophy of international relations by his response to the two grand challenges of the time: the "velvet revolutions" in Eastern Europe and German unification.

The logic that Gorbachev decided to apply to the countries of Eastern Europe became known in 1985 during his predecessor's funeral. He summoned the leaders of the Socialist states who attended the ceremony and promised that Moscow would stop interfering in their affairs. He also urged them to resolve their domestic problems on their own without asking Moscow's advice. This statement signified the end of the Brezhnev doctrine. Afterward, he consistently pursued that political line despite the continual pressure from some of the hard-liners in the Politburo. After the final disintegration of the Socialist camp in 1991, several conservatives questioned Gorbachev's reasons for "giving away" Eastern Europe, and he reasonably responded: "Gave away to whom? Bulgaria to the Bulgarians, Hungary to the Hungarians, Czechoslovakia to the Czechs and Slovaks? Do we have any right to regard them as our property?"

When Gorbachev came into power, Soviet relations with the Socialist countries were dominated by false stereotypes such as "eternal friendship," "the brotherhood of nations," and "Socialist internationalism." This "brotherhood" lasted for almost half a century, but events in 1953 in Berlin, in 1956 in Hungary and Poland, and in 1968 in Czechoslovakia revealed the truth. As the gap between Western and Eastern Europe was deepening, the dissatisfaction of Eastern Europe with its dependency on the Soviet Union increased. The party *nomenklatura* in Eastern Europe were greatly interested in preserving such dependent conditions, which only hindered Eastern Europe's socioeconomic and political development and damaged peoples' national dignity.

Gorbachev understood this, as did his predecessors. The primary motive behind his decision to change the policy course toward the Socialist states was moral. It made him speak out the way he did during Chernenko's funeral. However, a pragmatic motive was soon added. The Eastern European standard of living was higher than that in the USSR owing to Western aid and cheap natural resources from the Soviet Union. The discovery of abundant oil resources in western Siberia and high oil prices on the world market permitted the Soviet Union to sell oil and other natural resources to Eastern Europe at low prices. However, when oil prices fell in the 1970s and Eastern European demand for oil increased, the situation became intolerable. It was evident that the primary victims of such practices were the Soviet people. Soviet oil was often taken to Rotterdam and sold on the international market for hard currency. Moreover, financial aid to the Socialist countries amounted to 41 billion golden rubles each year (Cuba received 27 billion annually). In November of 1986, Gorbachev openly proposed to build economic relations with the Socialist allies on a mutually beneficial basis under real market conditions. Some Eastern European leaders, especially Nicolae Ceauşescu of Romania, Erich Honecker of the GDR, and Todor Zhivkov of Bulgaria, whose personal relationship with Gorbachev had significantly worsened, were opposed to changes in the Soviet approach toward the Socialist countries as well as internal transformations in the Soviet Union.

However, there was a broadening gap between the leaders of the Socialist states, the party elite, and the *nomenklatura* on the one hand and the people and the majority of ordinary party members on the other. The growing demand for reforms subsequently led to the "velvet revolutions" of 1989. They occurred peacefully everywhere with the exception of Romania. During a flight in 1989, Gorbachev spoke half-jokingly to a small circle of aides about "Socialist friends": "They became bored with us and we with them. Let some time pass. We may look back, think and build new relations." He was confident that, having been liberated from Soviet-style socialism, the countries of Eastern Europe would choose their own national version of socialism. He was mistaken. However, Gorbachev viewed that as a natural and unavoidable occurrence influenced by profound economic and political changes in the world. He remained true to the principle of noninterference, which he had pledged to follow from his first day in office as general secretary.

Gorbachev's contribution to the reunification of Germany was another manifestation of his new thinking policy. He started to deal with the German issue at the initial stage of perestroika, primarily because of the importance of Soviet economic ties with the FRG. During his numerous contacts with German politicians, such as Kohl, Brandt, Bahr, Genscher, Weizsäcker, and Strauss, Gorbachev gradually came to understand that the reunification of Germany was inevitable and even desirable. His visit to Germany in the summer of 1989 left a deep and lasting impression on him as he saw a country that had nothing in common with the one described by Soviet propaganda. The final trigger for Gorbachev's consent for German reunification occurred when millions of Germans living on both sides of the Berlin Wall got involved in the process of solving their national problem. Once Gorbachev became convinced that the movement in support of reunification was truly popular and democratic, he made his decision, and he intended to have it realized by peaceful means. This indicated that the principles of new thinking were firmly entrenched in Soviet foreign policy.

Amid the spiritual discord reigning throughout Russia, there are many different appraisals of Gorbachev's German policy. Some believe reunification should have been resisted. There were ways and means to achieve that, including a 500,000-strong Soviet army equipped with the best armaments. Some consider Gorbachev's failure to use these means as a betrayal of the Soviet Union's interests and its GDR friends. Some accept reunification, but think Gorbachev should have received much more in return for his agreement. A certain public figure suggested "making the Germans pay through the nose." Others maintain that Germany should not have been allowed to join NATO. Blackmailing both the Germans and the Americans could have slowed down or perhaps even stopped the process.

These are just a few of the many points of view and nuances of thinking on reunification. Yet Gorbachev could choose none of these solutions. His position on this issue, which was an integral part of the historic cause he took up in 1985, was natural for a statesman such as Gorbachev who developed his views during the era of perestroika.

Gorbachev raised international politics to a new level where morality played a meaningful part. Even if his efforts were not completely successful, they were not in vain, despite the caustic criticism he received from certain traditional cynics of diplomacy.

Most Germans, even those who lost their material and social benefits as a result of reunification, have strong positive feelings of appreciation, respect, and, in many cases, admiration for Gorbachev. But some journalists and politicians, not only German, still ask who, besides Kohl and Genscher, was the main hero of reunification. During the annual celebration of the event in Stuttgart on October 3, 1992, which was attended by George Bush, the Chancellor, and other figures who had taken part in the reunification process, the burgomaster said at the opening ceremony, "We are being told that we, Germans, owe America a lot for Germany's reunification. No. We owe America and President Bush everything, and only them!"

Gorbachev was in Leipzig, Germany, at the time of the event, which he had not been invited to attend, in all likelihood for fear of Yeltsin's anger. When journalists asked for his opinion of the burgomaster's statement, he answered, "I think that the German people are the main heroes of reunification."

Gorbachev's simple answer reflected once more the essence of his new thinking, the greatest historical achievement of which was putting an end to the Cold War.

The Soviet-U.S. summit in Malta in December of 1989 dealt a final blow to the four-decades-long confrontation between the two superpowers. As he prepared for the summit, Gorbachev was still uncertain about the possibility of establishing a relationship based on trust with the new U.S. administration. In his conversation with Prime Minister Giulio Andreotti of Italy, the Soviet leader remarked: "Americans are still undecided. This might be the biggest difficulty of [the] current transitional period." Therefore, even the most optimistic predictions about the result of this meeting were inaccurate. President Bush came to Malta with major proposals on the critical issues for both countries. His two arms control initiatives were to abandon the binary chemical-weapons program, subject to a bilateral agreement on major cutbacks in chemical-weapons arsenals, and to give up U.S. insistence on the prohibition of mobile intercontinental ballistic missiles (ICBMs). He promised to take steps to suspend the Jackson-Vanik Amendment, thus paving the way toward granting the Soviet Union Most Favored Nation status in trade, and the Stevenson and Byrd Amendments, which limited loans to the Soviet Union. Finally, he added that the

United States would no longer object to Soviet membership in GATT. During a friendly breakfast, a momentous discussion on economic transformations in the USSR took place in which President Bush and Secretary Baker clearly demonstrated their interest in the final success of perestroika. This discussion strengthened Gorbachev's confidence that the U.S. administration, including George Bush, James Baker, and Brent Scowcroft, had chosen to foster a positive relationship with the Soviet Union. The most impressive moment of the meeting came when President Bush and General Secretary Gorbachev rose from the negotiating table, shook hands, and stated that from then on they would no longer consider their countries to be enemies. Thus, starting with the Malta summit, the world entered a new post–cold war era.

At the all-European conference of 34 states, including the United States and Canada, held in Paris in late November 1990, Gorbachev declared, "We enter the world of different dimensions, where the human values become of equal meaning for everyone, where freedom and the value of human life should become the basis of everyone's security and the highest criteria of progress." The Charter for Europe adopted by the summit included almost all the postulates of the new thinking. The euphoria expressed in this statement revealed a passionate desire for the realization of this goal. Yet the Charter reflected the reality of the great transformation that had already taken place. Moreover, Gorbachev also mentioned the dangers still confronting Europe, such as militant nationalism and separatism, the danger of "balkanization," and the temptation to use historical and other advantages at the expense of weaker nations, among other concerns. Therefore, he paid special attention to the institutionalization of the European process and the mechanisms of international interaction. It was during this period that the NATO and Warsaw Treaty states signed an agreement in Paris on conventional armaments and armed forces in Europe.

All of these innovations reveal the gradual shaping of a radically new system of international relations for the future.

Concerted actions taken by Moscow and Washington to curb

Saddam Hussein's aggression gave graphic proof that the cold war had sunk into oblivion. I would add a proviso: the approach to the problem was common but the means employed to achieve the ultimate goal were permeated by the old thinking.

A summary of the major achievements of the new political thinking includes the following:

- breakthrough in U.S.-Soviet relations, which paved the path to disarmament and decreased the threat of nuclear war;
- formation of non-confrontational international relations; the introduction of dialogue between the leaders of various countries as the most important means of resolving global problems;
- liberation of the Eastern European states from Soviet hegemony and deep socio-political transformations in these countries under peaceful conditions;
- unification of Germany, which put an end to Yalta's division of Europe;
- the international community's response to Iraq's aggression against Kuwait, which, according to Gorbachev, was the sign of radical changes in world politics; and
- prospects for transforming Gorbachev's idea of the "European house" Mitterrand's "European confederation," or Bush's "European world order" through a political effort that Gorbachev thought transcended DeGaulle's "geographical limits from Atlantic to the Urals." In Gorbachev's view, the project would include "the Soviet Union, the United States and Canada, which are linked to [the] Old Continent by a common historical fate."

Three weeks before the August coup, Bush and Gorbachev signed the START I treaty in Moscow and discussed major parameters for a comprehensive security system. A NATO session in London mapped out a way to reform that cold-war organization, the Warsaw Pact dissolved on its own, the settlement of the Middle

East issue began, and Bush and Gorbachev co-chaired the Madrid Conference.

As for the new thinking concept, only one element was added to it during 1990–1991: orientation toward economic integration with the West without an alternative; namely, coexistence between economic systems instead of confrontation based on the previous and largely autarkic principle of class. There followed the Soviet Union's application for membership in the IMF and the World Bank and its appeal to the G7. Gorbachev participated in the London G-7 meeting in the summer of 1991.

The presence of the new thinking was markedly expressed in the international policies in the last two and one-half years of Gorbachev's tenure in office. Of course, this would have been impossible unless Western leaders, primarily the U.S. administration, had met him halfway. Bush and Baker displayed nobleness and understanding. Later, after a strange pause, they were willing to support perestroika. Thus, the logic of confrontation was replaced by the logic of interaction and cooperation.

One should in no way underestimate the contribution made to this effect by Reagan, Bush, Shultz, Baker, and a number of outstanding European statesmen of that political generation. But it was Gorbachev who took the initiative and expended boundless energy to achieve the objective. Success was attained by his uniquely conceived reform activities that led to the elimination of the totalitarian system in a superpower that had dominated world politics.

Today we would have a safer and more secure world if not for the breakup of the USSR. Foreign policy is not to blame. I do not assume that the Bush administration deliberately worked to destroy the Soviet Union, but they and those who replaced them in the White House took advantage of the USSR's breakup, and not in the best possible way from the viewpoint of the international community's interests, for they were carried away by the idea of victory in the cold war. Bush and Baker were not obliged to save the USSR at any cost. But as one who knew them well and thought highly of their personal and political merits, I still feel some bitterness.

As Gorbachev has said, $100 billion was quickly found to quell Hussein while $14 billion was barely scraped up for a partner in world affairs and notice was given only a week before the recipient vanished. It is now clear that neither 100 nor 200 nor even 500 billion dollars would have saved the USSR from its historically inevitable collapse. But perhaps that collapse would not have been so destructive and so disastrous to the Russian people. Moreover, it would have been easier for the international community to deal with the antagonisms, conflicts, and crimes of the new epoch if it had not lost a powerful buttress for a new world order in the land dividing Europe and Asia. Of course, the new Soviet Union would have been a different state, but it would have been strong and democratic. Under Yeltsin, Russia was unable to play that part.

I did not idealize Gorbachev as an international politician. Under his leadership, tactical moves were not always successful and cunning. Furthermore, he sometimes neglected the CPSU tradition. In addition, he made annoying mistakes in assessing partners, exhibited unwarranted optimism, exaggerated the effects of his personal charm, and made superficial forecasts, not to mention preposterous emotional outbursts.

Generally speaking, it was difficult for Gorbachev to scrape off the crust of a Soviet-type party boss, although he had less of it than others. His strong and healthy nature guided by principles that had been instilled in childhood gave him strength. This background formed the core of his philosophy toward life and his concepts of foreign policy.

Gorbachev's foreign policy was a precondition for a new era of peace and cooperation in the world. The only way to achieve it, however, is to follow the principles of "new political thinking," Gorbachev's greatest legacy to the world's future leaders.

David Holloway : *Moving to Globalization*

THE YEARS FROM 1985 to 1991 were an extraordinary period in the history of international politics. A breakthrough in U.S.-Soviet relations ended the cold war and the nuclear arms race; Soviet domination of Eastern Europe collapsed, allowing the countries of that region to choose their own paths of development; Germany was reunified; and the Soviet Union was dissolved at the end of 1991. It was clear at the time, and it is no less clear in retrospect, that these profound changes constituted an historic moment in international relations comparable to the reconfigurations of the international system caused by World Wars I and II. Moreover, these changes took place more peacefully than it would have been possible to imagine ten years earlier.

Mikhail Gorbachev was a key figure in this great transformation. It is inevitable that his role should be widely debated, especially in Russia, where there are many who deplore the results of his policies, most notably the breakup of the Soviet Union. In the West, where the transformation is regarded with overwhelming approval, the debated issues have more to do with Gorbachev's role in ending the cold war: How much credit does he deserve, and how much was he forced to do because of pressure from the West, and especially from the United States?

As Gorbachev's foreign policy adviser, Anatoli Cherniaev was especially well placed to provide insight into Gorbachev's policies. He ascribes a central role to the "new thinking," the main points of which he summarizes clearly. Cherniaev's essay raises three questions: Where did the new thinking come from? What was the relationship of ideas to power in Gorbachev's policies? And do these ideas have a continuing effect on international relations?

First, as Cherniaev points out, Gorbachev's post-Stalin predecessors understood that nuclear weapons made it necessary for them to be cautious in pursuing their rivalry with the West. But Gorbachev went far beyond that prudent conclusion. The new thinking rested on two key premises: that nuclear weapons necessitated a new approach to international politics and that such basic human interests as peace had primacy over the interests of any particular class. The new thinking marked a fundamental shift in the Soviet view of international relations.

The precepts of the new thinking were not novel in themselves. The idea that in the nuclear age security has to be mutual, for example, was widely, though not universally, shared throughout the world. But taken together, the principles of the new thinking did have profound implications for Soviet policy and world politics. The most important innovation in the Soviet context was abandonment of the Leninist analysis of imperialism, which placed the struggle between capital and labor at the center of international relations. The new thinking ultimately signaled that the Soviet Union no longer aimed to maintain an alternative system of international relations but instead wished to be integrated into a global system.

Gorbachev did not have a clear formulation of the new thinking in mind when he became general secretary. He developed his thinking in the course of his efforts to deal with the problems that faced the Soviet Union. In 1985 the Soviet Union appeared to be more powerful in military terms than ever before, but its economy was stagnant, its technology lagged, it was fighting a fruitless war in Afghanistan, and it was engaged in an apparently endless arms race with an economically stronger rival. The buildup of Soviet armed forces in the 1960s and 1970s had not created the more favorable international environment that Soviet leaders had hoped for but had led to more tense and hostile relations with the West and with China. Gorbachev developed his ideas as he sought to extricate the Soviet Union from this difficult situation.

What led Gorbachev to the new thinking, according to Cherni-aev, was a combination of pragmatic and moral considerations. The pragmatic element was an understanding of the danger of nuclear confrontation, and the moral element was empathy for Soviet citizens and the suffering and deprivation they had endured. Gorbachev had not had formal responsibility for foreign policy before becoming general secretary, but he was of course aware of the dangerously high level of tension in East-West relations in the early 1980s and the heavy burden that the arms race imposed on the Soviet Union. As the Central Committee secretary responsible for agriculture, he had been concerned about the resources allocated to the military-industrial complex.[1]

Cherniaev stresses the importance of Gorbachev's meetings with foreign political leaders, which have received less attention than they deserve.[2] These conversations not only helped to shape Gorbachev's views on foreign affairs but also moved him toward a more social-democratic concept of socialism. They helped to persuade him that it would indeed be possible to end the cold war and to move international relations onto a different footing. But Gorbachev's serious conversations with foreign leaders began only in 1983, when he was already a prospective candidate for general secretary. This leaves open the question of why he was predisposed to pursue the line that he did, in fact, follow.

Some party and government officials in the early 1980s were critical of Soviet foreign policy and open to new approaches. Cherniaev himself was one of them; so, too, was Georgi Shakhnazarov, who also came to play an important role as an adviser to Gorbachev.[3] An even more important figure, perhaps, was Aleksandr Yakovlev, whom Gorbachev met during a 1983 visit to Canada, where

1. Mikhail Gorbachev, *Zhizn' i reformy*, kniga 1 (Moscow: Novosti, 1995), 207.

2. But see Archie Brown, *The Gorbachev Factor* (Oxford: Oxford University Press, 1996), 115–117.

3. Anatoli Cherniaev, *Shest' let s Gorbachevym* (Moscow: Kul'tura, 1993); Georgi Shakhnazarov, *Tsena svobody* [The Price of Freedom] (Moscow: Rossika Zevs, 1993).

Yakovlev was ambassador. Gorbachev soon brought him back to Moscow to head IMEMO, the leading international affairs institute in the Academy of Sciences. Eduard Shevardnadze, too, was an important ally and influence, especially after his appointment as foreign minister in July 1985. Of course, these advisers did not determine the policy that Gorbachev followed, but they did help to define the direction of foreign policy in conceptual and practical terms. Besides, the presence of such people in the party and state apparatus indicates that the capacity for policy innovation existed. In other words, there were those who, like Gorbachev, understood the need for change not only at home but also in the Soviet Union's relations with the rest of the world.

Cherniaev plays down the role of the Academy of Sciences institutes in formulating the new thinking. He is right to criticize the emphasis that some scholars have put on the role of the *institutchiki*. The institutes, which were closely tied to the Central Committee apparatus and the Ministry of Foreign Affairs, did not provide Gorbachev with a clearly formulated set of ideas when he became general secretary. But the institutes had on their staffs knowledgeable specialists who had developed ideas on global issues and had views that were not always identical to those of official policy (though they were, of course, restricted in what they could say publicly). Some of these specialists took advantage of the political space Gorbachev opened up to elaborate elements of the new thinking. They were part of the international affairs community Gorbachev could draw on in developing his ideas about foreign and defense policy.

Cherniaev's essay raises a second question: What was the role of ideas in this great transformation in international politics? There are those who argue that Gorbachev did only what he was forced to do by the realities of power, by the decrepit state of the Soviet economy, and by pressure from the Reagan administration. Others, who have argued that Gorbachev's policies show that ideas do play an important role in world politics, have used the end of the cold war to critique the realist approach with its emphasis on the primacy of power in international relations.

Gorbachev was indeed responding to the difficult domestic and international circumstances in which the Soviet Union found itself in the mid-1980s. He understood that the Soviet Union had to craft a new relationship with the rest of the world, and the new thinking provided the intellectual framework—the guidelines and the justification—for doing just that. By the latter years of Gorbachev's rule, this framework had evolved into a radical revision of the premises of Soviet foreign policy, matching the transformation that was taking place inside the country. It marked a fundamental change in the Soviet Union's concept of the world and of its own place in it.

But Gorbachev's policy was not the only possible one. Other leaders might have made other choices. As Shakhnazarov has written, "Suppose that in March 1985 the Politburo of the CPSU Central Committee had elected as General Secretary Grishin, Romanov, or someone else from the 'old guard.' It is possible to imagine that in that case the reforms would have followed the 'Chinese variant,' and the Soviet Union, as well as the bipolar system of international relations, would have been preserved."[4] The nuclear arms race would have continued, writes Shakhnazarov, and the missile confrontation in Europe would have become more intense. It is open to debate whether someone other than Gorbachev might have become general secretary, but Shakhnazarov is surely right that there were different courses of action possible in 1985. Gorbachev's choices were therefore important, and so, too, were his ideas, insofar as they guided his policies.

It took some time for Western leaders to understand that Gorbachev was prepared to be much more radical than had been apparent in 1985. He did not have a detailed foreign policy plan or a fully elaborated theoretical framework when he became general secre-

---

4. Shakhnazarov, *Tsena svobody*, 579.

tary. His immediate goals—to end the war in Afghanistan and to reduce the nuclear danger, for example—could be interpreted as prudent rather than visionary. But as it developed in the late 1980s, the new thinking pointed the way to a far-reaching transformation of the international system. Conceptual innovation is important in politics, especially in societies with an official ideology. This was not immediately understood in the West, where suspicion of Gorbachev's motives persisted for a long time. The event that achieved the final breakthrough was Gorbachev's remarkable speech to the United Nations in December 1988, when he made one of his most cogent statements on the new thinking and announced deep unilateral cuts in Soviet forces, thereby removing the 40-year-old Soviet military threat to Western Europe.

The U.S. debate about the role of ideas in foreign policy is unnecessarily polarized in suggesting that explanations in terms of power are distinct from explanations that pay attention to ideas. The new thinking did not arise in a political vacuum and was indeed formulated as a way of dealing with the problems that the Soviet Union faced. But that does not mean that Gorbachev's ideas were unimportant. Ideas can provide a guide to action, they can help to create political support by giving a rationale for policy, and they can reassure other states by providing a context in which a state's policies can be understood. The new thinking played all of these roles in the Gorbachev years.

A third question is prompted by Cherniaev's essay: What legacy has the new thinking left? This question can be broken into two parts: the long-term impact of the changes that Gorbachev helped to bring about and the continuing influence of the new thinking as a set of ideas about international relations.

The legacy is enormous if we look at the effect of the transformation brought about by Gorbachev's policies. Of course, Gorbachev did not bring about these changes on his own; he had collaborators inside and outside the Soviet Union. Nor did Gorbachev intend everything that transpired; he desperately wanted to prevent the breakup of the Soviet Union, for example. Indeed, events went beyond his control. But what is striking is that this transformation took place much more peacefully than could have been envisaged 10 or 20 years earlier. The new thinking provided a vision of the Soviet Union's place in the world that reassured the Soviet public as well as foreign leaders and publics. It thereby exercised a calming influence on the process of change. In that sense, the new thinking had a lasting effect in making it easier for the cold war to end in a relatively peaceful manner.

The answer is much less clear if we ask whether the new thinking, understood as a set of ideas, continues to influence international politics. In Russia the term is hardly used at all, except to refer to Gorbachev's policies. Since many people judge his policies to have been a catastrophic failure, that association does not help to perpetuate the influence of his ideas. Gorbachev's policies came under increasing criticism while he was still in office, not because he had abandoned Leninism but because he was believed to be paying insufficient attention to the national interest. Putin is now stressing the need to strengthen the Russian state and pursue the Russian national interest with vigor. The emphasis of Putin's policy is very different from that of Gorbachev's policy and is more akin to traditional realpolitik. Yet, key elements of the new thinking continue to serve as premises of Russian policy, even though the term is rarely used today. Russian leaders, for example, have not resuscitated the class approach to international relations, they view security in the nuclear age as mutual, and they aim to secure for Russia what they regard as its rightful place in the global system.

In the West, the new thinking, as a set of ideas, is associated with Gorbachev and the specific circumstances of his time. Even in that context, most Western analysts ascribe only secondary importance to the role of ideas in shaping Gorbachev's policy. They put more weight on U.S. policy and on the defects of the Soviet system in limiting the options that Gorbachev had available to him. The starkest version of this approach is the one that credits Reagan's Strategic Defense Initiative with bringing the cold war to an end and causing the collapse of the Soviet Union. In that interpretation, ideas play a very small part in Gorbachev's policies. The popularity of this interpretation (which is quite misleading, in my opinion) helps to explain why some analysts relegate the new thinking to history and regard it as irrelevant today. Moreover, some of the tenets of the new thinking that appeared unshakable—notably the mutuality of security—have come under strain in the United States, where a unilateralist approach to national security has gained strength since the mid-1990s.

It would be wrong, however, to dismiss the new thinking as no more than a set of ideas associated with Gorbachev and the policies he pursued. The emphasis on global human values was the antithesis of the idea of socialism in one country or even in one system of states. By virtue of the role it played in Gorbachev's policies, the new thinking contributed to the breakdown of the alternative system of international relations that the Soviet Union had constructed among the Socialist countries. Gorbachev's policies gave a powerful impetus to the globalization that now characterizes the international state system. During the cold war, international politics revolved around the rivalry of two antagonistic systems. Now we have a single global system in which the key issues are who defines the rules of the game, who has influence in the system, who benefits from the system, and who does not. In our preoccupation with current politics, we sometimes forget Gorbachev's role in bringing this about. Moreover, in this new context, the premises of the new thinking are still relevant for international politics and are indeed growing in importance. The processes of globalization reinforce the need for a global perspective on world politics. The cold war may be over, but nuclear weapons are still with us, and the need for a new approach to international relations has not lost its urgency.

CHAPTER 4

Georgi I. Mirski : *Soviet-American*
: *Relations in*
: *the Third World*

AMONG THE FACTORS that led to the
end of the cold war, Soviet-U.S. relations in the third world are
certainly not predominant. Nevertheless, the third world proved
important in the process that culminated in what may be called a
second edition of détente initiated by Mikhail Gorbachev.

Developments in Asia, Africa, and Latin America in the 1970s
and 1980s helped create an atmosphere in which the superpower
rivalry came to be regarded by both sides as counterproductive and
obsolete. The growing disenchantment of both the Soviet and the
U.S. leadership regarding the possibility of achieving their global
aims by activist policies in the third world strengthened the desire,
first manifested by Gorbachev, to put an end to the worldwide
confrontation. Moreover, as Gorbachev increasingly focused on
accommodation with the West—first and foremost on terminating
the arms race, which had become an intolerable burden for the Soviet economy—the conviction was growing that the continuation
of the anti-imperialist drive in the third world was distinctly harmful for the newly formulated goals of Soviet policy. The traditional
militant pattern of Soviet behavior in the third world that had been
initiated by Nikita Khrushchev did not square with Gorbachev's
new political thinking, much less with the new concept of de-
ideologization of interstate relations. And it was not particularly
painful for the Kremlin to embark on a strategic retreat from the
third world. The point is that expansion in Asia, Africa, and Latin

America had never figured as a vital part of Soviet political thinking; it was subordinate to the overall design of undermining the West and strengthening the position of the socialist camp.

Moscow and the Third World

In order to understand the value of the third world for the Soviets, it is necessary to go back to the Khrushchev era. In the mid-1950s, it was already clear to the Kremlin that the confrontation between the two systems was deadlocked. No breakthrough in Europe was in sight, both sides being firmly entrenched to the east and west of the iron curtain and engaged in a positional warfare. The Leninist legacy of interests of world socialism dictated, however, the necessity of a relentless struggle against the imperialist forces. The only option was to try to undermine and sap those forces somewhere else. Encroachment in the third world, instead of a frontal assault, was quite promising as a means of bypassing the main bulwarks of the imperialist system.

The whole concept bears resemblance to a Maoist theory according to which the global village, or developing countries, would surround the global city, or the industrialized West, forcing the latter eventually to capitulate. In Moscow, however, nobody really expected to gain a decisive victory over the West by promoting socialism in Asia and Africa. Gone were the days when Soviet party ideologues and scholars seriously expounded the theory that the imperialist center was bound to collapse as soon as it was deprived of its colonial periphery. In the 1960s, it was abundantly clear that the liberated colonies remained dependent on the economy of their former masters and that Western monopolies were deriving even more profits from their dealings with Asian and African countries than in the past. It would be hard to believe in strangling Western capitalism by spreading Soviet influence and Socialist ideas in the third world.

The rationale for moving into the third world was different; in fact, it was of a rather defensive nature. Paradoxically, a certain feeling of insecurity and vulnerability was typical of post-Khrushchev leadership in the realm of foreign policy. How could rulers of a superpower fail to feel absolutely secure and self-confident? Yet they were always apprehensive about the global growth of U.S. power and influence, always on the alert, anxiously scanning and monitoring every U.S. move, ever preoccupied with the issue of maintaining parity with Washington regarding the military balance. This phenomenon can be explained only by the peculiar mentality of *Homo Sovieticus*, that deplorable blend of ancient Russian prejudices and Communist ideology.

The Soviet leaders' paranoia reflected a deep-rooted Russian distrust toward the West, exacerbated by a typically Soviet suspicion of foreign subversion. Although Soviet propaganda claimed that imperialism would hardly dare launch an attack against the USSR, given the new balance of forces, deep down the Kremlin rulers were not at all certain about that. The Politburo members, poorly educated and lacking first-hand knowledge of the outside world, were prone to ascribe to foreign governments their own patterns of political behavior. They believed that the West was just as capable of breaking its promises and obligations, of double-crossing and even outright aggression, as they were themselves. I remember Boris Ponomarev, head of the International Department of the CPSU Central Committee, saying in 1977: "Under no circumstances can we afford to let the Americans achieve even a small degree of military superiority, to rise just one notch above our level, because in this case the next U.S. president may be tempted to strike at our country. And we have no way of knowing who the next President will be, maybe some crazy warmonger like Reagan."

So deep suspicion and distrust were paramount in the Soviet leaders' attitude toward the West. Particularly maddening for them was the U.S. pattern of pact-building. I remember how furious the Central Committee officials were when the Baghdad Pact was founded. The Soviet obsession with encirclement was a major psychological factor of the Kremlin's foreign policy. Soviet leaders always felt as though they were in a state of ongoing war, always on the frontline, watching through binoculars the movements of enemy forces. Every American move anywhere in the world was an attack, to be repulsed immediately with a counterstroke. They also knew that if you could not crush the enemy, the thing to do was to bypass its forces and strike at its rear. Thus, the creation of the Baghdad Pact was the main issue behind Khrushchev's decision to strike a deal with President Nasser; it was simply a necessary riposte, a countermove. Very soon, however, the Kremlin boss realized that this tactical move could be an initial step in a vast enveloping movement designed to shift the battlefield from the frozen trenches of a rigidly divided Europe to the only area where maneuver warfare was still possible: the third world.

It was a bold and imaginative pattern, and Brezhnev did not hesitate to follow it through. In the eyes of the Soviet leaders, peaceful coexistence by no means abolished the class struggle of two systems and thus was quite compatible with attempts to improve and strengthen the position of the world Socialist forces, primarily in the third world. As for the notion of détente (in Russian it sounded like "the policy of defusing international tension"), it was regarded, first, as a means to save forces and minimize the cost of engagement and, second, as a strategy of low-level actions calibrated in such a way as to avoid major clashes capable of triggering a global military confrontation.[1]

China should not be overlooked. As the Chinese threat was perceived to be growing, the old specter of encirclement reemerged in Soviet thinking. This time around, it seemed there was a remote possibility of an unholy alliance between China and the Western powers.[2] To prevent this, Soviet leaders believed that steps had to

---

1. For a review of Soviet-U.S. relations in the third world prior to détente, see John Lewis Gaddis, *We Now Know: Rethinking Cold War History* (Oxford: Clarendon Press, 1997), 152–188.

2. This was a theoretically embarrassing situation. Marxism could not foresee the possibility of Socialist countries fighting each other. The way out of this deadlock was to assume that there was no socialism in China. Evgeni Primakov, with whom I studied at the Arabic department of the Moscow Institute of Oriental

be taken to normalize Soviet relations with the imperialist camp, particularly after Nixon's visit to China, which was an unpleasant surprise for Moscow.

U.S. Concepts of Détente in the Third World

The U.S. policy, as envisaged by President Nixon and Secretary of State Kissinger, was impressively designed. It aimed at containing the Soviet Union "through a network of linked rewards and punishments," ensuring world stability in a form that suited U.S. interests, and avoiding direct and costly U.S. involvement in regional conflicts, which, it was felt, might be instigated or promoted by the Kremlin unless it could be persuaded to desist.[3]

In the midst of the Vietnam imbroglio, the U.S. administration was anxious to prevent the Soviet Union from attempting to exploit regional conflicts that abounded in the third world. It was feared that the Kremlin, by fomenting unrest in the volatile areas of Asia, Africa, and Latin America, might try to sap U.S. influence worldwide and compel the United States to disperse and tie up its forces in local entanglements. In Kissinger's words, the Soviet practice was to "promote the attrition of adversaries by gradual increments."[4] He thought that the Soviet aim was to change the global balance of forces without a head-on collision with America. To counteract this, Kissinger assumed that an arrangement was possible whereby the Soviets could be persuaded that their interests could best be served by discarding their subversive strategy. At the same time, Kissinger, who was still saddled with the Vietnamese nightmare, supported cutting America's losses by withdrawal from Vietnam.[5]

Studies, told me sometime in the 1970s that he intended to prove beyond all doubt that Maoist China was not a Socialist country at all.

3. See Stanley Hoffmann, "Détente," in *The Making of America's Soviet Policy*, ed. Joseph S. Nye Jr. (New Haven, CT: Yale University Press, 1984), 231, 237.

4. Henry Kissinger, *White House Years* (Boston: Little, Brown, 1979), 118.

5. See Franz Schurmann, *The Foreign Politics of Richard Nixon: The Grand Design* (Berkeley, CA: Institute of International Studies, 1987), 87; Gerry Argyris Andrianopoulos, *Kissinger and Brzezinski* (London: Macmillan, 1991), 170.

It is not clear on what logic Kissinger based his assumptions or what led him to believe that the Soviets could somehow be talked out of their usual pattern of behavior. From the very beginning, it could have been surmised that Moscow had nothing to lose and much to gain by continuing what Kissinger called "the attrition of adversaries by gradual increments." Exploiting third world conflicts to strengthen the position of "the global forces of socialism" was something no Kremlin leader could neglect without being accused of failing to promote the Socialist cause. It is hard to imagine precisely what rewards America could promise to the Soviets in exchange for desisting from intervening in local conflicts; it is also difficult to fathom what punishment Washington could have meted out to Moscow in the event of the latter's bad behavior. As American author Stanley Hoffman put it, "The design was impressive but beyond reach, and the tools it used were inadequate."[6]

The most important concrete area where the Nixon-Kissinger doctrine was to be implemented was the Middle East. The foundation stones of U.S. Middle East policy were Israel and Iran, later to be joined by Egypt and Saudi Arabia. Israel's security and regular access to the region's oil were constant imperatives of every U.S. administration. For Washington, détente tactics in the Middle East were regarded as conducive to a substantive reduction in the level of Soviet involvement. Rivalry between the superpowers would go on in that region unabated, détente notwithstanding. In all likelihood, however, it was hoped that Moscow would refrain from instigating revolution in the Arabian Peninsula and from encouraging the Arab world to step up its anti-Israeli crusade.

There were similarities in the Soviet and U.S. concepts of détente. Both sides realized that the cold war was at a stalemate, yet there was no end in sight. So there emerged a tacit agreement to lower the level of conflict, to cease fighting to the hilt to ensure that the inevitable rivalry would not lead to a world war, and to avoid creating situations in which one of the conflicting sides would face a dreadful choice: to back down and lose face or to start a suicidal nuclear war.

---

6. Hoffmann, "Détente," in Nye, *The Making of America's Soviet Policy*, 231.

On a strategic level, the policy of both sides was defensive rather than offensive. The Soviet leaders, true to their Bolshevik paranoia, tried to thwart what they saw as an imperialist attempt to encircle Russia. The Soviet Union had to compensate for its geopolitical and economic weakness by reaching out to promising new areas to exploit the anticolonial inertia of Asian and African nations. The ultimate aim was not to beat America but to avoid being beaten. However, this defensive, or preemptive, strategy was translated into a tactical offensive. The Soviets tried to seize the initiative whenever and wherever they could.

The United States also appeared to have a defensive rationale aimed at containing Soviet expansion in gray areas. A deeper analysis would show, however, that America actually was much more on the offensive than was the Soviet Union. Successive U.S. administrations made persistent efforts to undermine Soviet positions in the third world, particularly in the Middle East. For instance, President Anwar Sadat's change of heart and his surprising reorientation was not just a result of his own reappraisal of the situation. He repeatedly said in the beginning of the 1970s that the United States held 90 percent of the trump cards in the Middle East, and it would be logical to assume that U.S. diplomacy reinforced this thinking. Subsequent events, including the 1973 Arab-Israeli war and the complicated political game that ensued, finally gave Sadat exactly what he had wanted all along: the restoration of Egyptian sovereignty over the Sinai and the reopening of the Suez Canal. By the same token, Henry Kissinger had no reason to be disappointed by the outcome of the confrontation Sadat had initiated, probably with tacit U.S. encouragement. Kissinger, who made brilliant use of the deadlock resulting from the Yom Kippur War, could claim a victory over the Soviets.

The Collapse of Détente

As the Middle East was the principal battlefield in the Soviet-U.S. rivalry in the third world, it would have been logical to expect that it was precisely in that area that détente would be destined to collapse, but this was not the case. The point is that the main lines of confrontation in the Middle East were clearly marked, and each side had its own allies, seemingly firmly committed and loyal. Moscow had a more advantageous position by the time détente was initiated. The most important country of the region, President Nasser's Egypt, seemed to be firmly under Soviet control. Together with its regional allies, Syria, Iraq, South Yemen, Algeria, Libya, and Sudan, Egypt was dependent on Soviet arms in anticipation of an inevitable new round of military confrontation with Israel. The Soviet Union lavishly supplied its local allies with arms, helping them build a position of strength vis-à-vis Israel.[7] Moscow also pinned its hopes on the nascent Palestinian resistance movement, backing Arafat's PLO. Except for Israel, the United States did not seem to have any bulwarks in the area. This situation was to change dramatically in America's favor in just a few years' time after the sharp rise in oil prices in the wake of the 1973 war, which resulted in the phenomenal growth of power and influence of Saudi Arabia and Iran. By the end of the 1960s, however, U.S. prospects appeared bleak. The Soviet Union was emerging as a key Middle Eastern power whereas U.S. influence in the area seemed to be waning.

President Nasser's death in the fall of 1970 changed everything. His successor, Anwar Sadat, continued to demand and receive more Soviet arms while beginning a subtle game of his own. Convinced that the United States held 90 percent of the trump cards in the Middle East, his challenge was to play skillfully and create a situation in which Washington would have no option but to put

---

7. Deliveries of Soviet military equipment by 1977 totaled more than $3.2 billion, and 23 percent of all the arms exports went to Egypt, which was the first non-Communist state to receive the SA-3 low-level SAM missile, the FROG tactical ground rocket, and the mobile ZSU–23–4 radar-controlled anti-aircraft gun. See Roger E. Kanet, ed., *Soviet Foreign Policy in the 1980s* (New York: Praeger, 1982), 154–161, 272–275, 285–287, 296–299; E. G. Feuchtwanger and Peter Nailor, eds., *The Soviet Union and the Third World* (London: Macmillan, 1981), 16, 124; Robert H. Donaldson, ed., *The Soviet Union in the Third World: Successes and Failures* (Boulder, CO: Westview Press, 1981), 157, 386–390.

pressure on Israel to return Sinai to Egypt. Sadat's first bold move was to expel Russian military advisers in July 1972, which took the Kremlin by surprise and produced a veritable shock.[8] This sent an unmistakable signal to Washington, and it worked. Kissinger clearly became interested in dealing with Sadat, and, when the latter made his next bold move, attacking Israel in October 1973, it was Kissinger who played a decisive role in settling the conflict.

Sadat's notion of America holding most of trump cards was convincingly validated as he followed through on his new pro-American policy and crowned his efforts with the Camp David agreement. Completely sidelined, Moscow was embittered and frustrated. Paradoxically, however, the Kremlin did not regard the whole affair as a treacherous U.S. ploy but rather as a setback within the framework of the mutually recognized rules of the game, and all its anger was directed at Sadat. Evgeni Primakov, a leading Soviet expert in the field, wrote a book a few years later titled *The Story of a Treacherous Deal.*[9] The treason in question, of course, was that of Sadat. Washington had every reason to be happy with the outcome of the whole process, and Kissinger was justified in saying, "The USSR suffered a major setback in the Middle East and accepted it; the conflicts between us, while real, were managed."[10]

So détente was destined to collapse not in the Middle East but in Africa. In November 1975, the Soviets began an airlift of arms and Cuban troops to Angola, where a civil war was raging between pro-Soviet leftist forces and their right-wing adversaries. In January 1978, Cuban troops along with the Ethiopian army began a counteroffensive in the Ogaden region, which had been invaded by Somalia six months earlier. In both cases, the Soviet-Cuban inter-

---

8. By that time, more than 12,000 Soviet military personnel were stationed in Egypt, and about 4,000 military instructors were involved in an advisory capacity. Also withdrawn were Soviet missile launchers, bombers, and several squadrons of MIG-21s. See Schurmann, *The Foreign Politics of Richard Nixon*, 290; Donald R. Kelley, ed., *Soviet Politics in the Brezhnev Era* (New York: Praeger, 1980), 265.

9. Evgeni Primakov, *The Story of a Treacherous Deal* (Moscow: Politizdat, 1985).

10. Henry Kissinger, *Years of Upheaval* (Boston: Little, Brown, 1982), 246.

vention proved effective: the leftist MPLA won the war in Angola while Ethiopia's proto-Communist regime led by Mengistu Haile Mariam succeeded in pushing back the Somalis and retaking the Ogaden. The question remains: Why did the Soviets decide to intervene in the first place, and why did Washington react so decisively?

The Soviet Union did not create the conflicts in Angola and Ethiopia. Moscow was naturally happy when, after the revolution in Portugal, left-wing forces appeared victorious in the newly independent Angola. One more nation was added to the already formidable list of countries with Socialist orientations. So when the MPLA was threatened by a hostile and decidedly anti-Communist political force that had launched an armed attack, the Soviet government could not afford to stand idly by and refuse aid to the Angolan left-wing regime without risking a serious loss of face.

In the Ethiopia-Somali conflict over the Ogaden, the Soviet position was much more delicate because, unlike in Angola, there was no clear-cut choice between the revolutionary and reactionary forces. Both republics had proclaimed their Socialist orientation, were friendly with the USSR, and were hostile to the United States. The choice Moscow finally made was based not on the degree of Socialist commitment and loyalty to Marxism but on thoroughly pragmatic grounds: Ethiopia was the bigger, stronger, and more important of the two.

In neither case did the Soviets risk sending their own forces to fight; the Cuban proxy was used instead. Moscow was obviously reluctant to jeopardize its relations with the United States. An important question arises: Did the Soviet leadership know beforehand about Castro's intention to airlift Cuban troops to Angola? Speaking at a conference titled "Global Competition and the Deterioration of U.S.-Soviet Relations, 1977–1980" held by the Carter-Brezhnev Project in March 1995, Karen Brutents, former deputy head of the International Department of the Central Committee of the CPSU, said that the Soviet leadership as a whole "was not informed about it. Furthermore, many members of the Soviet leadership were unhappy with what they regarded as the Cuban drive to show independent action." Nevertheless, "Soon they had adjusted to the circumstances, and even supported it. It was convenient in many respects: it was the Cubans, not us, who were involved . . ."[11] At another conference sponsored by the same project, "SALT II and the Growth of Mistrust," held in May 1994, Sergei Tarasenko, a senior staff member of the Soviet foreign ministry, said that as soon as news about the Cuban airlift reached the USSR, the foreign ministry in Moscow sent a telegram to Havana asking Castro "not to do it" and "to abstain." By that time, however, "The planes were already in the air. The planes were flying while the telegram was going to Havana."[12] However, at the same conference, General Sergei Kondrashov, special assistant to head of the KGB Yuri Andropov, admitted that the KGB "knew beforehand of the intentions of Cubans to help Angolans. That information went to Moscow; so, practically speaking, the whole leadership knew about this forthcoming development. . . . Nothing happened without knowledge of the leadership of the country. . . . We didn't want to be involved in the Angolan situation ourselves; but we knew about Cuban intentions."[13] So it appears that the Kremlin was informed about the planned Cuban action but, true to form, officially chose to pretend that it was ignorant of it. It even showed surprise so as to be able to convey the impression, primarily to the Americans, that it was purely the initiative of Fidel Castro, the Cuban leader.

Another angle that must be taken into consideration is Moscow's rivalry with Beijing, a bitter clash of two Communist giants over control of both the Communist and national-liberation movements. The Soviets were afraid that if they did not come to the aid of an embattled leftist regime, the Chinese would. At the 1995

---

11. "Global Competition and the Deterioration of U.S.-Soviet Relations, 1977–1980," Conference No. 3 of the Carter-Brezhnev Project, Harbor Beach Resort, Fort Lauderdale, FL, March 23–26, 1995, 50.

12. "SALT II and the Growth of Mistrust," Conference No. 2 of the Carter-Brezhnev Project, Musgrove Plantation, St. Simons Island, GA, May 6–9, 1994, 293–295.

13. Ibid., 300–301.

"Global Competition" conference, Oleg Troianovski, former Soviet ambassador to the United Nations, said that the Soviet Union "was under a constant fire from the Chinese side for not being active in the fight against imperialism. We were charged with appeasing the United States, and things like that. And sometimes this may have led to decisions which would not have been made under other circumstances."[14]

In view of the growing Chinese penetration in Africa, it was also useful to secure the loyalty of yet another young African state. I recall that a few years after the events in Angola and Somalia, I clashed with Valentin Falin, deputy head of the International Department of the CPSU Central Committee. Speaking at a party meeting, I voiced my indignation regarding our diplomacy's flirtation with the Ugandan tyrant Idi Amin. Falin's reply was, "Don't you realize that, after the Chinese had started a love affair with Tanzania, we just had to secure a friend nearby."

The United States was furious over Angola and Ethiopia, believing the Soviet-Cuban intervention to be part of a sinister pattern. Zbigniew Brzezinski, a strong advocate of a tough American response, maintained that "if the Soviets believe they could expand their influence with impunity, they might well do so next in the developing struggle in Rhodesia."[15] President Jimmy Carter and Secretary of State Cyrus Vance did not concur with him and preferred a more moderate line, and Brzezinski said later, "SALT lies buried in the sands of the Ogaden."[16] Kissinger, too, later said that "had they succeeded in Angola, there would have been no Ethiopia."[17] Although President Carter had rejected Brzezinski's tough line on Africa, he obviously felt humiliated later, and these two episodes certainly contributed to his growing coolness toward détente. Of course, other developments regarding both the SALT

---

14. "Global Competition," 79.
15. Alexander Moens, *Foreign Policy Under Carter* (Boulder, CO: Westview Press, 1990), 105.
16. Ibid., 103.
17. Andrianopoulos, *Kissinger and Brzezinski*, 173.

treaty and human rights issues affected him as well. By the end of his presidency, Carter had abandoned détente and returned to a cold war policy.[18]

The United States' outrage at the Soviet interventions in Africa is understandable. In the highly volatile conditions that abound in most African countries, there was no telling where violence would flare up next. Civil and ethnic conflicts could start at any moment in practically every part of the continent, and there can be no doubt that in the atmosphere of the 1970s, when the prestige of socialism was still high and rewards of an alliance with the Soviet Union quite tangible, pro-Soviet leftist movements calling for Soviet backing were likely to emerge anywhere. Brzezinski was not being paranoid when he voiced his concern over Rhodesia. Knowing the nature of Soviet leaders, it was easy to predict that if they met with feeble or token opposition from the West, they might be emboldened enough to undertake much larger-scale adventures, not only in Africa but in Asia and Latin America as well. Whereas in Angola and Ethiopia they simply reacted to crises they could not have been blamed for creating, in the future they could deliberately begin to provoke them.

Doesn't this suggestion invalidate the earlier thesis of the essentially defensive character of Soviet strategy in the third world? Not if we take into consideration the inherent duality of the Soviet leaders' mind-set. On the one hand, they no longer believed in the global victory of communism, they were quite apprehensive about the possibility of a new global war, and they were generally averse to taking risks. On the other hand, as true heirs to Lenin and Stalin, they would see themselves as unworthy of their predecessors' great legacy if they let slip an opportunity to promote the Socialist cause. This opportunity could be provided for them by the imperialist camp's weakness and lack of resolve. The weaker the Western resis-

---

18. William Stueck, "Placing Jimmy Carter's Foreign Policy," in *The Carter Presidency: Policy Choices in the Post–New Deal Era*, ed. Gary M. Fink and Hugh Davis Graham (Lawrence, KS: United Press of Kansas, 1998), 259; Hoffmann, "Détente," 257–259.

tance, the more arrogant and aggressive they would grow. Both Kissinger and Brzezinski intuitively realized this, and their anxiety over Soviet moves in Africa appears to be justified. Soviet politicians could always be counted on to use any opportunity to exploit every weakness in the enemy camp to gain an advantage, no matter how limited. For the Kremlin leaders, life in general, including international relations, was a constant and implacable struggle; fair play and honoring one's commitments were notions they could only despise in the old Bolshevik tradition of contempt for bourgeois values.

The collapse of détente occurred mainly, although not exclusively, because of developments in the third world. In the arms race and in the military balance between the USSR and the United States, nothing new and surprising could happen. In Europe, low-level confrontations continued without any dramatic developments. It was in the shifting sands of the third world, a battlefield of maneuver warfare, that new and unforeseen collisions between the superpowers could be expected, and they did not take long to materialize. Détente, characterized by Samuel Huntington as a "brief interlude in an otherwise consistently competitive relationship,"[19] was weakest where the interests were too sensitive, asymmetrical, or diffuse to be negotiated, such as Soviet involvement with the third world and Western involvement with human rights.

The final nail in the coffin of détente was the Soviet invasion of Afghanistan.[20] Contrary to widespread notions of the time, this aggression was by no means motivated by a desire to obtain access to the Indian Ocean, much less grab Persian Gulf oil. The Afghan revolution of 1978 was neither planned nor anticipated by the Kremlin, although, of course, cadres for this kind of contingency had been trained for years. A representative of the Khalq (People's) Party, in a meeting with Boris Ponomarev, head of the Interna-

---

19. Samuel R. Huntington, "Renewed Hostility," in *The Making of America's Soviet Policy*, ed. Joseph S. Nye Jr. (New Haven, CT: Yale University Press, 1984), 270.

20. Andrianopoulos, *Kissinger and Brzezinski*, 198–200.

tional Department of the CPSU Central Committee, explained the decision to strike at that precise moment: "We know what Lenin said about the timing of the October revolution in Russia: yesterday it was too early, tomorrow it would be too late. The right time is today. Arrests have already begun of our leading comrades, including the party leader Comrade Taraki, so we had to act swiftly." Karen Brutents, while speaking at the Nobel Symposium 95, "The Intervention in Afghanistan and the Fall of Détente" in September 1995, argued that "the Soviet Union had nothing to do with the April coup."[21] Thus, Brutents disagreed with Anatoli Dobrynin, former Soviet ambassador to the United States, who believed that the USSR supported the April coup for ideological reasons. In Brutents's view, "Ideological considerations did not play any major role whatsoever in our policy. State interests, as they were understood, were the main consideration. The ideological coloring remained."[22]

The ensuing events have been amply described elsewhere. Suffice it to say that the fatal decision to send Soviet troops to Kabul and kill President Hafizullah Amin was taken, against the advice of both the KGB and the army, by three Politburo members, Yuri Andropov, Dmitri Ustinov, and Andrei Gromyko, who succeeded in obtaining the consent of the frail and senile Leonid Brezhnev. General Valentin Varennikov, former deputy minister of defense, recalls that this decision was taken on December 10, 1979, and that Marshal Ogarkov, chief of the general staff, as well as two deputies of Minister of Defense Ustinov, were against the introduction of Soviet troops but were overruled by their boss. Ustinov told them bluntly that the political decision had already been made and that their duty was to obey. Ogarkov had already been reprimanded by Andropov, who told him at a Politburo meeting: "Comrade Ogarkov, we invited you here not because we wanted to hear your opin-

---

21. "The Intervention in Afghanistan and the Fall of Détente," Nobel Symposium 95, Lysebu, Norway, September 17–20, 1995, 6.
22. Ibid., 14, 29.

ion. You should take notes and follow orders."[23] Nor was the KGB enthusiastic about the decision to send Soviet troops to Afghanistan, but its opinion was disregarded. The International Department of the Central Committee of the CPSU was also apprehensive about the military intervention. Brutents recalls that as he was about to express "a negative opinion on the issue in a memo, he was told by Aleksandrov, Brezhnev's assistant, "So, do you suggest that we should give Afghanistan to the Americans?"[24]

General Aleksandr Diakhovski, who served at the Soviet Ministry of Defense at the time, mentions another factor: Brezhnev's personal animosity toward Amin, who had ordered the assassination of Mohammad Taraki. Brezhnev "could not forgive Amin, because he [Brezhnev] personally gave Taraki assurances that he would be able to help him, yet they disregarded him completely and murdered Taraki." Brezhnev used to say, "How could the world believe what Brezhnev says, if his word does not count?"[25]

Gromyko explained his position almost ten years later in an unsent letter to Gorbachev, quoted by Gromyko's son: "Comrades, you know well that American ruling circles have been planning to destabilize progressive regimes, friendly to us. . . . The American government aspired to destabilize the situation on the southern flank of the Soviet borders and threaten our security. . . . Brezhnev believed that . . . Amin's group might gang up with the USA."[26] It was the typical Soviet paranoid pattern, based on eternal suspicion, incredulity, and inner insecurity.

Brutents mentioned yet another aspect of the time and gave one more rationale for the Soviet intervention. He recalls that some of the conversations he heard at the end of 1979 "were along the lines of 'What have we got to lose?' Everything had already been lost. . . . What was Afghanistan for us? It was a coup de grâce for dé-

---

23. Ibid., 74.
24. Ibid., 177.
25. Ibid., 81.
26. Anatoli Gromyko, *Andrei Gromyko. V labirintakh Kremlia*, trans. as *Andrei Gromyko: In the Kremlin's Labyrinths* (Moscow: IPO "Avtor," 1997), 187, 188.

tente, nothing else."[27] Indeed, it was clear by that time that détente was all but dead.

On the whole, the Soviet rationale for moving into Afghanistan was not to take the country but to prevent others from grabbing it. The action was essentially of a defensive and preemptive nature; but the West had no time for psychological analysis. It justly saw the invasion as an aggression and a breach of international law.

The Soviet leadership reacted to the world's outrage in a characteristic way: it exiled leading dissident Andrei Sakharov from Moscow and resumed the jamming of foreign broadcasts. In a matter of just a few days, Moscow managed to do practically all that was needed to alienate world public opinion and to finish off détente.

The Cold War's End

By the end of the 1970s and the beginning of the 1980s, each of the superpowers had a mixed record of successes and failures in the third world. Moscow had lost Egypt, the linchpin of its Middle Eastern policy, and had become mired in Afghanistan. The United States had even more reason to feel gloomy; except for the Camp David accord, almost everything seemed to be going wrong. As Huntington put it: "[The] April 1978 coup in Afghanistan, the June 1978 coup in South Yemen, the toppling of the Shah and Khomeini's accession to power in Iran in February 1979, and the victory of the Sandinistas over Somoza in July 1979. All these developments could be considered, and by many were perceived as, American defeats. Yet all were almost entirely the product of domestic forces within the respective societies, with virtually no known Soviet involvement." Feeling was widespread "that the Carter administration could not or would not adequately protect American interests in the Third World."[28]

---

27. "The Intervention in Afghanistan," 99.
28. Huntington, "Renewed Hostility," in Nye, *America's Soviet Policy*, 275–276.

It was in this environment that Ronald Reagan assumed office. In an apt description by U.S. diplomat Samuel Lewis, "a deeply convinced ideological warrior against world communism, totally suspicious of Soviet intentions, Reagan was the United States' first true ideological president."[29] His administration, although initially obsessed with the third world, in practice focused less on regional issues than it did on countering the USSR's subversive designs. However, its obsession with the Soviet Union as the evil empire could be quite misleading in its approach to third world conflicts, particularly in the Middle East. Reagan's advisers constantly warned that the Soviets were poised to take advantage of all the upheaval and turmoil in the region, though the Soviets had been remarkably unsuccessful in exploiting Middle Eastern instability since the late 1960s.[30] The irony of the situation, however, was that neither of the two dangerous situations with which the Reagan administration had to cope in the Middle East, Iran and Lebanon, had anything to do with Moscow. A new force of militant Islamic fundamentalism emerged in the area, and its spread could be seen as potentially detrimental to Soviet interests as well.

Practically the only area of the third world where Reagan felt he had to combat Soviet interests was Central America. The upsurge of the Cuban-backed left-wing forces in Nicaragua and El Salvador became the administration's main concern for years to come. True to his world view, Reagan could not fail to regard Central American revolutions as part of a sinister Soviet design; the "domino theory" was revived, and great efforts were made to thwart the pro-Cuban leftist forces. Elsewhere in the third world, however, the situation was fairly stable with respect to Soviet-U.S. confrontation. After the Egyptian fiasco, Moscow could not present a seri-

---

29. Samuel W. Lewis, "The United States and Israel: Constancy and Change," in *The Middle East Ten Years After Camp David*, ed. William B. Quandt (Washington, DC: Brookings Institution, 1988), 227.

30. Philip S. Khoury, "The Reagan Administration and the Middle East," in *Reagan and the World*, ed. David E. Kyvig (Westport, CT: Greenwood Press, 1990), 73–74.

ous practical threat in the Middle East, although the Soviets, true to form, continued to meddle from time to time. All the attempts to "bury Camp David," a slogan loudly propagated in the early 1980s by Arabists of Primakov's school, proved ineffective, and the Front of Steadfastness and Confrontation, set up under Syrian and Soviet auspices, never became an efficient political instrument. Nor was there any real sign in Africa of the Soviets being up to some new intervention. Rather, the United States was suspected of indirectly backing, along with Saudi Arabia, the anti-government UNITA rebels in Angola who were waging war against the pro-Soviet regime. The Soviets, of course, were not slow in coming to the aid of their Angolan allies, but as détente was over anyway, this aid could be seen as something normal, even legitimate, within the framework of the renewed cold war.

By the time Gorbachev acceded to power in 1985, the Soviet-U.S. rivalry in the third world was by no means as acute as it had been a few years earlier. After Soviet successes and U.S. setbacks in the 1970s, things had dramatically changed all across the board: a spectacular revival of the Western economy, the end of the frustration in America caused by the Vietnam syndrome, a serious worsening of the Soviet Union's economic situation, and the Afghanistan quagmire. What was needed was a comprehensive reappraisal of policy both at home and abroad.

This reappraisal, which had begun surreptitiously prior to the Gorbachev era, was given a powerful boost as perestroika and glasnost managed to achieve something that had been utterly unthinkable just a few years earlier: to question some basic, traditional foundations of the Soviet world view. Such terms as "new political thinking" and "de-ideologization of interstate relations" symbolized a new approach to Soviet involvement abroad, particularly with regard to the third world. Numerous articles were published, some of them contributed by the present author, calling for a revision of usual Communist notions regarding patterns of development of Asian, African, and Latin American countries. Old clichés were being discarded one by one. This new approach was based on irrefutable facts that tended to confirm what had already been suspected for years: a fiasco of the Soviet third world strategy.

By this time, Moscow felt a certain weariness stemming from a deep disillusionment about Soviet prospects in Asia, Africa, and Latin America. It was evident that the great Khrushchev design had failed to bear fruit. No real breakthrough capable of shattering the West had been achieved. Afghanistan was by then a veritable quagmire, and African left-wing regimes had become largely irrelevant. Most of all, the Soviets were tired and disenchanted with the Arab world, upon which great hopes had once been pinned. When Eduard Shevardnadze took over as foreign minister in June 1985, this was the situation he found, as told by his American biographers: "Reductions in Western influence were not always accompanied by increased Soviet influence. Important Third World leaders accepted aid, then pursued policies contrary to Soviet interests. Seemingly promising situations proved disappointing."[31] The important last part of this gruesome catalogue of failed hopes was the failure of the whole pattern of Socialist orientation in the third world.

In 1987, I spoke at a conference convened by Shevardnadze and attended by, among others, approximately 100 Soviet ambassadors. I told them that in my view, the Socialist orientation had proved a failure. During the break, ambassadors who worked in Congo, Angola, and Mozambique came up to shake my hand. They said, "We knew it all along, we warned the Ministry that the situation in the countries we are accredited in was a total disaster, but nobody seemed to care."

Actually, Soviet policymakers had always been indifferent to the practical results of non-capitalist development in Asia and Africa. What mattered to them was the involvement of the states ruled by revolutionary democrats in a worldwide anti-Western coalition. Ideology as such, instrumental in bringing about a decisive change

---

31. Carolyn McGiffert Ekedani and Melvin A. Goodman, *The Wars of Eduard Shevardnadze* (University Park, PA: Pennsylvania State University Press, 1997), 208–209.

in the correlation of global forces, was secondary. Third world leaders who proclaimed their allegiance to socialism were committing to side with the USSR. Just how successful they actually were in the business of Socialist transformation of their countries was not very important. What was vital was that, by proclaiming their Socialist commitment, they could be counted as Soviet allies and a net loss to the United States in a zero-sum game.

The propaganda aspect was crucial, too. What mattered for Brezhnev was to be able to say in his report to the party congress: "Comrades, the period under review has demonstrated once more that the ideas of socialism are on the march throughout the planet; more countries are joining us under the banner of socialism."

As perestroika progressed and momentous events were taking place in the Soviet Union, third world affairs were increasingly sidelined to the point of becoming largely irrelevant. The de-ideologization of interstate relations was the name of the game. The time came to cut the Soviet Union's losses, and the most urgent issue was Afghanistan.

Studying the CPSU Central Committee archives makes it possible to follow the evolution of Politburo thinking. At the meeting on May 6, 1980, when Brezhnev was still in power, the Soviet invasion of Afghanistan was routinely justified by the necessity to combat the United States. "The termination of military invasions or any other forms of meddling into Afghanistan's internal affairs as well as guarantees against the resumption of such actions would remove the reasons that compelled Afghanistan to ask the USSR to send the above-mentioned contingent into its territory."[32] Three years later, with Andropov in charge, the same line persisted. At the Politburo meeting on March 10, 1983, Andropov said: "We are being confronted here [in Afghanistan] by American imperialism, which perfectly understands that it has lost its positions in this sector of international politics. This is why we cannot afford to back down." At the same meeting, however, the issue of the eventual

---

32. CPSU Central Committee archives, fond #89, 1983, list 34, file 8, 2.

withdrawal of Soviet forces seems to have been raised for the first time, as evidenced by Gromyko's words: "At present it is impossible to give Pakistan a pledge as to the concrete terms of the withdrawal of our troops from the country."[33]

As Gorbachev took over in 1985, the Soviet leadership's position began to change. Sometime in 1986, Evgeni Primakov told me that a *political* decision to pull out of Afghanistan had already been taken by the Politburo, implying that the next stage would be the working out of a military plan of withdrawal. Ambassador Jack Matlock recalls that in February 1986, Gorbachev called the war in Afghanistan "a running sore." He said that henceforth, "Soviet military involvement in Afghanistan was to be treated as a problem that needed to be solved."[34]

The remarks of political and military leaders at the Politburo meeting on November 13, 1986, revealed the new mood in the Kremlin.

Gorbachev: "We have been fighting in Afghanistan for six years. If we do not change our approach to the issue, we'll be fighting for twenty or thirty years more. . . . Shall we wage an endless war, making plain the inability of our troops to deal with the situation? We need to put an end to this process in the nearest future."

Gromyko: "Not very long ago we talked about the necessity of closing Afghanistan's borders with Pakistan and Iran. We failed to achieve this because of the difficult terrain, with hundreds [of] mountain passes. Today, we must say frankly that our strategy should be to move toward the termination of the war."

Gorbachev: "In the resolution to be adopted, we must stress the necessity of ending the war not later than one year from now, maximum two years."

Gromyko: "We have not received their [Afghanistan's] support from inside. The number of new conscripts in the Afghan army is equal to the number of deserters."

---

33. CPSU Central Committee archives, fond #89, 1983, list 42, file 51, 2.

34. Jack Matlock Jr., *Autopsy on an Empire* (New York: Random House, 1995), 94.

General Akhromeev, deputy defense minister: "We have lost the struggle for the Afghan people. The government enjoys the support of the minority of the population."

Gorbachev: "In October of last year, at a Politburo meeting, we made clear our position in regard to Afghan settlement. Our goal was to accelerate the withdrawal of our forces from Afghanistan while ensuring the existence of a friendly Afghanistan. To achieve this, we tried to combine military and political measures. We have failed, however, to make progress in either field."[35]

Thus, it appears that the preliminary decision to pull out of Afghanistan was taken as early as October 1985, just a few months after Gorbachev had assumed office. This was also confirmed during my conversations with Primakov and others close to the decision-making circles. This preliminary decision was made in broad and rather vague terms: to work toward withdrawal sometime in the near future, after the existence of a "friendly Afghanistan" was ensured. The idea was to achieve some degree of military preponderance and to start actual withdrawal from a position of strength. However, a whole year was wasted before the Politburo, in November of the next year, came to the conclusion that it was time to decide on withdrawal without waiting for any serious military achievements.

What were the motives behind Gorbachev's decision to pull out of Afghanistan? As can be seen from the Politburo protocols, the most obvious reason was the sheer impossibility of winning the war without large-scale operations aimed at closing Afghanistan's border with Pakistan. Such an operation would have required a gigantic effort involving armed forces and financial resources probably exceeding the level of what the Soviet government was prepared to assign to Afghanistan even at the best of times, much less at a time of growing economic and political strain that marked the perestroika period. A second reason, never mentioned at Politburo meetings, was the growing feeling that the Afghanistan adventure

---

35. CPSU Central Committee archives, fond #89, 1986, list 42, file 16, 1–3.

seriously hampered Gorbachev's efforts to achieve an understanding with the West. And this understanding was badly needed in order to carry out the new leader's economic reforms.

It was only when Gorbachev assumed office that he was fully able to realize the extent of his country's economic backwardness compared with the West. He understood that in order to put things right he had to cut drastically the enormous defense budget, especially after President Reagan announced his Strategic Defense Initiative program, which was clearly beyond the power of the Soviets to counter or to imitate. At least that was what the Soviet military thought at the time, despite what was to be disclosed later about SDI's practical feasibility.

The reduction of military expenditure was an absolute priority; nothing less could provide the financial resources necessary for the modernization of the civilian economy. As the bulk of this expenditure went into maintaining the huge Soviet nuclear arsenal, it was essential to cut down immediately on the kind of armaments that were the backbone of the Soviet military machine. Strategic parity with America had always been the name of the game. Since unilateral disarmament was out of the question, the only way to achieve parity was to reach an agreement with the West, and first and foremost with the United States, on the question of gradual mutual disarmament. As Gorbachev's bad luck would have it, however, precisely at that critical moment the United States and Great Britain had staunch anti-Communists, Ronald Reagan and Margaret Thatcher, as their leaders.

Thus, Gorbachev faced an uphill struggle trying to convince them that the Soviet Union was no longer an evil empire. His initial attempts to demonstrate a new spirit in Soviet foreign policy by proposing a nuclear test ban and a 50 percent reduction of strategic armaments were not good enough for the West. Something else was necessary: tangible and practical steps to prove that Moscow was really prepared to discard its traditional totalitarian and aggressive pattern. It amounted to liberalization at home and proof of genuinely peaceful intentions abroad. Such actions as the return of Andrei Sakharov from exile in Gorky, the go-ahead for a new round of de-Stalinization, and the introduction of multicandidate elections were largely dictated by Gorbachev's willingness to promote perestroika and defeat his diehard adversaries. It would be a mistake, however, to focus only on the domestic dimension of those crucial political decisions. They were also motivated, although to a lesser extent, by Gorbachev's need to convince Western leaders of his goodwill and his genuine desire to achieve the liberalization and humanization of the Soviet system. It is in this context that the decision to end the war in Afghanistan should be viewed.

While trying to disentangle himself from Afghanistan, Gorbachev attempted to minimize Soviet commitment in other Socialist-oriented countries of the third world as well. At its meeting on September 18, 1989, the Politburo decided against sending more weapons to Ethiopia in response to a plea by Ethiopian dictator Mengistu Haile Mariam, who appeared to be heading for defeat in his war against the rebels.[36] At the next meeting on November 17, 1989, the Politburo approved a memo signed by Shevardnadze, Yakovlev, Yazov (the defense minister) and Kriuchkov (KGB chief), which stated: "A further increase in military assistance to the Ethiopian regime would hardly result in making it stronger; at the same time such an increase could provoke an upsurge of anti-Soviet sentiment in that country and cause harm to political interests of the Soviet Union. . . . It is necessary to complete the withdrawal of Soviet military advisers and experts from combat areas in the north of Ethiopia during November of 1989."[37]

In Nicaragua, the ruling Sandinistas suffered an astounding electoral defeat in the spring of 1990. At its meeting on April 13, 1990, the Politburo approved a memo signed by Shevardnadze, Yakovlev, and Kriuchkov in which it was suggested that "the emergence of a new leadership in Nicaragua calls for substantial corrections in Soviet-Nicaraguan relations with the aim of making them more prag-

---

36. CPSU Central Committee archives, fond #89, 1989, list 10, file 43, 2.
37. CPSU Central Committee archives, fond #89, 1989, list 10, file 45, 1.

matic and de-ideologized."[38] No regrets were recorded as to the fiasco of the Sandinista "comrades."

At the same time, steps were being made toward restoring Soviet relations with Israel. At a meeting on December 29, 1989, the Politburo decided to upgrade the consular groups already in existence and to set up regular consulates.[39] The decision to restore relations with Israel may have been influenced by several considerations. First, it became apparent that the lopsided pro-Arab policy had brought no tangible results. After Sadat's maneuvers, culminating in the Camp David agreement, it was clear that no further deal with the Egyptian president could be possible; Sadat was no Nasser. So Egypt was out of the game for good and Iraq was completely engrossed in its confrontation with Iran. What remained was Syria, a rather enigmatic and unreliable ally, as well as the Palestinians, clearly unable at that time to influence events decisively. Thus, nothing could really be gained from continuing the old policy. Second, Gorbachev still wanted to retain some degree of influence in the Middle East. After all, the Soviet Union was, at least nominally, the United States' partner in the Geneva conference, and to be able to match the American influence it was necessary to play the game on the whole chessboard, not just on the Arab side of it. What was needed was the ability to "stand on both legs, not on one leg," as the Chinese say. The USSR could only hope to influence the inevitable peace process in the Middle East if it had some foothold in Israel, too. Third, as perestroika and glasnost progressed, old anti-Israeli stereotypes and clichés were becoming increasingly irrelevant. The rapprochement with the United States was logically leading to a softening of the Soviet position on Israel. It would have been less than serious to move to an accommodation with the United States while maintaining a hostile attitude toward one of America's allies and going on, as usual, about "Zionist aggressors," "puppets," and so on. Fourth, anti-Semitism, ever present in the Kremlin's attitude toward Israel, was

---

38. CPSU Central Committee archives, fond #89, 1990, list 9, file 117, 2.
39. CPSU Central Committee archives, fond #89, 1989, list 9, file 68, 2.

definitely on the wane in the new atmosphere in Moscow. Both Gorbachev and Shevardnadze seemed to lack anti-Jewish sentiments, so they could not be motivated by the traditional bias.

Elsewhere in the third world, no serious events took place during the perestroika years that involved high-level Soviet policy decisions directly bearing on Soviet-U.S. relations. Thus, two developments in the Middle East dominated the political scene: the civil war in Lebanon and the Iran-Iraq War. In neither of these cases were any major Soviet political decisions recorded, which does not mean, however, that those events were insignificant in Soviet political thinking. The Lebanese civil war demonstrated the depth of internal differences in the Arab world, thus contributing to the growing feeling that the hope of creating a powerful Arab bulwark against U.S. domination was in fact groundless. The Iran-Iraq War introduced two new elements into the Soviet perception of the Middle East. First, the adventurism and unpredictability of Saddam Hussein, one of the traditional Soviet allies in the area, was clearly seen as one more sign of the dubious value of any alliances with "countries of Socialist orientation" in the Arab world. Second, Islamic fundamentalism emerged on the scene close to the USSR's southern borders, and from then on both the Americans and Soviets appeared to have a common enemy. So political thinkers close to Gorbachev increasingly displayed distinctly anti–third world sentiments; some of them even went so far as to stress objective convergence of the interests of the Soviet Union and the United States in regard to a new common danger. While playing no major part in shaping the new political thinking, events in the Middle East, if anything, strengthened the conviction that it was high time that the traditional concept of an irreconcilable clash of U.S. and Soviet interests in the third world be discarded as obsolete, thus paving the way for the idea of ending the cold war.

As regimes of Socialist orientation began crumbling one after another, nobody in Moscow seemed to be unduly disturbed. Perestroika and glasnost overshadowed everything else, the fundamentals of socialism were being questioned, and the fate of the Socialist system was at stake. There is a Russian saying that "Once you have had your head cut off, there is no need to fret about the hair."

The practical effects of the new political thinking introduced by Gorbachev could probably be best illustrated by the Kremlin's stand during the Gulf crisis in 1990 and 1991. The former Soviet leader recalls in his memoirs: "It was a major test for new political thinking. During the Cold War, this conflict could have led the opposing blocs to a military, even a nuclear, confrontation. . . . I met President Bush in Helsinki. This meeting, undertaken at his initiative, was of fundamental importance. Its crux was the issue of maintaining and consolidating the American-Soviet partnership in the face of the crisis that had broken out. . . . I was in complete agreement with Bush's point that 'Saddam Hussein cannot be allowed to profit from his aggression.'"[40] This was a far cry indeed from Soviet thinking of the cold war era.

Conclusion

By the end of the 1980s, a whole era in international relations had come to a close, an era that in the Soviet Union was called peaceful coexistence and peaceful competition of the two world systems. The third world was bound to play a major role in world politics during the cold war if only because frontlines in the main battlefield, Europe, were frozen, with no chance for either of the opposing sides to achieve a breakthrough. Spreading Soviet influence in the third world looked quite promising; the idea was to strike at the soft underbelly of the imperialist camp, thus bypassing its main citadels in North America and Western Europe. The developing countries, seething with discontent and driven by the dynamics of anticolonial inertia, presented an excellent opportunity to undermine the imperialist system from within rather than engage it in an open clash.

This grand design was deeply flawed from the outset. Try as it

---

40. Mikhail Gorbachev, *Memoirs* (New York: Doubleday, 1996), 551, 553–554.

might, the Soviet Union could not substantially change the balance of global forces, which favored the U.S.-led Western coalition. The Soviets overplayed their hand, which resulted in an extraordinary squandering of resources.[41] The Socialist orientation proved a dismal failure; pro-Moscow left-wing regimes were just as corrupt and faction-ridden as almost all the others in the third world while being less efficient economically. Their downfall, which had always been just a matter of time, can be regarded as part of the same pattern that manifested itself in the demise of the Socialist regimes in Eastern Europe. As socialism crumbled in its main citadel, its collapse on the periphery was inevitable.

In the geopolitical and military struggle for the third world, the Soviet defensive and preemptive strategy proved just as inconclusive as the defensive and containment approach of the United States, no matter how many bold tactical moves Moscow could boast. For example, in Asia, the Soviet Union never had a chance of forging a real alliance with the pivotal state, India, however much Soviet diplomacy tried to play on Indian differences with U.S.-backed Pakistan. In the Middle East, the Kremlin proved unable to hold on to the key state, Egypt, in spite of being its main arms supplier. Attempts to secure a base on the African Horn for the benefit of a fast-growing Soviet navy so as to mirror American naval bases came to nothing as war broke out between Somalia and Ethiopia.

However, the United States soon had to part with the illusion that it was possible to transform the USSR into an honest and responsible partner, contain its expansion, and compel it to observe the rules of the game designed to ensure a U.S.-controlled stability in the third world. The United States lacked a sufficient supply of sticks and carrots; moreover, the third world had such an inexhaustible conflict potential that the United States could not expect

---

41. From 1954 through 1977 alone, the Soviet Union committed almost $13 billion worth of economic assistance to the countries of the third world. See Kelley, *Soviet Politics*, 240.

to cope with all the adventurous leaders, strongmen, and dictators who kept popping up everywhere, ready to condemn imperialism and proclaim their Socialist credentials in order to get Soviet jet fighters and tanks.

The former Soviet ambassador to the United States, Oleg Troianovski, admits that "in the context of the cold war, it was often enough for some warlord to say that he was going to build socialism in his country, and the Soviet Union would start helping him."[42] His assessment is reinforced by General Anatoli Gribkov, former chief of staff of the Warsaw Treaty Organization: "As soon as a leader in Mozambique, Angola, Ethiopia, or Somalia mentioned the word 'socialism,' our leaders immediately picked up on it and decided that this particular country would become socialist."[43]

Both Dobrynin and Troianovski maintain that neither of them ever heard anyone in the Soviet Union suggest that the third world was the main problem for the USSR.[44] But as the former high official in the Central Committee of the CPSU Georgi Shakhnazarov suggested, "It all reminded [one of] the soccer strategy known as man-to-man coverage: every player in one team has a player to follow from the opposing team. If a player from the other side moves, then one of our players must move with him. So it was with the United States: whenever they moved their forces, we had to move ours."

Shakhnazarov recalls a conversation with Andropov in 1965 during which Andropov said: "The future competition with the United States will take place not in Europe, and not in the Atlantic Ocean directly. It will take place in Africa, and in Latin America. We will compete for every piece of land, for every country. We need bases there, and then we will be able to enjoy an equal status with the Americans. We will not let them command there."[45]

At first, it might seem to be a contradiction: the third world was

---

42. "Global Competition," 12.
43. Ibid., 59.
44. Ibid., 47.
45. Ibid., 38, 39.

never a top priority for the Kremlin, but at the same time it was regarded as the main battlefield in the global competition. Actually, there is no contradiction here. The third world as such was not a major issue, but ever since Khrushchev's era it had been viewed as an area where the rival could be dealt the most painful blows. Countries in that area were just pawns in the game.

The third world refused to play to either the U.S. or the Russian tune; it was too heterogeneous, too volatile, and its traditions and mentality were too far from those of the two other worlds. It proved impossible to pigeonhole it and fit it into a pattern worked out in Moscow or Washington. Of course, it was possible to play on its formidable conflict potential, but this had its downside, too. Alliances all too often proved fragile, governments were prone to switch sides, and loyalties to superpowers were not binding. As the Arabs say, "The camel driver has his plans but the camel has his."

Neither side could win the third world, and deadlock could have continued for decades were it not for Mikhail Gorbachev and his perestroika. The last leader of the Communist Party intended to invigorate and rejuvenate the system. He probably never read Alexis de Tocqueville, who said that the most perilous hour for a bad government comes when it tries to mend its ways.

For Gorbachev, voluntary dismantling of the once-powerful Soviet positions in the third world was vital in the context of his new policy of rapprochement with the West. By 1986, he already had well-grounded hopes for reaching an understanding with President Reagan on major issues such as the end of the arms race, the reduction of strategic armaments, and the withdrawal of tactical missiles from Europe. This seemed to promise, first, a long overdue modernization and genuine transformation of the Soviet economy as the state budget would be freed from the burden of a truly monstrous military expenditure, and, second, a new boost to the process of humanization and democratization inside the country. Compared to such momentous benefits, continued clinging to Soviet positions in the third world was more trouble than it was worth. Asia, Africa, and Latin America had never been a priority in

Soviet foreign-policy guidelines; the third world had always been a secondary battlefield. Gorbachev, bent on striking a comprehensive deal with the West, would not want to see his great initiative compromised by the increasingly irrelevant concept of promoting socialism in distant tropical countries.

Once the idea of accommodation with the West and ending the cold war took hold in Moscow, it would have been futile to pretend that the overall goal—a crusade against imperialism as part of a universal class struggle—remained the same. In this situation, continued support of "class comrades" in the third world clearly lost its raison d'être.

The Reagan administration was wise enough to seek negotiated outcomes to the various third world conflicts then raging. An Afghan settlement was achieved in the Geneva framework; Chester Crocker and Anatoli Adamishin pursued an Angola/Namibia settlement that also involved South Africa and Cuba; and negotiations over Central America and Cambodia bore fruit later. Presidents Reagan and Bush accepted Gorbachev's good faith in seeking a new turn. Thus, it is possible to speak about a mutual interest in winding down third world conflicts, which amounted to an interaction of the two sides' policies.

In fact, Gorbachev's foreign policy, including its third world dimension, could be called a new détente. A fundamental difference between the first détente, initiated under Brezhnev, and that made possible by Gorbachev's fresh and imaginative approach to world affairs, is obvious: while the former merely served to disguise cardinal differences between Soviet and U.S. aims and resulted in attempts to achieve those aims under the cover of détente, the latter was based on completely new premises that ensured a genuine rejection of the very idea of confrontation. If the Brezhnev détente finally resulted in the resumption of the cold war and in increased international tension, the Gorbachev détente contributed to the end of the superpower rivalry and effectively signaled the termination of the cold war. In this context, events in the third world played a significant role, for they produced moral weariness and disenchantment in the attitude of Soviet policymakers that encouraged them to look for new foreign policy guidelines.

As Karen Brutents notes, "There was a certain contradiction in the concept of détente from the very beginning, because the most serious . . . basic elements of the Cold War remained intact." In his opinion, politicians on both sides should also be blamed; instead of trying to soften the basic contradiction of détente and smooth it over gradually, they deepened and sharpened it and as a result ruined détente. It happened "because of short-sightedness and excessive fighting spirit on both sides."[46] It is also worthwhile to quote the prominent American Sovietologist Robert Legvold, who, after listing all the contradictory issues of the era of détente, came to the conclusion that "it was the cumulative effect of all these things that really mattered, and the extent to which the whole process turned out to be more important than the sum of the parts."[47]

The cold war did not come to a close because of developments in the third world. These developments did, however, contribute significantly to the realization on both sides that a new page in history had to be opened.

46. Ibid., 27, 28.

47. News conference at the National Press Club, Washington, DC, March 27, 1995. The Brown University News Bureau, 3–4.

Peter W. Rodman : *Reversal of Fortune?*

AMERICAN ANALYSTS of the cold war competition in the third world have the greatest respect for Georgi Mirski as one of those perceptive (and courageous) scholars in Moscow who led an agonizing reappraisal of Soviet third world policies in the 1980s. Dr. Mirski describes this reappraisal well in his essay, though he is too modest about his own role.

His essay reflects the same forthrightness and insight. Undoubtedly he is correct in saying that both sides sometimes treated the competition in the third world as more important than it really was; in retrospect, it was clearly never as central to the cold war rivalry as the division of Europe or the strategic nuclear balance. Nonetheless, I continue to find the contest in the third world the most interesting intellectually. From the days of Woodrow Wilson and Lenin, the anticolonial struggle in the developing world seemed to both sides a moral as well as a strategic opportunity. The United States and Soviet Russia both considered themselves free of the taint of European colonialism, and indeed natural champions of the anticolonial cause. Both sides, accordingly, invested much of their self-esteem and historical self-confidence in the question of how this contest would turn out—which side the new nations would "choose." In the 1950s and 1960s, there were certainly many in America who imagined that the global balance of power would be decided there. Recall books and films of the 1950s such as *The Ugly American* that reflected Americans' angst about whether they were sufficiently sensitive to the new nations' needs.[1] Recall the

---

1. William J. Lederer and Eugene Burdick, *The Ugly American* (New York: Norton, 1958). The book was made into a film in 1963 by Universal Studios with George Englund, director.

"long twilight struggle" to which President John F. Kennedy repeatedly summoned the American people in the early months of his term.[2] Many of the bitterest domestic controversies over foreign policy during the cold war were over our engagement in third world conflicts in Korea, Vietnam, and Central America.

Dr. Mirski is also correct to point out two important historical moments when the third world contest did play a pivotal role in the East-West confrontation. He describes perceptively how Soviet overreaching in the third world doomed the détente efforts of the 1970s. And he is correct that in the 1980s the first practical evidence of the winding down of the cold war came in the negotiations that resolved a number of these conflicts (Afghanistan, Angola, and later Central America and Cambodia). The new inside information that Dr. Mirski presents about Soviet calculations (and miscalculations) makes this essay valuable.

An American observer is bound to offer some additional perspective, however. To Dr. Mirski, the prime mover in the endgame was Mikhail Gorbachev, who, he says, "initiated" and "first manifested" the policy of seeking an end to this dimension of competition. Both sides' third world policies had failed, he says, and it was Mr. Gorbachev whose "new political thinking" broke the stalemate and led to the resolution of these conflicts. The American perspective is somewhat different. No one can doubt Mr. Gorbachev's pivotal importance, but it is not chauvinistic of me to suggest that Dr. Mirski does not do justice to the interaction of the two sides' policies during the period.

This is especially true with regard to the climactic turning point of the 1980s, the central topic of this book. When future historians look back on this period, they will see a bigger picture and a bigger question that cries out for an answer: What accounts for the extraordinary reversal of fortune that occurred globally between 1975 and 1985?

---

2. John F. Kennedy, inaugural address, January 20, 1961; State of the Union address, January 30, 1961; Special Message to Congress on Urgent National Needs, May 25, 1961.

In 1975, despite its strategic successes with Egypt and China, the United States was reeling from a series of setbacks: defeat in Indochina, abdication in Angola, energy shocks and economic recession, and the resignation of a president in the constitutional crisis called Watergate. It was in this context that Leonid Brezhnev, addressing the Twenty-fifth Soviet Communist Party Congress in February 1976, could boast that the historical "correlation of forces" was shifting in favor of socialism.[3] This is indeed how things looked.

Ten years later, the pendulum of history had swung the other way. By 1985, the Western economy had recovered from recession and the information revolution had already begun. Western demoralization had ended, too; Ronald Reagan and Margaret Thatcher were in office. The Soviet Union, meanwhile, had gone through a prolonged, humiliating, and debilitating succession crisis, its economy had stagnated, and it was bogged down in Afghanistan. The global "correlation of forces" was no longer going its way. The transformation of the competition in the third world can best be understood in this broader historical context.

Dr. Mirski touches upon all of this, but he shrinks from drawing the appropriate conclusions about causation. Events were *forcing* on the Soviet system the need for a thoroughgoing reassessment of everything.

To be sure, Dr. Mirski is right to stress the policy reappraisal that took place inside research institutes and government offices in the Soviet Union. The internal pressures for change in foreign policy were becoming as inexorable as the pressures for change in domestic policy. After many decades, a large proportion of Soviets were reaching the conclusion that the "Socialist orientation" of many Soviet clients was a sham, that Soviet aid to these clients was going to waste, and that Soviet military commitments to some of

---

3. Leonid Brezhnev, "Report of the CPSU Central Committee and the Immediate Tasks of the Party in Home and Foreign Policy," February 24, 1976 (Moscow: Novosti Press Agency Publishing House, 1976), 10–12, 20–22.

these clients, especially Afghanistan, were dragging Moscow deeper into local quagmires.

This reappraisal began even before Gorbachev's appointment as general secretary in March 1985. Its signs were evident in the early 1980s during the brief tenure of Yuri Andropov. As early as 1982, a scholarly book entitled *Socialist Orientation of the Liberated Countries* appeared, arguing that, contrary to the exuberant optimism of the Khrushchev and Brezhnev periods, problems of social, political, and economic underdevelopment were often profound and intractable. Many supposedly Socialist countries in the third world were still closely tied to, and indeed integrated into, the capitalist world. This dry academic analysis had profound practical implications: not only were fundamental tenets of Marxist-Leninist analysis proving to be flawed, but, in addition, these countries were likely to be unreliable allies for Soviet foreign policy.[4]

Andropov himself, at a plenary meeting of the Central Committee on June 15, 1983, sarcastically called into question the ideological credentials of various Soviet clients and suggested rather dismissively that their economic development was their own responsibility: "It is one thing to proclaim socialism as one's goal and quite another thing to build it. . . . [O]n the whole their economic development, just as the entire social progress of those countries, can be, of course, only the result of the work of their peoples and of a correct policy of their leadership."[5]

Most importantly, the Reagan administration was noticing all this. In May 1984, a young Sovietologist on the National Security Council staff, Stephen Sestanovich, published an op-ed article in the *Washington Post* calling attention to the many signs that Moscow was increasingly disillusioned with its third world involvement

---

4. Karen Brutents, Rostislav Ulianovsky, Evgeni Primakov, and Anatoli Gromyko, *Socialist Orientation of the Liberated Countries: Some Problems of Theory and Practice* (Moscow: Mysl, 1982), cited in Elizabeth Kridl Valkenier, "New Soviet Thinking about the Third World," *World Policy Journal* 4, no. 4 (Fall 1987): 667.

5. Yuri Andropov, Speech at CPSU Central Committee Plenum, June 15, 1983, in FBIS-SOV-83–117, June 16, 1983, R9,11.

and was feeling the strain of overextension. He quoted the Andro-
pov remarks and cited some of the scholarly commentary.[6] The
Reagan administration identified this overextension as a significant
Soviet strategic vulnerability. Over the next two years, the Ameri-
cans increased their assistance to guerrilla movements resisting
Marxist-Leninist regimes in Angola, Afghanistan, Nicaragua, and
Cambodia, in what came to be known as the Reagan Doctrine. In
March 1986, a seminal White House document on regional policy
(of which Sestanovich was a principal draftsman) explicitly stated
that the rationale of the new U.S. policy was to raise the costs of
Soviet third world involvement and thereby to spur the reappraisal
that was under way: "Our goal, in short—indeed our necessity—is
to convince the Soviet Union that the policies on which it embarked in the 70s *cannot work*. . . . [T]here are reasons to think that
the present time is especially propitious for raising doubts on the
Soviet side about the wisdom of its client ties. . . . There is no time
in which Soviet policy reviews and reassessments are more likely
than in a succession period, especially when many problems have
been accumulating for some time."[7]

By 1988, Soviet commentaries on the subject were becoming
even more forthright and pessimistic. Dr. Mirski himself, in a 1987
paper, openly deplored the ideological blinders that had hindered
earlier Soviet analysis of third world complexities: "Years passed
before we understood the significance and influence of the middle
classes, the intelligentsia, the bureaucracy and the army, which indeed had been understood earlier by Western scholars. And years
passed before we sufficiently realized what enormous weight can
be attributed to traditions and non-class-related social institutions
like tribalism, the deeply rooted dividing lines in Asian and African

---

6. Stephen Sestanovich, "Do the Soviets Feel Pinched by Third World Adventures?" *Washington Post*, May 20, 1984, B1.

7. President Ronald Reagan, "Freedom, Regional Security, and Global Peace,"
White House statement, March 14, 1986 (emphasis in original).

societies according to ethnic, religious, caste and clan lines. . . ."[8] Historian Viacheslav Dashichev in a 1988 article scathingly denounced the "miscalculations and incompetent approach of the Brezhnev leadership" that had provoked "unprecedented new pressure from imperialism."[9] Brezhnev's offensive in the third world had derailed détente, Dashichev explained in a later interview, and triggered a U.S. arms buildup that was bankrupting the Soviet Union:

> [W]e launched an offensive against imperialism's positions in the Third World in the mid-seventies. We attempted to expand the sphere of socialism's influence to various developing countries which, I believe, were totally unprepared to adopt socialism. And what came of all this? A sharp clash of political contradictions with the Western powers (and that was not all—even China opposed our actions in the Third World). Détente was derailed, and we came up against a new and unprecedented explosion of the arms race.[10]

Andrei Kozyrev, then a junior official in the Soviet foreign ministry, lamented in the ministry journal in 1988 that Moscow's entanglement in third world conflicts was not only wasting resources but incurring "enormous" costs in poisoning relations with the West: "Unfortunately, there are no data concerning the price paid by the Soviet Union for providing assistance to those countries. . . . Furthermore, it is important to stress that aid itself is only the tip of

---

8. Georgi I. Mirski, "On the Question of the Developing Countries' Choice of Path and Orientation," *World Economy and International Relations* 11 (1987): 76, cited in Mammo Muchie and Hans van Zon, "Soviet Foreign Policy under Gorbachev and Revolution in the Third World: An Ideological Retreat or Refinement?" in *The New Détente: Rethinking East-West Relations*, ed. Mary Kaldor, Gerard Holden, and Richard Falk (London: Verso/United Nations University, 1989), 191–192.

9. Viacheslav Dashichev, "East-West: Quest for New Relations: On the Priorities of the Soviet State's Foreign Policy," *Literaturnaia Gazeta*, May 18, 1988, in FBIS-SOV-88–098, May 20, 1988, 7–8.

10. Viacheslav Dashichev, "Topical Interview," *Komsomolskaia Pravda*, June 19, 1988, in FBIS-SOV-88–118, June 20, 1988, 57.

the iceberg. Our direct or indirect entanglement in regional conflicts brings about enormous losses, exacerbating overall international tensions, justifying the arms race and hampering mutually beneficial economic ties with the West."[11] A later writer in the same journal lamented the military quagmires in which the Soviet Union was sinking on behalf of failed authoritarian regimes. Afghanistan loomed very large in this reassessment:

> [W]e waged an outright war in Afghanistan, we were deeply enmeshed in several acute regional conflicts . . . and we promoted the creation of regimes in different parts of the world that tried, under the banner of anti-imperialism, to implement in their own conditions the administer-by-command model and therefore counted on us for everything. The specifics of these regimes, the militarist bent typical of our domestic and foreign policy, and the backwardness of the Soviet civilian economy that was strongly manifest even then made for the fact that military cooperation and arms deliveries were the heart of our relations with developing states "friendly" to us. Their militarisation only pushed them even farther into participation in conflicts and into authoritarian rule and worsened the situation in the economy that was falling apart as it was."[12]

Dr. Mirski is correct to give the Reagan administration credit for seeking negotiated outcomes to the various third world conflicts then raging from Afghanistan and Angola/Namibia to Central America. In a speech to the UN General Assembly in October 1985, President Reagan urged the two sides to make a concerted effort for diplomatic solutions. These regional negotiations became an integral part of the U.S.-Soviet diplomatic agenda, at summits and in regular channels, from 1985 onward. The Arab-Israeli conflict and tensions in Korea and the Indian subcontinent were also regularly discussed. As Dr. Mirski says, Presidents Reagan and Bush accepted Mr. Gorbachev's good faith in seeking a new turn.

---

11. Andrei Kozyrev, "Confidence and the Balance of Interests," *International Affairs* (Moscow) 11 (November 1988): 7–8.

12. Andrei Kolosov, "Reappraisal of USSR Third World Policies," *International Affairs* (Moscow) 5 (May 1990): 35–36.

The interest in winding down these conflicts was indeed mutual, and thus credit goes to the interaction of the two sides' policies.

Many of the bitterest Soviet reappraisals, as we have seen, denounced the Brezhnev policies for harming Soviet interests by provoking a Western reaction. This seems to me to be an acknowledgment that U.S. responses—raising the costs of these policies when the Soviets were themselves reassessing them for a variety of reasons—had their impact. It is idle to deny this when it is so clearly stated in Soviet commentaries. The opportunistic blunders of Brezhnev, which Dr. Mirski so well documents, were blunders in large part precisely because they triggered a Western reaction. Had there been no Western reaction, including no Western support for resistance movements, some of these Soviet third world adventures might have succeeded, and different conclusions might have been drawn in the Politburo.

Therefore, it can be argued that Mr. Gorbachev's policies were as much the result as the cause of what was happening in the 1980s. The Soviet Union was on the defensive in the third world, and Mr. Gorbachev was drawing proper conclusions. He admitted this himself in remarks he made on October 15, 1985, seven months after he came to power. Explaining to a party plenum the need for a new party program, he argued: "It has been necessary to work out a new understanding of the changes in the correlation of forces that are occurring. . . ." There was a "very dangerous shift" in the policies of the imperialists, he said, in seeking military superiority and suppressing liberation movements. Thus, it was "imperative to take a realistic view." The new party program would demonstrate the party's "ability to take into account the changing situation in due time, face the reality without any bias, objectively appraise current events, and flexibly react to the demands of the moment."[13]

---

13. Mikhail Gorbachev, Report to the Plenary Meeting of the CPSU Central Committee, October 15, 1985, quoted in *On the New Edition of the CPSU Programme* (Moscow: Novosti Press Agency Publishing House, 1986), 13–15; also in FBIS-SOV-85–200, October 16, 1985, R3, 6.

"Realistic" was a compliment that Moscow often bestowed on Western leaders who were conciliatory; they were praised for accommodating themselves to the objective factors of history. We are entitled to return the compliment, especially because Gorbachev seems to have shared the assessment.

CHAPTER 5

Robert L. Hutchings : *Europe Between the Superpowers*

THE OPENING LINES of the Charter of Paris, signed by European and North American heads of state in November 1990, affirmed that Europe was "liberating itself from the legacy of the past."[1] And indeed self-liberation was the accurate designation, for it was the Poles and Hungarians, soon joined by others, whose peaceful democratic breakthroughs touched off the stunning events of 1989 and 1990. Yet the end of Europe's long division could not have occurred without the roles played by the Soviet Union and the United States. Liberation was not something bestowed on Europe by U.S. and Soviet leaders, but neither was it something that Europe could have achieved on its own. It was the *interaction* between superpower relations and developments in Europe, East and West, that brought about the end of the cold war.

By 1989 the bipolar world of the cold war had already broken down, and the leaders of the two superpowers both knew it in ways not true of their immediate predecessors. Preoccupied with the Soviet military and ideological threat, President Reagan accordingly held a Manichaean view of the world. Theirs was the evil empire against which the Western camp needed to be ever vigilant—a notion that looks positively quaint in light of what we now know of the Soviet system in its final years. By the same token, Konstantin Chernenko was a dogmatic throwback to a bi-

---

1. "Charter of Paris for a New Europe, Paris 1990," *New York Times*, November 22, 1990, A16.

polar world that no longer existed. For their successors, President Bush and General Secretary Gorbachev, the tasks of statesmanship were far different, calling for catalytic leadership rather than the assertive unilateralism that had characterized much of the cold war.

Europe was never as thoroughly bipolar as the cold war divide made it appear. Economically, the Bretton Woods system symbolized American hegemony up to the early 1970s, but, by the end of the 1980s, the global system increasingly reflected a tripolar distribution of economic power among North America, Europe, and East Asia. Politically, the junior European allies had long since slipped the leash in the Western camp and were poised to do so in the East as well. It was only in the military arena, especially in the nuclear field, that bipolarity remained dominant. The nuclear relationship generated rigidities that artificially preserved the formal bipolar structure of East-West relations and obscured the political and economic realities beneath the surface. It was a dynamic that John Lewis Gaddis once likened to the evolutionary history of the giant moose: just as the moose evolved ever more imposing antlers that intimidated other moose but were useless for other contingencies, so also did the vast U.S. and Soviet nuclear arsenals evolve within a cold war logic that was increasingly irrelevant to the realities of the late cold war.

By the end of the 1980s and indeed long before, this aspect of cold war confrontation—the prospect of nuclear war—had receded nearly to the vanishing point, taking with it superpower domination of East-West relations. Change was being driven by forces from below, springing from regime failure in the East and regime success in the West. It is something of a paradox that, whereas the relative decline of U.S. power in Europe pushed the Western Europeans closer together, the decline of Soviet power pushed the Eastern Europeans farther apart. And a more fluid East-West environment in the 1980s yielded new opportunities for intra-European engagement.

Eastern Europe in Crisis

By 1985, when Mikhail Gorbachev took power in Moscow, the countries of Eastern Europe were in deep crisis, brought on by a combination of economic decline, political malaise, and social discontent.[2] The economic strategies on which they had embarked in the 1970s—relying on Western trade and credits in hopes of promoting economic growth—had bought a few years of relative prosperity but soon produced a regionwide financial crisis. Trade with the West collapsed, new credits dried up, and Eastern Europe was facing a political as well as an economic crisis. By 1982, all of the Eastern European countries save Bulgaria and Czechoslovakia had been compelled to enter into refinancing negotiations with Western creditors. Despite massive rescheduling, Poland's debt continued to increase. Hungary managed to stay afloat only through periodic refinancing and short-term loans. The GDR survived the financial squeeze thanks to generous West German credits but was mortgaging its political future in the process. As Miklos Nemeth, Hungarian prime minister in 1989, later put it, "The killing of the socialist bloc or the communist system started with that moment when the Western banks gave some credits and debt loans to certain countries."[3]

Trade with the Soviet Union in the 1980s fared little better as Moscow raised oil prices to reflect rapidly rising prices on the world market, cut deliveries by 10 percent, and put increased pressure on the Eastern Europeans for higher-quality goods in return. For a Soviet economy that was itself in decline, the economic burdens of empire were becoming more onerous, and Politburo dis-

---

2. Robert L. Hutchings, "Soviet Dilemmas in Eastern Europe," in *United States—East European Relations in the 1990s*, ed. Richard F. Staar (New York: Crane Russak, 1989), 15–34.

3. CNN interview for its Cold War Series, October 1997, http://www.cnn.com/SPECIALS/cold.war/kbank/profiles/nemeth.

cussions of the time reflected Moscow's preoccupation with this concern. Poland was to some extent spared, owing to its fragile economic and political situation after the crushing of Solidarity in 1981, but the rest of Eastern Europe quickly felt the added financial squeeze from Moscow.[4]

As a consequence of this double economic bind from the East as well as the West, Eastern Europe as a whole experienced sharp economic decline during the 1980s, and some countries, notably Poland and Hungary, experienced multiple years of negative growth.[5] External economic pressures, in turn, took a heavy toll on material living standards in the region, jeopardizing the fragile social contract many of these regimes had struck with their disaffected populaces. Poland's downward economic spiral destroyed whatever hopes its regime had of creating a new stability after the Solidarity debacle. By 1986, the Polish leadership was obliged to begin thinking the unthinkable: that Solidarity might have to be relegalized as the price of gaining public support for an economic recovery program. By mid-1988, this thought had crystallized into the idea of an "anti-crisis pact" that evolved a year later into the historic Roundtable Agreement of early 1989.[6]

Elsewhere the decline was less catastrophic but still severe, with no turnaround in sight. To keep personal consumption from declining even more rapidly, the Eastern European regimes cut back sharply on investment, with the result that every country in the region endured negative growth in the 1980s. Rates of investment

4. Recently declassified Soviet documents reveal how sensitive Moscow was to Poland's economic bind and how skillfully the Polish side exploited its own weakness. For a detailed compilation, see Mark Kramer, *Soviet Deliberations During the Polish Crisis, 1980–1981*, Cold War International History Project, Special Working Paper No. 1 (April 1999), Woodrow Wilson Center, Washington, DC.

5. Joint Economic Committee, Congress of the United States, *East European Economies: Slow Growth in the 1980s*, Vol. 1 (Washington, DC: U.S. Government Printing Office, 1985), viii–ix.

6. See, e.g., the Chronology and Documents 4 and 6 (transcripts of meetings of the Political Bureau, August 21, 1988, and the Secretariat, October 4, 1988), in *Poland 1986–1989: The End of the System: International Conference, 20–24 October 1999*, Polish Academy of Sciences, Miedzeszyn-Warsaw, Poland.

in Poland and Hungary dropped by 4.9 percent and 5.2 percent, respectively, in the first half of the 1980s before leveling off; for East Germany the figure was a whopping 10 percent.[7] Sharply reduced investments had perpetuated the aging smokestack industries, further undermining Eastern European competitiveness in world markets, and failure to keep pace with the newly industrialized economies, much less the advanced Western democracies, had further mortgaged Eastern Europe's economic future. By the mid-1980s, some Hungarian reform economists were arguing that closing the scientific and technological gap was essential to Hungary's national survival. They seemed to mean that literally.

Adding to Eastern Europe's decline in the 1980s was the stagnation of its superannuated party leadership. The average age of the Eastern European party leaders was well over 70, and their average tenure in office was more than two decades. Political malaise in Eastern Europe had been accentuated by a prolonged period of drift in Moscow, stretching from the latter years of the Brezhnev era through the brief administrations of Yuri Andropov and Konstantin Chernenko and into the early experimental years of Mikhail Gorbachev. Thus, for most of the 1980s, the absence of clear and consistent Soviet leadership had left the Eastern European regimes largely to their own devices.[8] The more conservative among them—the East German, Czechoslovak, Bulgarian, and Romanian regimes—retreated into obsessive orthodoxy, eschewing any hint of reform for fear that it might stir their repressed populaces to action. At the other end of the spectrum, the cautiously reform-minded Polish and Hungarian regimes soon found their half-measures eclipsed by public calls for much more sweeping change.

For Gorbachev, the Eastern European situation presented sev-

---

7. CIA figures presented in "Soviet Policy toward Eastern Europe under Gorbachev" (Secret), NIE 11/12–9-88, May 1988; declassified in 1999 and reprinted in *At Cold War's End: U.S. Intelligence on the Soviet Union and Eastern Europe, 1989–91* (Washington, DC: Central Intelligence Agency, 1999), 154–177.

8. Robert L. Hutchings, special editor, "The Effects of 'Leadership Drift' on Communist Systems," *Studies in Comparative Communism* 22, no. 1 (Spring 1989): 1–55.

eral dilemmas. Severe economic decline implied a continued drain on Soviet resources as well as a growing threat of economically induced political crisis in the region. The hidebound regimes in East Germany, Czechoslovakia, Bulgaria, and Romania were also foreign policy liabilities, interfering with his efforts to promote a "common European home." Gorbachev obviously hoped that the example of his own reform agenda would have a persuasive effect in Eastern Europe and strengthen reform tendencies there as well. But his efforts to promote change by dint of his own example were having little impact on the entrenched hard-line leaderships in the region.

Yet Gorbachev was not as hands-off as he would have had us believe by his repeated assurances that interference in Eastern Europe was a thing of the past. His visit to Prague in April 1987 was a case in point. Although he avoided direct criticism of the Czechoslovak leadership during the trip, he nonetheless made plain his preference for a reform agenda modeled on his own. And when asked during the visit to explain the difference between Gorbachev's reforms and the Prague Spring, Soviet press spokesman Gennadi Gerasimov put it succinctly: "Nineteen years." Later in the year, as their frustrations mounted, Soviet officials interfered more directly in the Czechoslovak party leadership's internal machinations. One of Gorbachev's key advisers on Eastern Europe published excerpts of a November 1987 memorandum to Gorbachev that revealed a level of intrusion that would have made Stalin proud: "Given that maintaining [party leader Gustav] Husak . . . is hardly possible, . . . the most suitable scenario remains cooperation between Jakes and Strougal in the offices of General Secretary and Premier. . . . Bil'ak will have to go. . . . The only way . . . is to convince Jakes that it is necessary to find common ground with Strougal."[9]

---

9. Vadim A. Medvedev, *Raspad: Kak on nazreval v 'mirovoi sisteme sotsializma,'* excerpt published in Czech in *Soudobe dejiny* 5, no. 4 (1988): 541–545. (Stalin's blush would have been one of pride and not of embarrassment, of course.)

Just as Metternich, after the election of Pius IX, is said to have remarked that he had "bargained for everything but a liberal Pope," the Eastern European Communists were ill-equipped to handle the consequences of a reform-minded Soviet leader. The more dogmatic among them found it hard to rule with the same ruthlessness, and those predisposed to reform were unable to stay ahead of public demands for more sweeping change. It was also apparent that, just as Gorbachev's reforms in the USSR encouraged and legitimized the far more radical efforts taking shape in Poland and Hungary, successful challenges to Communist rule in Eastern Europe would eventually blow back on the Soviet Union, particularly among its restive nationalities.

Indeed, as I wrote in *American Diplomacy and the End of the Cold War*, "It is hard to imagine the Soviet enterprise unraveling in any other sequence than it ultimately did . . . first in Central and Eastern Europe, next among the Baltic states, then in Ukraine and other republics, and finally in Russia itself."[10] This sequence and logic, it should be noted, was the assumption of U.S. policy from the earliest days of the cold war, dating to National Security Council (NSC) Report 58/2 of December 1949, which considered Eastern Europe to be the "weakest link" in the Soviet empire.[11] J. F. Brown nicely captured its implications for the Soviet system: "One of the ironies of 1989 and after was the way reform in Eastern Europe, made possible by Gorbachev, interacted with Soviet developments much to his embarrassment and political disadvantage. Would the East European revolution devour its own patron?"[12] The question anticipated the answer.

---

10. Robert L. Hutchings, *American Diplomacy and the End of the Cold War: An Insider's Account of U.S. Policy in Europe, 1989–92* (Baltimore, MD: Johns Hopkins University Press, 1997), 8.

11. "Report to the President by the National Security Council (NSC 58/2): United States Policy toward the Soviet Satellite States in Eastern Europe," December 8, 1949, in *The Foreign Relations of the United States, 1949*, 5 (Washington, DC: U.S. Government Printing Office, 1976), 42–54.

12. J. F. Brown, *Surge to Freedom: The End of Communist Rule in Eastern Europe* (Durham, NC: Duke University Press, 1991), 59.

Soviet and U.S. Assessments

What did Soviet and U.S. leaders make of these developments?
Newly declassified documents from the Soviet and U.S. archives
reveal strikingly similar conclusions about the crisis of Communist
rule in Eastern Europe. A secret memorandum from the International Department of the Central Committee of the CPSU to Aleksandr Yakovlev, dated February 1989,[13] described the "prolonged
crisis of the model of socialism" in Eastern Europe and the "lack
of legitimacy" of those political systems. "The ruling parties cannot rule in the old way any more," yet "new 'rules of the game' . . .
have not been worked out." In this precrisis situation, the memorandum continued, three future scenarios presented themselves: a
peaceful path of democratization led by the ruling parties, regime
capitulation following a political crisis, and preservation of the existing system through repression. Of the three—reform, revolution, or repression—the first was seen as preferable, in that the
analysis presumed that the ruling parties would be able to retain
control of the situation internally and would remain allied with
Moscow externally.

Another memorandum written for Yakovlev by Marina Silvanskaia of the Bogomolov Institute, also dated February 1989,[14] likewise described "crisis symptoms . . . in all spheres of public life"
in Eastern Europe. It distinguished between those countries where
crises had broken out into the open (Poland, Hungary, and Yugoslavia) with all the others (Czechoslovakia, GDR, Bulgaria, and
Romania), where conflict was also acute even if less easily detected.

---

13. From the National Security Archive, George Washington University,
Washington, DC.

14. From the National Security Archive, George Washington University,
Washington, DC. A similar but more cautious treatment of the same topic by the
Bogomolov Institute (The Institute of Economics of the World Socialist System)
was presented at a conference held in Alexandria, Virginia, July 6–8, 1988, and
published in *Problems of Communism* 37, nos. 3–4 (May–August 1988).

In the first group, the analysis contrasted the "most favorable" scenario of regime-led reform with the "pessimistic scenario" of conservative retrenchment. However, the memorandum found the situation in countries in the second group more dangerous as the failure of their regimes to undertake long overdue reforms had made a popular explosion more likely. These trends could well lead in some countries to internal power sharing and external "Finlandization," in which "they would pass from the sphere of monopolistic influence of the USSR into the sphere of mutual and joint influence of the Soviet Union and the European 'Common Market.'" Then came the sanguine conclusion that "this process not only poses no threat to the interests of the USSR" but, on the contrary, could facilitate Soviet ties with the whole of Europe.

On the U.S. side, a National Intelligence Estimate issued in May 1988 reached similar conclusions. It found that Gorbachev's policies had "increased the potential for instability in Eastern Europe" but also "expanded the scope for diversity and experimentation." Its three scenarios of popular upheaval, sweeping reform, or conservative backlash all pointed to diminished Soviet influence in the region. The Estimate did not exclude Soviet military intervention but noted that sweeping reforms pushed from below and led, at least nominally, by the ruling party would be hard to arrest. The Estimate waffled on how Gorbachev would respond to such a challenge: "His choice—by no means a foregone conclusion—would hinge on the scope of change and the perceived challenge to Soviet influence in the region."[15]

In an October 1988 memorandum for Gorbachev, Georgi Shakhnazarov asked essentially the same question: "What shall we do if the social instability that is now taking an increasingly threatening character in Hungary will combine with another round of troublemaking in Poland, demonstrations of 'Charter 77' in Czechoslova-

---

15. "Soviet Policy Toward Eastern Europe Under Gorbachev," *At Cold War's End.*

kia, etc.? In other words, do we have a plan in case of a crisis which
might encompass the entire socialist world or a large part of it?"[16]
Clearly, Gorbachev had no such plan, nor did he appreciate the
consequences of his policies for the fragile regimes in Eastern Europe. As I put it in 1987, "For many in Eastern Europe, Gorbachev
represented fresh hope for the gradual transformation of their political systems toward greater efficiency, diversity, and openness . . .
[but] he projected a self-confidence that struck some as self-delu-
sion in his ability to manage the process of change he had unleashed."[17]

Meeting with Hungarian Communist Party leader Karoly Grosz
in Moscow in March 1989, Gorbachev stressed the need to "draw
boundaries." He told Grosz, "Democracy is much needed," but
"the limit . . . is the safekeeping of socialism and assurance of stability."[18] Those boundaries were soon to be toppled, as Gorbachev's foreign policy adviser Anatoli Cherniaev foresaw in May
1989: "Inside me depression and alarm are growing, the sense of
crisis of the Gorbachevian Idea. He is prepared to go far. But what
does it mean? . . . He has no concept of where we are going."[19]

Meanwhile, pressures were building in Hungary and Poland,
where change was driven by revolutionary pressures from below
and reform sentiment from above, by some segments of the ruling
establishment, to produce a "refolution," to use Timothy Garton

---

16. Georgi Kh. Shakhnazarov, *Tsena Svobody* [The Price of Freedom], 368–
369. Trans. Vladislav Zubok for the National Security Archive.

17. Robert L. Hutchings, *Soviet-East European Relations: Consolidation and
Conflict*, rev. ed. (1983; repr., Madison, WI: University of Wisconsin Press, 1987),
xxvi–xxvii.

18. Memorandum of conversation between Mikhail Gorbachev and Karoly
Grosz, General Secretary of the Hungarian Socialist Workers Party, Moscow,
March 23–24, 1989 (Top Secret), from *Political Transition in Hungary, 1989–90;
International Conference, June 12, 1999,* Hungarian Academy of Sciences, Buda-
pest; A Compendium of Declassified Documents.

19. Excerpts from the diary of Anatoli Cherniaev, May 2, 1989, from Anatoli
Cherniaev, *The Diary of an Assistant to the President of the USSR,* trans. Vladislav
Zubok, (Moscow: TERRA, 1997).

Ash's term.[20] In Hungary, the ouster of veteran Communist leader Janos Kadar in May 1988 was a delayed acknowledgment of the collapse of "Kadarism," the tacit social contract that had evolved in the decades after the Hungarian Revolution and its bloody suppression. The deteriorating economy meant that the regime could no longer fulfill public expectations of steady improvements in material living standards. Moreover, the passing of the 1956 generation, coupled with the demonstration effect of Soviet reforms, meant that the sense of self-imposed limits was giving way to a new impatience for fundamental change. Rival centers of power sprang up as reformist figures within the Communist Party joined forces with dissidents outside the ruling establishment. By early 1989, the Hungarian regime had lost its capacity to govern and was obliged to enter into roundtable negotiations with the democratic opposition.

Karoly Grosz told a meeting of the Hungarian Communist Party's Political Committee in early 1989 that he envisioned a political opening that would lead to a "transition period" lasting until around 1995 before real power sharing would take place. Another speaker disagreed with this sanguine forecast, noting that "we are sometimes accused, not only by orthodox party members, of being . . . a Political Committee which aims at liquidating its own party."[21] A month later, Gorbachev declined to interfere when Hungarian prime minister Miklos Nemeth informed him that Hungary intended to remove its border controls with Austria. "Of course," Nemeth added, in anticipation of the East German emigration tide he was about to unleash, "We will have to talk to comrades from the GDR."[22]

---

20. Timothy Garton Ash, "Refolution: The Springtime of Two Nations," *New York Review of Books*, June 15, 1989.

21. Record of conversation between Mikhail Gorbachev and Miklos Nemeth, March 3, 1989, Doc. 13 from *Political Transition in Hungary, 1989–90.*

22. Meeting of the Political Committee of the MSzMP (Hungarian Socialist Workers Party), February 7, 1989, Doc. 9 from *Political Transition in Hungary, 1989–90.*

In Poland, nearly a decade after the delegalization of Solidarity and the imposition of a "state of war," the regime of General Wojciech Jaruzelski had yet to establish political authority or implement a reform program to arrest the alarming deterioration of the economy. Having failed to suppress Solidarity, and having seen its reform program roundly repudiated in a national referendum in 1987, the Jaruzelski regime was forced to open direct talks with the Solidarity-led opposition. As mentioned earlier, the "anti-crisis pact" of 1988 gave way to the Roundtable Agreement of 1989 and soon thereafter to the rout of communism in Poland.

Western Europe: Toward Greater Unity

While the countries of Eastern Europe increasingly were going their own ways, the European Community was embarking on a bold new drive for unity, heralded by the Single European Act of 1986. The political impetus came, in part, from two seemingly contradictory perceptions of U.S. power: that the decline of U.S. power obliged the Europeans to assume a larger leadership role, and that continued and unwelcome U.S. dominance in European affairs could only be offset by a more cohesive and effective European policy. Yet the two perceptions were not as contradictory as they might have appeared. Well before 1989, the transatlantic relationship was in a state of flux in which the institutional relationships created in the early cold war period no longer reflected the real balance of U.S. and European power and influence. U.S. predominance was preserved institutionally even while it was receding in actuality. Thus, however annoying it may have been for U.S. policymakers, it was not altogether illogical for Western Europeans to conclude that the United States was both retreating and overbearing.[23]

Similarly, U.S. attitudes toward European unity had always been ambivalent, fluctuating along a spectrum from partnership

---

23. The French in particular were prone to argue one day that the United States was retreating into isolationism and the next day that the United States was bent on perpetuating its domination of Europe through NATO.

to rivalry. In the immediate postwar period, the United States had given strong support to the goal of European unity. Future secretary of state John Foster Dulles was the secretary of the American Committee for a United States of Europe in 1947 and 1948, and Marshall Plan aid explicitly required European coordination through the Organization for European Economic Cooperation and so created a framework for the future European Economic Community. Before the signing of the Treaty of Rome in 1957, President Eisenhower remarked that this would be "one of the finest days in the history of the free world, perhaps even more so than winning the war."[24] Of course, even in those early days and certainly later, U.S. attitudes about European unity were ambivalent. The United States wanted a more capable Europe but not necessarily a more willful one; U.S. administrations often seemed to support European unity in the abstract but to oppose it in practice when European aspirations collided with U.S. aims. Toward the end of the cold war, it was U.S. resistance to a more united Europe, rather than encouragement of it, that provided the impulse for greater unity.

The Single European Act, which targeted 1992 as the date for the achievement of Economic and Monetary Union, had its genesis in the global recession of the early 1980s and the period of "high Reaganism" in U.S. foreign policy. The driving forces behind "1992" were many and varied,[25] but the most salient was that the global recession and the ensuing period of stagflation in Western Europe had led EC leaders to a common conclusion: that no European economy could successfully pursue national economic goals without careful coordination with its partners. As negotiations entered the final stage, European thinking was influenced by the European Commission's White Paper as well as the so-called Cecchini

---

24. Alan S. Milward, *The European Rescue of the Nation-State* (London: Routledge, 1992), 375.

25. For a review, see Andrew Moravcsik, *The Choice for Europe: Social Purpose and State Power from Messina to Maastricht* (Ithaca, NY: Cornell University Press, 1998), 314–378.

Report prepared for the Commission under the title "The Costs of Non-Europe."[26] Citing the growing interdependence of Western European economies as well as their vulnerabilities if they acted alone in a more competitive global economy, the report helped galvanize political and corporate support for the single market.

There was a parallel and reinforcing political dynamic springing from European alarm over the unpredictability and unreliability of U.S. foreign policy—beginning with the erratic twists and turns of the Carter administration to the early bellicosity of the Reagan administration. The final straw for many Western European governments was the U.S.-Soviet summit in Reykjavik, at which President Reagan negotiated away, without so much as consulting his NATO allies, the very INF (intermediate-range nuclear force) missiles the Americans had insisted on deploying shortly before. (As will be seen, there was a similar and equally divisive INF controversy in the Warsaw Pact, as a Soviet-led "peace offensive" aimed against INF deployments in Western Europe boomeranged into Eastern Europe instead.) Thus, as was the case with respect to economic policy, Western European leaders increasingly came to the judgment that concerted action within and by the European Community was required to provide an effective counterweight to U.S. policy.

The reversal in French policy was particularly abrupt as President François Mitterrand, having tried and failed after his election in 1981 to address France's economic woes through national policies, had done a complete turnaround by 1983. Influenced by his finance minister, Jacques Delors, Mitterrand made the historic decision to embrace the single market and to fuse France's political and economic future with Europe's.

As president of the European Commission after 1985, Delors also played a key role in projecting a vision of a Grand Europe—a new European ideology few politicians save Prime Minister

---

26. Paolo Cecchini, *The European Challenge 1992* (Aldershot, England: Wildwood House, 1988). Although this abbreviated version was not published until 1988, the preparation of the multivolume sectoral studies influenced Western European thinking just as the Single European Act was being considered.

Thatcher had the temerity to challenge.[27] Less obviously, Delors and the EC were overseeing a process of "informal integration"—from the bottom up, as it were—whereby more political and economic activities were being taken over by EC agencies in Brussels. As a legal matter, Title III of the Single European Act codified European Political Cooperation (EPC), that is, foreign policy coordination, as a recognized act under international law and renamed it the Common Foreign and Security Policy (CFSP).[28]

Apart from aiming to counter U.S. preponderance, the evolution of European foreign policy coordination from EPC to CFSP was responding to new opportunities and challenges in Europe. EPC had been created in 1970 to provide a mechanism for coordinating EC approaches through the Conference on Security and Cooperation in Europe (CSCE), and CFSP was a political counterpart to the rapidly developing relationship between the EC and the countries of Eastern Europe. Thus, the Community's internal development and its external evolution—"deepening" and "widening"—always went hand in hand, although the Americans were slow to discern this linkage.

From the beginning, the very existence of a peaceful and cooperative European Community served as a magnet for the countries of Eastern Europe—or, better, as a beacon, to use the English translation of the EC's PHARE program of economic assistance to the region.[29] EC efforts to establish formal relations with the region

27. See, e.g., Delors' speech at the opening ceremony of the College of Europe at Bruges, October 1989, and compare it with Prime Minister Thatcher's speech at that ceremony a year before, as excerpted in Trevor Salmon and Sir William Nicoll, eds., *Building European Union: A Documentary History and Analysis* (Manchester: Manchester University Press, 1997), 208–220. See also Margaret Thatcher, *The Downing Street Years* (New York: HarperCollins, 1993), esp. 727–754.

28. Simon Nuttall, "Two Decades of EPC Performance," in *Foreign Policy of the European Union: From EPC to CFSP and Beyond*, ed. Elfriede Regelsberger, Philippe de Schoutheete de Tervarent, and Wolfgang Wessels (Boulder, CO: Lynne Rienner Publishers, 1997), 20–23.

29. PHARE simultaneously served as an acronym for Poland/Hungary Aid for Restructuring of Economies.

began with the period of détente in the early 1970s. In 1974, the EC Council offered to negotiate bilateral trade agreements as well as extend Most Favored Nation status to individual Eastern European countries. Only Yugoslavia and Romania accepted; the others hewed to the Soviet position that an agreement with the Moscow-led and controlled Council for Mutual Economic Assistance (CMEA) had to precede and supersede any agreements with individual countries. There matters stood until Gorbachev opened the way for the signing of an EC-CMEA declaration that allowed individual CMEA members to negotiate bilateral trade agreements with the EC. While these negotiations were beginning, the EC member countries were busy implementing the terms of the 1986 Single European Act.[30] This exerted a powerful magnetic pull, conveying to Eastern European governments the benefits of economic cooperation with a rapidly integrating EC market as well as the costs of failing to do so.

It is not that the European Community had an overarching political strategy with respect to Eastern Europe; indeed, in early 1989 Delors expressed his personal regret that political cooperation was lagging behind and that the 12 EC member countries could not agree on common positions.[31] Yet the gradual, piecemeal progress toward bilateral trade agreements had created a process for East-West economic negotiation and for an unparalleled degree of EC intrusion into key economic sectors in Eastern Europe. With domestic remedies long since exhausted and with Moscow in no position to help, the Eastern European economies had nowhere else to turn but westward, and they had to do so on Western political and economic terms.

Thus, by 1989, Henry Kissinger could ask a disconcerted Gorbachev, "How are you going to react if Eastern Europe wants to

---

30. See Alan Mayhew, *Recreating Europe: The European Union's Policy Towards Central and Eastern Europe* (Cambridge: Cambridge University Press, 1998), 6–20; and Karen E. Smith, *The Making of EU Foreign Policy: The Case of Eastern Europe* (London: St. Martin's Press, 1999), 22–42.
31. Smith, *The Making of EU Foreign Policy*, 46.

join the EC?" Gorbachev had no answer but later told his own Politburo, "The peoples of those countries will ask: 'What about the Soviet Union, what kind of leash will it use to keep our countries in?' They simply do not know that if they pulled this leash harder, it would break."[32]

East-West Relations in the Era of "Divisible Détente"

In the 1970s, U.S.-Soviet relations and East-West relations were in plausible harmony. Although the premises of the two approaches differed, the Nixon administration's détente policy coincided with and largely supported West German *Ostpolitik* under Chancellor Willy Brandt. After the cooling of U.S.-Soviet relations in the wake of the Soviet invasion of Afghanistan and the imposition of martial law in Poland, however, superpower relations and intra-European relations increasingly diverged.

Fearing the advent of a new ice age in East-West relations, Western European and especially West German leaders aimed to insulate intra-European détente from the vagaries of superpower relations. In a May 1980 meeting (on the occasion of Marshal Tito's funeral), Chancellor Helmut Schmidt and East German party boss Erich Honecker confirmed their shared interest in insulating inter-German relations from superpower conflicts and agreed to use their influence within their respective alliances to improve U.S.-Soviet relations. After the meeting, Schmidt said, "I was moved to hear from Honecker and [Polish party leader Edward] Gierek the same things that I told them: that we shouldn't let ourselves be pulled in if we can avoid it somehow."[33] By the end of the 1980s, the West German Social Democrats were proposing various schemes for a

---

32. Gorbachev's remarks from a meeting of the Politburo, January 21, 1989, from the notes of Anatoli Cherniaev, Archive of the Gorbachev Foundation, Moscow, trans. Svetlana Savranskaia.

33. Klaus Boelling, *Die fernen Nachbarn: Erfahrung in der DDR* (Hamburg: Gruner & Jahr, 1983), 78–82, as cited in Eric C. Frey, *Division and Détente: The Germanies and Their Alliances* (New York: Praeger Publishers, 1987), 146n3.

nuclear-free zone in central Europe in the spirit of "common security."[34]

"Divisible détente" it was called, and West German initiatives were reciprocated on the other side of the East-West dividing line, particularly after the Soviet walkout from the Geneva disarmament talks in late 1983. Trying to forestall West European INF deployment, the Soviet Union launched a massive "peace offensive" that failed in Western Europe but reverberated unexpectedly in Eastern Europe. For most of the Eastern European regimes, the preservation of European détente was no longer negotiable; it had become an essential element of political and economic stability. What ensued was an unprecedented and public breakdown of Warsaw Pact unity. Romania refused to join the Soviet-led boycott of the 1984 Olympic Games in Los Angeles, the East Germans expressed their determination to "limit the damage" to inter-German relations, and the Hungarians and others defended the "role of small states" in promoting détente.[35] This made for some odd political bedfellows in Eastern Europe, with the dogmatic East Germans aligning themselves on foreign policy issues with the reform-minded Hungarians.[36]

These trends were reflected in the structure of East-West relations as well. The Helsinki process had offered new opportunities for intra-European interaction in arms control and other arenas. Owing partly to the European Community's political cooperation

---

34. Timothy Garton Ash, *In Europe's Name: Germany and the Divided Continent* (New York: Random House, 1993), 312–330.

35. See, e.g., Ronald D. Asmus, *East Berlin and Moscow: The Documentation of a Dispute* (Munich: Radio Free Europe Research, 1988); Charles Gati, "The Soviet Empire: Alive but not Well," *Problems of Communism* (March–April 1985): 73–86; Frey, *Division and Détente*, 88–118.

36. At a meeting with Hungarian party chief Karoly Grosz in September 1988, Honecker recalled that "at the time of the stationing of the missiles in western Europe, the SED (East German Communist Party) was pleased with how the fraternal Hungarian party reacted by adopting a position similar to that of the SED." Zentrales Parteiarchiv, J IV/931, *Stiftung Archiv der Parteien und Massenorganisationen der DDR im Bundesarchiv*, Berlin, trans. Catherine Nielsen, National Security Archive.

and coordination within the CSCE context, what started as a bloc-to-bloc affair (with the neutrals and nonaligned countries in the middle) soon broke free of the bipolar framework. By the late 1980s there had emerged a "configuration that no longer fit the original dramaturgical scheme" of East-West competition within the CSCE framework. A new "sociogram" of support for the CSCE process developed, consisting of the two German states, the neutral and nonaligned Caucus, central European countries that urgently needed détente (Poland and Hungary), and other countries, such as Romania and France, that simply wanted to loosen the grip of the two superpowers. Thus, CSCE as a "field of strategic interaction" had evolved considerably by the late 1980s. Where once there had been "Western proposals" or "Eastern proposals," arms control and other initiatives increasingly came out of ad hoc sponsor groups transcending the East-West divide.[37]

Thus, paradoxically, what appeared to signal a resumption of East-West confrontation in the early 1980s disguised a profound loosening of cold war tensions as Europeans, East and West, carved out new areas of cooperation. What looked like a new ice age turned out to be the beginning of a profound thaw.

West European Perspectives on the Eve of Revolution

The major European powers were divided over how to respond to the opportunities and challenges posed by Mikhail Gorbachev's new thinking. Where the Germans saw new opportunities in the East and were eager to exploit them, the British saw new dangers for the West and were at pains to offset them, while the French saw new opportunities for "overcoming Yalta" but doubted their capacity to contain a newly resurgent Germany.

British perspectives were informed by a deep, enduring skepticism of the reformability of Communist systems, whether in the

---

37. Heinrich Schneider, "The Twelve/Fifteen's Conference Diplomacy," in Regelsberger et al., *Foreign Policy of the European Union: From EPC to CFSP and Beyond* (Boulder, CO: L. Rienner Publishers, 1996), 237–241.

Soviet Union or among the countries of Eastern Europe. Prime Minister Margaret Thatcher turned this perspective into a paradox: these systems must change but cannot. They must change, given the manifest superiority of liberal democracy and the conspicuous failures of Soviet-type systems; yet they cannot do so from within because the same rigidities that produced failure also engendered a reactionary immobility in the ruling apparatus.[38] While believing these systems were doomed to collapse in the longer term, she had little sense of *how* this might occur—save, one assumes, through revolutionary upheaval—and was therefore more impressed than most with their staying power in the short term. Meanwhile, her focus was on assuring the cohesion of the Western alliance during what was likely to be a prolonged and skillful Soviet "peace offensive"; her worry was that a lax and irresolute West, above all West Germany, would be seduced by high-sounding but empty Soviet peace initiatives.

British analysis coincided neatly with British interests, for the UK had less reason to want to disrupt the status quo than most of its continental partners. Its preoccupations were with managing a difficult process of adjustment with the European Community in ways that preserved British freedom of maneuver while maintaining the integrity of the Western Alliance and the "special relationship" with the United States. It is not quite right that the British "never developed a grand design for Europe," as one writer suggested.[39] The design, offering consistency if not imagination, was status quo in the West and "status quo plus" in the East, where the hope was that gradual political liberalization would lead to a more secure, though essentially conflictual, East-West relationship. Execution of this design hinged on U.S. leadership; hence Mrs. Thatcher's impatience with the Bush administration's initial slowness to engage Gorbachev, which she felt was eroding Western resolve and

---

38. Thatcher, *Downing Street Years*, 452–453.

39. Edwina Moreton, "The View from London," in Lincoln Gordon et al., *Eroding Empire: Western Relations with Eastern Europe* (Washington, DC: Brookings Institution Press, 1987), 246.

common purpose. (Her efforts to mediate between the two leaders were reminiscent of similar attempts by previous British prime ministers, from Macmillan on, to serve as "honest broker" between Washington and Moscow.)

If Thatcher betrayed occasional impatience with the Americans, her real antagonism was directed at the West Germans, whom she believed had "gone wobbly" on security and were succumbing to public antinuclear pressures. The immediate issue of contention—Bonn's push for early negotiations to reduce short-range nuclear forces (SNF)—was part of a larger worry about the complete denuclearization of Europe, leaving Western Europe hostage to Soviet conventional forces. British thinking in early 1989, in short, saw few prospects for meaningful change in the East and many dangers for the cohesion of the West. The main task for British diplomacy was to prod the Americans into organizing a cogent, coordinated Western response to Gorbachev that would both test the seriousness of Soviet new thinking and rein in those, like the Germans, who might be tempted down the garden path of denuclearization.

"Gorbymania" never caught on in France as it did in Germany or Italy. In many ways, France shared British skepticism about the prospects for change in the East and certainly shared British concerns about further denuclearization. Having launched early on a campaign of "disintoxication" to cleanse the French Left of delusions about Franco-Soviet friendship, President Mitterrand had remained cool to Soviet blandishments even after Gorbachev chose Paris for his first official visit to a Western country. Additionally, he worried that further nuclear force reductions would diminish the significance of France's independent *force de frappe*, even as a more fluid situation in central Europe threatened to upset the vision of an EC-centered Europe under French and German co-leadership. As one French analyst put it in late 1988, "De Gaulle's France of the mid-1960s was a revisionist power, intent on modifying the existing European security system. Today France is, at heart, a status-quo power, whereas Germany's deepest hope must be to transcend the division of Europe between East and West. . . .

As long as Germany's hope remains France's fear . . . the French-German nucleus of Europe will . . . remain central but inadequate."[40]

To consider the France of the late 1980s a "status-quo power" makes sense only in the context of two seemingly contradictory factors: undiminished French ambitions to "overcome Yalta" and the substantial evolution in French strategic thinking, particularly during the 1980s, toward fusing France's future with that of Europe.[41] As Mitterrand put it in a November 1988 interview, "Yalta is the symbol of the division of Europe into zones of power and influence between the Soviet Union and the United States. I cannot make do with it. My dream is of a reconciled and independent Europe."[42] Yet, in French thinking, this ambition had to be deferred until "European construction" was complete, and this was still a long way off. While remaining deeply dissatisfied with the status quo in this larger sense, France was even more hesitant than Great Britain to disturb it in the near term, lest rapid change in the East undermine EC integration before Germany had been safely tied up in a more federalized Europe.[43] Thus France pursued the deliberate aim of decelerating the process of change in the East while accelerating integration in the EC. It was an approach that had much to recommend it from the point of view of French interests, but it presumed vastly more influence than France actually had to retard history's course. It was a race against time, and France was losing.

The West Germans, meanwhile, were not to be restrained. Their attitudes were expressed in Foreign Minister Hans-Dietrich Genscher's controversial speech in Davos in 1987 entitled *"Nehmen Wir Gorbatschows 'Neue Politik' beim Wort."* It is interesting that

---

40. Dominique Moisi, "French Foreign Policy: The Challenge of Adaptation," *Foreign Affairs* 27 (Fall 1988): 157–158.

41. Steven Philip Kramer, "The French Question," *Washington Quarterly* (Autumn 1991): 83–96; and Samuel F. Wells Jr., "Mitterrand's International Policies," *Washington Quarterly* (Summer 1988): 59–75.

42. *Liberation*, November 23, 1988.

43. Ronald Tiersky, "France in the New Europe," *Foreign Affairs* 71, no. 2 (Spring 1992): 131–146.

the title—literally, "Let's Take Gorbachev's 'New Policy' at Its Word"—was rendered in the foreign ministry's official English translation as "Let's Put Mr. Gorbachev's 'New Policy' to the Test." The latter, tougher-sounding title was actually closer to the sense of the text, which did not imply that Gorbachev should be taken at face value but rather called on the West to take his policies seriously and challenge him to translate his words into concrete actions. It was the more provocative "at its word" that took hold, however, and gave rise to fears that the Federal Republic had succumbed to "Gorbymania." (Much was made of opinion polls showing that only 24 percent of the West German public considered the Soviet Union a military threat,[44] but polls in Italy, the UK, and even the United States yielded similar results.)

To understand German approaches in terms of an assessment of Gorbachev is to get the analytic cart before the strategic horse. Policy toward the Soviet Union was part of a larger German *Ostpolitik*, which in turn was driven by *Deutschlandpolitik*, aimed at expanding ties with the "other" Germany. Facilitating the ultimate goal of German unity, or at least doing nothing to retard it, was the determining objective. *Ostpolitik*, as it had evolved, pursued "change through rapprochement." Its logic was that reassuring Moscow would allow it to relax its grip on Eastern Europe, giving reformers there greater leeway to pursue gradual change. Regime-led reform, in turn, would produce greater stability and confidence, which would encourage Eastern Europe and Moscow alike to undertake further steps toward reform. The result of this "virtuous circle" of reassurance and reform would be an easing to the division of Europe and of Germany, making possible eventual rapprochement between the two German states.

Thus, West German policy was not wedded to "stability" any more than France's was wedded to the status quo. The German aim, in best dialectical fashion, was stable change, born of the belief that positive change could occur only under conditions of stability.

---

44. *Economist*, May 27, 1989, 47, citing a 1988 West German poll.

The strategy depended on reassurance, gradualism, and predictability: West German goals, as Helmut Kohl put it in early 1988, were "long-term stable cooperation with the Soviet Union" and its emergence as a "more predictable security partner."[45] In this concept, too much détente was as risky as too little, for rapid change could be seen as threatening to Eastern European and Soviet leaders and risked converting the "virtuous cycle" into a "vicious cycle" of revolt and repression.[46] (This predisposition stood in marked contrast to the approach, favored in American conservative circles, of doing nothing to help or reassure the Eastern European and Soviet regimes but rather letting them be hoisted by their own petards.)

Although some on the West German left had argued, as has been seen, for the *Trennbarkeit* (divisibility) of East-West détente, both Kohl and Genscher proceeded from the conviction that *Deutschlandpolitik* and *Ostpolitik* could not be divorced from broader Western approaches toward the East. As Horst Teltschik, Kohl's national security adviser, put it in June 1989, "The West German government knows . . . that its freedom of action with respect to the Soviet Union or the other Warsaw Pact countries basically depends on the superpowers' relationship to one another. The better and more constructive the relationship between the USA and the USSR, the greater the freedom the small and mid-size countries in Eastern and Western Europe to cultivate relations with the leading power of the other alliance and among each other."[47]

---

45. Speech at the Twenty-fifth International *Wehrkunde* Conference, February 6, 1988, as cited in Guenter Muechler and Klaus Hofmann, *Helmut Kohl, Chancellor of German Unity: A Biography* (Bonn: Press and Information Office of the Federal Government, 1992), 144–145.

46. Josef Joffe, "The View from Bonn," in Gordon et al., *Eroding Empire*, 151–153.

47. Horst Teltschik, "Gorbachev's Reform Policy and the Outlook for East-West Relations," *Aussenpolitik* 40, no. 3 (June 1989): 210. Interestingly, at the beginning of the 1980s, East German party leader Erich Honecker told his party congress essentially the same thing: "We do not dream of the possibility of maintaining good relations with the Federal Republic of Germany . . . when relations between the USA and the USSR are aggravated." *Neues Deutschland*, April 12, 1981.

Hence German ambitions required bringing the Americans and their European partners around to a new, coordinated pattern of engagement with the East. Kohl's meeting with Gorbachev in Moscow in October 1988 and Gorbachev's reciprocal visit to Bonn in June 1989 were designed to accomplish just that. In Washington, anticipation of the Gorbachev visit, together with Teltschik's admonition that "we ought not to ask too much of Gorbachev,"[48] lent urgency to the articulation of a U.S. strategy. Indeed, between German eagerness, British skepticism, and French ambivalence, there was ample room for a U.S. tactic that could weld a coordinated Western approach toward Gorbachev and test the limits of Soviet new thinking.

U.S. Diplomacy at the End of the Cold War

For policymakers in Washington, the April 1989 Polish Roundtable Agreement, which called for freely contested national elections, was the mobilizing event. It was apparent then that the Roundtable Agreement, if fully implemented, would be the beginning of the end of Communist rule in Poland. And if communism was finished in Poland, it was finished everywhere in Eastern Europe, including East Germany, which in turn meant that German unification had just leapt onto the international agenda.[49] These, of course, were very large questions; Washington's appreciation of the potential for such sweeping change was by no means a prediction that it would actually occur, much less that it could occur in a matter of months. Yet the potentialities inherent in these events underscored how much was at stake and how critical the U.S. role would be.

---

48. Teltschik, "Gorbachev's Reform Policy," 203.

49. Hutchings, *American Diplomacy*, 9. Outside of government, William Hyland had come to a similar judgment: "If there is some kind of new order in Hungary, Poland, and perhaps Czechoslovakia, with less of a Soviet presence . . . then the question is whether that can be applied to East Germany. And if it is, aren't you just a step or so away from the unification of Germany . . . ?" Cited by Don Oberdorfer in *From the Cold War to a New Era: The United States and the Soviet Union, 1983–1991* (Baltimore, MD: Johns Hopkins University Press, 1998), 346.

Accordingly, the Bush administration developed in early 1989 an overarching strategic design aimed at bringing about the end of the cold war. As I put it in *American Diplomacy*,

> American grand strategy involved a sequence of steps. The first was to alter the psychology of East-West relations away from an accommodation based on existing "political realities" toward a much more radical vision of Europe's future. The second was to restore the cohesion of the Western alliance . . . and to begin building a new transatlantic partnership that encouraged and accommodated a stronger, more united Western Europe. The third was to place Eastern Europe. at the top of the international agenda and to engage American leadership on behalf of political liberalization and independence. Then, as U.S.-Soviet relations had been put on hold while the first three steps were being carried out, the fourth was to challenge the Soviet leadership to respond to specific proposals. These proposals were consistent with the spirit and promise of Gorbachev's "new thinking" but went well beyond its practice to date; they would address the sources rather than the consequences of East-West conflict.[50]

Thus the various strands of policy were all connected. Eastern Europe had logical priority: it was, as President Bush argued in his first foreign policy address, where the cold war began and where it had to end.[51] Improved U.S.-Soviet relations, as Bush elsewhere noted, "would reduce the pressure on the nations of Eastern Europe, especially those on the cutting edge of reform" and so facilitate their self-liberation.[52] And forging the closest possible unity in the Western alliance called for unequivocal U.S. support for the proposition that a "strong, united Europe means a strong America."[53] Within Europe, as a March 1989 memorandum to

---

50. Hutchings, *American Diplomacy*, 46.
51. Speech in Hamtramck, Michigan, April 17, 1989, cited in *American Diplomacy*, 38.
52. Speech in Leiden, the Netherlands, July 17, 1989, cited in *American Diplomacy*, 70.
53. Speech in Boston, May 21, 1989, cited in *American Diplomacy*, 42.

President Bush argued, "the top priority for American foreign policy . . . should be the fate of the Federal Republic of Germany. . . . Even if we make strides in overcoming the division of Europe through greater openness and pluralism, we cannot have a vision for Europe's future that does not include an approach to the 'German question.' "[54] It was from this analysis that the idea of the United States and Germany as "partners in leadership" arose, not as a rhetorical flourish but as a serious judgment about Germany's role in Europe then and in the future.

The ultimate hope, as President Bush put it in a July 17 speech in Leiden, the Netherlands, was "that the unnatural division of Europe will now come to an end—that the Europe behind the wall will join its neighbors to the West, prosperous and free. . . ." Citing Winston Churchill's 1946 speech at the same pulpit in Leiden's Pieterskerk, Bush looked to the belated vindication of Churchill's vision for Europe: "The great wheel has swung full circle. . . . Let freedom reign."[55]

---

54. Memorandum from National Security Adviser Brent Scowcroft to President Bush entitled "The NATO Summit," March 20, 1989, as cited in Philip Zelikow and Condoleezza Rice, *Germany Unified and Europe Transformed: A Study in Statecraft* (Cambridge, MA: Harvard University Press, 1995), 28.

55. Speech in Leiden, cited in *American Diplomacy*, 70.

Commentary

Karen Brutents | *Europe Between the Superpowers: A Soviet Perspective*

ROBERT HUTCHINGS WRITES that the end of the cold war resulted from "the *interaction* between super-power relations and developments in Europe" and "was not something bestowed on Europe by U.S. and Soviet leaders, but neither was it something that Europe could have achieved on its own." Nevertheless, he suggests that the accurate term for these events is "self-liberation."

Indeed, the emergence of the popular and opposition movements ultimately served as the major factor in the liberation of Eastern Europe. The materials at our disposal show that the effect of perestroika in the Soviet Union, along with Mikhail Gorbachev's policy line and practical steps, played a decisive role in transforming latent discontent into a mass movement in the majority of Eastern European nations. Even in Poland and Hungary, where democratic demonstrations were more active, the Communist regimes still maintained a foothold. That foothold was particularly firm in Bulgaria and Czechoslovakia. As for the German Democratic Republic (GDR), a key country in the Warsaw Treaty Organization, its citizens began to rise up only when it became clear that Gorbachev not only sympathized with them but would never allow the use of force against them. Before that, most of them remained silent, apparently out of guilt rooted in World War II and a related fear that disturbances in the GDR might cause the Russians and their troops stationed in Germany to seek revenge. It is also possible that some of the intelligentsia were restrained by a sense of responsibility and an understanding that the use of force in the GDR could lead to a global military confrontation.

Yet these factors do not give an accurate picture of events. The decisive influence of perestroika and Gorbachev's policies, which helped discredit Communist regimes in Eastern Europe, evoked a massive response that later acquired the character and dynamism of a new movement that transformed the original intentions and goals of its founders. Perestroika and Gorbachev's attitude toward Eastern Europe could not, by themselves, guarantee either the rise or the success of the liberation movement.

Robert Hutchings correctly points out that Western Europe, often acting on its own, actively developed relations with Eastern European countries, and he might have added that this effort extended to the Soviet Union. He emphasizes Europe's intention to curb U.S. dominance. However, he writes, "By 1989 the bipolar world of the cold war already had broken down." Furthermore, he applies his assertion to an earlier period, stating that "Konstantin Chernenko was a dogmatic throwback to a bipolar world that no longer existed." His contention that "the nuclear relationship generated rigidities that artificially preserved the formal bipolar structure of East-West relations and obscured the political and economic realities beneath the surface" is, in my view, an exaggeration. I would have agreed, however, if he had said that the grip of those rigidities on East-West relations was no longer as firm as before.

In my opinion, the Soviet Union of the 1980s remained a superpower in terms of its territory, population, and resources; in its huge arsenals of weapons; in its global presence and interests; and in its messianic ambitions even though its obligations were becoming increasingly burdensome. It was well known that the Soviet Union had great military potential but lagged considerably behind the United States economically and was experiencing serious internal problems, so the opening of the Soviet archives revealed few surprises.

On the other side of this bipolar system was the United States, the superpower leading the Western world and essentially defining its policies. Nevertheless, its influence over its allies had weakened, just as the Soviet Union's influence had diminished.

Robert Hutchings believes that long before the end of the 1980s, "this aspect of cold war confrontation—the prospect of nuclear war—had receded nearly to the vanishing point, taking with it superpower domination of East-West relations." In my opinion, the threat persisted, albeit to a lesser extent, until Gorbachev rose to power and consolidated his position. Moreover, had Reagan pursued his aggressive policy line with the USSR, led by Yuri Andropov, who was not inclined to retreat, the risk of such confrontation could have escalated to its highest level since the Cuban crisis. It was Gorbachev's policies and subsequent changes in Soviet-U.S. relations that removed the threat of nuclear confrontation.

Thanks to the U.S. nuclear umbrella, Western Europeans were able to engage in their own line of diplomacy separately from the United States, although that diplomacy was limited in scale and lacked far-reaching goals. For example, under Margaret Thatcher, Great Britain grew stronger after its recovery from economic crisis and attempted to reaffirm its position as a great power by developing relations with the USSR. At the same time, Mrs. Thatcher was trying to prod the Americans into organizing a coordinated Western response to Gorbachev and Eastern Europe so that the Western Europeans' activities would be conducted under a U.S. political umbrella. Hutchings quotes a statement by Horst Teltschik, Helmut Kohl's national security adviser, which is quite revealing in this respect.

Hutchings expresses a number of interesting and accurate ideas about Eastern European problems and developments and Gorbachev's approach to them. He correctly infers that "clearly, Gorbachev had no such plan [with regard to Eastern Europe], nor did he appreciate the consequences of his policies for the fragile regimes in Eastern Europe." Gorbachev's approach to Eastern Europe was affected by a variety of factors and motives that did not constitute a consistent strategy and were even, at times, contradictory. The inevitable conclusion that arises is that there was neither a clear concept, as Hutchings points out, nor was there a purposeful and coherent policy in relation to the Warsaw Treaty Organization.

Hutchings refers to Georgi Shakhnazarov, Gorbachev's adviser, who admitted, "At that time [July 1988] our leadership did not give much thought to the fact that perestroika would lead to such a rapid disintegration of the military and political bloc used by the Soviet Union to control Eastern Europe."[1] The documents to which Hutchings refers confirm how inaccurate certain Soviet power structures and progressive scholars were in their assessment of development prospects in Eastern Europe. The authors of those memoranda took into account the mood of their superiors and tried to placate them. In fact, judging by the National Intelligence Estimate of May 1988 mentioned by Hutchings, as well as other well-known documents, the U.S. analysis was not much better.

Perhaps it was hard to imagine future developments in Eastern Europe because of the extraordinary nature of the process and the absence of close analogies in the past. In a conversation with Karoly Grosz, Gorbachev said, "The Americans are closely following the developments in Hungary and would like to take advantage of the moment to strengthen their influence. They believe the Soviet Union is itself changing and does not care about its allies. Here is an interesting dialectic: by changing and renewing, we do not weaken but enhance our role and our influence on the course of events in the world."[2] Apparently, Gorbachev hoped that the example of his reforms in the USSR would cause a "wave of imitation" in Eastern Europe because its elites had already become used to following the Soviet Union. In addition, he actively promoted those processes during his visits and through his efforts to replace the leadership in almost every Eastern European country. Hutchings mentions as examples the ouster of Gustav Husak and the fact

---

1. Georgi Kh. Shakhnazarov, *Tsena Svobody* [The Price of Freedom]. Record of a conversation between Mikhail Gorbachev and the General Secretary of the Hungarian Socialist Workers Party, March 23–24, 1989, 111.

2. Record of a conversation between Mikhail Gorbachev and Karoly Grosz.

that the day after the Council for Mutual Economic Assistance
(CMEA) summit in November 1986, Janos Kadar was also advised
"to go."[3] Moscow played a part in the removal of Todor Zhivkov
and Erich Honecker as well. Contrary to the Soviet Union's original intentions, this reshuffling led to weakening of the regimes
rather than stimulating reforms from the top. The ousters impaired
leadership in general, undermined confidence that had already been
eroded by an unclear Soviet policy, and launched internal controversies. The new leaders lacked the seniority and stability of their
predecessors, and with those old leaders gone, struggles for power
broke out in high places. Thus, the ouster of the former leaders
signaled a crisis and gave strong encouragement to the opposition.

Skepticism about Gorbachev, at least among some Eastern European leaders, was generated not only by conservatism and self-
preservation (in this respect they proved to be more farsighted than
he was) but also by Gorbachev's lack of notable achievements.
Aware of their doubts, Gorbachev often refrained from giving rec-
ommendations and advice to these leaders. In addition, Eastern European leaders were often confused because they had only a vague
understanding of Gorbachev's plans and goals. They were per-
plexed over the obscurities and vacillations of his policies, and his
actions often startled them. The Warsaw Pact, unlike NATO, had
no procedures or mechanisms to coordinate its members' activities.
Its summits usually boiled down to a formal exchange of information. In fact, the bloc leaders were kept on a starvation diet in terms
of information. For example, after a meeting with Reagan, Gorbachev would give them no more than a general report.

Perhaps the most important point is that, hoping to transfer perestroika processes to Eastern Europe, the Soviet leadership and
Gorbachev himself overlooked or underestimated the fact that the
regimes in those countries were regarded by the majority of their
citizens as having been imposed from outside. Therefore their po-

---

3. *Vneshniaia politika SSSR I Rossii 1985–1995: k desiatiletiyu perestroiki*
(Moscow: Aprel-85, 1995), 60–61.

tential for stability and transformation, regardless of the leadership's sentiments, was limited, and their chances for success were smaller than those of the USSR. The Soviet leadership was mistaken in its expectation that liberalization in the Warsaw Pact countries would stop at an acceptable threshold and remain within the framework of democratization of the Socialist system.

Gorbachev's policies also revealed another tendency: to see the Warsaw Pact countries as a burden. His attitude intensified as the Eastern European leaders showed a reluctance to accept Soviet policy innovations. As the Soviet leadership lost interest in Eastern Europe, some leaders ventured mild reproaches. For instance, East German party leader Egon Krenz told Gorbachev, "We proceed from the idea that the GDR is a child of the Soviet Union. Yet decent people always recognize their children, at least they give them their inheritance."[4]

These developments influenced the Soviet Union's decision to switch to hard currency in trade relations with the CMEA, a move that dealt a serious blow to Eastern European, as well as Soviet Union, economies and forced them to increase their efforts to look for markets in the West. By this time, the Eastern European countries were alienated from Moscow, a fact that Gorbachev acknowledged when he said, on a flight from Kiev to Moscow in July 1990, "They are pretty sick of us, and we are of them too."

Hutchings presents an attractive scholarly and logical sequence for the unraveling of the Soviet enterprise "first in Central and Eastern Europe, next among the Baltic states, then in Ukraine and other republics, and finally in Russia itself." Yet if we examine the facts, we will realize the need to reorder some of the elements in this sequence. For example, Russia should come before Ukraine and some of the Central Asian republics. Russia led both politically and practically in initiating the "parade of sovereignties" as part of the struggle against the center. Yeltsin promoted the primitive nationalist idea, popular among some Russian leaders, that other

---

4. Record of a conversation between Mikhail Gorbachev and Egon Krenz.

republics were weights chained to Russia's legs, and that if a loco-
motive (Russia) were unhooked from its cars (the republics), Russia
would live in abundance. The majority of the Ukrainian electorate
voted to preserve the Union as late as March 1991, whereas sovereignty was declared in the summer of 1990.

Based on these goals, the Russian leadership roused secessionist
sentiments in other republics. Kazimira Prunskene, head of the
Lithuanian government in 1988 and 1989, told me that Yeltsin had
a special agreement with Vytautus Landsbergis that the Lithuanian
leader would reject any compromises with the Soviet president.[5]
One should not overestimate the effect of Eastern European developments on the Soviet Union "blowback," as other factors were
also at work.

Hutchings describes the Western European attitude, and especially the German position, on divisible détente. The aim was to
prevent the strengthening of bloc discipline, especially within the
Warsaw Pact countries, which would impede the implementation
of the general strategy directed at Eastern Europe.

But divisible détente had many contradictory aspects. It cannot
be regarded as a mere counterbalance to superpower competition
and confrontation; it was part of the superpowers' strategy. They
wanted to use divisible détente to promote their own interests, primarily to soften their opponent's camp and, at the same time, to
prevent allies from acquiring excessive freedom and independence.
In other words, the allies were to take appropriate steps under the
superpowers' general control. Thus the issue boiled down to the
degree of control that would benefit a superpower rather than its
adversary or even some of its allies. It was therefore no surprise
that Moscow, which was itself oriented toward a comprehensive
development of relations with Western Europe and encouraged its
allies' controllable steps in that direction, was nonetheless suspicious of Honecker's contacts with his Western European partners.

---

5. Karen Brutents, *Tridtsat let na Staroi Ploshchadi* (Moscow: Mezhdunarodnye Otnosheniya, 1998).

However, the superpowers' allies pursued their own goals and interests, including economic benefits and improved relations among the opposition camp. As a deterioration of Soviet-U.S. relations would impede their freedom, these participants in divisible détente supported improved interaction between the superpowers. Horst Teltschik's statement, quoted by Hutchings, is entirely in keeping with this spirit.

Problems and differences did exist within the Warsaw Treaty Organization, as in any other bloc, but Hutchings's point about "an unprecedented and public breakdown of Warsaw Pact unity" dating back to the mid- or even early 1980s seems an exaggeration. For example, he cites Romania's refusal to participate in the Moscow Olympic Games, but Bucharest had often demonstrated its disagreement with the Soviet Union on more serious matters. Its refusal to join the military intervention in Czechoslovakia and its position on relations with China were merely aimed to get benefits from outside the Warsaw Pact. Nor do other examples support Hutchings's conclusion. For instance, certain so-called controversies over positions taken by Warsaw Pact countries were, in fact, preliminarily agreed upon with Moscow.

Hutchings's description of U.S. military strategy unquestionably reflects essential elements of the Bush administration's policy, but it lacks consideration of the Soviet element. His conclusion that this strategy was "put on hold while the first three steps were being carried out" is hardly well founded. Hutchings may have been inspired to some extent by Brent Scowcroft, who said, "There were two major areas of relations that justified far-reaching steps, helped us regain initiative, and promoted our interests. The first was Eastern Europe, where the emergent steps toward reforms could give us an opportunity to benefit from a new thinking in the Soviet Union to loosen Moscow's grip on its satellites. The second was nuclear and conventional arms control."[6] This statement not

---

6. George Bush and Brent Scowcroft, *A World Transformed* (New York: Vintage Books, 1998), 15.

only contains a major disarmament aspect but also links the United States' Eastern European policy with the new thinking in the USSR, or, in other words, relations with Gorbachev.

In January 1989, Henry Kissinger met with Gorbachev in Moscow, where he offered a deal. He proposed that the United States develop extensive political contacts with the Soviet Union and help it by relieving its burden of arms spending and by other means in exchange for U.S. freedom of action in Eastern Europe. It remains unclear whether this suggestion was initiated by the new administration or by Kissinger himself, but Gorbachev was skeptical and declined the offer. The proposal met the same reaction at the subsequent Politburo meeting.

There was then a pause in Soviet-U.S. relations, attended by soothing statements addressed to Gorbachev. Finally, Secretary of State James Baker brought an extensive set of proposals to Moscow. Apparently, Washington had come to the conclusion that the situation in Eastern Europe could only be influenced by improving Soviet-U.S. relations and by working through Moscow. And, since the United States saw Gorbachev as "a man we can deal with," this was a realistic perspective. The administration understood that the alternative was that Moscow could close the door.

The United States and some other Western countries began to emphasize that they would not act to the detriment of the USSR's interests, a theme that President Bush discussed during his visit to Poland. Thatcher, in turn, told Gorbachev in London on September 23, 1989:

> Neither are we interested in destabilization in Eastern Europe and breakup of the Warsaw Pact. Of course, domestic changes in all the East European countries have become imminent. But we want them to be exclusively domestic processes, and we shall not interfere in them or support decommunisation in Eastern Europe. I can say that the position of the U.S. President is the same. He sent me a message in which he asked me to tell you that the USA would not do any-

thing that would threaten the Soviet Union's security or would be taken as a threat in Soviet society.[7]

In short, the political logic adopted after Baker's visit was put into operation: changes in Eastern Europe took place in connection with changes in the USSR in conformity with its new interests. Baker points out in his book that in order to achieve its goals in Eastern Europe, the United States needed the best possible relations with Gorbachev and his minister of foreign affairs, Eduard Shevardnadze.[8]

I would like to make a final comment about one of Hutchings's assertions. He writes that the Nixon administration "largely supported West German *Ostpolitik* under Chancellor Willy Brandt." This assertion lacks foundation. On the contrary, the administration responded to Brandt's initiatives cautiously and even with suspicion, especially in the beginning. Washington's attitude toward Brandt himself was reserved. However, some elements of Chancellor Brandt's policy, such as preparation of a quadrilateral agreement on Berlin, were supported by the United States.

---

7. Record of a conversation between Mikhail Gorbachev and Margaret Thatcher (translated from Russian).

8. James A. Baker III, *Politics of Diplomacy: Revolution, War and Peace, 1989–1992* (New York: Putnam, 1995), 7:158.

CHAPTER 6

Philip Zelikow and : *German Unification*
Condoleezza Rice :

THE EXAMINATION of historical turn-
ing points usually involves some tension between different levels of
analysis. Large-scale causes are easy to identify and discuss without
much specialized knowledge. In the case of Germany, for instance,
a typical large-scale candidate for analysis might be the weakening
grip of coercive power in the Eastern bloc. This factor can be accompanied by other explanations ranging from generational
change to the information age to the epistemic community of new
thinkers around Mikhail Gorbachev. In this examination of German unification, our bias is toward the micro-scale of analysis.

Many people have asked us about the knotty problem of whom
to credit with ending the cold war peacefully. Abundant credit
should be awarded to those who contributed to "a turning point in
the more than seventy-year history of antidemocratic and totalitarian systems that emerged after World War I."[1] The events of 1989
and 1990 can and should be placed in a well-defined setting already
shaped by the operation of large-scale historical forces. But, granting these underlying circumstances, many outcomes were still possible. The former Soviet foreign minister and ambassador to the
United States, Aleksandr Bessmertnykh, stated at a recent conference that "the story of reunification seems simple after you've
heard what everybody has to say about it. In fact, it was not that
simple, it was not that naïve, and it was not that placid. There were

---

1. Hans-Dietrich Genscher, quoted in Richard Kiessler and Frank Elbe, *Ein
runder Tisch mit scharfen Ecken: Der diplomatische Weg zur deutschen Einheit*
(Baden-Baden: Nomos, 1993), 14–15; Timothy Garton Ash, *In Europe's Name:
Germany and the Divided Continent* (New York: Random House, 1993), 343.

a lot of nerve-wracking situations in Moscow."[2] And not only in Moscow.

Some recent books have put forward particular Germans, Americans, or Soviets as winners of the prize for having made a difference in the ending of the cold war. However diverting, such a contest tends to shed more heat than light. We are more interested in the interaction of perceptions and choices by the various governments. Though some individuals had more influence than others, we found the spotlight shifting from person to person and from country to country at different times and on different issues.

We would like to offer another way of thinking about the challenge of assigning credit to one particular individual or to one individual's favorite cause. To do this, we have adopted a rather formal causal analysis. The following points might be thought of as constituting a map of causal variables in the unification of Germany. First, we specify our dependent, or outcome, variables:

- *Unification and its timing.* The two German states are unified into one before the Federal Republic of Germany elections at the end of 1990.
- *The fundamental nature of the new German state.* Unification occurs according to Article 23 of the West German constitution, destroying the German Democratic Republic and making the new state an expanded FRG without any fundamental changes in the system of government or principles for the organization of society.
- *The political alignment of the new German state.* The united Germany is a full member of the North Atlantic Alliance, with all German territory protected by NATO, all German forces remaining integrated within NATO's multinational military

---

2. For "greatest triumph," see Karl Kaiser, *Deutschlands Vereinigung: Die internationalen Aspekte* (Bergisch Gladbach: Bastei Lübbe, 1991), 16; for "most hated developments," see Aleksandr Bessmertnykh, quoted in a 1991 interview in Michael Beschloss and Strobe Talbott, *At the Highest Levels: The Inside Story of the End of the Cold War* (Boston: Little, Brown, 1993), 240.

command, and without placing unique legal limits on German forces.

- *Asymmetrical treatment of NATO and Soviet forces.* All Soviet forces leave Germany; Western forces, including U.S. nuclear forces, stay.

German and European history since 1990 would be quite different if any of these variables had acquired a different content.

Next, we offer a set of independent, or explanatory, variables. We believe these variables must meet three criteria:

1. But for the specified content of the variable (that is, in a counterfactual condition with this variable being absent), the content of one or another dependent, or outcome, variable would have been materially different;
2. The above-mentioned counterfactual condition must be reasonable, in that there must be a genuine possibility of the variable being absent; and
3. The causal variable is independent, in that the decisive content of the variable is indeterminate even after the contents of preexisting (but not simultaneous) variables have been established.

At least 13 variables appear to meet these criteria. To help the reader apply the third criterion cited above, we list them in chronological order, although several of them overlap in time.

1. The USSR and the GDR divide sharply and publicly on the need for and direction of reform communism (1988–1989).
2. Hungarian decisions on borders are made and misunderstood; Hungary then reverses its policy toward Romanian and East German refugees (May–September 1989).
3. East Germans decide against the "Chinese solution" for domestic protest and choose, with Soviet backing, the reform Communist government of Egon Krenz (October 1989).

4. Responding erratically to a surge in domestic unrest, the Krenz government's policies culminate in the unplanned opening of the Berlin Wall (October–November 1989).

5. Chancellor Helmut Kohl, with President George Bush's encouragement, reverts from the *Ostpolitik* paradigm of *Wandel durch Annäherung* (change through rapprochement) back to the Adenauer paradigm of *Wandel durch Kraft* (change through strength); Kohl destabilizes the East German governments of Krenz/Modrow, spurring popular contemplation of unification; the United States helps deflect international attempts to curb Kohl and restrain popular expectations in the GDR (October–December 1989).

6. Kohl spurns confederative negotiations with Hans Modrow and the Roundtable, and, with U.S. backing, decides to seek direct economic and political annexation of Eastern Germany (January–February 1990).

7. The United States chooses maximal objectives for unifying Germany in NATO and the "Two-plus-Four" plan for negotiating international aspects of unification (January–February 1990).

8. Kohl's agenda for rapid unification, propelled by indicators that it is internationally viable, produces a surprising electoral victory for his cause in the GDR election (March 1990).

9. Soviet diplomatic reactions to German developments are ineffective as "Two-plus-Four" activity is deliberately delayed and constrained and the United States and the FRG rally the West behind common objectives for unification (February–May 1990).

10. The FRG offers limited financial aid to the USSR and spurs positive but inconclusive multilateral consideration of a much larger assistance package (January, May–July 1990).

11. The United States and the FRG shape and deliver commitments on German armed forces and significant change in NATO's political and military stance that nevertheless re-

main consistent with preexisting U.S. and FRG objectives (June–July 1990).

12. Gorbachev makes a series of connected decisions: he avoids an invasion of Lithuania, begins to abandon structures of collective leadership, and starts changing his stance on the German question during and after the Washington summit. Yet he successfully fends off challenges at the Twenty-eighth Soviet Communist Party Congress (May–July 1990).

13. Complex political-military negotiations of linked political and economic agreements, consistent with preexisting U.S. and FRG objectives, are accomplished among "Two-plus-Four" states and specifically among the USSR, Germany, and the United States (July–September 1990).

Our narrative attempts to reconstruct the intricate details of each of these variables, which are themselves clusters of choices and interactions. But for the reader anxious to get to the story, we offer a sample of the empirical data underlying the fifth independent variable from the preceding list. This story focuses on the way in which America worked to shield Kohl and keep the GDR pot bubbling at a full rolling boil.

President Bush had been a firm supporter of German unification since the first time he was asked about this issue in May 1989.[3] As December 1989 began, he met with General Secretary Mikhail Gorbachev on the island of Malta and did his part to ease Soviet anxieties about East-West relations in general and German developments in particular. Chancellor Helmut Kohl had responded to the opening of the Berlin Wall and the new government in East Berlin by working to further destabilize the East German state. Even before the wall opened, Kohl had concluded that "cosmetic

---

3. See George Bush and Brent Scowcroft, *A World Transformed* (New York: Knopf, 1998), 188–189; Philip Zelikow and Condoleezza Rice, *Germany Unified and Europe Transformed: A Study in Statecraft* (Cambridge, MA: Harvard University Press, 1995), 24–29, 80–81, 92–95.

corrections [in East Germany] weren't enough. We didn't want to stabilize an intolerable situation."[4] On this point, Bush agreed.

As President Bush flew from Malta to Brussels to tell Allied leaders what had happened, he faced another formidable task. Having determined that Soviet policy on Germany was still relatively quiescent, he now needed to accomplish the remaining operational objectives for his trip. Most crucial was rallying Allied support behind the Ten-Point Plan for unity that Helmut Kohl had announced on November 20, thus sheltering Kohl. Meanwhile, as Kohl himself later put it, Bush's "calculation was to make himself a spokesman for the German side and in return to secure our firm assurance that we would stick strongly by membership of a united Germany in NATO."[5]

Soon after his plane touched down in Brussels, President Bush met with Chancellor Kohl. Secretary of State James Baker chose not to attend the dinner meeting, deliberately permitting the two heads of state to talk without the presence of West German foreign minister Hans-Dietrich Genscher (Baker's counterpart). Genscher's absence would allow Kohl to speak more freely.[6] To the Germans, Bush and his national security adviser, Brent Scowcroft, seemed tired. But Bush launched into a detailed report on the talks in Malta. The U.S. president warned Kohl that Gorbachev thought the chancellor was in too much of a hurry. Kohl said he had reassured Gorbachev that no one wanted events in the GDR to get out of control.

Kohl then thanked Bush for his "calm" reception of the Ten-

---

4. Helmut Kohl, *Ich Wollte Deutschlands Einheit*, ed. Kai Diekmann and Ralf Georg Reuth (Berlin: Propylaen, 1996), 117.

5. Ibid., 189; see also Bush and Scowcroft, *A World Transformed*, 196–197.

6. For the German account of this meeting, see Horst Teltschik, *329 Tage: Innenansichten der Einigung* (Berlin: Siedler, 1991), 62–64; for the U.S. notes, see memcon of meeting with Chancellor Kohl at Château Stuyvenberg, Brussels, December 3, 1989; the account that follows also draws on the Zelikow interview with Scowcroft, Washington, DC, June 1991, and Bush and Scowcroft, *A World Transformed*, 198–200. See also Scowcroft to President Bush, "Scope Paper—Your Bilateral with Chancellor Kohl" (trip briefing materials).

Point Plan and promised not to do anything reckless. There was no timetable. The FRG was part of Europe and part of the European Community (the EC, now called the European Union, or EU). The chancellor said he always worked carefully with French president François Mitterrand. Continued integration with the West was a "precondition" for the ten points. After free elections in the GDR, the next step was confederation, but with two independent states. The third phase, federation, lay in the future. It would take years, perhaps as many as five, to reach this goal.

Bush summarized Gorbachev's attitude as one of uncertainty. That, he said, was why "we need a formulation which doesn't scare him, but moves forward." Kohl assured Bush that he did not want Gorbachev to feel cornered. The newspapers were full of nonsense, he said. Former secretary of state Henry Kissinger had written that East and West Germany might come together within two years, but that was obviously impossible, Kohl said, as the economic imbalance between the two states was too great. However, he added, Bush should not misunderstand; the unification question was developing "like a groundswell in the ocean." West European reactions were mixed. "I need a time of quiet development," Kohl remarked, sounding somewhat drained by the extraordinary events of November, when the Berlin Wall had opened.

Both the White House and the chancellery considered this dinner conversation significant. The Americans found Kohl clearly determined to move forward toward unification. The Germans felt somewhat relieved about the way Gorbachev had approached the unification issue with Bush at Malta. Scowcroft felt sure Kohl now understood that the United States would stand by him, and Scowcroft was right.

The NATO summit meeting of 16 heads of government, to be held in Brussels on December 4, would consist of two main sessions. In the morning President Bush would debrief his counterparts on his meetings in Malta. In the afternoon he would offer a general overview of the future of Europe that his NSC staffers, Robert Blackwill and Philip Zelikow, had drafted before the trip.

They had started with a paper originally prepared when Blackwill was first flirting with the idea of a landmark joint statement by Presidents Bush and Gorbachev and then turned it into a statement of U.S. policy toward Germany and Europe. It included an outline of NATO, the Conference on Security and Cooperation in Europe (then the CSCE; it is now the OSCE), and the EC as the central institutions for Europe's future. The draft welcomed the possibility of German unification. Scowcroft had circulated the draft to Secretary of Defense Cheney, who endorsed it with enthusiasm.

On the road, Bush's planned policy statement was significantly revised, principally by Baker's counselor, Robert Zoellick, along with Blackwill. The revisions on Germany were especially important. In late November, Baker had endorsed four clear guidelines for U.S. policy on German unification, which had been put together for him by Dennis Ross and Francis Fukuyama of his policy planning staff. Although the press took little notice, Secretary Baker first publicized an initial version of these four principles in his pre-Malta briefing for the White House press corps in Washington on November 29.[7] During the trip, Zoellick suggested that Baker's four principles be inserted into Bush's statement. Blackwill agreed, and the traveling party worked on the language, strengthening its endorsement of German unification. The draft was reviewed and approved by Scowcroft, Baker, and Bush.

President Bush began the afternoon session before the NATO leaders with his policy statement about "the future shape of the new Europe and the new Atlanticism." The alliance, he said, faced great choices in consolidating the peaceful revolution in the East and providing the "architecture for continued peaceful change." He stated that the United States and NATO had never accepted the "painful" division of Europe; all had supported German reunification. The president continued:

---

7. See PA transcript, Press Conference by Secretary Baker on Bush-Gorbachev Malta Meeting, the White House, Washington, DC, November 29, 1989, 7–8.

In our view, this goal of German unification should be based on the following principles:

- *First,* self-determination must be pursued without prejudice to its outcome. We should not at this time endorse nor exclude any particular vision of unity. [The earlier State Department addendum, which said that the outcome must also be acceptable to Germany's neighbors, had been dropped.]

- *Second,* unification should occur in the context of Germany's continued commitment to NATO and an increasingly integrated European Community and with due regard for the legal role and responsibilities of the Allied powers.[8]

- *Third,* in the interests of general European stability, moves toward unification must be peaceful, gradual, and part of a step-by-step process.

- *Lastly,* on the question of borders we should reiterate our support for the principles of the Helsinki Final Act.

Bush added: "An end to the unnatural division of Europe, and of Germany, must proceed in accordance with and be based upon the values that are becoming universal ideals, as all the countries of Europe become part of a commonwealth of free nations. I know my friend Helmut Kohl completely shares this conviction." Then, following up on the "Europe whole and free" rhetoric of his May 1989 trip, Bush proposed that the alliance should make the promotion of greater freedom in the East a basic element of its policy. At the same time, NATO should continue to be the guarantor of stability in this period of historic transition. In this context, Bush said, "I pledge today that the United States will maintain significant mil-

---

8. The earlier Ross-Fukuyama formula included a qualifier: "if there is unification." That phrase was dropped. The language referring to four-power rights was new, added because the embassy in Bonn had complained of Kohl's persistent failure to refer to these rights and because of the Americans' care to mention their legal obligation for Berlin and "Germany as a whole." See Bonn 37736, "Kohl's Ten-Point Program—Silence on the Role of the Four Powers," December 1, 1989.

itary forces in Europe as long as our Allies desire our presence as part of a common security effort. . . . The U.S. will remain a European power." Bush also praised the European Community's "intensified" integration and said that the United States would seek closer ties with the EC.[9]

When Bush completed his statement, Kohl remarked that no one could have done a better job of summarizing the alliance approach and said, "The meeting should simply adjourn."

Following an awkward pause, Italian prime minister Giulio Andreotti asked to continue with his presentation. He warned that self-determination, if taken too far, could get out of hand and cause trouble. Kohl snapped back that Andreotti might not hold the same view if the Tiber divided his country.

The Dutch prime minister, Ruud Lubbers, interrupted the skirmish between the Germans and the Italians to support Bush's approach. British prime minister Margaret Thatcher could not let the matter rest there. She said that she shared Andreotti's concerns and wanted to study Bush's proposal more carefully. But one by one, other Allied heads of state supported the general thrust of the Bush approach.[10]

---

9. The text of the intervention was subsequently released to the public. "Outline of Remarks at the North Atlantic Treaty Organization Headquarters in Brussels," December 4, 1989, in *Public Papers of the Presidents: George Bush* (Washington, DC: U.S. Government Printing Office, 1990), 2:1644–47. Bush passed along his four principles on Germany directly to Gorbachev. See President Bush to President Gorbachev, December 8, 1989. For a sense of the positive press reactions to Bush's handling of the Malta-Brussels trip, see News Conference in Brussels, December 4, 1989, in *Public Papers*, 1989, 2:1647–49; and Scowcroft to President Bush, "European Press Reaction to the NATO Summit and Your Speech on the Future of Europe," December 6, 1989.

10. Teltschik, *329 Tage*, 64–67; Blackwill, interviewed by Zelikow, Cambridge, MA, 1991. Despite growing calls for U.S. troop cuts in Europe, American public support for military commitment remained solid in late 1989. In 1982, about 66 percent of Americans wanted to maintain or increase U.S. troop strength in Europe; in November 1989, despite the political changes on the continent, this figure had shrunk by only 8 points to 58 percent. The success of the May 1989 NATO summit may have played a part, as did wariness about future Soviet intentions and the uncertain political situation—themes repeatedly emphasized by President

Thatcher felt defeated by both the U.S. stance on Germany and Washington's strong support for the further integration of Europe. After the NATO meeting in Brussels, she wrote: "[I knew there] was nothing I could expect from the Americans as regards slowing down German reunification [and] possibly much I would wish to avoid as regards the drive towards European unity."[11]

Kohl and his advisers, by contrast, were elated. The NATO framework would now dominate the treatment of Germany at the EC summit four days later. The world leaders would not derail Kohl's plan. "On the contrary!" Horst Teltschik wrote, "The signal stayed green—caution will be admonished, but the railway switches are all thrown the right way."[12]

The NATO allies were not the only ones to get the news from Malta. Warsaw Pact heads of government also gathered on December 4 to hear Gorbachev's report.[13] All these states were now ruled by Communist "reformers" except for Poland and Romania. Gorbachev praised the Malta summit and President Bush. He said that Bush did not lecture him as Reagan had sometimes done, but instead formulated careful positions "slowly, thoughtfully." In Gorbachev's book of his public and private statements, the chapter on

---

Bush. On the polling data, see Tutwiler to Baker, "Support for NATO and U.S. Troops in Europe," December 8, 1989.

11. Margaret Thatcher, *The Downing Street Years* (New York: HarperCollins, 1993), 795–796.

12. Teltschik, *329 Tage*, 67.

13. For the official Soviet report on the Warsaw Pact summit meeting, an account of which follows, see "Vstrecha rukovoditelye godsudarstvuchastnikov Varshavskogo Dogovora" [Meeting of the leaders of the Warsaw Pact members states], *Vestnik* (December 31, 1989), 42–45. For the account of a participant as told to a journalist, see Don Oberdorfer, *The Turn: From the Cold War to a New Era—The United States and the Soviet Union, 1983–1990* (New York: Simon & Schuster, 1991), 384–386. Although Krenz insisted on going to Moscow with Modrow, the Soviets pointedly publicized Gorbachev's meeting with Modrow, treating the now discredited Krenz as a nonperson. Ralf Georg Reuth and Andreas Bönte, *Das Komplott: Wie es wirklich zur deutschen Einheit kam* (Munich: Piper, 1993), 185–186. Modrow later described the message from Gorbachev in a conversation with Rudolf Seiters. See Teltschik, *329 Tage*, 68.

Malta is titled "A Historic Breakthrough." Privately, too, Gorbachev felt he could trust Bush.

But Gorbachev was displaying second thoughts about the German issue. According to one participant, he told the Eastern European delegates that both NATO and the Warsaw Pact must be maintained to preserve Europe's security. Kohl's Ten-Point Plan speech, he said, had gone too far. Gorbachev asked for comments. There were none, except for a bitter tirade from Romania's dictator, Nicolae Ceauşescu,[14] a man whose overthrow and execution by his own people was then only three weeks away. East Germany's new premier, Hans Modrow, in Moscow for the Warsaw Pact meeting, was able to meet with Gorbachev, who told the premier that his "treaty community" idea was acceptable—but only if it did not lead to German unification.

Storm clouds were forming around Modrow's once hopeful government. By early December it was clear that the East German people would force their leaders to allow free elections, whatever this choice might mean for the future or for socialism in the GDR. On December 1, the East German parliament, the *Volkskammer*, voted to revoke the constitutional guarantee of the governing party's leading role in politics. The country was rocked by disclosures of top-level corruption. Shortly afterward, the entire party Politburo, and then the full Central Committee, resigned their positions.

The arrests of former top officials, charged with corruption and

---

14. See Deutschland Archiv, *Chronik der Ereignisse in der DDR* (Cologne: Verlagwissenschaft und Politik, 1990), 33–34; Elizabeth Pond, *Beyond the Wall: Germany's Road to Unification* (Washington, DC: Brookings Institution, 1993), 140–145; and Konrad H. Jarausch, *The Rush to German Unity* (New York: Oxford University Press, 1994), 70–76. In Washington, Blackwill convened a meeting of CIA and DIA analysts to review the situation in the GDR on December 7, 1989, and the U.S. government closely monitored developments for signs of a breakdown of public order. Soviet forces remained quiet. See Benko (analyst attached to Blackwill's office) through Blackwill to Scowcroft, "Intelligence Community Assessment of Current Tensions in the GDR," December 7, 1989.

abuse of power, began on December 3. Egon Krenz resigned his post as head of state on December 6, leaving Modrow alone at the top. Civil authority began to break down. Some citizens' committees seized public buildings in order to stop secret police destruction of incriminating government records.[15] There were several attacks on East German, and then Soviet, military installations in the GDR. The Soviet press angrily warned that "attacks on military property would not be tolerated." The situation became so unstable that, on December 7 or 8, Soviet military commanders ordered Soviet forces in the GDR to undertake "emergency measures to protect themselves and property."[16]

Ambassador Yuli Kvitsinski was recalled from Bonn to Moscow to help prepare a lengthy, highly secret interdepartmental paper on upcoming Soviet negotiations with the government of the GDR. The paper contained his still controversial proposal to persuade the East German government to press the idea of a German confederation as an alternative to unification. Kvitsinski reminded his colleagues that the paper could be put forward only after it had been formally approved by the Politburo of the USSR. Two of Gorbachev's top advisers, Aleksandr Yakovlev and Valentin Falin, flew to East Berlin, where, on December 8, Modrow's beleaguered party was holding a congress to plan their next moves. The visiting Soviets, Falin in particular, offered their frustrated hosts little beyond philosophical musings about the need for two German states.[17]

15. See *Krasnaia zvezda* and *Izvestia*, December 5 and 6, 1989. For reports on emergency measures taken by Soviet troops, see the same newspapers for December 8 and 9, 1989.

16. Julij A. Kwizinskij, *Vor dem Sturm: Erinnerungen eines Diplomaten*, trans. Hilde and Helmut Ettinger (Berlin: Siedler, 1993), 17; Wjatscheslaw Kotschemassow, *Meine letzte Mission* (Berlin: Dietz, 1994), 195–196.

17. According to both Shevardnadze aide Sergei Tarasenko and Cherniaev, the Soviet leadership was becoming worried that the real problem for them if Germany unified would be a witch hunt carried out against those who had "lost East Europe and Germany." Tarasenko claims that, by the end of 1989, he and others knew that the unification of Germany was inevitable and were trying to devise a strategy to keep this development from bringing down Gorbachev's government. See Rice interviews with Tarasenko, Moscow, October 1991, and Cherniaev, Mos-

On December 5, Gorbachev abruptly abandoned his philosophical detachment. His appeals to history and to Kohl's "sense of responsibility" had not worked. Bush and Kohl had received the impression from Gorbachev that he was not anxious about Germany's future, perhaps because, as Gorbachev's foreign policy aide Anatoli Cherniaev noted, Gorbachev liked to avoid confrontation in personal discourse. But now Gorbachev seemed frustrated and angry that they had misread his message. To Cherniaev, Gorbachev seemed angriest of all about Kohl's failure to consult him before presenting his Ten-Point Plan. Yet when Gorbachev had had the chance to voice his concerns directly to President Bush, he had not done so.

Perhaps there was no single cause for the shift in Gorbachev's mood. The situation in Eastern Europe was continuing to deteriorate. Czechoslovakia, Bulgaria, and Romania were all in the throes of crises. At home, pressures from the republics and from a relentlessly outspoken Boris Yeltsin were building. Now, with the GDR trembling again with internal crisis, yet another Gorbachev gamble—this time on Modrow—was on the verge of collapse. The stakes were high. As the situation worsened in the GDR, Gorbachev had reason to worry that a loss of face on Germany might be the final straw in his situation at home in the Soviet Union, a development that could radically alter the domestic balance of power in Moscow and bring down all that he had worked for there.[18]

---

cow, June 1994. This evidence is not reliable as a characterization of the whole Soviet diplomatic effort, but it does offer insight into the way domestic concerns were already shadowing Soviet policy.

18. This discussion is based on Soviet memcon, "Zapis besedy M. S. Gorbacheva s Ministrom inostrannykh del FRG G. D. Gensherom," December 5, 1989, made available to the authors by Aleksandra Bezimenskaia. See also Anatoli Cherniaev, *Shest' let s Gorbachevym: po dnevikovym zapisiam* (Moscow: Progress Publishers, 1993), 306–309. The "left no doubt" quotation is from Kiessler and Elbe, *Ein runder Tisch mit scharfen Ecken*, 70. Shevardnadze's reference to Hitler was in the context of an alleged German diktat in forcing the annexation of a neighbor. For Genscher's own account to his counterparts of his meeting in Moscow, see State 3834, "12/13/89 Quadripartite Ministers' Meeting," January 5, 1990. See also *Pravda*, December 6, 1989, 1, and *Izvestia*, December 6, 1989, 4.

West German foreign minister Hans-Dietrich Genscher was the first target of his wrath. In an extraordinary meeting that Cherniaev thought went "far beyond the bounds" of Gorbachev's usual discussions with statesmen, Gorbachev treated Genscher like an errant child.[19] He told Genscher at the start that the conversation would be serious and Genscher would not be spared, especially because the two men knew each other well. Genscher delivered a general presentation about Soviet-German rapprochement. Gorbachev said he welcomed such comments, but more needed to be said. This was a test of history, Gorbachev remarked, and he could not understand why Kohl had come out with his Ten-Point Plan. Kohl's demand for revolutionary political change in the GDR as a condition for German assistance outraged him. "One should say this is an ultimatum, a 'diktat,'" he fumed. The move had been an "absolute surprise" to Gorbachev, who thought that he and the chancellor had reached an understanding in their telephone conversation on November 11. He remarked, "And after that—such a move!"

Perhaps the chancellor did not need this understanding anymore. "Perhaps," said Gorbachev, "he thinks that his melody, the melody of his march, is already playing and he is already marching to it." This attitude could not be reconciled with the talk of con-

---

Shevardnadze's public criticism of Genscher was especially sharp. Teltschik was surprised by the Soviet hard line after Bush's report of his more temperate talk with Gorbachev in Malta (*329 Tage*, 68). Echoing Gorbachev's line (which he may have helped write), Valentin Falin told the British ambassador in Moscow on December 7 that the USSR thought Kohl, demonstrating "national egoism," had broken a promise to Gorbachev not to undertake any pan-German initiatives. On the hardening Soviet line, see the analysis sent urgently to Washington in Moscow 35285, "Soviet Concerns about Germany," December 9, 1989. The Falin comment was passed along by the British to their U.S. colleagues in Moscow. Soviet deputy foreign minister Anatoli Adamishin also went out of his way on December 11 to convey a message in Paris to Richard Schifter, assistant secretary of state for human rights, that, in part because of domestic criticism, Moscow was "deeply concerned" over the possibility of early German reunification. Schifter heard concerns from senior officials in the French foreign ministry as well. See Schifter to Baker, "Soviet Concern over German Reunification and French Thoughts Thereon," December 15, 1989.

19. See TASS reports, December 5, 1989, in *FBIS-SOV* 89–233, December 6, 1989, 51. The *Pravda* reports for the next day, December 6, are similar.

structing a common European home. Kohl had promised a balanced, responsible policy. But Gorbachev attacked the Ten-Point Plan in detail. He asked what confederation ideas meant for defense and alliance membership and whether the FRG would be in NATO or the Warsaw Pact. "Did you think this all through?" he demanded of Genscher.

Genscher loyally defended the Ten-Point Program, though in fact he had been as surprised by it as Gorbachev. He pointed to the qualifying language, to the vague assurances, and to the goodwill of the German people, who, Genscher said, had learned from their mistakes. It was a proposal, not an ultimatum. Gorbachev would not be assuaged. "Never mind all that," he said. The German chancellor was treating citizens of the GDR as if they were his subjects. Shevardnadze interjected dramatically, "Even Hitler didn't permit himself this." Gorbachev made it clear that Kohl's conditions for helping the GDR amounted to demands for revolutionary change. Genscher tried to explain, but Gorbachev said he was not fooled. This line of thinking from Kohl "was a political blunder." The Soviets "left no doubt" that the GDR must remain an independent state and a member of the Warsaw Pact.

Breaking with what had become a practice of downplaying differences between Western and Soviet leaders, the Soviet press went out of its way to emphasize that Genscher's meetings with Gorbachev, Shevardnadze, and Yakovlev had been "extremely frank."[20]

Gorbachev formally reported on his German policy to the Communist Party's Central Committee in a plenum on December 9. "We underscore with all resoluteness," he declared, "that no harm will come to the GDR. It is our strategic ally and a member of the Warsaw Treaty." He harshly attacked Western attempts to "influence the processes under way in socialist countries" and promised to "neutralize attempts at such interference, in particular, in regard to the GDR."[21]

20. See reports of the Gorbachev speech in *Pravda*, December 10, 1989, 1–3.

21. Soviet memcon, "Zapis besedy M.S. Gorbacheva s preszidentom Frantsii F. Mitteranom," December 6, 1989, made available to authors by Aleksandra Bezimenskaia. For French foreign minister Dumas's account of the meetings in Kiev, see State 3834, "12/13/89 Quadripartite Ministers' Meeting," January 5,

Meeting Gorbachev in Kiev the day after the Soviet president had savaged the West German foreign minister, French president François Mitterrand heard firsthand about the Soviets' anger over Bonn's behavior. At the end of November, Gorbachev had phoned Mitterrand and reportedly told him that, on the day Germany unified, "a Soviet marshal will be sitting in my chair."

Mitterrand did not need much prompting. At their meeting in Kiev, Gorbachev began with a philosophical discussion, but Mitterrand replied bluntly, "Today the problem is Germany." Mitterrand emphasized the all-European process. The German component should be a part of all-European politics, "not overrun it." He was not afraid of a unified Germany, but the four powers had to safeguard the balance of power in Germany's relationship to Europe.

Mitterrand, like Gorbachev, thought that Kohl was hurrying. When he said so to Genscher on November 30, Genscher had not seemed to disagree. Gorbachev recounted how "rudely" he had handled Genscher the day before, criticizing Kohl's plan as a "diktat." Mitterrand expressed his surprise and pressed Gorbachev for the details. Mitterrand mentioned his plan to visit East Germany and asked if Gorbachev would like to join him there. Though this move would have been a tremendous boost for Modrow, Gorbachev seemed too astonished by the suggestion to even muster a reply. Mitterrand asked at one point, "What should we do concretely?" But neither leader had answers to that question, and the meeting ended inconclusively.[22]

With Soviet concerns ringing in his ears, Mitterrand flew back to France to prepare for another EC summit, a meeting of the European Council, that he would chair in Strasbourg on December 8. Mitterrand soon found another ally. The British wanted him to

---

1990. Mitterrand told Kohl, over breakfast during the EC summit on December 9, that Gorbachev had displayed "astonishing" inner peace about Germany but might react differently if developments moved too quickly toward unification. The Germans noticed that Mitterrand said nothing about the French side of this conversation. As usual, Kohl tried to downplay any concern about unification taking place anytime soon. Teltschik, *329 Tage*, p. 71.

22. Thatcher, *The Downing Street Years*, 796.

help open up a second front against Kohl's plan. Though discouraged by Bush's handling of the NATO summit meeting, Thatcher had not given up. Her attention turned to Paris. "If there was any hope now of stopping or slowing down reunification," she recalled, "it would only come from an Anglo-French initiative."[23]

Mitterrand and Thatcher had two private meetings in Strasbourg on the margin of the summit. The subject was Germany. Thatcher recalls Mitterrand as being "still more concerned than I was." That was true. Mitterrand had already warned Genscher that Kohl's rash policies might lead to the revival of the Triple Entente of France, Britain, and Russia, which had been formed before World War I. He cautioned that such an alliance might rally once more against Germany. Now the French leader drew an analogy from the years before World War II: "We find ourselves in the same situation as the leaders in France and Britain before the war, who didn't react to anything. We can't repeat Munich!"[24] Mitterrand criticized Kohl's plan and commented disparagingly on the Germans. So what could be done? Mitterrand said that Kohl had already gone well beyond the assurances he had offered EC colleagues in Paris a few weeks earlier. According to Thatcher, Mitterrand commented that at times of great danger France and Britain had always established special relations. Such a time had come again. But the two leaders could not agree on a plan of action.[25]

At least France could ease its worries by assuring itself that steps toward German unity could be matched by equally large steps toward European union. This was just the approach Jacques De-

---

23. Ibid., 796–797.

24. See Jacques Attali, *Verbatim: Tome 3, Chronique des années 1988–1991* (Paris: Fayard, 1995), 337, 369.

25. Genscher, interview by Zelikow, Wachtberg-Pech, December 1994; and Conclusions of the Presidency, European Council, Strasbourg, December 8 and 9, 1989. See also Scowcroft to President Bush, "Mitterrand and the Strasbourg Summit," December 13, 1989 (drafted by Blackwill). The CIA pointed out the similarities between the president's four principles on Germany and the EC's Strasbourg statement in an informal chart, "Conditions for German Reunification," which Blackwill passed to General Scowcroft on December 13.

lors, president of the European Commission, had chosen to adopt. On these points Kohl was ready to agree; Mitterrand would be pushing on an open door. So France was able to accomplish its most important operational objectives for the Strasbourg summit of the European Community. Mitterrand won Kohl's support for convening, in late 1990, an intergovernmental conference to amend the Treaty of Rome, which had created the European Community, in order to prepare a new treaty adopting economic and monetary union. In return, the EC endorsed Germany's movement toward unification in terms similar to the guidelines proposed by President Bush at the December 4 NATO summit.

Yet the language on Germany was contested. The German negotiators, led by political director Dieter Kastrup, sought unequivocal support for self-determination. The French and the Italians objected that Germany's future could not be determined by the Germans alone. Genscher thought that the German attitude toward monetary union would be the test for earning Mitterrand's support. Bonn passed the test. After a sometimes heated discussion, the EC heads of government agreed on a single modest paragraph:

> We seek the strengthening of the state of peace in Europe in which the German people will regain [their] unity through free self-determination [the traditional formula]. This process should take place peacefully and democratically, in full respect of the relevant agreements and treaties and of all the principles defined by the Helsinki Final Act, in a context of dialogue and East-West cooperation. It also has to be placed in the perspective of European integration.[26]

Kohl commented later on the "icy climate" he had encountered among his fellow leaders in Strasbourg. The winds from Moscow were chilly, too. The United States had been watching with alarm as pressure was being put on Kohl. He seemed to be isolated on all fronts. Gorbachev may have been calm at Malta, but now he

---

26. Teltschik, *329 Tage*, 70.

seemed furious. In Bonn, though, Teltschik was still discounting the Soviet worries as nothing but "appeals and warnings." After all, when West Germany had accepted deployment of new U.S. nuclear forces in 1983, "the Soviet leadership had threatened us with war and missiles."[27] Fortunately for Bonn, the Soviet, British, and French governments seemed to have an attitude without a policy.

The most important priority for the United States was to keep the path for Kohl open—free of conditions that Moscow, or the French or British for that matter, might attach. In early December, the only addendum to Bonn's goals was the set of principles articulated by Bush, putting Kohl on the record in support of continued German alignment with NATO. As one of Genscher's top advisers put it, "In this way Bush had made Germany's NATO membership an unequivocal prerequisite for the later process of unification, like the solution of the border question with Poland."[28]

A week after the Strasbourg summit, Mitterrand flew to St. Martin in the Caribbean to review European developments in person with President Bush.[29] They discussed the future of Germany at some length. Again Mitterrand tried to find the proper balance. Though not projecting the alarm Thatcher recalls from the Strasbourg summit, Mitterrand was clearly troubled about developments in Germany. This time he agreed with President Bush that Germany could unify with "a proper transfer" of power. But the

---

27. Kiessler and Elbe, *Ein runder Tisch mit scharfen Ecken*, 55.

28. The account that follows is drawn from the Zelikow interview with Baker, Houston, TX, January 1995, and memcon of meeting with President Mitterrand, St. Martin, December 16, 1989. See also Scowcroft to President Bush, "Scope Paper—Your Meeting with President Mitterrand," December 15, 1989 (drafted by Basora and Blackwill); and Scowcroft to President Bush, "Mitterrand, the Germans, U.S.-EC Cooperation, and the CSCE," December 15, 1989 (drafted by Blackwill).

29. See CIA, "East Germany: Movement Toward Democracy and Reunification," December 11, 1989; Munich 4955, "Bavarians and the Reunification Question," December 15, 1989; Bonn 38006, "Kohl's Ten-Point Program: A Burst of Criticism and then More Embracing," December 5, 1989; Claus Gennrich, "Genscher Pledges Respect for Soviet Security Interests," *Frankfurter Allgemeine Zeitung*, December 13, 1989, 4; Bonn 38015, "The SPD and the German Question," December 5, 1989; and other U.S. intelligence reports.

objections of the Soviets, Poles, Czechs, Belgians, Danes, Italians, and others could not be ignored. Mitterrand had told Kohl at their recent meeting in Switzerland that Germany should go no faster than the EC, or the whole thing "will end up in the ditch." Mitterrand repeated that, for him, developments in Germany were linked to developments in NATO and the EC. He could understand what the Germans wanted and it was hard to stop them. But if Kohl went too fast, he could cause a diplomatic crisis. It would have the wrong effect, complicating East-West relations at a time when the West was winning hands down.

Secretary of State Baker pointed out that the NATO and Strasbourg summits had shown the way to a common position. Mitterrand claimed to agree with Bush but said he was trying to manage the contradictions of the situation. Fast movement could disrupt the equilibrium in Europe and on the frontiers. Like Gorbachev, Mitterrand had been annoyed by Ambassador Walters's speculation that reunification could occur in as little as five years. Bush replied that Walters's view was not official and would not be repeated. Nevertheless, Mitterrand argued, Walters said it in Germany and the Germans had heard it. We should not encourage more speed, he said. Movement on arms control, EC integration, and Euro-American relations was also required. Mitterrand's anxiety seemed to spill over as he spoke of the need for a new Europe if the continent was to avoid slipping back to where it had been in 1913 (an analogy Mitterrand had also used with Gorbachev and with his own advisers). Everything could be lost.

The fact that Mitterrand did not air these views in public shows the powerful but silent effect of the clear U.S. stance. With President Bush openly saying he supported German aspirations for unification, Mitterrand and Thatcher were acutely inhibited from publicly voicing their concerns. That enforced reticence, in turn, made it harder for them to rally a countervailing political momentum against the West German and U.S. plans.

Secretary of State Baker then made his own trip to Berlin, where he reassured Kohl about a meeting of the ambassadors from the four powers that the Soviets, British, and French had requested. Then he made a brief visit to East Germany, where he linked any Western economic assistance for the GDR to fundamental political and economic reform. He stressed the importance of genuinely free elections. Immediately after his meetings in Potsdam, Secretary Baker traveled on to Brussels, where he met with EC foreign ministers on December 13, principally to discuss the status of economic assistance for Eastern Europe.

Most important, on the evening of December 13, Baker had a working dinner with foreign ministers Hurd, Dumas, and Genscher to discuss Berlin and German issues. The ministers responded positively to the broad vision for Europe's future that Baker had explained in a speech in Berlin. But the Germans were still angry about the sight of the ambassadors from the four powers standing together in Berlin. Genscher felt that there should never be another such meeting at which the Germans were left sitting at the "cat's table." Behind the scenes, Genscher's advisers began to warn of the danger of a new peace treaty "like Versailles." Baker put his hand on Genscher's arm and said, "Hans-Dietrich, we have understood you."[30]

Other European statesmen pursued their own efforts to moderate the quickening pace toward German unity. Mitterrand, completing his energetic round of diplomatic consultations, met with Modrow in East Berlin on December 21. Breaking with the U.S. approach, the French president offered a multiyear program of aid for the existing East German government and proclaimed his support for closer GDR ties to Western Europe. One of Mitterrand's advisers privately warned Teltschik again that Kohl was going too fast.[31]

---

30. For accounts of this dinner and the next morning's breakfast, see Kiessler and Elbe, *Ein runder Tisch mit scharfen Ecken*, 74–75 (quoting Genscher and Baker; Elbe was present); State 3934, "12/13/89 Quadripartite Ministers' Meeting," January 5, 1990.

31. On the comment from Mitterrand's adviser, Jean-Louis Bianco, see Teltschik, *329 Tage*, 96.

Nevertheless, as 1989 drew to a close, Helmut Kohl clearly held the reins in determining Germany's future. Bush and Baker had deliberately decided to legitimize Kohl's program, and the United States had succeeded in adding its own objective: Germany's continued membership in NATO, anchoring the FRG firmly to the West. The U.S. diplomatic strategy was intended to calm the Soviets and keep the Allies from descending into renewed national hostilities so that the goals of Washington and Bonn could be achieved.

Chancellor Kohl tried to reassure the Soviets. He sent a message to Gorbachev promising not to destabilize the situation in Europe. It was the people, he wrote, who were putting the German question back on the agenda. Any developments would be embedded in all-European structures. He recognized the legitimacy of Soviet security interests. As this message was being delivered, Gorbachev was sending his own letter to Kohl. Its tone was cold. Gorbachev said that the USSR would do all it could to "neutralize" intervention in the GDR's internal affairs. East Germany was a strategic partner of the Soviet Union, and the existence of two German states was a historic fact.[32]

Kohl tried to meet with Gorbachev as he had told Baker he would, but the Soviet leader rebuffed him, saying that he did not have time. According to several officials, the Soviets were trying once again to reevaluate their policy options.[33] Perhaps Gorbachev was still angry and wanted to keep Kohl waiting. But once more, Moscow forfeited a chance to define the agenda. When the two leaders finally met in February 1990, the German Democratic Republic was a walking corpse.

Undaunted by Gorbachev's slight, Kohl pressed on with the first steps of his Ten-Point Plan, meeting with Modrow in Dresden

---

32. Kohl's message was sent to Moscow on December 14, 1989. Gorbachev's message was waiting when Kohl returned on December 18, 1989, from a visit to Hungary. Teltschik, *329 Tage*, 80–81, 85.

33. Tarasenko, interview by Rice, Moscow, October 1991. Teltschik was told this by the Soviets as well. Teltschik, interview by Zelikow and Rice, Gütersloh, June 1992.

on December 19, 1989, to begin negotiating new agreements on social, cultural, and economic ties between the two German states.
Kohl indicated a readiness to help Modrow stabilize the GDR and
listened sympathetically to his request for billions of marks in aid.
The leaders announced that they would open the Brandenburg
Gate in Berlin as a border crossing and lift the remaining restrictions on cross-border movement in time for Christmas.

The Dresden trip was important for Kohl, bringing home the
momentum of East German opinion and providing an opportunity
to seize the moment. Addressing cheering crowds in Dresden,
Kohl spoke emotionally of the German nation and was met with
chants for unification. Kohl had rallied political support for his
cause within his party, he had kept his program for unity on the
table, and now, as he had hoped, the East German people were rallying to the dream he had told them could come true.

In Washington, even the Americans were beginning to fear that
the FRG was acting imprudently. Conceding that Kohl had scored
a public relations coup by his visit to East Germany, Secretary
Baker advised President Bush that Kohl's activities "may raise
again the question with some, however, of whether the chancellor's
domestic political interest is leading him too far, too fast on the
issue of unification; he's tapping emotions that will be difficult to
manage."[34]

It was clear that the frenzied diplomacy in the month after the
opening of the Berlin Wall had dramatically altered the political
landscape. Genscher's adviser, Frank Elbe, captured the change
when he recalled that in the middle of November he had told Zoellick that "the tempo of German unification cannot be permitted to
endanger the stability of Europe." By early December, however,
Elbe told Zoellick, "If German unity *doesn't* come, *that* will endanger the stability of Europe."[35]

---

34. Baker to President Bush (for his evening reading), December 20, 1989. On
Kohl's trip to the GDR, see Teltschik, *329 Tage*, 87–96.

35. Kiessler and Elbe, *Ein runder Tisch mit scharfen Ecken,* 47 (emphasis
added). Elbe remembers that Zoellick replied to the December warning by agreeing, "We also see it that way."

As pressure mounted in 1990, there was no longer any doubt that the two German states would come together in some fashion. The most difficult challenge now was to determine when and how unification would occur and to balance these plans against the danger of a new East-West crisis that could plunge Europe back into a cold war. An authoritative German history rightly judges that, by the end of 1989, "The constellation of interests had quickly crystallized: The Federal [German] government and the U.S. administration as real advocates of unification against a large, clear group of doubters and brakemen, with France and Great Britain also declared enemies of unification along with the GDR and the Soviet Union."[36] To meet that challenge, the U.S. and West German governments rushed in the first weeks of 1990 to develop a whole new strategy to bring about unification, this time on a timetable of months rather than years.

Returning to the opening argument of this essay, the preceding story turned a magnifying glass on the December 1989 diplomacy that partly determined the content of only one of 13 such independent variables in this turning point of the cold war. In this brief story, the content was not predetermined. A more timid West German policy or a more passive Bush administration policy during this period is quite imaginable and could well have slowed the process and dampened popular expectations inside East Germany. Perhaps, too, a different set of policies might have been adopted by the opposing powers. But the effect of the December maneuvers on the volatile German crisis was that, instead of wielding a fire extinguisher, Kohl and Bush were adding judicious splashes of gasoline. Yet this outcome still did not preordain the content of our dependent variables. Instead, the content of this specific variable opened up new choices and possibilities and another spectrum of potential outcomes in a succession of pivotal moments.

---

36. Werner Weidenfeld with Peter M. Wagner and Elke Bruck, *Aussenpolitik für die deutsche Einheit: Die Entscheidungsjahre 1989/90*, vol. 4, *Geschichte der deutschen Einheit* (Stuttgart: Deutsche Verlags-Anstalt, 1998), 208.

For analysts of international relations, illustrations such as these can be humbling. They suggest that within one large turning point, a number of smaller turning points can be discerned, each deserving careful study before causal explanations for the whole can be offered confidently. The burden of required knowledge may seem forbidding. But just as analogous developments in the science of physics and human biology have liberated understanding and creativity, so a renewed appreciation for the significance of microchoices in the even less determinate realm of human behavior can add essential understanding.

Vladislav Zubok : *German Unification from the Soviet (Russian) Perspective*

PHILIP ZELIKOW and Condoleezza Rice caution researchers who seek to analyze turning points leading to the end of the cold war and the reunification of Germany that they face a daunting task. Indeed, under scrutiny, so-called milestones and decisive factors dissolve into a maze of intertwined circumstances and events that constitute the fabric of the complex and elusive phenomenon of human history. The same ambiguity applies to two essential aspects of research on the end of the cold war: sources and interpretations. New sources and new angles may significantly alter our perceptions of the past.

In particular, this effect can be expected from the Soviet perspective of German reunification, including judgments, mistakes, and rationales that guided Soviet policy and especially Soviet leader Mikhail Gorbachev. Zelikow and Rice's essay sheds light on the Soviet perspective, which they analyze in greater depth in their book, *Germany Reunified and Europe Transformed: A Study in Statecraft.*[1] Relying on records stored at the Gorbachev Archive in Moscow, including transcripts of conversations that Gorbachev had with other Soviet leaders, his advisers, and foreign leaders, the authors reveal Gorbachev's "philosophical detachment" on the German question, his delays in formulating diplomatic positions,

---

1. Philip Zelikow and Condoleezza Rice, *Germany Reunified and Europe Transformed: A Study in Statecraft* (Cambridge, MA: Harvard University Press, 1995).

and the reactive, shifting nature of those positions. In a footnote, they observe that "domestic concerns were already shadowing Soviet policy" in 1989. Yet the reasons for Soviet behavior are not independent variables in their story. Zelikow and Rice's analysis (and this can be said about other books written by veterans of the Bush administration)[2] implies that the Soviet leadership did not have much of a choice, given the fast pace of events, the disappearance of their key ally, the German Democratic Republic regime, and the firm, skillful, and bold policies of Chancellor Helmut Kohl and the Bush administration.

Soviet policies, however, deserve careful attention as factors in German reunification. Gorbachev's attitudes and policies played a no less important role in the peaceful outcome of this process than did Washington's firm backing of Kohl. After all, Moscow was the parent of the GDR and for decades regarded it as the cornerstone of Soviet presence in Europe. The motives for relinquishing the GDR without a fight can be as revealing and important for historical interpretation as the outcome itself.

Therefore, the list of independent variables proposed by Zelikow and Rice should be accompanied by other factors that reflect the Soviet perspective, Soviet foreign policy, and the domestic context that determined Gorbachev's attitudes toward German unification. Chronologically, they are as follows:

1. Gorbachev delivers a speech at the UN in December 1988 in which he recognizes the right of self-determination without exception and renounces the use of force in international relations.
2. Gorbachev meets with Chancellor Kohl in Moscow in October 1988 and in the Federal Republic of Germany in June

---

2. See George Bush and Brent Scowcroft, *A World Transformed* (New York: Knopf, 1998); and Robert L. Hutchings, *American Diplomacy and the End of the Cold War: An Insider's Account of U.S. Policy in Europe, 1989–1992* (Washington, DC: Woodrow Wilson Center Press and Johns Hopkins University Press, 1997).

1989. The Soviet leader regards relations with West Germany as a cornerstone of his policy of East-West integration.

3. Gorbachev and Foreign Minister Eduard Shevardnadze turn blind eyes to the opening of the Hungarian-Austrian border that destabilizes the GDR.

4. The Kremlin leadership, immersed in domestic crisis, particularly the issue of Baltic independence, misjudges the consequences of the fall of the Berlin Wall (November–December 1989).

5. Gorbachev fails to address the issue of German reunification with President Bush and his team at the Malta summit in December 1989.

6. The Soviet leadership is left in diplomatic isolation at the "Two-plus-Four" negotiations in February and March 1990.

7. In talks with Secretary of State James Baker and President Bush in February and June 1990, Gorbachev accepts their position on a unified Germany as a part of NATO without explicit security guarantees.

8. Gorbachev accepts Kohl's draft treaty between the USSR and a unified Germany without explicit security guarantees from a unified Germany in July 1990.

Naturally, this brief essay cannot address each of these episodes in detail. Fortunately, in one way or another most of them have already been described in scholarly literature.[3] This allows me to focus on a few key issues related to these variables. Where did the issue of German reunification fit in Gorbachev's policy agenda? What was the impact of domestic instability on Gorbachev's control over Soviet foreign policy and its German policy in particular? What was the impact of the Gorbachev factor, that is, the Soviet

3. Zelikow and Rice, *Germany Reunified and Europe Transformed*; Angela E. Stent, *Russia and Germany Reborn: Unification, the Soviet Collapse, and the New Europe* (Princeton, NJ: Princeton University Press, 1999); Jacques Lévesque, *The Enigma of 1989: The USSR and the Liberation of Eastern Europe* (Berkeley, CA: University of California Press, 1997).

leader's choices, preferences, and errors? To what extent did U.S. foreign policy constrain Gorbachev in promoting his agenda on Germany?

It is impossible to understand the dynamics of Soviet policy regarding Germany without taking seriously the assumptions and goals of Gorbachev's "new thinking." Among Western scholars, only a few acknowledge that in Gorbachev's relations with the West from 1988 to 1991, the new thinking in effect replaced traditional diplomacy rooted in realpolitik. As Jacques Lévesque notes, one of Gorbachev's principal objectives was "precisely to integrate the USSR into Europe structurally, and as solidly as possible. The disarray and obstinacy which the Soviet leaders demonstrated throughout all the discussions and negotiations surrounding German reunification must be understood in this context."[4]

The renunciation of force was a most important ideological innovation that enabled peaceful reunification of Germany. In internal communications among trusted officials (Shevardnadze, Yakovlev, Dobrynin, Falin, and Cherniaev), Gorbachev said in late October 1988 that he wanted his UN address to "present our worldview philosophy based on the results of [the] last three years. We should stress the process of demilitarization and humanization of our thinking."[5] Western and Eastern Europeans still doubted Gorbachev's sincerity, but the evidence as well as subsequent events demonstrate that he was earnest about renouncing the Brezhnev doctrine. In May 1989, after the publicized use of troops against civilian demonstrators in Tbilisi, Gorbachev said to the Politburo: "We have accepted that even in foreign policy force does not help

---

4. Lévesque, *The Enigma of 1989*, 225. The best Western study on the evolution and importance of the new thinking is by Robert D. English, *Russia and the Idea of the West: Gorbachev, Intellectuals and the End of the Cold War* (New York: Columbia University Press, 2000).

5. Anatoli Cherniaev's notes, October 31, 1988, Archive of the Gorbachev Foundation; also see Pavel Palazhchenko, *Gorbachev and Shevardnadze: The Memoir of a Soviet Interpreter* (University Park, PA: Pennsylvania State University Press, 1997), 103–104.

(*nichego ne daiet*). So especially internally—we cannot resort and will not resort to force."[6]

The new thinking was also relevant to German reunification for another reason. It left the German question, a key issue of Soviet foreign policy at least until the early 1970s, in limbo.[7] Fixated on his plan to integrate the USSR into Europe, Gorbachev began to look at the division of Germany not so much as a cornerstone of the geopolitical status quo but as an antiquated problem inherited from the past that was a major obstacle to his grand multilateral diplomacy of pan-European integration. While his relations worsened with the GDR's conservative and obstinate leader, Erich Honecker, his gaze shifted to the FRG's leadership. After years of boycotting Helmut Kohl because of his support for U.S. missile deployment in Europe and his unfortunate comparison of Gorbachev to Joseph Goebbels, Hitler's minister of propaganda, in October 1986, Gorbachev decided to make the chancellor his friend. A breakthrough came on October 28, 1988, when Kohl met Gorbachev for the first time in the Kremlin. The leaders quickly established a relationship of mutual trust. During his return visit to West Germany on June 11–15, 1989, Gorbachev believed he had secured Kohl's support for perestroika and his idea of a "common European home." In return, he took a tolerant stand when Kohl in effect suggested a joint interference in the affairs of the GDR in order to remove Honecker and encourage changes. Anatoli Cherniaev believes there was a deliberate double meaning in the joint FRG-USSR declaration that singled out from other principles and norms of international rights the "respect for the right for national self-

6. Cherniaev and Medvedev's notes at the Politburo, May 11, 1989. Discussion of the memorandum of six Politburo members on the situation in the Baltic Republics, Archive of the Gorbachev Foundation, fond 4, opis 1, and fond 2, opis 3, published in *The Union Could Be Preserved: The White Book: Documents and Facts about the Policy of M. S. Gorbachev to Reform and Preserve the Multi-National State* (Moscow: April Publishers, 1995), 52, 55.

7. Stent, *Russia and Germany Reborn*, 72.

determination.''[8] At the same time, Kohl privately assured Gorbachev that he and his government did not want "any destabilization" of the GDR.[9] This relationship was as crucial to the subsequent peaceful reunification of Germany as the relationship between Willy Brandt and Leonid Brezhnev had been to détente in the early 1970s.

Gorbachev and his advisers chose to trust Kohl because they needed his friendship. As a result, the Soviet leadership overlooked Kohl's exploitation of the growing instability in Eastern Europe to promote his agenda. On August 25, 1989, Kohl reached an understanding with the reformist leadership of Hungary to open the Hungarian-Austrian border to defectors from the GDR. In return, Hungary received DM 1 billion to cover its budget deficit. The details of this understanding, fateful for the GDR, came to light only years later.[10] What intelligence Moscow received is still unknown. But during Gorbachev's trip to Berlin to celebrate the fiftieth anniversary of the GDR, Honecker told him that Miklos Nemeth had received from the Social Democratic Party (SDP) a loan of DM 550 million on the condition that "Hungarians opened a border with Austria."[11] One may guess that Gorbachev, skeptical about anything that Erich Honecker said, dismissed this information.

When the crisis erupted in the GDR, Mikhail Gorbachev continued to rely on Kohl's personal assurances. As Lévesque points out, his major goal at the time remained the same, "but the whole problem was in the synchronization" between the Soviet-European

---

8. Third conversation of General Secretary Gorbachev and Chancellor Kohl, Bonn, (June 1989), notes of Cherniaev provided to the National Security Archive, Washington, DC.

9. Ibid.

10. Conversations of Chancellor Kohl and Foreign Minister Genscher with Prime Minister Nemeth and Foreign Minister Horn, Palais Gymnich, August 25, 1989, published in *Dokumente zur Deutschlandpolitik: Deutsche Einheit: Sonderedition aus den Akten des Bundeskanzleramtes 1989/90*, ed. Hanns Juergen Kusters and Daniel Hoffmann (Munich: R. Oldenbourg Verlag, 1998), 377–382.

11. Gorbachev's conversation with Erich Honecker, October 7, 1989, Archive of the Gorbachev Foundation, document provided to the National Security Archive, Washington, DC, by Cherniaev.

integration and the creation of a new security system on the one hand, and the pace of German reunification on the other.[12] In a telephone conversation with the Soviet leader on October 11, 1989, Kohl said: "The only thing that we want [is] that the GDR joins your course, the course of progressive reforms. . . . We do not intend to agitate them [the population of the GDR], urge them to any actions that later might lead others to criticize us." Gorbachev eagerly accepted the renewed reassurances.[13]

In another telephone conversation after the collapse of the Berlin Wall, Kohl reaffirmed his rejection of any course "for radicalization" of dynamics in the GDR "in any form." Gorbachev responded that relations among the USSR, the FRG, and the GDR should be "a triangle where everything should be well-considered and well-balanced. I believe that our present relationship allows [us] to do it this way." He warned that any "forced acceleration of events" might lead to "chaos."[14] When Kohl unilaterally proclaimed his Ten-Point Plan in December 1989 and shifted to the policy of *Wandel durch Kraft* (change through strength) with regard to the GDR, Gorbachev at first interpreted it as a preelection maneuver by the chancellor. He could not believe that Kohl had betrayed his trust.[15] When he realized his mistake a few days later, he expressed his feelings to Hans-Dietrich Genscher rather than to Kohl himself. It would be incorrect to ascribe Gorbachev's displeasure merely to his realization that he had no countermeasures against Kohl's program, a realization that came only at the end of January 1990. Rather, this shows that Gorbachev continued to put

---

12. Lévesque, *The Enigma of 1989*, 227.

13. From a telephone conversation between General Secretary Gorbachev and Chancellor Kohl, October 11, 1989, Archive of the Gorbachev Foundation, provided to the National Security Archive, Washington, DC, by Cherniaev.

14. From a telephone conversation between General Secretary Gorbachev and Chancellor Kohl, November 11, 1989, Archive of the Gorbachev Foundation, provided to the National Security Archive, Washington, DC, by Cherniaev.

15. From a telephone conversation between General Secretary Gorbachev and Giulio Andreotti, Chairman of the Council of Ministers of Italy, Rome, November 29, 1989, Archive of the Gorbachev Foundation, provided to the National Security Archive, Washington, DC, by Cherniaev.

his other goals well above the German question and for that reason saw no alternatives to partnership with Kohl, despite his intense displeasure with his actions.

The primacy of the integrationist agenda over the dangers of the German question may also explain the otherwise inexplicable failure of Gorbachev to address the events in Germany in a systematic manner. There was no "fire brigade" or "crisis group" on Germany in the Soviet leadership. Nor was Gorbachev interested in engaging Bush on this issue at the Malta summit on December 2–3, 1989. He also "forfeited a chance to define the agenda"[16] when he rebuffed Kohl's proposal to come to Moscow for a talk after he announced his Ten-Point Plan. The first special meeting on Germany took place on January 27, 1990, two and one-half months after the collapse of the Berlin Wall.

A second issue is the impact of the domestic crisis on Gorbachev's German policy. President Bush frequently expressed his conviction that there could have been a much more aggressive and violent reaction to the collapse of the Berlin Wall from the Soviet side. In particular, he pointed to the hard-liners in the Soviet leadership and the frustrated military. Most scholars of German reunification imply that Gorbachev had to look over his shoulder at Egor Ligachev and other hard-liners in the Politburo and elsewhere. Also, Shevardnadze and his assistant Sergei Tarasenko later recalled their concern that the German question might undermine Gorbachev and his policies. The memories of war with Nazi Germany still colored public opinion in the Soviet Union, and there was a potential threat that Gorbachev might be blamed for selling the shop in dealing with the GDR.[17]

Indeed, by early 1990, government officials and military leaders carried on an open discussion in the Soviet media regarding available options for dealing with the German issue. Yet, the available

---

16. Quote from Zelikow and Rice, *Germany Unified and Europe Transformed*, 147.

17. Stent, *Russia and Germany Reborn*, 101; Zelikow and Rice, *Germany Unified and Europe Transformed*, 445, fn 118.

evidence does not indicate any real danger to Gorbachev's position from any opposition groups from the winter of 1989 through the spring of 1990. While it is true that Gorbachev unleashed forces that he ultimately could not control, those forces had the temporary effect of rallying the old political and bureaucratic elites around their leader. The party functionaries raised in the tradition of total obedience to the supreme leader could not think of expressing any political opposition to Gorbachev. As a result, despite growing domestic criticism of his leadership, Gorbachev retained firm control over Soviet foreign policy. He made decisions on most important questions not at the Politburo but among his narrow circle of advisers or, in some cases, together with Foreign Minister Shevardnadze. As this method of decision making was a natural prerogative of the general secretary, it was not contested. Leading figures with hard-line reputations, such as Egor Ligachev, had no foreign policy experience and did not contest, either then or later, Gorbachev's right as the party's general secretary to monopolize foreign affairs.

Only in the spring of 1990 did the domestic backlash begin to focus on the "loss" of the GDR.[18] Preemptively, Gorbachev threatened at a stormy Politburo meeting on May 3, 1990, to scuttle, if necessary, the Vienna arms control talks and strategic weapons talks in order to prevent a unified Germany from gaining membership in NATO. A milder position developed by Shevardnadze and his assistant Tarasenko was cosponsored by Aleksandr Yakovlev, Minister of Defense Dmitri Yazov, and KGB chairman Vladimir Kriuchkov, who accepted Gorbachev's stance without argument.[19]

Nevertheless, even at that time domestic pressure for a hard line was counterbalanced by another domestic concern: the rapidly developing economic and financial crisis of the USSR. By early 1990,

---

18. Cherniaev, *Shest Let s Gorbachevym: Po dnevnikovym zapisiam* (Moscow: Progress-Kultura, 1993), 347.

19. On this episode, see Zelikow and Rice, *Germany Reunified and Europe Transformed*, 224–245.

the Soviet economy was practically bankrupt and in desperate need of Western loans. As Gorbachev threatened a tough stand on German membership in NATO, Cherniaev reminded him that this "blackmail" would have been "too risky, above all from [an] economic viewpoint."[20] Zelikow and Rice note that the Soviets contacted Bonn with requests for a large loan on May 7–8.[21] Yet Gorbachev began to solicit Bush for money as early as the Malta summit.

Domestic pressures affected Gorbachev's German policies in other indirect ways. In the fall of 1989 he was immersed in domestic politics, particularly at the sessions of the Congress of People's Deputies that he chaired, and other crisis situations at home. The main issues that determined Gorbachev's political future were failing political and economic reforms (perestroika) and growing domestic instability, particularly the calls for independence in the south Caucasus and the Baltic states. Characteristically, on November 9, 1989, a few hours before the Berlin Wall fell, the Politburo was in session discussing the separatist claims of the Baltic republics.[22] This continued to be the hottest issue during the key months of January through March 1990, when the outlines of German reunification were taking place. For Moscow policymakers, the preservation of the Soviet Union psychologically overshadowed issues of foreign policy.[23] It is plausible that domestic issues, including the crisis in the Baltic states, prevented Gorbachev and

---

20. Cherniaev's notes to General Secretary Gorbachev, May 4, 1990, Archive of the Gorbachev Foundation, fond 2 (Cherniaev's papers), opis 1. For the excellent exploration of the financial crisis in the USSR see: Egor Gaidar, *Gibel Imperii. Uroki dlia sovremennoi Rossii* [Demise of the Empire. The Lessons for Today's Russia] (Moscow: Rosspen, 2006).

21. Zelikow and Rice, *Germany Unified and Europe Transformed*, 256–259.

22. Minutes of Cherniaev, Archive of the Gorbachev Foundation, fond 2, opis 3, published with excerpts in A. B. Veber and A. S. Cherniaev, *Soiuz mozhno bylo sokhranit* [The Union Could be Preserved] (Moscow: Aprel'-85, 1995), 75–77.

23. The diaries of Gorbachev's main foreign policy assistant, Anatoli Cherniaev, from the spring of 1989 to the spring of 1990 are peppered with pessimism, even despair, regarding the future of the Soviet Union and Gorbachev's reforms. See Cherniaev, *Shest Let*, 294–295, 337–338.

the Soviet leadership from focusing sufficiently on the German crisis.

Increasingly, Gorbachev devoted himself to the business of building personal relationships with foreign leaders and pursuing the general goal of ending the cold war on the basis of East-West integration. He delegated to Shevardnadze and his assistants the tactics and modalities of Soviet policies on particular foreign policy issues, including the German question. Many important specific issues were discussed and resolved along back channels between Horst Teltschik and Cherniaev, as well as between Shevardnadze, his assistant Sergei Tarasenko, and James Baker, Dennis Ross, and Robert Zoellick.[24] It is unclear to what extent Gorbachev kept track of all this.

This growing laxness accompanied by elements of chaos in the formerly centralized Soviet foreign policy may explain the enigmatic episode at the Ottawa negotiations in February 1990 when Shevardnadze accepted the Western change from the "Four-plus-Two" to the "Two-plus-Four" formula. In the war of recollections, Valentin Falin claimed this was done unilaterally and without instructions, while Cherniaev argued that the whole issue made no sense because it was already politically impossible to insist on the occupation rights of the four powers over East and West Germany. In the discussion on January 27, however, it was Cherniaev who corrected Gorbachev (who apparently saw no difference between the two formulas) and proposed the "Four-plus-Two" version as the basis for Shevardnadze's instructions.[25] And it was Cherniaev who wrote to Gorbachev on May 4 to say that Shevardnadze indeed "arbitrarily agreed to change the formula into 'Two-plus-Four,' although both Thatcher and Mitterrand were ready to support us."[26] Shevardnadze apparently got away easily with this and other mistakes.

---

24. Sergei Tarasenko and Robert Zoellick, in conversations with the author.

25. Cherniaev's notes of the meeting, which he provided to the Thomas Watson Institute of Brown University and the National Security Archives.

26. Cherniaev's notes to General Secretary Gorbachev, May 4, 1990, Archive of the Gorbachev Foundation, fond 2 (Cherniaev's papers), opis 1.

The Soviet Union's remarkable acquiescence with the destruction of the GDR and unified Germany's membership in NATO is ultimately explained by Gorbachev himself—his personality, choices, judgments, and temperament. Western leaders were frequently amazed and overjoyed that the Soviet leader voluntarily gave them what they had expected to obtain only through hard bargaining and mutual concessions. As a result, the United States and West Germany achieved optimal political results without having to accept any binding legal commitments or limitations on their future behavior.[27]

It is tempting to explain Gorbachev's attitudes from the angle of realism. Zelikow and Rice write that the U.S. and West German governments discreetly decided in February 1990 to proceed with the annexation of the GDR within the framework of NATO, even if the Soviets stalled.[28] Indeed, by early 1990 the Soviet leadership had few levers left beyond the presence of their troops in the GDR. Gorbachev's advocates also claim that he understandably misjudged the situation in the GDR after the collapse of the wall. Indeed, in November and December no one expected that the GDR would begin to disintegrate so quickly that there would be no transition period at all.[29]

Gorbachev's conversations at the time and Cherniaev's notes to Gorbachev support these explanations, yet much of Gorbachev's behavior remains difficult to understand. In general, as I have argued earlier, Gorbachev's belief in his new thinking allowed him to see German developments in a light that was radically detached from traditional geopolitical worries. In November and even December of 1989, Thatcher and Mitterrand appeared to be more

---

27. See Cherniaev, "Ob'edineniie Germanii: Politicheskiie mekhanizmy i psikhologicheskie stereotipy," *Svobodnaia Misl*, August 1997, 25–34; Alexander Galkin and Anatoli Cherniaev, "Pravdu, i tolko pravdu: Razmyshleniia po povodu vosppominanii," *Svobodnaia Misl*, January-February 1994, 19–29.

28. Zelikow and Rice, *Germany Unified and Europe Transformed*, 246.

29. Galkin and Cherniaev, "Pravdu," 23.

concerned than Gorbachev was about the fall of the wall and the future of the GDR. Gorbachev took his own ideas too seriously and was too detached from pragmatic considerations. New thinking took precedence over not only the immediate interests of the negotiating process but also Soviet interests.

From the very beginning of the German crisis, Gorbachev voluntarily renounced both direct and indirect use of force. He also refrained from political and economic pressure on the GDR and other Eastern European states. This left the Soviet leadership with only diplomatic means to influence the situation in Germany on the eve of reunification. When Kohl launched his campaign for reunification, Gorbachev never consistently pursued a campaign of counterpressure. Despite encouragement from Thatcher and Mitterrand to bolster the GDR leadership and confront Kohl, Gorbachev never exerted serious effort on either count.

Gorbachev's friends argue that the Soviet leader demonstrated a high moral standard of statesmanship and global responsibility by rejecting the art of diplomacy and narrow gamesmanship.[30] It is not clear, however, why one excluded the other. Gorbachev's partners in the West managed to combine the same degree of responsibility and statesmanship with considerable skills in achieving their diplomatic aims. The explanation lies not so much in the realization of the unfavorable balance of forces (by his inaction, Gorbachev made this balance even more unfavorable) as in the combination of personal predilections and the ideological self-image of the Soviet leader.

With his messianic streak, Gorbachev viewed himself not only as a Soviet leader but as a global statesman. Cherniaev, in many ways an alter ego of Gorbachev, though more direct, jotted in his diary after the fall of the Berlin Wall: "A total dismantling of socialism as a world phenomenon has been taking place. This may be inevitable and good. For this is a reunification of mankind on the

---

30. Ibid.

basis of common sense. And a common fellow from Stavropol [Gorbachev] set this process in motion."[31]

Gorbachev had a personal aversion to confrontation and forceful projection of power. He preferred compromise and consensus in both domestic and foreign policy. The Bush administration relied on Gorbachev's commonsense acceptance that the United States had won the cold war and could dictate its outcome. On October 11, 1989, Bush told NATO Secretary General Manfred Wörner that the main objective was to persuade the Soviets to allow continued change in Eastern Europe and the GDR. When Wörner warned that Gorbachev would not let the GDR leave the Warsaw Pact, Bush wondered if he could persuade Gorbachev that the military value of the Warsaw Pact was no longer essential and he should let it go. "That may seem naïve," Bush said, "but who predicted the changes we are seeing today?"[32] One could hardly imagine any U.S. leader trying to persuade Stalin, Khrushchev, Brezhnev, or Andropov to relinquish Soviet influence in Europe.

At Malta, Gorbachev, who was eager to develop a personal partnership with Bush, avoided taking a confrontational stance on Germany. After criticizing Kohl's Ten-Point Plan, he sidestepped the issue of the military and political status of a unified Germany, stating that "it would be *premature to discuss now one* [neutrality] *or the other* [membership in NATO] *scenario.*" He continued by saying, "There are two German states, so history ordered. And let history now decide how the process should evolve and where it should lead to in the context of [a] new Europe and the new world."[33] From the U.S. perspective, Gorbachev did not exclude the option of NATO's advance to the East.

---

31. Archive of the Gorbachev Foundation, fond 2, opis 2. This entry was omitted from Cherniaev, *1991 god: Dnevnik Pomoschnika Prezidenta SSSR* (Moscow: TERRA, 1997).
32. The record of the meeting is cited in Zelikow and Rice, *Germany Unified and Europe Transformed*, 398–399.
33. Soviet record of a one-on-one conversation between General Secretary Gorbachev and President Bush, December 2, 1989, Archive of the Gorbachev Foundation.

Returning to Zelikow and Rice's thesis about the limited choices Gorbachev had by February 1990, one may wonder what would have happened if the Soviet leadership had consistently advocated binding legal commitments for NATO not to advance to the East. Given the complexities of European and German public opinion, particularly widespread uneasiness about Germany's expansion and the position of Mitterrand and Thatcher, it is not at all clear that Kohl and Bush would have been able to proceed while totally ignoring Soviet demands for security guarantees.

Gorbachev's performance during German reunification was as much a reflection of his personal political style as of his domestic policy of perestroika. Foes and friends alike highlight Gorbachev's "ad hocism," his characteristic lack of a long-range strategic plan, and his aversion to the practical details of governance. They all recognize that perestroika had no plan and the new thinking was vague and could not be a practical guide for reform. Gorbachev's favorite phrases, in addition to "unpredictability," were "let processes develop" and "processes are on the run" (*protsessi poshli*). In the judgment of one of his sympathizers, Gorbachev's leadership mirrored his excessively optimistic view of people in general, and the Russian populace in particular. "It always seemed to him that people could not help but be glad to organize their own lives for themselves."[34] Gorbachev addressed the German question with similar historic optimism and "ad hocism," as abundantly illustrated by his repeated allusions to history. Zelikow and Rice describe how, on his visit to Berlin in October 1989, Gorbachev oddly quoted the Russian poet Fedor Tiutchev, who wrote that instead of "iron and blood . . . we will try to forge [German unity] with love." While it certainly inspired Wim Wenders, it was, as U.S. scholars and politicians note, "a strange way for the leader of the Soviet Union to warn the FRG to respect the 'postwar realities.'"[35]

---

34. Dmitri Furman, "Fenomen Gorbacheva," *Svobodnaia Misl*, November 1995, 65.

35. Zelikow and Rice, *Germany Unified and Europe Transformed*, 83.

Gorbachev's advocates assert that there was "a conceptual-moral, if one may use this term, recognition that it is abnormal to divide forcibly a great nation and it is wrong to condemn the entire people forever for the crimes of its leaders."[36]

Gorbachev's moral standing paid off for him personally and for the future relationship between Germany and Russia. In the meantime, however, the Soviet Union and then Russia were marginalized in the process of European integration and building European security.

Finally, a few words on the impact of U.S. leadership on the Kremlin during the process of German reunification. In the months leading to the collapse of the Berlin Wall, the Bush administration displayed as little foresight as Gorbachev and his assistants concerning the dynamics in Germany. No U.S. officials predicted the rapid developments that led to the fall of the Berlin Wall. Even after the event, only a few of them, particularly Ambassador Vernon Walters, believed that German reunification would take place within a few years, and nobody foresaw that it would occur within one year. The Bush administration, however, gained a huge strategic advantage over Gorbachev when Bush decided to stand firmly behind Kohl in support of his course of annexation of the GDR. Bush was also as effective in quelling the brewing antiunification sentiments among NATO allies as Gorbachev was ineffective in exploiting them.

Zelikow and Rice point persuasively to several levers that the Bush administration possessed by January 1990. They include:

- the commitment of Bush since the summer of 1989 to avoid destabilization of Eastern Europe, demonstrated during his visit to Poland and Hungary;
- the commitment of Bush at the Malta summit in December 1989 to give direct and indirect assistance to Gorbachev and his course of perestroika; and

---

36. Galkin and Cherniaev, "Pravdu," 22.

- the agreement of Bush at the Malta summit to maintain neutrality toward the movements for national liberation in the
  Baltic states as long as Gorbachev refrained from the use of
  force there.

The U.S. impact on Gorbachev and Soviet policy, however, was
exerted more through persuasion than containment and coercion,
much to the credit of President Bush and his assistants. Bush's style
reassured Gorbachev while helping him make concessions without
looking like a pawn in American hands. The most important moments in this regard were the Malta summit, a meeting with Secretary James Baker in February 1990, and the Washington summit of
June 1990.

U.S. tactics of persuasion would not have been so effective had
Gorbachev and certain members of his team not been eager to become close partners with Bush. This was a unique, perhaps unprecedented, time when the politicians and analysts of the dying Soviet
superpower developed psychological dependence on their former
enemies and geopolitical rivals. This undoubtedly was the product
of Soviet domestic pressures, which also played a role in the talks
on German unification. Increasingly beleaguered at home and es-
tranged from conservative, hard-line colleagues, Gorbachev, Shevardnadze, Yakovlev, Cherniaev, and Tarasenko began to look at
their foreign counterparts as allies and trusted friends. With the exception of Gorbachev himself, they also feared an imminent collapse of the USSR and the reform movement. In late February
1990, Cherniaev noted in his diary that he had spoken with
Thatcher's foreign policy assistant, Percy Cradock, "without any
self-censorship" and completely forgot he was not one of the
"comrades."[37] U.S. as well as West German statesmen and diplomats exploited this unique mood without fully understanding its
nature and causes. A similar forthcoming and candid attitude from
their side would have qualified as treason.

---

37. Cherniaev, *1991 god*, 28.

Gorbachev, Shevardnadze, and their assistants dismiss the notion that there were significant events following the collapse of the Berlin Wall that stimulated the German people to express their will for unification. With the wisdom of hindsight, they deny that different Soviet policies could have produced different outcomes. At the same time, in an essay published in 1997, Cherniaev regrets that the collapse of the USSR and other radical changes in the international environment precluded "the Moscow-Berlin axis." This, he writes, would have become "the decisive factor of the real European process" in integration, but it "degenerated into the process of NATO expansion."[38] However, in January 1990, long before the Soviet Union collapsed, Cherniaev predicted the same result: "It is increasingly obvious that [a] 'Common European Home' will exist (if it will!) without us, without the USSR, and for a while we will live as 'neighbors.'"[39]

It is hoped that this modest analysis will help to restore the notion that diplomacy was important after all. The Russian perspective, informed by international research, allows us to discern the moments when a more energetic, systematic, pragmatic, and realist form of Soviet diplomacy might have altered the process of German reunification and the future course of European history. If Gorbachev had possessed the will and foresight for preemptive diplomacy, perhaps his partners in the United States would feel somewhat less dominant today. Contempt for the "cynical traditionalists of diplomacy," as expressed by some of Gorbachev's friends in an effort to protect him from later criticism, is irrelevant in a balanced historical analysis.

---

38. Cherniaev, "Ob'edineniie Germanii," 25, 34.
39. Cherniaev, *1991 god*, 27.

CHAPTER 7

Michael McFaul *Boris Yeltsin: Catalyst for the Cold War's End*

INDIVIDUALS MATTER. Ironically, this simple hypothesis about politics receives little attention in the social sciences today. Although we have many well-developed theories about the role of institutions, classes, modernization, and power in the social sciences, we have very few theories that give a causal role to the individual. Structures—not agents—still enjoy a privileged position in the modern canon of social science theory. Even rational choice theory—a model of how individual choices produce social outcomes—reduces the role of the individual to a utility maximizer. In this role, the personality, beliefs, and actual decisions of a *specific* individual do not matter since the aim of the rational choice project is to provide a *general* theory for all human behavior.[1] In place of historical figures with first and last names, individuals become faceless players in strategic situations, usually represented by the variables x or y.

One consequence of this explanatory approach is that much theoretical work in political science focuses on elucidating equilibria phenomena.[2] Rational choice methodologists have devoted particu-

---

1. In their search for general theories, social scientists end up focusing their energies on repetitive, static phenomena rather than unique, dynamic situations.

2. Regarding legislative theories, representative and overview works include Kenneth Shepsle and Barry Weingast, "Structure-Induced Equilibrium and Legislative Choice," *Public Choice* 37 (1981): 503–519; Barry Weingast and William Marshall, "The Industrial Organization of Congress; or Why Legislatures, Like Firms, Are Not Organized as Markets," *Journal of Political Economy* 96, no. 11 (1988): 132–163; and Terry Moe, "An Assessment of the Positive Political Theory

lar attention to modeling and explaining stability. As Robert Bates and Barry Weingast write, "The greatest achievement of rational choice theory has been to provide tools for studying political outcomes in *stable* institutional settings."[3] Theorists of equilibria phenomena tend to downplay, dismiss, or ignore moments of rapid change, such as the end of the cold war, especially when the change in question is unexpected, radical, and hence, by definition, exogenous to models concerned with representing static and recurrent outcomes. Kenneth Waltz has gone so far as to assert that theories should not even *aspire* to explain change because "a theory explains continuities. It tells one what to expect and why to expect it. Within a system, a theory explains recurrences and repetitions, not change."[4] Consistent with Waltz's recommendation, many of our most robust theories seek to explain the lack of change: why the rules of the U.S. Congress "make public policy stable and predictable when it might be expected to be arbitrary," why countries do not go to war even when the anarchy of the international system permits, if not encourages, them to do so, or why political systems persist even when they stunt economic growth.[5] In Soviet studies,

---

of 'Congressional Dominance,'" *Legislative Studies Quarterly* 12, no. 4 (November 1987): 475–519. As Moe writes, in summarizing this literature, "Its contributors have been concerned, most abstractly, with moving from models of voting—especially models of pure majority rule with their attendant emphasis on voting cycles and system instability—to an understanding of how institutional rules can shape collective choice and induce the kinds of stability we actually observe in politics." (476). In international relations, see Kenneth Waltz, *Theory of International Politics* (Reading, MA: Addison-Wesley, 1979); and Hans Morgenthau, *Politics Among Nations: The Struggle for Peace* (New York: Alfred Knopf, 1954). In comparative politics, see Carl Friedriech and Zbigniew Brzezinski, *Totalitarian Dictatorship and Autocracy* (Cambridge, MA: Harvard University Press, 1956); and Juan Linz, "Totalitarian and Authoritarian Regimes," in *Handbook of Political Science*, ed. Fred Greenstein and Nelson Polsby (Reading, MA: Addison-Wesley, 1975), 3.

3. Robert Bates and Barry Weingast, "Rationality and Interpretation: The Politics of Transition," unpublished manuscript, June 1996. Emphasis added.

4. Waltz, *Theory of International Politics*, 69.

5. The summary quote about American institutional approaches to the study of Congress comes from Robert Bates, "Macropolitical Economy in the Field of Development," in *Perspectives on Positive Political Economy*, ed. James Alt and Kenneth Shepsle (Cambridge: Cambridge University Press, 1990), 46.

as well, there was a "theoretical bias in the direction of stability."[6] Explaining change in these systemic equilibria—be it the Gingrich revolution of 1994, the collapse of the bipolar international system in 1989, or the sudden end of the Soviet regime in 1991—is beyond the domain of static theories. And the role of the individual in bringing about these rapid, unexpected changes receives almost no attention whatsoever.[7]

The absence of real, live people in social science theory today stands in sharp contrast to how practitioners, journalists, and even historians describe and explain history. The memoirs of former presidents and prime ministers are filled with anecdotes about the importance of individual relationships or key (and unique) decisions. The recent explosion of millennium lists focused almost entirely on the role of great men and women in the making of history. In their careful study of causality, historians are not afraid to evaluate the role of individuals as one of several factors that produce specific historical outcomes. Moreover, these accounts of history often focus on unique, unexpected events rather than static phenomena or recurrent behavior. For instance, historians have produced hundreds and hundreds of volumes on World War II, many of which include detailed accounts of the roles of individuals such as Hitler, Stalin, Churchill, and Roosevelt, but very few international relations specialists have devoted serious attention to explaining this unique event.

These two views of politics need to be integrated. Obviously, structures and strategic situations shape, constrain, and mediate the decisions and actions of individuals. At the same time, individuals do make specific decisions in unique contexts that shape the course of history.

---

6. Thomas Remington, "Soviet Political Studies and the Problem of System Stability," in *Beyond Soviet Studies*, ed. Daniel Orlovsky (Washington, DC: Woodrow Wilson Center Press, 1995), 180.

7. A notable, important exception is Paul Hollander, *Political Will and Personal Belief: The Decline and Fall of Soviet Communism* (New Haven, CT: Yale University Press, 1999).

In certain contexts, individuals make these decisions not only out of self-interest but also because of an attachment to certain ideas. This is the second hypothesis of this essay: ideas matter. The beliefs, ideas, or even ideologies that individuals embrace can have a causal influence on political outcomes. If powerful individuals embrace these ideas, then they can change the very course of a state's history and the very structure of the international system. Alone, individuals and ideas do not alter the course of history. Power and interest always come into play. Under certain conditions, however, this fusion of unique individuals and new ideas can catalyze revolutionary change.

Such a fusion occurred in the late 1980s in the Soviet Union when Boris Yeltsin embraced anti-Communist ideology. Soviet economic decline and Gorbachev's response to it—perestroika, glasnost, and democratization—created the permissive conditions conducive to the emergence of both a historical figure such as Yeltsin and revolutionary ideas such as democracy and capitalism. Without Gorbachev and his reforms, there would have been no Yeltsin and no revolution. Yet, the converse is probably also true; without Yeltsin and the revolutionary ideas he embraced, the Soviet Union might have avoided or at least prolonged its collapse, the basic institutions of the Soviet economy and polity might have survived, and, in turn, the cold war might not have ended when and how it did. To be sure, the cold war was well on its way to ending before the rise of Yeltsin. And the Soviet Union was bound to collapse someday. However, as Michael Dobbs has written, "There was nothing inevitable about the timing of the collapse or the manner in which it occurred."[8] Soviet and U.S. competition fueled by competing world visions would have lingered well beyond 1991 if the coup plotters in August 1991 had succeeded. At a minimum, Yeltsin and his ideas accelerated the process of Soviet domestic change, which in turn helped to end the cold war.

---

8. Michael Dobbs, *Down with Big Brother: The Fall of the Soviet Empire* (New York: Alfred A. Knopf, 1997), 451.

This chapter makes this argument in three increments. Section one recounts how and why Yeltsin became a challenger to the Soviet *ancien régime*. Section two then chronicles how and why Yeltsin came to embrace liberal, anti-Communist ideas championed by Russia's democratic movement, a marriage that was not inevitable. Section three demonstrates how the combination of Yeltsin and these revolutionary ideas helped to destroy communism, dissolve the Soviet empire, and thereby facilitate the end of the cold war.

Boris Yeltsin, Accidental Rebel

For the first three decades of his professional career, it would have been impossible to predict that Boris Yeltsin would one day help to destroy the Soviet Union.[9] Whereas Vaclav Havel in Czechoslovakia and Lech Walesa in Poland focused their energies on undermining communism, Yeltsin was devoted to making communism function better. Havel and Walesa served time in jail for their efforts; Yeltsin won promotion. Yeltsin had a reputation within the CPSU as a populist crusader who worked hard to fulfill the plan, improve the economic well-being of his people, and fight corruption. It was his reformist credentials, after all, that compelled Mikhail Gorbachev to bring him to Moscow to become the capital's first secretary. As Dusko Doder and Louise Branson wrote in 1990, "Boris Yeltsin in many ways typified the new 'perestroika gang' assembled by Gorbachev."[10] Yet Yeltsin was not a dissident. During his years as a rising star within the Soviet Communist Party, Yeltsin was not reading Thomas Jefferson, Friedrich Hayek, or Robert Conquest. His embrace of democratic, market, and anti-imperial ideas came only after his fall from grace within the Communist Party.

That fall occurred soon after Yeltsin arrived in Moscow in 1985.

---

9. The definitive biography, especially detailed in these early years, is by Leon Aron, *Yeltsin: A Revolutionary Life* (New York: St. Martin's Press, 2000).

10. Dusko Doder and Louise Branson, *Gorbachev: Heretic in the Kremlin* (New York: Futura Publications, 1990), 103.

That year, Gorbachev directed Yeltsin to leave his post as CPSU first secretary in Sverdlovsk Oblast and assume the position of head of construction within the Central Committee. Only six months later, Gorbachev asked Yeltsin to become the first secretary of the Moscow Communist Party, replacing Viktor Grishin, a potential rival to Gorbachev.[11] Curiously, Yeltsin was not made a Politburo member but instead was appointed as a candidate member, even though first secretaries from lesser regions, such as Egor Ligachev from Tomsk, had been promoted to the Politburo before him.

Upon his arrival in Moscow, Yeltsin immediately seized upon Gorbachev's anticorruption slogans and pushed openly for more radical changes.[12] Yeltsin's anticorruption speeches, coupled with his populist proclivities (he used to ride the metro and the bus to work) earned him immediate popularity in Moscow. Whether for personal or ideological reasons, Yeltsin became increasingly incensed by Gorbachev's lack of attention to corruption issues and he began to make bolder statements that threatened the core principles of Communist Party rule.[13] In response, Gorbachev removed Yeltsin as first secretary and demoted him to deputy chairman of the Ministry of Construction in 1987. Gorbachev, however, was not satisfied with simply removing Yeltsin. In a dramatic episode, he ordered Yeltsin out of the hospital and forced him to convene a plenum of the Moscow Party Committee in order to admit to his mistakes as first secretary. Gorbachev personally attended the meeting to watch the humiliation.[14] This event crystallized the per-

---

11. John Morrison, *Boris Yeltsin: From Bolshevik to Democrat* (New York: Dutton Books, 1991), 43.

12. See, for instance, Matlock's description of Yeltsin and his views at an August 1987 meeting in Matlock, *Autopsy on an Empire: The American Ambassador's Account of the Collapse of the Soviet Union* (New York: Random House, 1995), 112–113; and Aron, *Yeltsin*, chapter four.

13. In Fedor Burlatski's estimation, Yeltsin wanted to be included in Gorbachev's inner circle of liberal reformers within the Politburo, but was never invited to join. See Fedor Burlatski, *Russkie Gosudari: Epokha Reformatsii* (Moscow: Shark, 1996), 214–215.

14. Yeltsin exacted his revenge in August 1991 when he made Gorbachev sit through a humiliating session of the Russian Congress of People's Deputies at which Gorbachev's role in failing to prevent the coup attempt was discussed.

sonal animosity between the two men, a hatred that eventually had consequences for the fate of the Soviet Union itself.[15] Yeltsin also felt betrayed by the Communist Party as an organization, a grudge upon which he later had the opportunity to act.

The so-called Yeltsin affair was a single incident without immediate consequences. Analysts in the West, for instance, predicted that Yeltsin's political career was over. In the past, such a demotion signaled the end of one's political career in the Soviet system. According to memoirs written by his aides at the time, Yeltsin's behavior after this demotion indicated that he himself believed his political career had ended. He began drinking heavily, and some report that he even attempted suicide.

Reviving an Old Enemy: Gorbachev's Democratization

Gorbachev, however, inadvertently resuscitated Yeltsin's political prospects by introducing pluralist reforms in the summer of 1988. Yeltsin's greatness as a political leader and his role in helping to end the cold war would not have been realized without changes in the political institutions of the Soviet Union—changes over which he had little control or influence. Structure most certainly shaped Yeltsin's opportunities and actions as an individual political actor. Once these political changes occurred, Yeltsin took advantage of the new context in ways never predicted by the designers of the institutional reforms, including Gorbachev himself.

As Gorbachev makes clear in his own memoirs, he initially introduced limited democratic reform not as an objective in itself but rather as a means for pursuing economic reform. Even before becoming general secretary, Gorbachev took a more critical view of the health of the economy than most of his Politburo colleagues.

---

15. Gorbachev himself explains the "Yeltsin affair" as a scandal concocted by Yeltsin himself to win popular support. See Mikhail Gorbachev, *Memoirs* (New York: Doubleday, 1996), 242–248; Boris Yeltsin, *Ispoved' na Zadannuiu Temu* (Leningrad: Sovetskii Pisatel, 1990); and Fedor Burlatski, *Russkie Gosudari: Epokha Reformatsii*, 216–218.

When he became general secretary in the spring of 1985, economic reform was his primary focus. Gorbachev's first attempts at reform resembled other Soviet reform efforts that focused on making the current system work faster and more efficiently.[16] When these strategies did not produce results, Gorbachev introduced more radical ideas under the rubric of perestroika. Though short on specifics, Gorbachev conceptualized perestroika as a revolutionary reordering of economic and social life within the Soviet Union. The very word, "perestroika" (restructuring), implied sweeping and fundamental change in the economic organization of the Soviet system.

Gorbachev and his government did introduce some important economic reforms, including self-financing and increased autonomy for enterprises, and eventually even partially private property in the form of collectives. However, Gorbachev was not satisfied with the pace of economic change, and he blamed the entrenched *nomenklatura* within the CPSU as the chief impediment. Even after he succeeded in purging the party's upper echelons, Gorbachev still worried that the CPSU was a hindrance rather than a vanguard for perestroika.[17] Consequently, Gorbachev believed that political reform had to be introduced as a strategy for weakening the conservatives within the CPSU. In other words, he saw political reform as a means to spur further economic reform.[18]

By allowing greater freedom of the press and new rights of assembly, Gorbachev hoped to stimulate societal allies for perestroika. Most dramatically, however, he spelled out a radical program for political reform at the Nineteenth Party Conference in the summer of 1988, which included a new, semicompetitive electoral system for selecting deputies to the Soviet Congress of Peo-

---

16. Mikhail Gorbachev, *Politicheskii Doklad Tsentral'nogo Komiteta KPSS XXVII S'ezdu Kommunisticheskoi Partii Sovetskogo Soiuza* (Moscow: Polizdat, February 25, 1986).

17. Gorbachev, *Memoirs*, 282.

18. For elaboration, see part one of Michael McFaul, *Russia's Unfinished Transition: Political Change Under Gorbachev and Yeltsin* (Ithaca, NY: Cornell University Press, 2001).

ple's Deputies.[19] Gorbachev essentially wanted to strengthen the mandate of these so-called legislative institutions and weaken the power of the party. If the party could not become the instrument of economic change, then perhaps a revitalized state could. Approved at the twentieth session of the USSR Supreme Soviet in December 1988, the constitutional amendments governing elections to the 1989 Soviet Congress of People's Deputies outlined a freer and fairer process for elections than ever before witnessed in Soviet history.[20]

Yet these elections were only partially free and competitive.[21] A third of the seats were not open to competitive elections but were reserved for social organizations. Some of these social entities did allow for competition within their organizations, but most did not. The CPSU and its allies also controlled the nominations process. Nonetheless, the elections to the Soviet Congress of People's Deputies, held during the spring of 1989, provided Yeltsin with an opportunity to resurrect his political career. He took full advantage of it.

Although encouraged to compete in several regions of Russia by voter initiative groups, Yeltsin decided to run in the largest electoral district in the country, the all-city district in Moscow. He ran an essentially antiestablishment campaign, calling the party's leadership corrupt and vowing to roll back the privileges of the party's ruling elite.[22] However, his attacks, aimed at the party-state bureau-

19. *Materialy XIX Vsesoiuznoi konferentsii KPSS*, 120.

20. For a summary and discussion of the law, see the interview with Central Electoral Commission Chairman V. P. Orlov in *Sovetskaia Rossiia*, March 14, 1989, 1. For a chronicle of the electoral reform process leading up to the 1989 elections, see Peter Lentini, "Reforming the Electoral System: The 1989 Elections to the USSR Congress of People's Deputies," *The Journal of Communist Studies* 7, no. 1, 69–94.

21. For comprehensive discussions of nondemocratic features of the law, see M. L. Gerver, "Predlagaiu izmenit' nashu izbiratel'nuiu sistemu," *Sovetskoe Gosudarstvo i Pravo* 7 (1990): 78–85; and Nikolai Biriukov and Viktor Sergeev, *Russia's Road to Democracy: Parliament, Communism and Traditional Culture* (Aldershot, Hants, England: Edward Elgar Publishing, 1993), 96–100.

22. For the blow-by-blow account of the campaign, see Boris Yeltsin, *Against the Grain: An Autobiography* (London: Pan Books, 1991).

cracy, fell short of calling for a new political or economic system altogether. In 1989, Yeltsin had not formed a coherent set of political or economic ideas, but was instead tapping into the high levels of public resentment toward the ruling elite.

At this stage in his new career, Yeltsin's allies were members of voter clubs from large enterprises located in working-class neighborhoods of Moscow who loved Yeltsin's antiprivilege message. These groups eventually formed a coalition called the Committee of 19. Leaders of this coalition were populists, not intellectuals or dissidents. Likewise, few liberal ideas jumped out of Yeltsin's campaign speeches.[23] Like the other sweeping successes in this election, former state prosecutors Telman Gdlian and Nikolai Ivanov, Yeltsin was a populist, not a democrat or neo-liberal reformer, and most certainly not an anti-imperial crusader. By championing antiestablishment themes, Yeltsin shocked the country and the world by winning 90 percent of the popular vote in this election.

Forging the Yeltsin-Democrat Alliance

Yeltsin was not the only beneficiary of Gorbachev's political liberalization. Paralleling Yeltsin's rehabilitation, informal social associations also sprouted throughout the Soviet Union. At first, these groups advocated modest, apolitical aims such as more attention to Russian cultural traditions. Over time, however, these independent associations, called "informals," eventually became more overtly political. Still, liberal ideas did not dominate. On the eve of the 1989 elections, the range of ideologies represented within the informal movement included radical anti-Communists such as the Democratic Union, militant neo-Communists such as the United Workers Front, and strident nationalist organizations such as the *Pamiat* groups.[24] Before the 1989 vote, Yeltsin personally had only

---

23. Boris Yeltsin, *Ispoved' na zadannuiu temu* (Vilnius: INPA, 1990).

24. For details on all of these groups, complete with interviews of their leaders, see Sergei Markov and Michael McFaul, *The Troubled Birth of Russian Democracy: Political Parties, Programs, and Profiles* (Stanford, CA: Hoover Institution Press, 1993).

limited contacts with these informal groups. In 1987, he had given permission to the local *Pamiat* branch to hold a public demonstration in Moscow. Some interpreted Yeltsin's approval of this demonstration—the first public gathering on the streets of Moscow by an independent political organization in decades—as a sign of his nationalist inclinations. At the time, radical pro-Western groups did not trust Yeltsin. After all, he had devoted his whole career to working for the enemy, the Communist Party of the Soviet Union.

During the course of the 1989 campaign, however, Yeltsin and the voter associations supporting him came in contact with Moscow's leading democratic movement at the time, the Moscow Popular Front. Front leaders opportunistically initiated the contact. Front campaign managers wanted to tie the electoral prospects of their unknown candidates to Yeltsin's extraordinary popularity. Sergei Stankevich, a young leader of the Moscow Popular Front and a Congress candidate from a Moscow electoral district, was particularly aggressive in attaching his electoral fortunes to Yeltsin's coattails.[25] Stankevich sent a telegram to Yeltsin supporting his candidacy. Then his campaign team reproduced and distributed the telegram throughout their district as a way to identify the unknown Stankevich with the wildly popular Yeltsin. Voters in his district were led to believe that Stankevich and Yeltsin were close political allies even though they had never met.

Soon thereafter, campaign managers from both teams began to coordinate their efforts with a set of interactions that eventually produced the alliance between Yeltsin and Russia's democratic movement.[26] The alliance was based not on shared norms but on a mutual enemy—the Communist Party of the Soviet Union. Both candidates ran on protest platforms, but the campaign staffs supporting Yeltsin and Stankevich came from very different strata of

---

25. Stankevich was running in Cheremushkinski district, a subsection within Moscow, whereas Yeltsin was running in a national electoral district, which included the entire city of Moscow. Consequently, Yeltsin was campaigning throughout the city, including Stankevich's district.

26. Eventually, Stankevich served as a political adviser to Yeltsin.

Soviet society. Stankevich's supporters from the Moscow Popular Front were highly educated, liberal-minded activists from the informal movement who had little or no experience with the CPSU. Many, in fact, were ardent opponents of the CPSU and the Soviet system more generally. Yeltsin's entourage, on the other hand, was a mix of former members of the ruling elite—including Yeltsin himself—and populist, grassroots leaders of voter clubs primarily from working-class neighborhoods in Moscow. At this stage, no forward-looking ideas united the two campaign staffs. Instead, they shared a feeling of opposition to the party-state. This common *ideology of opposition* served as a focal point for these antisystemic forces and constituted the basis of the alliance.[27]

The results of the 1989 elections could not be interpreted as a victory for this new opposition alliance. Some CPSU leaders, such as Soviet premier Nicolai Ryzhkov, understood the embarrassing defeats of senior party leaders (including several who ran unopposed) as a sign of a shift in power away from Gorbachev and the Communist Party he headed.[28] Nationalist victories in Estonia, Latvia, and Lithuania also strengthened the cause of independence in the Baltic republics. Gorbachev, however, claimed that the election results represented a big victory for the CPSU, in part because 85 percent of the deputies were CPSU members and in part because the process demonstrated that the CPSU was not afraid of competitive elections.

In Moscow, Yeltsin's landslide victory signaled that the protest vote against the Soviet system was growing. In major metropolitan areas, the population appeared to be demanding more than Gorbachev's reforms of the Communist system. Several other progressive deputies also obtained seats in the Soviet Congress through social organizations. However, these electoral victories for radicals were the exception and not the rule. In Moscow, only one leader of the

---

27. In other words, the idea that united these groups was negative rather than positive. On the role of focal points in solving coordination problems, see Thomas Shelling, *Strategy of Conflict* (Cambridge, MA: Harvard University Press, 1980).

28. Nikolai Ryzhkov, interview by Michael McFaul, June 1992.

informal movement, Stankevich, had won. In Leningrad, informal groups did organize successful negative campaigns against conservative CPSU members and elected to the Congress a couple of ardent reformers—Anatoli Sobchak and Yuri Boldyrev. CPSU officials and their allies, however, won the vast majority of seats within the Russian Federation and formed a solid majority within the Congress as a whole. Independent of Yeltsin, Russia's democratic movement was still very weak.

The first session of the Soviet Congress of People's Deputies provided the next major catalyst for strengthening the alliance between Yeltsin and the democrats. The most progressive deputies organized themselves into a bloc called the Inter-Regional Group of People's Deputies (MDG). With human rights activist Andrei Sakharov as the informal leader and the Club of Voters of the Academy of Sciences providing ideological and logistical support, the MDG quickly assumed a distinctly intellectual, urban profile. Initially, populists such as Yeltsin and Gdlian kept their distance from this assembly of the intelligentsia. Within the Congress, however, Yeltsin soon realized that these academics could be useful allies and he eventually decided to join their parliamentary faction. In fact, the MDG was the only non-Communist political association within the Congress because nationalist and neo-Communist groups failed to win significant numbers of seats in the 1989 vote. Had Yeltsin had the opportunity to ally with a nationalist coalition, one wonders what choice he might have made.

The intellectuals that dominated the MDG, as well as their allies in the rapidly expanding grassroots democratic movement outside of Congress, also had a choice to make about Yeltsin. Some argued that the former party boss was a populist demagogue who neither understood nor embraced democratic principles. (At the time, there was little discussion about economic reform so his views on the economy were not as central.) Others complained that Yeltsin's Communist Party career disqualified him as a legitimate leader of Russia's democratic movement. Pragmatists countered these historical and ideological worries by recognizing that Yeltsin's popularity could not be matched by any other leader within the democratic movement, including Sakharov. Yeltsin's charismatic orations and populist connections with broad segments of the Russian population were assets that could not be ignored. Without a political figure like Yeltsin, so the argument went, the democratic movement within Russia would always be relegated to minority status. Consequently, these advocates of cooperation argued instead that liberals had to try to shape Yeltsin's thinking in the "right" direction rather than oppose Yeltsin altogether.

In addition to Moscow intellectuals and populists associated with Yeltsin and Gdlian, leaders of nationalist liberation movements from other republics constituted a third component of the Inter-Regional Group.[29] For the first time, the MDG fused leaders of Russia's intelligentsia and the human rights movement, such as Sakharov, with populist "dissidents" from the *nomenklatura* such as Yeltsin and Gdlian and leaders of the independence struggles in several republics. At the height of its popularity, the MDG had less than 20 percent of all Congress deputies. These contacts proved vital in forging an anti-imperial alliance between Russian liberals with their new leader, Boris Yeltsin, on the one hand, and leaders of the national liberation movements of the non-Russian republics on the other.

The MDG's representation within the Soviet Congress, however, was far short of a majority. As Gorbachev and his allies asserted their control over the agenda of the Congress, Inter-Regional leaders realized the difficulties they faced, as a minority, of promoting radical change from within. Frustrated by their lack of power, radical voices within the MDG advocated abandoning Union politics altogether in favor of seizing state power at the lowest levels of gov-

---

29. The faction's leadership reflected the balance of power of these three different groups as the original five cochairs were economist Gavriil Popov, historian Yuri Afanasiev, physicist and human rights activist Andrei Sakharov, Estonian academician Viktor Palm, and Boris Yeltsin. Other prominent members included Telman Gdlian, Arkadi Murashev, Anatoli Sobchak, Sergei Stankevich, Galina Starovoitova, and Ilia Zaslavski.

ernment.[30] This group called upon USSR people's deputies to focus their attention on the upcoming 1990 elections at the republic, oblast, city, and district levels. Driven by fading prospects for reform from within the Soviet Congress, Russian democratic opposition groups moved to seize power at lower levels of government. This strategic decision eventually produced dire consequences for the future of the Soviet Union. In agreeing to compete for a seat in the Russian Congress, Yeltsin spearheaded the charge.

The 1990 Elections to the Russian Congress of People's Deputies

In 1990, Soviet and U.S. negotiators were ironing out the details of German unification, an important milestone in ending the cold war. Equally important to the end of the cold war, though almost totally unnoticed by U.S. and Soviet diplomats, were the 1990 elections for deputies to soviets at the republic, oblast, city, and district levels. Even more amazingly, the original designers of Soviet political reform devoted little attention to these elections. Top Communist Party officials did not engage strategically either in writing the rules governing these elections or campaigning for *their* candidates. As had always been the case in Soviet history, they assumed that the most important institutions of political power were located at the highest levels. They were wrong. More than any single event during the Gorbachev era, these elections empowered anti-Soviet fronts in the Baltic republics, Georgia, and Armenia.[31] The same was also true in Russia. Above all else, these elections gave Yeltsin the chance to win another popular contest and then gain independent control of a government institution.

---

30. Ilia Zaslavksi, interview by Michael McFaul, July 1995.

31. In a report on the Lithuanian elections, the U.S. Commission on Security and Cooperation in Europe concluded that the Sajudis' electoral victory "paves the way for a dramatic confrontation, possibly within a week, between Vilnius and Moscow over questions of independence." U.S. Commission on Security and Cooperation in Europe, "Report on the Supreme Soviet Elections in Lithuania" (Washington, DC: U.S. Congress, March 6, 1990), 1.

The 1989 election experience fueled greater popular participation in the 1990 elections.[32] Almost 7,000 candidates competed in 1,068 electoral districts.[33] In 1989, 49 percent of all electoral district seats had been contested; in 1990, 97 percent of all districts had at least two candidates. With almost two years of experience in organizing political demonstrations, Russia's opposition forces were much more cohesive as a national political organization in these elections. In the interval between the 1989 and 1990 elections, the collapse of communism in Eastern Europe, the calls for independence in the Baltic states, and the rapidly declining Soviet economy created a much greater sense of crisis within Russia, a condition that helped the opposition to consolidate and grow. Yeltsin and his allies had the momentum.

By the spring of 1990, Yeltsin was the unquestioned leader of Russia's anti-Communist movement, and Democratic Russia—a new coalition of dozens of proto-parties, civic groups, and trade unions—was the hegemonic anti-Communist organization. Yeltsin never formally joined Democratic Russia because his virulent antipathy toward the Communist Party gave him an uneasy feeling about political organizations.[34] In addition, the former Politburo candidate member, Sverdlovsk chief executive, and construction foreman had little in common with the non-Communist urban intellectuals who dominated Democratic Russia. At the same time, Yeltsin realized the importance of this alliance in defeating their common enemy, the Soviet *ancien régime*, but he never saw the necessity of creating new political parties as a component of a new Russian democracy. His embrace of liberal ideas was both tactical and limited.

---

32. For accounts, see M. Steven Fish, *Democracy From Scratch* (Princeton, NJ: Princeton University Press, 1993); and Geoffrey Hosking, *The Awakening of the Soviet Union* (Cambridge, MA: Harvard University Press, 1991).

33. N. A. Mikhaleva and L. A. Moroza, "Reforma respublikanskogo izbiratel' nogo zakonodatel'stva," *Sovetskoe Gosudarstvo i Pravo* 6 (1990): 34.

34. After quitting the Communist Party of the Soviet Union in the summer of 1990, Yeltsin never joined another party or formed his own political party, a strategic decision that has had negative consequences for party development and democratic consolidation in Russia.

Even if Yeltsin did not formally join the organization, Democratic Russia did fuse together two disparate but radical parts of Russia's nascent democratic movement: the intelligentsia and human rights advocates on the one hand and populist groups associated with Yeltsin and Gdlian on the other.[35] Human rights leaders associated with Andrei Sakharov, such as Lev Ponomarev, Father Gleb Yakunin, and Dmitri Kataev, constituted one part of the movement's leadership, whereas activists from the Committee of 19 closely associated with Yeltsin, including Lev Shemiaev, Aleksandr Muzykanski, Sergei Trube, and Vladimir Komchatov, constituted a second core group. A third set of allies came from Russia's new parties, who realized at the time that they were better off allying with a national coalition headed by Boris Yeltsin than seeking to win votes for their unknown political parties.

The formation of Democratic Russia as an electoral bloc before the 1990 elections did not mean that Russia's democrats shared a common political platform or plan for political and economic reform. On the contrary, anti-communism was the only concept that united them. This banner included everyone from radical Westernizers to militant Slavophiles. In addition to ideological incoherence, the Democratic Russia bloc also faced several difficulties competing in these elections. Because the Communist Party still controlled all mass media, Democratic Russia had no easy way to publicize its existence. The group also had limited financial resources as few independent sources of funding for anti-state activities existed in an economy still dominated by the state.[36] Momentum, however, provided a countervailing force to offset these financial and structural obstacles. As the only organized societal voice for reform in these elections, Democratic Russia had little trouble tapping into the growing protest sentiment within the Russian electorate. The

---

35. Vladimir Pribilovski, ''Moskovskoe Ob'edinenie Izbiratelei (MOI),'' mimeo, 1990.

36. Vladimir Bokser, Democratic Russia leader, interview by Michael McFaul, May 1995.

election eventually became polarized into two camps, Communists and democrats.

The principal campaign strategy for Democratic Russia candidates in the 1990 elections was to ride Yeltsin's coattails, just as Stankevich had done in 1989. Once the bloc had endorsed a candidate, she or he was then allowed to print a personal leaflet with signatures of endorsement from Democratic Russia's most popular national figures, such as Yeltsin, Popov, and Stankevich. Given the thousands of new, unknown candidates competing in these elections, such endorsements proved decisive. Yeltsin, in effect, helped hundreds of anti-Communist deputies at all levels get elected.

Like the 1989 vote, 85 percent of all deputies elected to the Russian Congress of People's Deputies were members of the CPSU. But this percentage communicated little about the real balance of forces within the Congress. Democratic Russia asserted that candidates endorsed by their electoral bloc won roughly a third of the seats to the 1,000-member Congress.[37] Conservative Communists won roughly 40 percent of all seats and subsequently formed the Communists of Russia, the largest and best-disciplined group in the Congress. Though conservative Communists still won the largest number of seats, momentum in these elections had definitely swung to the democratic opposition.

In its first consequential act in May 1990, the new Russian Congress of People's Deputies elected Boris Yeltsin as chairman, though only by a paltry victory margin of four votes. Despite Democratic Russia's careful planning and the Communists' lack of strategy, the vote nonetheless reflected the precarious balance within the Congress. Democrats were a minority in this body. At the peak of its strength, Democratic Russia still had no more than

---

37. In preparatory meetings leading up to the First Congress, Democratic Russia organizers counted 35 percent of deputies as solid supporters and another 20 percent as soft supporters. (Aleksandr Sobianin, interview by Michael McFaul, July 1995). See also Sobianin and Yuriev, *S'ezd narodnykh deputatov RSFSR v zerkale poimennykh golosovanii* (Moscow, 1991); and Dawn Mann, "The RSFSR Elections: The Congress of People's Deputies," *Report on the USSR*, April 13, 1990, 11–17.

400 deputies loyal to its cause out of the 1,068 total seats in the Congress.[38] Yeltsin secured a majority only by reaching out to other nonliberal constituents within the Congress, including many regional representatives and nationalists who sought greater autonomy from the Soviet Union for the Russian Federation.

Yeltsin's Embrace of Anti-Communist, Pro-Western Ideas

Yeltsin and his allies in Democratic Russia knew well what they stood against but had very vague ideas regarding what they stood for. Because of his "betrayal" in 1987, Yeltsin detested the Communist Party *nomenklatura* as a group and Mikhail Gorbachev in particular. Everything that Gorbachev advocated, Yeltsin opposed. Given Gorbachev's essentially reformist orientation—an orientation that included greater economic and political autonomy for individuals in the Soviet Union and greater integration with the West—Yeltsin could have easily gravitated to the opposite ideological direction if his hatred of Gorbachev had been the only motivating factor. Instead, however, Yeltsin opted to outflank Gorbachev on the reformist ledger. In part, Yeltsin probably made this tactical move because his allies in the democratic movement also held these views. Other anti-Communist ideologies such as nationalism or fascism had neither mobilized mass followings nor produced electoral victories for their proponents. Given his own history with the Communist Party, Yeltsin was unlikely to embrace neo-Communist ideas, and neo-Communists did not embrace him. Consequently, Yeltsin's only real choice was to be more radical than Gorbachev himself. Although initially vague, several antisystemic themes

---

38. Lev Ponomarev and Gleb Yakunin, Democratic Russia leaders in the Russian Congress, interviews by Michael McFaul, July 1995. Ponomarev expressed frustration that both the Russian public and the West did not fully appreciate their weak position within the Congress and therefore expected too much from this body by way of reform. For analysis of the changing balance of support for Democratic Russia and its causes within the Congress, see Sobianin and Yuriev, *S'ezd narodnykh deputatov RSFSR v zerkale poimennykh golosovanii.*

eventually crystallized to help situate these challengers in diametric opposition to Gorbachev's *ancien régime*.[39]

Demand for national sovereignty was most salient. According to Democratic Russia leaders, the 1990 elections gave them a mandate to seek greater autonomy for Russia.[40] As Boris Yeltsin stated in May 1990, "The problems of the [Russian] republic cannot be solved without full-blooded political sovereignty. This alone can enable relations between Russia and the Union and between the autonomous territories within Russia to be harmonized. The political sovereignty of Russia is also necessary in international affairs."[41] This rhetoric about sovereignty helped Yeltsin cobble together the majority that elected him chairman of the Russian Congress. It also appealed to Russian democrats, who saw Yeltsin's declaration as a peaceful way to dissolve the Soviet empire; to Russian nationalists, who embraced the idea for ethnic reasons; and to mid-level Communists, who saw sovereignty as a way for them to gain independence from CPSU bosses in Moscow.[42] Two months later, in June 1990, the Russian Congress of People's Deputies voted to declare the Russian Federation a sovereign state.[43] Obviously, such ideas

---

39. During revolutionary transitions, moderate opposition ideas are often replaced by more radical ideas over the course of time. See Michael McFaul, "Southern African Liberation and Great Power Intervention: Toward a Theory of Revolution in an International Context." PhD diss., Oxford University, 1991.

40. See the comments by Viktor Sheinis from May 1990, as reported in John Dunlop, *The Rise of Russia and the Fall of the Soviet Empire* (Princeton, NJ: Princeton University Press, 1993), 95–96.

41. Boris Yeltsin, speech to the Russian Federation Congress of People's Deputies, Moscow, May 22, 1990, reprinted in *The Soviet System: From Crisis to Collapse*, ed. Alexander Dallin and Gail Lapidus (Boulder, CO: Westview Press, 1995), 410.

42. Anatoli Shabad, interview by Michael McFaul, July 1995. Shabad, a Jew, was deeply offended by the kinds of conversations he overheard during the deliberations on this declaration but saw this alliance as a tactical necessity. In contrast, Russian nationalist Ilia Konstantinov recalls that he voted for Yeltsin and sovereignty but then deeply regretted his votes. Ilia Konstantinov, interview by Michael McFaul, May 1995.

43. "Declaration on the State Sovereignty of the Russian Soviet Federation Socialist Republic," reprinted in Dallin and Lapidus, *The Soviet System*, 404.

cut against the grain of Gorbachev's quest to reform but preserve the Soviet Union.

Capitalism constituted a second, but underdeveloped, component of Yeltsin's (and Democratic Russia's) ideology of opposition. During deliberations over the 500-Day Plan—a blueprint for market reform for the USSR as a whole—Yeltsin and his aides adopted increasingly radical positions on free prices, private property, and international trade liberation. If Gorbachev sought to revitalize the Soviet command economy by introducing some modest market mechanisms, Yeltsin wanted to introduce radical new market reforms as a means to destroy the Soviet Union. However, whether Yeltsin's objective was the destruction of the Soviet empire, the Communist Party, Mikhail Gorbachev, or the Socialist economy remained unclear at this stage. Likewise, within Democratic Russia, advocates of Eurocommunism and neoliberalism coexisted. Yeltsin himself never articulated a coherent economic program,[44] and on some issues, such as price reform, Yeltsin championed populist, antimarket views. Only when the Soviet economy edged toward collapse in the winter of 1991 did the opposition's call for a new economic order grow increasingly militant.[45]

Democracy was a third component of the ideology of opposition. In fact, Russia's revolutionaries effectively captured this term in labeling themselves "democrats" and their movement the "democratic opposition." The term helped to crystallize Russia's political spectrum into two camps—democrats and Communists—though the so-called democratic camp included many non-democrats and the Communist camp included several promoters of the democratic process. To clearly delineate this democratic versus antidem-

---

44. Egor Gaidar, Russia's eventual architect of radical economic reform, recalls in his memoirs that he was very troubled by Yeltsin's early statements on economic reform. Egor Gaidar, *Dni Porazhenii i Pobed* (Moscow: Vagrius, 1996), 61.

45. *Materiali: II S'ezda Dvizheniia Demokraticheskoi Rossii* (Moscow: DR-Press, November 1991).

ocratic cleavage, the opposition promoted and carried out the election of their leader, Boris Yeltsin, to the newly created post of president of Russia in June 1991. Yeltsin's election in June 1991 was his third landslide victory in as many years, whereas the leader of the Soviet Union, Mikhail Gorbachev, had never even participated in a general election. Respect for individual liberties, a free and independent press, and the rule of law: all were themes propagated by Russia's democratic movement. Russia's democratic opposition also used mass events to contrast their democratic credentials and popular support with the authoritarian practices and waning popular appeal of Gorbachev's regime. As with capitalism, however, the opposition's—and especially Yeltsin's—commitment to democracy was neither firm nor comprehensive. Generally, Russia's informal political organizations practiced internal democracy, at times to a fault. Yet the speed of change and the minimal time in opposition (a few years as compared with several decades for the African National Congress in South Africa or even a decade for Solidarity in Poland) meant that democratic principles did not have time to mature within these organizations. Yeltsin did not spend years thinking about democratic ideals. National debates about the virtues and vices of a democratic polity did not occur.

A fourth component of this ideology of opposition was a stridently pro-Western orientation regarding international affairs. Because Western capitalist democracies were prosperous and opposed communism, they were perceived by Yeltsin and Russia's democratic movement as allies in their common struggle against the Soviet system.[46] Besides democracy and capitalism, there were no

---

46. This analysis echoes the arguments on transnational relations and epistemic communities with the caveat that my argument incorporates the structure of the international system as a determining factor for understanding which ideas travel and which do not. For elaboration, see McFaul, "Southern African Liberation and Great Power Intervention." On the Soviet and Russian case, see Matthew Evangelista, "The Paradox of State Strength: Transnational Relations, Domestic Structures, and Security Policy in Russia and the Soviet Union," *International Organization* 49, no. 1 (Winter 1995): 1–38; and Sarah Mendelson, *Changing*

other attractive models or ideologies in the international system with which Russian revolutionaries could identify. Relations with the Western world, however, posed a particularly difficult dilemma for Yeltsin and his supporters as Gorbachev had already acquired a formidable reputation as a friend of the West in most European and American capitals. To win over Western favor, Yeltsin tried to be even more pro-Western than Gorbachev, compelling him to articulate radical positions such as the dissolution of the Soviet Union and Russian membership in NATO. Without question, Yeltsin and his allies aimed to end the cold war.

From Ideas to Action: The Collapse of the Soviet Union and the End of the Cold War

Ambiguous ideologies of opposition are common in revolutionary situations. Tactically, ambiguity helps to unite disparate groups. Revolutionaries generally know better what they are against than what they desire. Over time, ideologies of opposition also tend to become more radical and more antithetical to the ideas of the regime in power. Moderate ideas and centrist politicians lose sway as attempts at compromise fail.[47]

Such revolutionary ideas become consequential only if the revolutionaries win. In the year leading up to the collapse of the Soviet Union, Russia's revolutionaries did not always seem to be gaining power. Within Yeltsin's entourage and especially within the democratic movement that backed Yeltsin's actions, the fall of 1990 and the winter of 1991 were uncertain times, marked by dispute, division, and doubt.[48] At the same time that the democratic opposition

---

Course: Ideas, Politics, and the Soviet Withdrawal from Afghanistan (Princeton, NJ: Princeton University Press, 1998).

47. Crane Brinton, *Anatomy of a Revolution* (New York: Vintage Books, 1938).

48. This observation is based on dozens of meetings and discussions between the author and leaders of the Russian democratic movement at the time.

in Russia appeared to be splintering, conservative forces appeared to be consolidating.[49] In the fall of 1990, Gorbachev purged his government of most liberals and centrists and strengthened the hand of conservatives, especially those affiliated with the military-industrial complex. In protest against this conservative turn, one of Gorbachev's most loyal allies, Foreign Minister Eduard Shevard-nadze, quit the government in December 1990, warning in his res-ignation speech of an impending coup.[50] In response to Shevardnadze and others, Gorbachev claimed that he was carving "a centrist po-sition, trying to keep the state organs committed to the mainte-nance of order in the country, away from the swing of rightist or leftist extremes."[51] Increasingly, however, Gorbachev's regime sounded and acted reactionary, not reformist or centrist.[52]

The implications of this change in the balance of forces at the top was first manifest in January 1991, when Soviet troops seized control of the publishing plant of the main newspaper in Riga, Lat-via, attacked the printing house in Vilnius, Lithuania, and then stormed the television station there. Upon capturing the television station, members of a "committee for national salvation" pro-claimed that they were the new government and pledged their loy-alty to the Soviet government. Fourteen people died in the raid and hundreds more were injured. The following week, special forces (OMON) of the ministry of the interior killed four people in Riga.

From January to August 1991, the balance of power between radicals and reactionaries swayed back and forth several times. Large demonstrations throughout Russia to protest the invasion of

49. Such a backlash had been predicted by careful Soviet observers for some time. See, for instance, Peter Reddaway, "The Quality of Gorbachev's Leader-ship"; and Andranik Migranyan, "The Quality of Gorbachev's Leadership: A So-viet View," both in *Soviet Economy* 6, no. 2 (1990): 125–140 and 155–159, respectively.

50. Shevardnadze's speech before the Soviet Congress, reprinted in *FBIS-SOV-90–245*, December 20, 1990, 12.

51. Gorbachev, *Memoirs*, 584.

52. Serge Schmemann, "The Tough New Leaders in Moscow Have Kremlinol-ogists Up and Guessing," *New York Times*, January 27, 1991.

the Baltic states reinvigorated the democratic movement, which then organized several massive demonstrations throughout the year. In the first part of 1991, Soviet conservative forces also scored victories, including major changes in the Soviet government and an electoral victory in March 1991, when a solid majority of Russian voters (and Soviet voters in republics that participated) passed a referendum to preserve the Soviet Union.[53] In June 1991, Yeltsin won a landslide victory to become Russia's first elected president, a vote that returned momentum to Russia's anti-Communist forces.

Sensitive to the momentum swing, Soviet conservatives attempted to strike back. After a prolonged set of negotiations during the spring of 1991, Yeltsin and most of the other republican leaders were prepared to join Gorbachev in signing a new Union treaty, scheduled to take place on August 20, 1991. Soviet conservatives saw this treaty as the first step toward total disintegration of the USSR[54] and therefore preempted its signing by seizing power. While Gorbachev was on vacation, the State Committee for the State of Emergency (GKChP) announced on August 19, 1991, that they had assumed responsibility for governing the country. Gorbachev, they claimed, was ill and would return to head the Emergency Committee after he recovered. The GKChP justified their move as a reaction against "extremist forces" and "political adventurers" who aimed to destroy the Soviet state and economy.

We can only speculate about what would have happened had this junta succeeded in seizing power. Had they prevailed, the process of ending the cold war rivalry between the United States and the Soviet Union would have lingered much longer than it did.[55] The

---

53. On hints of an impending coup, see Dunlop, *The Rise and the Fall of the Soviet Empire*, 192–194.

54. Gennadi Yanaev and Anatoli Lukianov, two of the principals in the coup attempt, interviews by Michael McFaul, November 1993. See also Anatoli Lukianov, *Perevorot: Mnimyi i Nastoiashchii* (Voronezh: Vorenezhskaia oblastnaia organizatsiia Soiuza zhurnalistov Rossii, 1993), 46.

55. Since the fall of the Berlin Wall, U.S. and Russian leaders have declared the cold war over many times, suggesting that the end of the historical period was a process and not a single event or moment. Even George W. Bush and his administration felt compelled to declare the cold war over more than a decade after the

GKChP pronouncements were flavored with heavy doses of Soviet nationalism. These leaders seemed committed to preserving the Soviet Union. Some of them, it should be remembered, had already authorized the use of military force in January 1991 against Latvia and Lithuania. From these actions, it seems safe to predict that they would have resisted Soviet dissolution, most certainly would have delayed Russian troop withdrawals from places like the Baltic states, and would have been much less cooperative with Western countries that promoted Russian military withdrawal and Western alliance expansion. Some of the coup leaders also represented interest groups, such as the military-industrial complex, the KGB, and the military, that subsequently became the loudest anti-American voices in post-Soviet foreign policy debates in Russia. Had the coup succeeded, the new Soviet dictators would have been beholden to these interest groups, rather than to the people, to stay in power. Subsequent political activities of the participants in the failed coup also reveal what might have occurred had they stayed in power. For instance, Anatoli Lukianov became one of the Communist Party's most articulate anti-American representatives in parliament after his release from jail. He and other coup participants became the darlings of militant nationalist and Communist groups in post-Communist Russia.

These people did not stay in power, however, because Yeltsin and his allies stopped them. After learning about the coup attempt, Yeltsin immediately raced to the White House, the building that housed the Russian Congress of People's Deputies, and began to organize a resistance effort. As the elected president of Russia, he called on Russian citizens—civilian and military alike—to obey his decrees rather than those of the GKChP. At the time, each of the two independent governments claimed sovereign authority over the same territory. The Russian Supreme Soviet convened an emer-

---

Soviet collapse. Those late declarations imply that lingering elements of the cold war persisted well beyond the fall of the wall and the dissolution of the USSR. The argument here is that these lingering elements would have lingered longer had the coup plotters succeeded.

gency session to approve Yeltsin's decrees. This legal alternative to the coup leaders' decrees gave military commanders the necessary excuse not to fulfill orders issued by the Soviet authorities. While Yeltsin orchestrated the resistance at the White House, Democratic Russia and its allies assumed responsibility for mobilizing popular resistance on the streets of Moscow.[56] Democratic Russia activists quickly assembled hundreds of supporters outside the White House only a few hours after news of the coup had been announced. The following day, two massive demonstrations took place on the streets of Moscow in which tens of thousands of Muscovites defied Red Army regiments. By the third day, the coup plotters lost their resolve and began to negotiate an end to their rule.

The failed coup attempt and Yeltsin's victory rapidly accelerated the pace of change within the Soviet Union. Gorbachev, imprisoned in his vacation home in Crimea for the three days of emergency rule, returned to a different country when he flew back to Moscow. Believing that they had a new mandate for change, Yeltsin and the Russian Congress of People's Deputies in effect seized power themselves. They pressured the Soviet Congress of People's Deputies to dissolve, assumed control of several Soviet ministries, and compelled Gorbachev to acquiesce to these changes. Most dramatically, Yeltsin then met with the leaders of Ukraine and Belarus in early December to dissolve the Soviet Union. On December 31, 1991, the Soviet empire disintegrated. Historians continue to de-

---

56. Without question, the outcome of the coup would have been vastly different had it taken place in 1988 or even 1990. Analyses that focus only on splits within the military tend to forget that opposing positions within the armed forces would not have crystallized without clearly defined choices as to which political group to support. If, for instance, Yeltsin had been arrested immediately and popular resistance had not taken to the streets to defend the Russian parliament building, who would defecting Soviet military units have supported? For an interpretation focusing on the military and downplaying the role of democratic political movements, see Stephen Miller, "The Soviet Coup and the Benefits of Breakdown," *Orbis* (Winter 1992). On the politicization of the Soviet military, see Stephen Miller, "How the Threat (and the Coup) Collapsed: The Politicization of the Soviet Military," *International Security* 16, no. 3 (Winter 1991–92).

bate about when the cold war actually ended. The day the Soviet Union died most certainly has to rank as one of the important milestones in ending this historical era.

Conclusion

Gorbachev initiated the crucial reforms within the Soviet Union that began the process of ending the cold war. He then refrained from intervening to protect Communist regimes in Eastern Europe in 1989, a nonevent that was as important as any direct action in ending the cold war. After the fall of the Berlin Wall, it was difficult to imagine how the cold war could have been restarted.

But think again. Imagine if the coup leaders had prevailed in August 1991 and a leadership determined to preserve the Soviet empire, the command economy, and Communist dictatorship were still in the Kremlin today. The battlefronts of the cold war might have moved farther east, but the war itself might not have ended. In fact, the failed August coup and the collapse of the Soviet empire still might not have ended the cold war completely as Russia's relationship with communism and the West was not clarified until several years after 1991 when market and democratic institutions began to take hold. Some have speculated that only the emergence of a new common enemy—terrorism—after September 11 finally ended the cold war. And even after September 11, the fragile footing of Russian democratic institutions still allows for the possible reemergence of dictatorship in Russia. The return of an autocrat to the Kremlin would most certainly fuel competition, if not conflict, between the United States and Russia.

Yet, even if Russian democracy collapses and Russian capitalism continues to sputter, the reemergence of a *Soviet* or *Communist* threat to the West is highly unlikely. Yeltsin made some disastrous mistakes as Russia's first post-Communist leader.[57] He and his

---

57. For a review of this list, see Michael McFaul, "Yeltsin's Legacy," *The Wilson Quarterly* (Spring 2000): 42–58.

team achieved only limited success in building new political and economic institutions. Nonetheless, he still deserves credit for destroying the dangerous institutions of the Soviet Communist and imperial system. Yeltsin's leadership and the democratic, capitalist, and pro-Western ideas he embraced, in combination with the support of his allies in Russia's democratic movement, proved to be a powerful catalyst for speeding the process of Soviet disintegration. This same configuration of leaders, ideas, and organizations also provided the critical check to those who attempted to preserve the Soviet system. Russia's democratic movement has not proven strong enough to build liberal democratic institutions, but it was powerful enough to help destroy Soviet autocratic institutions.[58]

Would the Soviet Union have collapsed and the cold war ended without Yeltsin? We will never know the answer to this question, but thinking through counterfactual concepts helps to isolate Yeltsin's personal contribution as well as the role of ideas in these events.

First, if Yeltsin had not emerged as the leader of the democratic movement, others most certainly would have tried to fill his shoes. Yet, Yeltsin embodied several important leadership characteristics that few others, if any, exhibited. Whether in the service of communism or anti-communism, he was a bold, charismatic, and forceful leader. Within the democratic movement, few could match his leadership qualities. Until his death in December 1989, Andrei Sakharov had greater authority than Yeltsin within the democratic movement because of his integrity and ideals. But even had he survived, Sakharov lacked two other leadership qualities that Yeltsin possessed: the ability to speak to the masses and the capacity to work with Communist Party apparatchiks. If Russia's leading democrat had emerged from the dissident community, Russia's anti-Communist forces probably would not have gained control of the Russian Congress of People's Deputies in the spring of 1990,

---

58. On the illiberal flaws of Russia's political regime, see McFaul, *Russia's Unfinished Transition,* chapter nine.

but would have remained a minority group in this body and more generally for years to come. Subsequent post-Communist elections in Russia after the Soviet collapse demonstrated that the electoral base for liberal parties was always much smaller than Yeltsin's own following.[59] Yeltsin's CPSU background also gave him the skills to navigate the peaceful dissolution of the Soviet system, a balancing act that grassroots leaders of Russia's democratic movement might not have managed well. It is important to remember that the distribution of power between Communists and anti-Communists was always much more equal in Russia than in Poland. Consequently, the transition from communism in Russia was not and could not have been as clean and abrupt as Poland's transition.[60] A reformed Communist such as Yeltsin, rather than unequivocal democratic leaders such as Walesa or Havel, might have been a necessary evil of Russia's anti-Communist revolution.

A second counterfactual idea has to do with the historical contingency that brought together Yeltsin and democratic concepts. What if Boris Yeltsin had adopted a different ideology of opposition and a different set of allies who associated with those ideas? That Russia's revolutionary ideology of opposition became prodemocratic, pro-market, and, by association, pro-Western was not inevitable. Many alternative ideologies of opposition were articulated and discussed during this transitional period. Nationalist organizations had cultivated an anti-Western ideology that was anticapitalism and anti-communism, as they considered communism a Western, cosmopolitan, Jewish ideology. Their anti-Western and pro-imperial ideology was radically different from the approach of the liberal and pro-Western Democratic Russia. Yet, even within Democratic Russia, several prominent leaders advocated national-

---

59. Stephen White, Richard Rose, and Ian McAllister, *How Russia Votes* (Chatham, NJ: Chatham House Publishers, 1997).

60. For elaboration, see Michael McFaul, "The Fourth Wave of Democracy and Dictatorship: Noncooperative Transitions in the Postcommunist World," *World Politics* 54, no. 2 (January 2002): 212–244.

ist, rather than liberal, ideologies.[61] Likewise, many Socialist and social-democratic organizations that were both anticapitalist and anti-Soviet flourished in the early days of Gorbachev's liberalization.[62] In several respects, the alliance between Russia's liberals in Democratic Russia and Boris Yeltsin, the Communist boss turned populist, was an accident of history forged by common enemies, the Soviet Communist system and later Mikhail Gorbachev.[63] Had Yeltsin's rise to power been buoyed by a different ideology or backed by a different set of allies, Russian democratization might have produced a more belligerent foreign policy—not an end to the cold war, but a different variation of the old East-West confrontation.[64]

Yeltsin's identification with liberal ideas was not totally random, nor was it entirely determined by internal alliance politics, as the balance of ideologies within the international system also shaped choices made by Yeltsin and his allies. But it would be wrong to assume that his embrace of liberal, pro-Western values was inevitable. The slow pace by which Western leaders engaged Yeltsin as a potential ally suggests that Yeltsin's own actions made him suspect as a democratic revolutionary. Yeltsin's spotty record as a demo-

---

61. McFaul and Markov, *The Troubled Birth of Russian Democracy*, chapters four and five. The Democratic Party of Russia (headed by Nikolai Travkin), the Russian Christian Democratic Movement (Viktor Aksiuchits), and the Constitutional Democratic Party of Russia (Mikhail Astafiev) left Democratic Russia when the organization decided to endorse the dissolution of the Soviet Union.

62. Boris Kagarlitsky, *Farewell Perestroika* (London: Verso, 1990).

63. Democratic Russia founders Vladimir Bokser, Viktor Dmitriev, Lev Ponomarev, and Gleb Yakunin, interviews by Michael McFaul, Summer 1995. At the time, Democratic Russia leaders debated the alliance with Boris Yeltsin as some claimed he was a Communist while others thought he was a nationalist. In 1992, Democratic Russia co-founder Yuri Afanasiev quit the organization, claiming that it identified too closely with the antidemocratic Yeltsin. Russian liberals divided again over their support for Yeltsin during the October 1993 events and the Chechen war.

64. For a discussion of such cases, see Edward D. Mansfield and Jack Snyder, "Democratization and the Danger of War," in *Debating the Democratic Peace*, ed. Michael Brown, Sean Lynn-Jones, and Steven Miller (Cambridge, MA: MIT Press, 1996).

cratic promoter in the post-Soviet era suggests that his acceptance or understanding of these liberal ideas was not complete.[65] Consequently, it is not unreasonable to assume that Yeltsin could have adopted a different set of ideas, which in turn would have resulted in a different trajectory in Russia's relations with the West.

As a final counterfactual idea, consider what would have happened if the coup plotters in August 1991 had succeeded. This group held anti-Western views and illiberal ideologies and enjoyed close ties to the military, the KGB, and the military-industrial complex. Had they prevailed, civil war might have ensued and interstate war would have been more likely. At a minimum, Russia would have become an opponent, if not a belligerent enemy, of the West. In retrospect, their failure seems inevitable. At the time, however, support for their actions throughout Russia and parts of the Soviet Union seemed significant. Only Moscow and St. Petersburg staged large anticoup demonstrations, only three regional heads of administration openly sided with Yeltsin, and Yeltsin's call for a national strike went unanswered.[66]

Here again, Yeltsin played a critical leadership role. He inspired Democratic Russia activists, mobilized support within the Russian Congress, and perhaps most importantly, persuaded a handful of Russian officers and soldiers to join his side of the barricade. Without this charismatic leader armed with democratic ideas, the August 1991 coup might have succeeded.

Yeltsin's role in destroying communism and ending the cold war provides a powerful policy lesson for future American decisionmakers who must deal with rogue states. The lesson is simple: domestic politics matter. Internal changes in the composition of a regime can have a profound influence on the international behavior

65. See Lilia Shevtsova, *Yeltsin's Russia: Myths and Realities* (Washington, DC: Carnegie Endowment for International Peace, 1999).
66. Koordinatsionyi Sovet "Demokraticheskoi Rossii, Vsem, Vsem, Vsem," mimeo, August 19, 1991. According to a poll of 1,746 Russian residents conducted by VTsIOM on August 20, 1991, only 34 percent supported the idea of an immediate strike while 48 percent opposed such an idea. See VTsIOM, "Data-express" Ekstrennyi Vypusk, mimeo, August 21, 1991.

of that regime. Today, the United States faces security threats from a small but menacing set of states: Iraq, Iran, and North Korea. U.S. leaders are prepared to spend billions of dollars to defend our borders and skies from these states. At the same time, the lesson from the end of the Soviet menace is that the threats emanating from Iran, Iraq, and North Korea are most likely to end when the Yeltsins of these three countries emerge to challenge and eventually topple these autocratic, anti-Western regimes.

In theory, therefore, U.S. foreign policymakers should seek to court and then support the Boris Yeltsins of Iran, Iraq, and North Korea. The problem with this strategy, however, is that U.S. leaders will always be slow to recognize the Yeltsins of the world. They could also hurt the political prospects of such revolutionary challengers by embracing them too quickly. And finally, U.S. leaders can pick and then identify too strongly with the wrong leader. This inability to select winners and this clumsiness in intervening in the domestic affairs of other countries suggests that U.S. leaders should focus instead on promoting the right ideas and then hope that the right leaders will eventually embrace them.

Individuals matter. But they matter most when they are acting as individuals and not as the puppets of outside powers. Ideas also matter. And the beauty of democratic ideas is that they cannot be owned or controlled by anyone.

Nikolai Petrov : *Boris Yeltsin: Catalyst for the Cold War's End?*

TOLSTOY'S *War and Peace* illustrates how personalities can influence the course of history.

This is especially true if one happens to be in the right place at the right time.[1] Michael McFaul demonstrates this point using the example of Boris Yeltsin and his fight against communism. But Yeltsin appears to be a much less convincing example of McFaul's second point: the importance of ideas.

In my opinion, it would be presumptuous to say that Boris Yeltsin was an advocate of "liberal, pro-Western values." The universal lesson Michael McFaul draws from "Yeltsin's role in destroying communism and ending the cold war"[2] seems quite ambiguous, especially in light of what the author himself says: "The slow pace by which Western leaders engaged Yeltsin as a potential ally suggests that Yeltsin's own actions made him suspect as a democratic revolutionary. Yeltsin's spotty record as a democratic promoter in the post-Soviet era suggests that his acceptance or understanding of these liberal ideas was not complete. Consequently, it is not un-

---

1. A system that finds itself at a crossroads may start developing further along different paths. In that case, it takes a relatively modest effort or a willful decision to set the system's development in motion along one path or another. This process is not irreversible. The development path is not a railroad track but rather a normal road on which one can always make turns.

2. McFaul writes, "The lesson from the end of the Soviet menace is that the threats emanating from Iran, Iraq, and North Korea are most likely to end when the Yeltsins of these three countries emerge to challenge and eventually topple these autocratic, anti-Western regimes."

reasonable to assume that Yeltsin could have adopted a different set of ideas, which in turn would have resulted in a different trajectory in Russia's relations with the West."

Let us try, however, to look into the substance of this theme, following Michael McFaul's reasoning in a sequential manner. Let us start with the question: Why and how did the cold war end? Did it end with democratization of the mighty USSR, a giant that suddenly turned peaceful and voluntarily renounced the policy of opposing the West? Yes and no. Yes, because the notorious evil empire actually did become more humane. No, because the process of becoming more humane resulted in the collapse of the evil empire rather than in its transformation from a hostile power to a friendly one. Once it became less malevolent, the evil empire collapsed. There are no such things as good empires, at least in our time.

When did the cold war end? Did it end in 1989 with the fall of the Berlin Wall, or in 1991 with the collapse of the Warsaw Pact and Gorbachev's unilateral force reductions, or later the same year with the collapse of the USSR and the Soviet military? Regardless of the answer, Yeltsin's role would not have been decisive. At one point, McFaul says, "Imagine if the coup leaders had prevailed in August 1991 and a leadership determined to preserve the Soviet empire, the command economy, and Communist dictatorship were still in the Kremlin today. . . . The failed August coup and the collapse of the Soviet empire might still not have ended the cold war completely as Russia's relationship with communism and the West was not clarified until several years after 1991 when market and democratic institutions began to take hold."[3]

---

3. Returning to the role of personality in history, and to Yeltsin's role in particular in the collapse of the Soviet empire, it is useful to quote William Odom: "At some point during the last couple of years of the Gorbachev period, the forces of dissolution began to outweigh the forces of centralization. Perhaps Dunlop [John Dunlop, *The Rise of Russia and the Fall of the Soviet Empire* (Princeton, NJ: Princeton University Press, 1993)] is right that the GKChP, if it had stormed the White House, could have saved the Soviet Union. No doubt it could have gained control of Moscow, but reversing all the centrifugal forces in the republics and the far-flung regions of the RSFSR would not have been easy. The bureaucracies that held the Soviet Union together for so long were no longer effective—

Boris Yeltsin actually did play an important role in the breakup of the Soviet Union and, through it, the ending of the cold war. However, he played that role at the final stages of the process, and that role, albeit important, was not the decisive one. This view is supported, on the one hand, by the fact that Western leaders and analysts have long held that Gorbachev, not Yeltsin, was the revolutionary leader of the Soviet transformation (unlike McFaul, I do not think they were mistaken), and, on the other hand, by the fact that it is Mikhail Gorbachev, not Boris Yeltsin, whom the Russian public has traditionally blamed for the collapse of the Soviet Union. On the latter point, there may be doubts or different assessments, but they do not change the substance of the issue: Gorbachev made the breakup of the Soviet Union possible, and Boris Yeltsin's actions transformed that possibility into reality and accelerated the process. Thus, Yeltsin's catalytic role was not to enable, but to hasten, the reaction. In any event, the cold war's end represents a by-product of the power struggle that led the Soviet Union to its collapse.

Yeltsin's Path to Power: Myths and Reality

The perception of Yeltsin as a fighter against the Communist system is a great myth. That myth is based on the banning of the CPSU, anti-Communist statements by Yeltsin himself, and the propaganda campaign during the 1996 presidential elections. It is important, however, to distinguish between substance and facade. Based on outward appearances only, if one looks at the situation in 1999, the last year in which Yeltsin was in power, it would be odd, to put it mildly, to speak of Yeltsin's successful struggle against the Communist system. That year, the president was a former candi-

---

particularly the military, which was the last line of defense, the 'embodiment' of the sovereignty and stability of empire. Had the GKChP been victorious against the White House, it might have postponed the dissolution of the Soviet Union for a while, but not for long." William E. Odom, *The Collapse of the Soviet Military* (New Haven, CT: Yale University Press, 1998), 395–396.

date member of the Politburo of the CPSU Central Committee, Prime Minister Evgeni Primakov and Federation Council Chairman Egor Stroev were former Politburo members, Duma Speaker Gennadi Seleznev was the former editor-in-chief of the main Komsomol publication and then of the principal Communist Party newspaper, and he was number two on the Communist Party ballot during the 1995 and 1999 Duma elections.

Taking a closer look, one will see that the Soviet *nomenklatura*, or Communist, system, actually changed very little under Boris Yeltsin, despite all declarations to the contrary.[4] *Nomenklatura* perks and privileges made officials dependent on their superiors within a huge bureaucratic apparatus, allowing the state to dominate society and the party leadership to dominate the state. (Under Yeltsin, the role of party leadership was taken over by the presidential administration, which symbolically moved into the offices of the former CPSU Central Committee on Staraia Ploshchad.) All of this led a number of analysts to insist, as early as 1992, that the *nomenklatura* system had gained revenge.[5] Thus, to a large extent, Yeltsin maintained the system that, like a lizard, had cast away its tail to keep its head.

Yeltsin's appointment to Moscow in 1985 was not at all incidental. Partly, it was an element of the natural process of bringing fresh blood into the system in the same way that Gorbachev, former first secretary of the Stavropol Regional Party Committee, Egor Ligachev, former first secretary of the Tomsk Regional Party Committee, and many others before them had made their way into the Communist Party's central apparatus. It was also partly a result of Gorbachev's attempt to secure his own power base by pushing aside the party gerontocracy, including Viktor Grishin, Yeltsin's

---

4. Whether Yeltsin was indeed capable of building an alternative system or restructuring the old *nomenklatura* system into something new is an important question. His position was similar to that of an armory worker who, having spent a lifetime producing machine guns and having no skills to produce anything else, is suddenly instructed to produce a pram.

5. See, for example, V. Varov, A. Sobianin, and D. Yuriev, *Nomenklaturnyi revansh* [*Nomenklatura's Revenge*] (Moscow: RF Politika, 1992).

predecessor as head of the country's largest and most influential party organization and Gorbachev's rival in the general secretary election. Ligachev, who had overseen regional party organizations in his capacity as CPSU Central Committee secretary since December 1983, traveled to Sverdlovsk to become better acquainted with Yeltsin. Ligachev liked what he saw, and Yeltsin received an offer to move to Moscow and join the Central Committee apparatus. At the April 1985 plenary meeting of the Central Committee, which is traditionally viewed as the starting point of perestroika, Ligachev was elected a full member of the Politburo. Yeltsin became a Central Committee secretary three months later. The paths of Ligachev, the number two man in Gorbachev's entourage, and Yeltsin, a protégé of both Gorbachev and Ligachev and a would-be career rebel, were destined to cross more than once.

The start of Yeltsin's career in Moscow coincided with the political demise of Grigori Romanov, Gorbachev's former rival in the power struggle, who had moved from Leningrad to Moscow two years earlier. The career of Viktor Grishin, another candidate for the post of general secretary, came to an end at the beginning of 1985, when Yeltsin replaced him as head of the CPSU Moscow City Party Committee.

Researchers normally tend to ignore the period when Yeltsin was at the helm of the Moscow City Party Committee, the country's largest and most influential such organization. That period, however, is quite important for understanding the personality of the future "fighter against the system." When, at the very start of sweeping changes, he found himself heading the Moscow City Party Committee, Yeltsin realized that Moscow, always so much in the public eye, could become a great springboard for his career. He needed tangible and obvious successes and the popularity he had enjoyed back in the Urals, and Yeltsin started to act at once.[6] He

---

6. Boris Nemtsov, another individual from the provinces who was in the focus of public attention in the capital city, would find himself in a similar situation ten years later. Being much younger and better prepared, it took Nemtsov two years to adapt to the Moscow climate.

did so in the traditional ways he had mastered when heading a large industrial region in the Urals. He called for extraordinary overtime work, tongue-lashed and maltreated officials at lower levels, and socialized with the "commoners."

Young and energetic, the new master of Moscow and his emphatic ways of running the city were a sharp contrast to the anemic management style of the "stagnation" years. The problem was that Moscow, ever prominent in the public eye and more prestigious than any other regional posting, could not provide the full autonomy that Yeltsin had enjoyed as the party overlord of the Urals. Besides, Muscovites never considered the power of city-level party leadership to be distinct from that of the Central Committee.

What did Yeltsin do? He fired two-thirds of district-level party bosses in less than a year, and in some districts he started a second wave of dismissals.[7] He organized grandiose autumn food fairs at which refrigerated vans carrying fruit to Moscow became makeshift retail outlets instead of simply unloading their goods and heading back. He rubbed shoulders with the masses, spending hours with workers and gladly answering copious questions, some of which had been prepared by his assistants well in advance. The arsenal of ploys he used to gain popularity included such simple tactics as demonstrating his Russian-made shoes ("costing 23 rubles") and jackets. In the same manner, Yeltsin would travel by limousine and then transfer to the tram to ride the last two stops

---

7. "Yeltsin fired 23 out of Moscow's 33 district Party secretaries and some of them were fired two times in a row because the new appointees proved to be no better than the old cadres. 'Trading bad for worse,' Yeltsin used to joke later. One of the fired district Party secretaries jumped to his death from a seventh-story apartment window. Yeltsin took this incident very close to heart. When he was blamed for ruining the cadres, he referred to Gorbachev's experience who dismissed 66 percent of provincial Party bosses across the country, while he fired only 60 percent of district-level Party secretaries in Moscow. In the Moscow City Party Committee, Yeltsin fired 40 percent of the CPSU *nomenklatura* cadres, 36 percent of municipal government officials, and 44 percent of trade union leaders. The respective numbers of Gorbachev's dismissals stand at 60 percent of ministers and 70 percent of heads of CPSU Central Committee departments." Vladimir Soloviev and Elena Klepikova, *Boris Yeltsin: A Political Biography* (London: Weidenfeld and Nicolson, 1992), 37–38.

before visiting a factory or plant, or he would turn up at his local medical clinic instead of going to the Kremlin hospital. Such mingling with the general populace received generous coverage in municipal mass media controlled by the City Party Committee and by Yeltsin personally.

Yeltsin's more senior Politburo colleagues were growing increasingly irritated by his populist policies, love of theatrical gestures, arbitrariness, attacks on the very fundamentals of the *nomenklatura* system,[8] and growing popularity. First, Yeltsin was refused the expected promotion, instead remaining an alternate rather than a full Politburo member, which he should have become by virtue of his position.[9] Later, in the fall of 1987, he was first dismissed as head of the Moscow Party organization and subsequently as candidate member of the Politburo. It was at that moment that Gorbachev vowed he would never allow Yeltsin to return to politics. However, Yeltsin did receive a *nomenklatura* sinecure, being appointed deputy chairman of the State Construction Committee with a ministerial portfolio.

Yeltsin's expulsion from the pinnacle of party leadership immediately turned him into a hero in the eyes of the public. Rumors started to spread that, at a plenary meeting of the CPSU Central Committee, the Moscow Party leader denounced Gorbachev's indecisive and palliative policies, called for more radical reforms of the party and society, and blasted the *nomenklatura* system. The popular perception of Yeltsin was that of a fighter for good and

---

8. It is important to stress that Yeltsin's challenge to the *nomenklatura* system with slogans about combating privileges and corruption was strictly limited by the time period of his ascent to power. Once he took power, however, Yeltsin developed that system and made it more comprehensive rather than demolishing it.

9. In this regard, the comparison with the former Tomsk region secretary, Egor Ligachev, made by McFaul is inaccurate. However, three Moscow and Politburo newcomers, former masters of remote regions, Mikhail Gorbachev (Stavropol), Egor Ligachev (Tomsk), and, to a lesser degree, Boris Yeltsin (Sverdlovsk), pushed away the Kremlin gerontocracy representing national capitals, Viktor Grishin (Moscow) and Grigori Romanov (Leningrad), and defined the fate of the CPSU and the USSR itself.

against evil. He was even said to have urged Gorbachev to sharply reduce the visibility and role of his wife Raisa, who was extremely unpopular with the general public. When the plenary meeting documents were published a few years later,[10] they revealed that Yeltsin's speech was not as iconoclastic as expected. As for the "revolutionary" speech that was unofficially circulated in 1987, it was, in fact, written by a team of journalists close to Yeltsin, as Mikhail Poltoranin, who headed the group, admitted in an NTV channel production titled *Tsar Boris*.

Two other interesting episodes are closely connected with this turning point in Yeltsin's career, and they portray him as "a persecuted advocate of justice." They are Yeltsin's penitential speech at the plenary meeting of the Moscow City Party Committee of the CPSU at which he was dismissed as first secretary,[11] and his plea for "life-time rehabilitation" at the Nineteenth Party Conference in 1988. These two episodes do not fit well with the perception of Yeltsin as a man who had conscientiously and resolutely severed ties with his Communist past.

Had Yeltsin not been lucky in subsequent events that brought him back into political prominence in 1988, he would have spent the rest of his life in oblivion like Aleksandr Shelepin and Dmitri Polianski before him. The system itself had to bend so that a politician expelled from the leadership could stage a comeback to the very top. Yeltsin's failing party career suddenly became a step up, not down, when the whole system of power capsized.

Yeltsin as a Popular Tribune

In April 1989, Yeltsin was elected a people's deputy of the USSR representing the Moscow city constituency, although at the party

---

10. *Izvestia TsK KPSS*, no. 2, 239–241.

11. Yeltsin accounted for his incoherent and pleading speech by referring to his poor health (he had been hospitalized) and the influence of strong sedatives, which had paralyzed his willpower. Three years later, Yeltsin would say that the footage showing him in a state of intoxication while on a visit to the United States

conference a year earlier he had represented Karelia, and at the
Congress of People's Deputies of Russia a year later, he represented the Ural region. There are at least two factors that make Yeltsin's choice of his constituency interesting. Nominated as a
candidate for people's deputy in a number of constituencies, it appeared that he had a broad choice. However, considering the fact
that candidate registration decisions were made by constituency-
level election commissions, most of which were under party control, the real choice was between the Moscow and Sverdlovsk Na-
tional-Territorial *okrugs*, or NTOs (the former including the city
of Moscow, and the latter the Sverdlovsk Oblast), and about 50
constituencies in Moscow and the Sverdlovsk Oblast. What Yeltsin
needed was not simply election to the Congress but a triumphant
victory. That was why he chose the Moscow city NTO, thus
blocking the way, deliberately or not, of academician Andrei Sakharov, for whom Moscow was the only alternative to the Academy
of Sciences ballot list. The main political feature of those elections
was the opposition between the party *nomenklatura* candidates
and a broad front encompassing political forces ranging from the
democratic platform within the CPSU to dissidents. Therefore,
there was nothing surprising in the situation whereby Yeltsin, a
Communist who had fallen out of favor, found himself on the same
side of the barricade with Sakharov, a democrat and anti-Communist. Yeltsin and Sakharov were even nominated together by a democratically minded gathering at Moscow's House of Cinema.

Yeltsin's rival in the constituency was Evgeni Brakov, general director of the Likhachev auto plant. Brakov was an obscure candidate generally viewed as the personification of the party
apparatchik rather than an individual contender. In the context of
relatively free voting, there was effectively no way Brakov could
defeat Yeltsin.

---

had been tampered with and shown in slow motion. After some time, the explanations of his repeated antics would make him a laughingstock.

Two important aspects must be stressed here. First, the phenomenon of early Yeltsin is, to a large extent, propagandistic in nature, and anti-Yeltsin propaganda may have easily played a more important role than pro-Yeltsin propaganda in his rise to power. The anti-Yeltsin propaganda was clumsy and crude; the population was generally disappointed with the authorities of the day, and Yeltsin must be given credit for his skillful manipulation of that disappointment.[12] Yeltsin finally assumed the right image of a popular hero, a fighter for justice who challenged the system and was victimized by it. All these factors combined in the public consciousness to generate the Yeltsin myth, which could not be dispelled by any rational reasoning. What was needed was either another myth or time for the Yeltsin myth to dissipate.[13]

Second, all stages of Yeltsin's rise to power, from his invitation to Moscow to his election as Supreme Soviet Chairman and, later, as president of the Russian Federation, were invariably connected to Mikhail Gorbachev. One cannot fail to notice a number of chance situations that were extremely fortunate for Yeltsin. They include having convenient contenders (Brakov in 1989, Ivan Polozkov in the 1990 election of the Supreme Soviet Chairman, and Ni-

---

12. The antigovernment sentiments of the populace were most clearly manifested during the 1989 and 1990 elections of people's deputies of the USSR and the RSFSR. Voting against apparatchiks of all levels was the main feature of electoral behavior, while a clear division along political lines was still missing. The "protest" nature of the vote found its most eloquent manifestation in 1989 in Leningrad, where a number of party bosses, including the first secretaries of the oblast and city party committees, lost the election even though they had no rivals. As for the Leningrad NTO, the country's second largest after Moscow, the election there was won by an obscure populist, Nikolai Ivanov, who, in tandem with Telman Gdlian, won prominence for his investigation of the cotton and other corruption scandals.

13. The myth of General Aleksandr Lebed (1996–1997) is the second such instance in Russia's modern history. It is peculiar that Yeltsin himself saw a certain similarity between himself and the brave general: "A. Lebed reminded me of someone: myself. Only he was a caricature of me, as if I were looking in a fun house mirror." Boris Yeltsin, *Midnight Diaries* (New York: Public Affairs, 2000), 67.

colai Ryzhkov in the presidential elections); his "miraculous" election to the Supreme Soviet of the USSR,[14] where Yeltsin secured himself one of the leading positions; and, most importantly, his 1987 transformation from a candidate member of the CPSU Central Committee Politburo to a potential opposition leader. It is not incidental that a number of Sovietologists, including Jerry Hough, continued to regard Yeltsin as "Gorbachev's man" even after the 1991 presidential elections.[15]

The fact remains that Yeltsin, a *nomenklatura* man himself, headed the anti-*nomenklatura* revolution in the USSR and guided it to its ultimate conclusion in favor of the *nomenklatura* system. One can find certain similarities with the regional "velvet revolutions" of the late 1980s, when first secretaries of regional party committees were replaced by second and third secretaries, as well as with a number of gubernatorial elections in the second half of the 1990s, when the regional systems of power were preserved through the sacrifice of the first persons and their immediate entourages.

Yeltsin and Democrats

The alliance between Yeltsin and the democrats was created in the spring of 1989 during the election campaign of the Congress of People's Deputies of the USSR and, most importantly, during the preparation for the First Congress of the Moscow Initiative Group, which later become the core of the Inter-Regional Group of Deputies. The alliance against the common enemy—the party of power

---

14. The Supreme Soviet was formed at the Congress out of people's deputies to work on a consistent basis. Yeltsin did not get enough votes that time to be elected on his own. It was owing to one of the Siberian deputies, Aleksei Kazannik, who refused to release his mandate in favor of Yeltsin, that the latter became an MP and chaired the Supreme Soviet Committee on Construction. Later, when Yeltsin came to power, provincial lawyer Kazannik was awarded the position of prosecutor general, a post he lost in 1994 when he let Ruslan Khasbulatov, Aleksandr Rutskoi, and other leaders of the 1993 deputies' opposition to Yeltsin out of prison despite Yeltsin's pressure not to do so.

15. Jerry Hough, in discussion with the author, July 1991.

represented by the Communist *nomenklatura*—was a mutually beneficial one; the democrats needed a popular hero to use as a battering ram, and Yeltsin, who was entering public politics, needed secure massive electoral backing to support him in his campaign. "The democrats wanted to use Yeltsin for their own ends, but ultimately he used them for his own ends," was the way this cooperation was later expressed. But this description is too simplistic. It would be more accurate to speak about a tactical alliance in which most participants lacked a vision of strategic objectives.

As a kind of epilogue to the story of Yeltsin's early history with the democrats, it is interesting to trace what happened to the democratically minded intellectuals in Moscow who forged an alliance with him in 1989. Michael McFaul mentions seven individuals; some are no longer alive and others have dispersed. Andrei Sakharov died in the fall of 1989 under circumstances that still are not completely clear. In 1992 Yuri Afanasiev left the leadership of the Democratic Russia movement, which he believed had associated itself too strongly with the antidemocratic Yeltsin. He abandoned politics and currently heads the Russian State University of Humanities, which he founded. Gavriil Popov became Chairman of the Moscow City Soviet in 1990 and mayor of Moscow in 1991. In the middle of 1992 he unexpectedly resigned, and in 1993, as one of the leaders of the Russian Movement for Democratic Reform, he tried but failed to win a seat in the Duma. Currently serving as a university rector, Popov is involved in politics only in a consulting capacity; he is seen as one of the leaders of the Social Democrats. Until her assassination in 1998, Galina Starovoitova was the leader of the Democratic Russia movement, serving as the presidential adviser on ethnic issues. She remained with Yeltsin until 1992, the year in which she was considered as a potential candidate for the vice presidency and even for the post of minister of defense. Sergei Stankevich spent some time working as deputy chairman of the Moscow City Soviet and then served as Yeltsin's adviser on political issues. He left the country in 1993, was prosecuted on corruption charges, and currently lives in Poland. Arkadi Murashev spent some time working as head of the Moscow police force and was dismissed by Yuri Luzhkov in 1992; he currently heads the Liberal and Conservative Policy Center. He lost two elections to the state Duma (in 1995 and 1999); between Duma elections, he ran unsuccessfully for the Moscow city Duma. Ilia Zaslavski, who was included in this group by chance in the wake of the democratic movement of the late 1980s, did not stay long in politics.

As the foregoing list reveals, none of the real leaders of the first-wave democrats have remained in politics, either in power or in opposition. Many democratic leaders were appointed by Yeltsin to various positions, but they were forced to leave politics the year after he took over the Kremlin. Many left political life, and others passed away. The death of Andrei Sakharov, spiritual leader of the democratic opposition and uncompromising representative of the democratic movement, was the most negative event affecting the future of democracy in Russia.

Speaking of non-Moscow politicians, Michael McFaul mentions Anatoli Sobchak, who might easily have been the most successful among the founding fathers of the democratic movement outside Moscow. He served as mayor of St. Petersburg from 1991 to 1996, played an important role in the 1993 Constitutional Assembly, and at one point was even considered a possible successor to Yeltsin. However, having lost the 1996 mayoral election, Sobchak became politically marginalized and was even forced to emigrate after criminal charges (including abuse of office and illegal apartment distribution) were brought against him. When Sobchak returned to Russia in mid-1999 following the appointment of Vladimir Putin, his former deputy, as prime minister, Sobchak was nominated to the Duma in one of the St. Petersburg constituencies, but he lost the election. He died suddenly in early 2000 while serving as one of Putin's representatives in the presidential elections.

Having allied himself with the democrats, Yeltsin started to mount an opposition to centrist Gorbachev and the conservative wing of the party *nomenklatura*. Yeltsin's own democratic convictions were situation-specific (although similar situations had repeatedly emerged since 1989) and position-specific, his position usually being against, rather than for, a particular idea or movement. First, he opposed the conservative wing of the CPSU, then the conservative and pro-Communist faction in the Russian Congress of People's Deputies headed by Ruslan Khasbulatov, and finally the Communist majority in the Duma and the virtual "Red menace" of Gennadi Ziuganov's Communist Party of Russia.

Yeltsin had four major onsets of democratic sentiment in 1989, 1991, 1993, and 1996, and each time, he pursued a specific goal: to come to power, to avert an economic collapse, to secure full power, and to stay in power. Each time he had new democratic allies: democrats of the first wave, Egor Gaidar and his team, Gaidar once again with Sergei Kovalev, and Anatoli Chubais and the "St. Petersburg team." Thus for Yeltsin, democracy was a means rather than an end, and he was quick to forget his democrat loyalties as soon as he attained specific political goals. It is not surprising, then, that in 1992 prominent political expert Aleksandr Sobianin spoke of "the *nomenklatura* revenge,"[16] and today Michael McFaul speaks of Yeltsin's periodic lapses into antidemocratic and anti-Western policies.

The process of creation and affirmation of Yeltsin's image as a democrat was promoted by both the existence of the Communist opposition and the absence of a democratic opposition. The latter factor is only partially connected to Yeltsin's skillful political maneuvering and his ability to avoid turning his associates into enemies; once they were forced out of active political life, Yeltsin found ways to secure their silence and neutrality. It is equally important that, in an environment in which the spontaneous public enthusiasm of the late 1980s receded while the state continued to rigidly control all economic activities, no independent economic actors came forward, and political parties free of ties to clans within the ruling elite simply could not emerge.

---

16. Varov, Sobianin, and Yuriev, *Nomenklaturnyi revansh*.

Yeltsin Promotes Democracy:
Steps Forward and Backward

The picture of Russia's democratic development and Yeltsin's role in it would not be complete if, in addition to analyzing the motivations and intentions of political actors, we did not analyze the process of democratization with its major milestones and achievements. They are: direct elections of (1) members of parliament, (2) the president, (3) regional legislatures, (4) regional governors, and (5) heads of municipalities; referendums; liquidation of the Soviets; ban of the CPSU and nationalization of party assets; mass media and freedom of information; the constitution; freedom of travel; federalism; and horizontal division of power.

What was Yeltsin's role in securing these main achievements of Russian democracy? A distinction should be made between mainstream development and momentous steps that did not necessarily modify overall progress but nevertheless played an important part. Such steps include:

- 1991–1993: Ignoring the will of the people expressed directly at the 1991 all-Union and 1993 all-Russia referendums.
- 1991–1996: Postponing direct elections of regional governors for five years.
- 1991–1996: Weakening the role of institutions and strengthening the role of individuals; creating a system of favoritism with a succession of *eminences grises*, and generally pursuing a Byzantine style of leadership. The nontransparent and autocratic system of appointments to and dismissals from the highest government positions, which demonstrated utter contempt for public opinion, existed throughout Yeltsin's rule but became especially pronounced in 1998 and 1999. Yeltsin ignored gross violations of the constitution and federal legislation by regional barons in such places as Kalmykia in 1998, Tatarstan in 1996, and Bashkortostan in 1998, and engaged in

continued political bargaining with them, trading the center's noninterference in regional affairs and the support of regional leaders for their demonstrated loyalty to the president.

- 1993: Ignoring the Constitutional Court decision that confirmed the authority of the Cheliabinsk Oblast governor, Petr Sumin, whom Yeltsin refused to recognize; and using force in September to oust the Cheliabinsk and Briansk Oblast governors who had been popularly elected six month before. Yeltsin halted functions of the Constitutional Court itself for six months, and the court's composition was changed.
- 1993: Using crude force to resolve the conflict with the Supreme Soviet; trampling upon the constitution; bringing in tanks to shell the Supreme Soviet building in downtown Moscow, resulting in numerous casualties; pushing through his own version of the constitution instead of the one previously agreed on by the Constitutional Assembly, in violation of the effective referendum law; demonstrating contempt for the idea of a national referendum by calling elections for bodies that were not specified by the effective constitution simultaneously with the adoption of the new constitution; abolishing the right to vote "against all" on the very eve of the elections, thus preventing voters from blocking powerful but unpopular candidates; and allowing massive fraud in the 1993 elections and the constitutional plebiscite.
- 1994: Breaking his promise to hold an early presidential election as a kind of a vote of public confidence after the 1993 coup d'état.
- 1994–1996, 1999: Unleashing and waging an all-out war in Chechnya without declaring a state of emergency and without the approval of the Federation Council.
- 1995: Illegitimately prolonging by two years the term of regional legislature members elected in 1993 and 1994.
- 1995, 1999: Ignoring constitutional provisions and the opinion of the Federation Council when appointing and dismissing Prosecutors General Aleksei Iliushenko and Yuri Skuratov.

- 1996: Using the full might of the state to secure his election for the second term; exceeding the legally permitted amount of campaign funds by tens, if not hundreds, of times; and selling state property cheaply to finance his presidential campaign.
- 1999: Bestowing power on his successor in an antidemocratic way while securing immunity from criminal prosecution for himself and his family members.

The list of other wrongdoings includes Yeltsin's failed attempt to restore the KGB-FSB in 1994; the planned dissolution of the Duma in 1996 to avoid presidential elections; the firing of some elected officials at the municipal level in 1997 and 1998; and expanding influence of the coercive apparatus during his second term, including mass appointments of secret service and police officers to high civilian positions.[17]

During the full six years from December 1993 to December 1999, Yeltsin, whose political career in the new Russia started with the position of parliament chairman, visited the state Duma, the Russian parliament's lower chamber, only twice. First, in 1997, he personally delivered a state award to Speaker Gennadi Seleznev on the occasion of Seleznev's fiftieth anniversary, and second in 1998, when he assisted in the approval of the anticrisis plan of Sergei Kirienko's government. Yeltsin's attitude toward parliament and its members was clearly expressed when he said in the spring of 1998, as the Duma was discussing Kirienko's appointment to the post of prime minister, "I gave an instruction to Pavel Borodin to resolve the problems of the Duma deputies."[18]

One must conclude that Yeltsin advocated democracy only when

---

17. Three out of four prime ministers appointed by Yeltsin in 1998 and 1999—Evgeni Primakov, Sergei Stepashin, and Vladimir Putin—had the experience of heading either foreign intelligence or FSB. The new wave of presidential representatives in regions appointed in 1998 and 1999 consisted mainly of FSB officers.

18. See, for example, Peter Reddaway and Dmitri Glinski, *The Tragedy of Russia's Reforms: Market Bolshevism Against Democracy*, United States Institute of Peace Press, http://www.usip.org (2001).

he was aspiring to power and abandoned it once power was in his hands. He understood democracy as limiting not his own power, but that of others. His concept of democracy was expressed by the goals he declared, not by his methods. Evidence that Yeltsin's idea of democracy was destructive rather than constructive is contained in his memoirs.[19]

With regard to democracy, especially in the Russian context, the question of ends and means becomes quite important. In Russia, democracy is often understood as power of the self-styled democrats; the means employed, especially when dealing with Communists and other ideological adversaries, are considered unimportant. This is why the terms "democrat" and "Communist" are often enclosed in quotation marks, for they share a genetic code and both groups often act in similar ways.[20] Not surprisingly, when the conflict between Yeltsin and the Supreme Soviet ended in bloodshed in 1993, it was widely remarked that "one wing of the Bolshevik party had defeated the other."

Conclusion

There is no doubt that Boris Yeltsin was an outstanding personality—a bright, strong, inventive man who destroyed all obstacles blocking his ascent to power.[21] Unfortunately, attaining power was Yeltsin's only agenda. Once he possessed absolute power, he

---

19. Boris Yeltsin, *Midnight Diaries.*

20. For a detailed description, see Alexander Lukin, *The Political Culture of the Russian "Democrats"* (Oxford: Oxford University Press, 2000).

21. Yeltsin in general was a reactive, revolutionary type of politician for key moments of history, but not for everyday life. His extraordinary activist outbursts were followed by long periods of passivity or total absence from the political scene. As time went by, his activism became more artificial and less positive. I can remember him on the evening of January 13, 1991, when, at the celebration of the Moscow News jubilee, he got a message about the Vilnius events described by McFaul and left for the airport to fly to Vilnius immediately. At the time, Gorbachev did not react at all, but later he explained that he had been sleeping and thus had not been informed. Less than four years later, at the beginning of the first Chechen war, the president and commander in chief was absent from Russia for an entire week due to a "planned operation on his nose."

proved unable to use that power for the benefit of the country. Yeltsin is guilty of, and has to be pitied for, having squandered a tremendous amount of public confidence by betraying the expectations of those who supported him, however unrealistic those expectations might have been. By the end of 1993, Yeltsin had fully played out his historic role, and for the six years that followed he simply lingered in the political arena.

Boris Yeltsin was a person of great integrity. He was never a renegade, neither in the late 1980s nor in the mid-1990s. He adapted to changing political situations and entered into political alliances with the enemies of his enemies. He accepted the famous call to "Take as much sovereignty as you can swallow!" which was perfectly consistent with the logic of the moment because sovereignty would then be taken away from Mikhail Gorbachev and union authorities, not himself. At various points in time, Yeltsin's allies included the so-called democrats, leaders of ethnic regions, striking miners, the Baltic republics, and the West.[22] Yeltsin often reversed his relations with such allies and maintained no lasting relationships. Instead of working for the interests of Russia or democracy, he pursued his own ambition for power. Only at certain stages did Yeltsin's self-interest coincide with interest in democracy for Russia.

Returning to Michael McFaul's analysis of the role of personality and ideas in Russia's modern history, I believe one may conclude that both Gorbachev and Yeltsin played extremely important roles in the democratization of Russia and bringing about the collapse of the old regime,[23] but the conflict between the two leaders was even more important. This was a perfectly institutional conflict with a personal touch. With Gorbachev gone in 1991, a new con-

---

22. It is widely known that once the Belovezhskaia Pushcha Accords (which dismantled the Soviet Union) were signed in 1991, Yeltsin called President George H. W. Bush in an attempt to secure Western support. Only later did he inform President Gorbachev.

23. The difference is that, when he came to power, Gorbachev started to modernize the system, which eventually led to its collapse, whereas Yeltsin forced the system's disintegration as a vehicle to bring himself to power.

flict, also institutional, started to drive the democratization process: the conflict between Boris Yeltsin and the Supreme Soviet. It is to that conflict that the country owes the process of federalization, the first elections of regional governors, and the referendum. Once the conflict was over, so was the initial stage of the democratization process. Further democratization weakened the state and all its institutions.

I fully agree with McFaul that Yeltsin essentially shaped the peaceful transition out of communism in Russia. Without Yeltsin, this transition from the former *nomenklatura* system to the present neo-*nomenklatura* system might have proceeded in a different direction. With regard to Yeltsin's adoption of democratic ideology, I would give more credit to Russian society than to Yeltsin himself. Yeltsin skillfully rode the powerful democratic wave from 1988 to 1991. It was a rational choice inspired by external political circumstances, and had he adopted a different ideology of opposition and a different set of allies, he would have failed to grasp power.

There is not necessarily a rigid link between Yeltsin's embrace of democracy and his relations with the West. His honeymoon with the West ended at the beginning of 1996 when Evgeni Primakov replaced Andrei Kozyrev as foreign minister. Yeltsin interpreted the electoral success of the Russian Communist Party in the 1995 Duma elections as a signal of growing left-wing and superpower sentiments in society. After that, he effectively shared the Communists' foreign policy agenda while retaining certain domestic policy differences with them. Thus, Yeltsin was "pro-Western" only until he entered the 1996 presidential campaign for his second term; hence, the fate of START II.

Boris Yeltsin was a man of many facets. A democratically elected tsar, he played the role, acting autocratically and on impulse, with little respect for democratic processes or even for the laws he himself had established. At the same time, he was never simply a political machine devoid of idealistic aspirations. Yeltsin may not deserve blame, for the problems he faced as a leader were essentially with Russian society, but neither does he merit praise.

CONTRIBUTORS

Alexei Arbatov is a scholar-in-residence at Carnegie Moscow Center and Program Co-chair on Nuclear Nonproliferation. He served as a member of the Russian parliament (State Duma) and as Deputy Chairman of the Defense Committee from 1994 to 2003. Dr. Arbatov has authored a number of books, including *Russia and the West: The 21st Century Security Environment* with Karl Kaiser and Robert Legvold (1999), and *Beyond Nuclear Deterrence: Transforming the U.S.-Russian Equation* with Vladimir Dvorkin and with a foreword by John D. Steinbrunner (2006). He has written numerous articles and papers on global security, strategic stability, disarmament, Russian military reform, and various issues of current domestic and foreign policy.

Karen Brutents, Ph.D., served as deputy head of the International Department at the Central Committee of the CPSU and as an adviser to the president of the Soviet Union, Mikhail Gorbachev. He is the author of a number of books and many articles on international relations. His latest books are *Thirty Years at the Old Square* (1998) and *Unfulfilled* (2005).

Anatoli Cherniaev is an associate at the Gorbachev Foundation in Moscow. For most of the glasnost period he was the chief foreign policy adviser to Mikhail Gorbachev, the leader of the Soviet Union. Prior to working for Gorbachev, Cherniaev served for twenty years in the International Department of the Central Committee of the Communist Party. His latest books include *Did Rus-*

sia Have a Chance? It Was the Last One (2003); *Eternity of Woman* (2000); *My Six Years with Gorbachev* (2000); *1991: The Diary of the Aide to the President of the USSR* (1997); and *My Life and My Time* (1995).

Oleg Grinevsky served as Ambassador of the Russian Federation to Sweden from 1991 to 1997. He served as head of the Soviet delegation to the Vienna Negotiation on Conventional Armed Forces in Europe (CFE) from 1989 to 1991. Ambassador Grinevsky was Director of the Middle East Department in the Soviet Foreign Ministry and headed the Soviet delegation to the CSCE Stockholm Conference from 1984 to 1986. Ambassador Grinevsky has published numerous articles and papers on issues of international security, disarmament, arms control, Soviet and Russian foreign policy, and modern Middle East policy. His latest books include *The Break: From Brezhnev to Gorbachev* (2004), *Scenario for World War Three* (2002), and *Secrets of Soviet Diplomacy* (2000).

David Holloway is Professor of Political Science, Raymond A. Spruance Professor in International History, and senior fellow at the Freeman Spogli Institute for International Studies, Stanford University. He is the author of *Stalin and the Bomb: The Soviet Union and Atomic Energy, 1939–1956* (1994).

Robert L. Hutchings is Diplomat in Residence at Princeton University, where he has also served as Assistant Dean of the Woodrow Wilson School of Public and International Affairs. During a public service leave from the university in 2003–05, he was Chairman of the U.S. National Intelligence Council in Washington, D.C. His combined academic and diplomatic career has included service as Fellow and Director of International Studies at the Woodrow Wilson International Center for Scholars, Director for European Affairs with the National Security Council, and Special Adviser to the Secretary of State, with the rank of ambassador. He has also served as deputy director of Radio Free Europe and on the faculty of the

University of Virginia, and has written widely about U.S. foreign policy and European politics. He is the author of *American Diplomacy and the End of the Cold War: An Insider's Account of U.S. Policy in Europe, 1989–1992* (1997).

Jack F. Matlock Jr. was the George F. Kennan Professor at the Institute for Advanced Study from 1996 to 2001. Subsequently, he served as visiting professor at Princeton University and Sol Linowitz Professor of International Relations at Hamilton College. He served as U.S. Ambassador to the Soviet Union from 1987 to 1991 and as Special Assistant to the President for National Security Affairs and Senior Director for European and Soviet Affairs on the National Security Council staff from 1983 to 1986. His recent books include *Reagan and Gorbachev: How the Cold War Ended* (2004) and *Autopsy on an Empire: The American Ambassador's Account of the Collapse of the Soviet Union* (1995).

Michael McFaul is the Peter and Helen Bing Senior Fellow at the Hoover Institution, Professor of Political Science at Stanford University, and the director of the Center on Democracy, Development, and the Rule of Law at the Freeman Spogli Institute for International Studies at Stanford. His latest books include *After the Collapse of Communism: Comparative Lessons of Transitions* with Kathryn Stoner-Weiss (2005) and *Russia's Unfinished Revolution: Political Change from Gorbachev to Putin* (2001).

Georgi I. Mirski is a chief research fellow at the Institute of World Economy and International Relations in Moscow, Russian Academy of Sciences. He is also a member of the board of advisers of Russia in Global Affairs. His books include *On Ruins of Empire: Ethnicity and Nationalism in the Former Soviet Union* (1997).

Pavel Palazhchenko is adviser to the President of the Gorbachev Foundation. He served at the Soviet Ministry of Foreign Affairs beginning in 1987 and was an interpreter for Mikhail Gorbachev during all Soviet-American summits. His latest book is *My Years with Gorbachev and Shevardnadze: The Memoir of a Soviet Interpreter* (1997).

Nikolai Petrov is a scholar-in-residence at the Carnegie Moscow Center, where he co-chairs the Russian Domestic Politics program and the Civil Society Project. He was adviser and analyst for the Russian parliament (Supreme Council) and government from 1991 to 1993 and served the presidential administration from 1994 to 1995. From 1993 to 1994 he was a scholar at the Kennan Institute for Advanced Russian Studies. His latest books include *Between Dictatorship and Democracy: Russian Post-Communist Political Reform* with Michael McFaul and Andrei Ryabov (2004), and contributions to *The Dynamics of Russian Politics: Putin's Reform of Federal-Regional Relations* (2006).

Condoleezza Rice has served as U.S. Secretary of State since January 2005. She was National Security Adviser to President George W. Bush from 2001 to 2005 and Senior Director of Soviet and East European Affairs in the National Security Council from 1989 to 1991. Dr. Rice is on a leave of absence from Stanford University, where she was a Professor of Political Science from 1993 to 2000 and a Senior Fellow at the Hoover Institution from 1999 to 2000. Her books include *Germany Unified and Europe Transformed: A Study in Statecraft* with Philip Zelikow (1995) and *The Soviet Union and the Czechoslovak Army, 1948–1983: Uncertain Allegiance* (1984).

Peter W. Rodman is a senior fellow in the Foreign Policy Studies program at the Brookings Institution. He served as Assistant Secretary of Defense for International Security Affairs from 2001 to 2007. During the administrations of Presidents Ronald Reagan and George H. W. Bush, Mr. Rodman was Director of the State Department Policy Planning Staff (1984–1986), Deputy Assistant to the President for National Security Affairs (1986–1987), and Special

Assistant to the President for National Security Affairs and National Security Council Counselor (1987–1990). He was a member of the NSC staff during the Nixon and Ford administrations (1969–1977). He is the author of *More Precious than Peace: The Cold War and the Struggle for the Third World* (1994).

George P. Shultz is the Thomas W. and Susan B. Ford Distinguished Fellow at the Hoover Institution, Stanford University. Mr. Shultz served in four cabinet positions: Secretary of Labor (1969–1970), Director of the Office of Management and Budget (1970–1972), Secretary of the Treasury (1972–1974), and Secretary of State (1982–89). His numerous books include *Economic Policy Beyond the Headlines* with Kenneth Dam (1977) and *Turmoil and Triumph: My Years as Secretary of State* (1993).

Kiron K. Skinner is an associate professor of international relations at Carnegie Mellon University and a research fellow at the Hoover Institution, Stanford University. She serves on the Chief of Naval Operations Executive Panel and the National Security Education Board. She is a coauthor of the *New York Times* best-sellers *Reagan, In His Own Hand: The Writings of Ronald Reagan that Reveal His Revolutionary Vision of America* with Annelise Anderson and Martin Anderson (2001) and *Reagan, A Life in Letters* with Annelise Anderson and Martin Anderson (2003).

Philip Zelikow holds the White Burkett Miller chair in the Department of History at the University of Virginia. He served as counselor of the Department of State from 2005 to 2007. He has also served as the Executive Director of the 9/11 Commission. A former foreign service officer, he worked on the staff of the National Security Council from 1989 to 1991. His books include *Essence of Decision: Explaining the Cuban Missile Crisis* with Graham Allison (revised edition, 1999), *The Kennedy Tapes: Inside the White House During the Cuban Missile Crisis* with Ernest May (1997), and *Ger-*

many Unified and Europe Transformed: A Study in Statecraft with Condoleezza Rice (1995).

Vladislav Zubok is Associate Professor of History at Temple University. His latest books include *Anti-Americanism in Russia: From Stalin to Putin* with Eric Shiraev (2000), *Inside the Kremlin's Cold War: From Stalin to Khrushchev* with Constantine Pleshakov (1996), and *A Failed Empire: The Soviet Union in the Cold War from Stalin to Gorbachev* (2007).

ACKNOWLEDGMENTS

THIS BOOK BEGAN as an ongoing discussion that Condoleezza Rice and I had during the late 1990s about the final decades of the cold war, and particularly the key turning points related to its end. We became interested in producing a candid conversation on this topic between Americans and Russians by inviting a few scholars and statesmen to submit essays and enlisting specialists from the other side of the cold war divide to provide commentary. The idea was endorsed by John Raisian, director of the Hoover Institution, and Charles Palm, then deputy director of Hoover, and Palm conferred with Victor Kuvaldin, a member of the Executive Committee of the Gorbachev Foundation in Moscow. Kuvaldin and Palm agreed that a unique project was in the making. I would like to thank Kuvaldin, Raisian, and Palm for their encouragement and support throughout this project.

I would also like to thank each of the essayists and commentators for submitting first-rate pieces of writing for this book and for their willingness to make the numerous revisions that are central to producing an intellectual conversation about some of the most significant international events of the twentieth century.

It is a pleasure to thank Pavel Palazhchenko, interpreter to Mikhail Gorbachev during all Soviet-American summits and now adviser to the president of the Gorbachev Foundation, and George Shultz, secretary of state during the Reagan era and currently a distinguished fellow at the Hoover Institution, for writing forewords that are in keeping with the book's theme of parallel analyses of the ending of the cold war.

The authors benefited from the close reading of the entire manuscript by William C. Wohlforth, chair of the Department of Government at Dartmouth College and a leading scholar on the cold war.

A debt of gratitude is owed to numerous colleagues at the Hoover Institution who facilitated the production of this book: Pat Baker, former editor of the Hoover Press, Jeff Bliss, William Bonnett, Frank Coronado, Claudia Hubbard, Denise Elson, Don Meyer, Rita Ricardo-Campbell, Richard Sousa, Celeste Szeto, Deborah Ventura, Dan Wilhelmi, and E. Ann Wood.

I would also like to praise those who provided invaluable assistance with research, editing, and transliteration: Emily Clise, Ioan Ifrim, Leslie Johns, Serhiy Kudelia, Kaiting Chen, Neil Guzy, Lela Gibson, Lauren Ingram, Jennifer LaCoste, Alex Porfirenko, Natasha Porfirenko, Susan Schendel, and Inyoung Song.

This book could not have been written without the generous support provided by the Hoover Institution, the Earhart Foundation, Tad and Dianne Taube, and the Taube Family Foundation.

INDEX

Able Archer maneuvers, 74–75
ABM. *See* anti-ballistic missile
Abrasimov, Petr, 76
Academy of Sciences, 144, 314
    Club of Voters of, 285
Adamishin, Anatoli, 180, 243n18
Adenauer, Konrad, 232
Afanasiev, Yuri, 286n29, 303n63, 317
Afghanistan, 169–73, 188
    Andropov and, 163
    antiterrorism in, 61
    Brezhnev and, 163
    Carter and, 11–15, 102
    coup in, 11, 163–65
    CPSU and, 44
    détente and, 14, 15, 40–41, 162
    Dobrynin and, 163
    Geneva Accords and, 130
    Gorbachev and, 128–31, 146, 170–73
    Gromyko and, 65, 163
    KGB and, 163, 164
    mujahedeen in, 1
    Pakistan in, xv
    Poland and, 76
    U.S. and, xxi, 186
    USSR and, ix, xv, 1, 5, 11, 14, 46, 65–66, 75, 79, 128–31, 142, 146, 155, 159–60, 162–65, 167–171, 173, 180, 184, 185, 188, 207
    Ustinov and, 163
    warnings about, 65

Africa, 19, 65–66, 149–50, 153, 155–162
    Carter and, 160–61
    China and, 160
    Cuba in, 15, 157–59
    national liberation movements in, 66
    in third world, 79
    unrest in, 153, 157–58
    USSR in, 1, 5, 11, 13, 44–46, 52, 65, 66, 79, 102, 155, 162–65, 177
    warnings about, 65. *See also* Angola; Egypt; Ethiopia
Akhromeev, Sergei, 81–82, 171
    Gorbachev and, 121
ALCM missiles, 49, 51
Aleksandrov-Agentov, Andrei, 14, 70, 164
Algeria, 156
Allen, Richard, 65, 110
    in Group B, 48
All-Union KGB meeting, 72
American Committee for a United States of Europe, 203
American Diplomacy and the End of the Cold War (Hutchings), 197, 216
American Enterprise Institute, 65, 65n2
Amin, Hafizullah, 11, 163, 164
Amin, Idi, 160
ancien régime, 277, 288, 292

Andreotti, Giulio, 136, 238

Andropov, Yuri, xix, 63, 64, 65, 75, 76, 88, 115, 159, 185, 186, 195, 268

 Afghanistan and, 163, 169

 diplomacy, 7

 INF deployments and, 31

 KGB and, 72–73

 on Middle East, 79, 83–84

 Reagan and, 2, 26–27, 41, 66, 70, 90–91, 93, 94, 103, 105, 220

 on SDI, 72, 93, 101

 third world and, 79, 178

Angola, 157–59, 161, 167, 168, 180, 188

 anti-Communists in, 158

 KGB and, 159

 U.S. and, 160, 184, 186

anti-ballistic missile (ABM), 42, 50

Anti-Ballistic Missile Treaty, 22, 67, 100, 101, 107

 congressional rejection of, 53

 U.S. withdrawal from, 59. *See also* Strategic Defense Initiative

anti-Communists, 302

 in Angola, 158

 Democratic Union as, 282

 Nixon as, 64

 in Reagan administration, 65

 Reagan as, 90, 172

 Thatcher as, 172

 Yeltsin as, 276–77, 288, 290–95, 308, 314

antimissile defense system. *See* Strategic Defense Initiative

Arafat, Yasser, 156

Arbatov, Alexei, xv, xxii, 4

 on Gorbachev, 8

Arbatov, Yuri (Georgi), 132

Armenia, 287

al-Asad, Hafez, 77, 79, 80

 USSR and, 80

ASAT systems, 42

Ash, Timothy Garton, 200–201

astrodynamics, 55

Austria, Hungarian border and, 257, 260

Baghdad Pact, 151–52

Bahr, Egon, 134

Baker, James, xv, 226, 227, 265, 271

 German unification and, 234, 236, 249–251, 257, 265

 Gorbachev and, 120–21, 139, 257, 271

 perestroika and, 137

balkanization, 137

Ball, James, 83

Baltic republics, 197, 223, 257, 259n6, 264, 271, 284, 287, 297, 298, 324. *See also* Estonia; Latvia; Lithuania

Bates, Robert, 274

Belarus, 299

Belovezhskaia Pushcha Accords, 324n22

Berlin Wall, 135

 Bush, G.H.W. and, 270–71

 German unification and, 272

 opening of, 232–33, 235, 252, 257, 261, 262, 264, 266, 267, 270, 272, 297n55, 300, 307

Bessmertnykh, Aleksandr, 93, 229, 230n2

Bil'ak, Vasil, 196
Bishop, Maurice, 31
Blackwill, Robert, 235, 236, 240n14
Bogomolov Institute, 198
Bokser, Vladimir, 303n63
Boldyrev, Yuri, 285
Bolshevik Revolution, 42
bombers
    B-1, 67
    B-1B, 49
    Backfire, 51, 68
    Bear, 69
    Blackjack, 69
    in Global Shield, 74
    Tu-22M, 51
Borodin, Pavel, 322
Brakov, Evgeni, 314, 315
Brandenburg Gate, 252
Brandt, Willy, 134, 207, 227, 260
Branson, Louise, 277
Bremer, L. Paul, III, 98n12
Bretton Woods system, 192
Brezhnev Doctrine, 7
    renunciation of, 132, 258
Brezhnev, Leonid, xv, xix, 7, 185, 187, 189, 195, 260
    Afghanistan and, 75, 76, 163, 164
    death of, 26
    failing health of, 79, 80
    foreign policy of, 112, 114, 152, 180, 268
    Nixon and, 11, 15, 114
    propaganda and, 169
    Reagan and, 41, 102, 103
    on socialism, 184
Brown, J.F., 197
Brutents, Karen, 6, 158, 163, 164, 181

Brzezinski, Zbigniew, 160–61, 162
Buckley, William, Jr., 106
Bulgaria, 133, 134, 193, 195–96, 198, 218
    in crisis, 242
Bureau of Intelligence and Research, 69
Burt, Richard, in Group B, 48
Bush, George H.W., xvii, xix, 34, 48, 99n15, 121, 216, 225, 226, 238, 256, 270, 297n55, 324n22
    Berlin Wall and, 270–71
    German unification and, 136, 216, 217, 232–35, 246–250, 252, 253
    Gorbachev and, 2–3, 116, 136, 137, 139, 176, 180, 188, 210, 216, 233, 235, 236, 239, 240, 242, 243n18, 257, 262, 264, 268
    perestroika and, 137
    statesmanship of, 192
    Thatcher and, 9, 210, 246
Bush, George W.
    disarmament agreements and, xv
    Putin and, xiv
Byrd Amendment, 136

Cambodia, U.S. and, 180, 186
Camp David accord, 157, 165, 167, 174
capitalism, 114, 118
    Russian, 300
    socialism and, 117
    Yeltsin and, 276, 293–94
Carter, Jimmy, xxi, 1, 11, 13, 165, 204
    Afghanistan and, 102

Carter, Jimmy (*continued*)
Africa and, 160–61
Reagan and, 13
USSR and, 63, 67
Carter-Brezhnev Project, 158
Casey, William, 34, 65, 68
in Group B, 48
Castro, Fidel, 158–159
Ceauşescu, Nicolae, 134, 240
Cecchini Report, 203–4
Center for Strategic and International Studies, 65
Central America, 166, 180, 188
El Salvador, 168. *See also* Nicaragua
CFE treaty. *See* Conventional Armed Forces in Europe Treaty
CFSP. *See* Common Foreign and Security Policy
Charter for Europe, 137
Charter of Paris, x, 191
Chechnya, 321
chemical weapons, 136
Cheney, Richard, 236
Chernenko, Konstantin, xxii, 115, 116, 133, 191–92, 195, 219
Reagan and, 41
Cherniaev, Anatoli, xii–xiii, xx, 6, 200, 241n17, 242, 243, 258, 259, 264–65, 266, 267, 271, 272
new thinking and, 141–43
on Reykjavik, 8
China, 152n2, 225
Africa and, 160
Russia and, 62
threat of, 152–53

U.S. and, 184
USSR and, ix, 42–43, 142, 152, 159–60, 187
Chubais, Anatoli, 319
Churchill, Winston, 217, 275
CIA Estimate, 68
Clark, William P., 98
class struggle, 38, 45, 114, 152, 180
Gorbachev and, 6–7
Club of Voters, 285
CMEA. *See* Council for Mutual Economic Assistance
Cobra Dane program, 85
Committee of 19, 282, 289
Committee of Scientists for Peace, 44
Committee on the Present Danger, 48, 65, 65n2
Common Foreign and Security Policy (CFSP), 205
communism, 18, 113
collapse of, 40, 277, 288
in Czechoslovakia, 277
eventual victory of, 45, 161
goals of, 66
in Poland, 202, 215, 277, 302
Reagan on, 18–19, 97
reform, 231
Yeltsin and, 301, 304, 306–7, 325. *See also* anti-Communists
Communist Party of the Soviet Union (CPSU), 44, 46, 72, 114, 116–18, 140, 145, 151, 158, 163–64, 169, 198, 201, 244, 277, 279, 280–85, 289–92, 301–2, 308–13, 319–20, 325
Afghanistan and, 44

Gorbachev and, 5, 8, 116–17,
280–81
Grishin and, 145
nomenklatura of, 5
Yeltsin in, 277–78, 288n34,
312–13
complex of 1941, 47, 115
Comprehensive Test Ban Treaty
(CTBT), 59
compromise
by Gorbachev, 53
new thinking and, 113
Conference on Security and Cooperation in Europe (CSCE), 5,
88, 121, 205, 209, 236
review by, 30
Congressional Medal of Honor, to
Reagan, xiii
Conquest, Robert, 277
Conventional Armed Forces in Europe (CFE) Treaty, 53, 58, 92
conventional arms, 42, 56, 60–61,
96, 120–21
agreement on, 137
reduction of, 44, 92
"Costs of Non-Europe, The"
(Cecchini Report), 204
Council for Mutual Economic Assistance (CMEA), 206, 222,
223
Council of Ministers, 44
coup
in Afghanistan, 163–65
in Russia, 138, 276, 296, 298–
300, 299n56, 304, 307, 321
in South Yemen, 165
CPSU. *See* Communist Party of
the Soviet Union

Cradock, Percy, 271
Crocker, Chester, 180
CSCE. *See* Conference on Security
and Cooperation in Europe
CTBT. *See* Comprehensive Test
Ban Treaty
Cuba, 15, 166
in Angola, 157–59, 180
financial aid to, 133
Kennedy, John F. and, 38
Khrushchev and, 114
missile crisis in, 63, 220
Czechoslovakia, 75, 133, 193, 195–
96, 198–99, 218, 225
communism in, 277
in crisis, 242
military withdrawal from, 127
Prague Spring, 196

Dashichev, Viacheslav, 187
Dead Grip system, 72
defense industry
in USSR, 42–43, 115. *See also*
military-industrial complex
de-ideologization, xiv, 6n7, 113
of interstate relations, 149, 167,
169
of Soviet foreign policy, 113, 118
DeLauer, Richard, in Group B, 48
Delors, Jacques, 204–5, 205n27,
206, 246–47
democracy
in Poland, 75
Reagan and, 59
USSR and, 59
in Warsaw Pact, 2
Yeltsin and, 276, 293–94, 320–23,
325

Democratic Russia, 288–91, 293, 299, 302, 304, 317
  founding of, 303n63
Democratic Union, 282
  as anti-Communist, 282
Deng Xiaoping, x
derzhavnye, 45
détente, 14–15, 43, 162, 180, 181, 260
  Afghanistan and, 40–41, 162
  collapse of, 40–41, 155–65
  divisible, 207–9, 224–25
  Germany and, 213–14
  Kissinger and, 110, 153
  Nixon and, 153
  Reagan and, 66, 108
  SALT I and, 40–41
  Soviet notion of, 149, 152
  of superpowers, 1, 180–81
  third world and, 152, 155–65, 187
  U.S. and, 153–55
deterrence, 35, 96, 108
  MAD and, 100
Deutschlandpolitik, 213–14
Diakhovski, Aleksandr, 164
Dimona Nuclear Research Center, 81
diplomacy, 5
  by Andropov, 7
  confrontational, 119
  Gorbachev and, 135, 259, 267, 272
  new thinking and, 258
  preemptive, 272
  by Reagan, 7
  strength and, xx–xxiv

  by U.S., 155
  by USSR, 177
  by Western Europe, 220
disarmament, 9, 51, 53, 57, 89, 91, 116–17, 126, 226
  Gorbachev and, 172
  negotiations on, 65
  nuclear, xv, 58, 138
Dmitriev, Viktor, 303n63
Dobbs, Michael, 276
Dobrynin, Anatoli, xx, 178, 258
  Afghanistan and, 163
  Haig and, 66
  O'Neill and, 37n26
  Reagan and, xxi, 27, 39, 70
Doder, Dusko, 277
domino theory, 166
Dulles, John Foster, 203
Duma, 309, 317–22, 326
  dissolution of, 322
Dumas, Roland, 244n21, 250

East Germany, 134, 193, 195–96, 198–99, 202, 209, 215, 218, 232, 240, 250–53, 255
  Hungary and, 201
  USSR and, 231. *See also* Honecker, Erich
Eastern Europe, 132–34, 177, 197, 204–06, 208, 213, 215, 216, 218, 224–27, 268, 288
  assessments of, 198–202
  in crisis, 192–98
  Finlandization of, 199
  Gorbachev and, 112, 120, 132–34, 138, 196–97, 199, 200, 220, 222, 260

Most Favored Nation status to, 206

velvet revolutions and, 132, 134, 316

Western Europe and, 131–2, 138, 209–15, 219. *See also* Baltic republics; Bulgaria; Czechoslovakia; East Germany; Hungary; Poland; Romania; Yugoslavia

Economic and Monetary Union, 203

Egypt, 154

U.S. and, 184

USSR and, 156, 156n7, 157, 157n8, 165, 166, 177

Eisenhower, Dwight D., 96, 203

El Salvador, 166

Elbe, Frank, 252

elections

antigovernment sentiments and, 315n12

Gorbachev and, 294

in Lithuania, 287n31

of Reagan, 34n25, 63

to Russian Congress of People's Deputies, 287–92

in USSR, 280–81

Yeltsin and, 281–84, 294, 318–19, 321–22

encirclement, 151–52

energy exports, controversy in, 62

EPC. *See* European Political Cooperation

equilibria phenomena, 273–74

Estonia, 284

Ethiopia, 158, 160, 161, 173

EU. *See* European Union

Europe, 191–227

divisible détente and, 207–9

between superpowers, 218–27

U.S. troops in, 238n10

USSR integration into, 259. *See also* Eastern Europe; Western Europe

European Community (EC) 203–7, 210–12, 235–39, 245, 247, 249

Cecchini Report, 203–4

Eastern Europe and, 206–7

EC Council, 206

PHARE program, 205

European confederation, 131–32, 138, 139, 196, 243, 259

European Political Cooperation (EPC), 205

European Union (EU), 202, 203, 235

European world order, 138

evil empire, 1, 2, 70, 88, 103, 166, 172, 191, 307

unlabeling of, 127

excessive use of force, 60

exports, to USSR, 12

Falin, Valentin, 160, 241, 243n18, 258, 265

financial aid

to Cuba, 133

to USSR, 232, 264

first-nuclear-use doctrine, 58, 61, 70, 72

500-Day Plan, 293

Ford, Gerald, 16

fortress under siege, 114–15
four-part agenda, 37, 99, 99n15
Four-plus-Two plan, 265
France, 82, 202n23, 204, 209, 211–
13, 215, 243n18, 246–8, 250,
253
See also Mitterrand, François
freedom of press, 280
Front of Steadfastness and Confrontation, 167
Fukuyama, Francis, 236

G7, 139
Gaddis, John Lewis, 97, 192
Gaidar, Egor, 293n44, 319
GATT, 137
Gdlian, Telman, 282, 285–86,
286n29, 289, 315n12
GDR. *See* East Germany
Genscher, Hans-Dietrich, 9, 136,
212–14, 229n1, 234, 242n18,
244, 246–47, 250, 252
Gorbachev and, 134, 243–45, 261
Georgetown University, 65n2
Georgia, 287
Gerasimov, Gennadi, 196
German Democratic Republic
(GDR). *See* East Germany
German unification, xvi–xviii, 4, 6,
9–10, 57, 141, 212, 213, 215,
229–72
Baker and, 234, 236, 249–251,
257, 265
Berlin Wall and, 272
Bush, G.H.W. and, 136, 216, 217,
233
Gorbachev and, 112, 132, 134–
36, 138, 240, 242, 266, 269

Great Britain and, 132, 246, 253
Kissinger on, 235
Kohl and, 9, 134, 256
Malta summit and, 257
new thinking and, 266–67
pace of, 252
principles of, 237
from Russian perspective,
255–72
timing of, 230
Germany
military withdrawal from, 127
in NATO, 6, 74, 135, 230–31,
263–64
Shevardnadze on, 262. *See also*
East Germany; German uni-
fication; Kohl, Helmut;
Schmidt, Helmut; West Germany
*Germany Reunified and Europe
Transformed: A Study in Statecraft* (Zelikow and Rice), 255
Gierek, Edward, 207
GKChP. *See* State Committee for
the State of Emergency
GKES. *See* State Committee on
Foreign Economic Coopera-
tion
glasnost, 125, 167, 174–75, 276
GLCMs. *See* ground-launched
cruise missiles
"Global Competition and the Deterioration of U.S.-Soviet Re-
lations, 1977–1980" (Carter-
Brezhnev Project Confer-
ence), 158
Global Shield, 74
globalization, 10, 141–48

Goebbels, Joseph, 259

Goldwater, Barry, 110

Gorbachev, Mikhail, xvii–xix, 8,
    25–30, 53, 56, 175, 183, 185,
    189, 193, 209, 211, 213, 220,
    222, 227, 227n7, 229, 233, 294,
    296, 303, 309, 312n9, 323n21
  Afghanistan and, 128–31, 146,
    170–73
  Akhromeev and, 121
  Baker and, 120–21
  Bush, G.H.W. and, 2–3, 121, 136,
    176, 236, 239, 240, 243n18,
    257, 264, 268
  on class struggle, 6–7
  common European home, 131–
    32, 138, 139, 196, 243, 259
  diplomacy and, 135, 259, 267,
    272
  Eastern Europe and, 132–34,
    195–97, 199, 200, 207, 218–24,
    226
  elections and, 294
  foreign policy of, 111–41
  Genscher and, 243–44, 261
  German unification and, 134–36,
    215, 233, 239n13, 240, 241n17,
    242, 245, 247–48, 255–72, 266,
    269
  as global statesman, 267
  Gorbymania, 211, 213
  Grosz and, 221
  Honecker and, 259, 260
  Hungarian-Austrian border and,
    201, 257
  Hungary and, 201
  Kissinger and, x, 206, 226

Kohl and, 134, 215, 235, 240,
    241, 243, 243n18, 251, 256–57,
    259–61, 268
  Middle East and, 174
  Mitterrand and, 122, 245–46
  Nixon and, 122
  optimism of, 269
  popularity of, 60
  Raisa, 313
  Reagan and, xxiii–xxiv, 38–39,
    106, 116, 117, 122–24, 139,
    179, 180, 222
  as revolutionary leader, 308
  SDI and, 119
  Shevardnadze and, 144, 263, 265
  Shultz and, xxii, 116, 125–26
  Soviet press and, vii–viii
  statesmanship of, 192
  Ten-Point Plan and, 242–44,
    261–62, 268
  Thatcher and, 111, 132, 226
  third world and, 149, 167, 175,
    179–81, 183
  in *Time,* 116
  transformative role of, 141–48
  at United Nations, 111–12, 127–
    28, 146, 256
  Yeltsin and, 276–82, 291, 293,
    297, 299, 315, 316. *See also*
    new thinking

Gordievsky, Oleg, 32n23

Gosplan, 44

grain sales, to USSR, 12, 28

Great Britain, 132, 209, 212, 215,
    220, 246
  German unification and, 248,
    250, 253
  See also Thatcher, Margaret

Grenada, 31–32, 91
Gribkov, Anatoli, 178
Grinevsky, Oleg, xi, xix, xxii, 5, 7,
    93–96, 98, 101, 110
  conventional arms and, 121
Grishin, Viktor, 145, 278, 309, 310,
    312n9
Gromyko, Andrei, xx, xxii, 64, 76,
    79, 80, 119
  Afghanistan and, 163, 164, 170
  Haig and, 65
  KAL-007 and, 88
  Shultz and, 30, 89–90
Grosz, Karoly, 200, 201
  Gorbachev and, 221
  Honecker and, 208n36
ground-launched cruise missiles
    (GLCMs), 21n14, 50, 55
Group B, 48
Group of Seven, x
GRU, surprise attack and, 72

Haig, Alexander, 17, 21, 65
  Dobrynin and, 66
  Gromyko and, 65
  in Group B, 48
  as secretary of state, 25
Havel, Vaclav, 277, 302
Hayek, Friedrich, 277
Helsinki Final Act, 15, 237, 247
Helsinki Process, 114, 208
Hersh, Seymour, 87
Hitler, Adolf, 242n18, 244, 259, 275
Hoffman, Stanley, 154
Holloway, David, xii, xx
  on Gorbachev, 10
Homo Sovieticus, 151

Honecker, Erich, 75, 76, 134, 207,
    214n47, 222, 224, 259–60
  Gorbachev and, 259
  Grosz and, 208n36
Hoover Institution, 65, 65n2
Hough, Jerry, 316
Human Events, 108
human rights, 37, 89, 289
  Reykjavik summit and, 124–25
  in USSR, 15, 114. *See also* Pente-
    costals
Hungary, 75, 133, 191, 193, 194,
    197–200, 201, 208–9, 218, 221,
    231, 270
  Austrian border and, 257, 260
  East Germany and, 201
  investment in, 195–96
  Kohl and, 260
  military withdrawal from, 127
  refugees in, 231
Huntington, Samuel, 162, 165
Hurd, Douglas, 250
Husak, Gustav, 196, 221
Hussein, Saddam, 3, 137–38, 140,
    175, 176
Hutchings, Robert, xv, 5, 197, 216,
    218–27
  on Thatcher, 9
Hyland, William, 215n49

ICAO. *See* International Civil
    Aeronautics Organization
ICBMs. *See* intercontinental ballis-
    tic missiles
ideology of opposition, 284
Ikle, Fred, 65n2
  in Group B, 48

Iliushenko, Aleksei, 321
IMEMO, 44, 115
   Yakovlev and, 144
IMF. *See* International Monetary
   Fund
imperialism, 114, 142, 151, 160,
   178, 180
   to encircle Russia, 155
   propaganda about, 151
   by U.S., 66, 124, 169
   by USSR, 26, 98
India, 177
INF. *See* intermediate nuclear
   forces
INF treaty, x, xv, 44, 53, 126–27
   conclusion of, 92
   negotiations on, 30, 123, 124
informals, 282
INF-SRF, 52, 53
institutchiki, 115, 144
Institute of Europe, 44, 132
Institute of U.S. Studies, 44
intercontinental ballistic missiles
   (ICBMs), 22, 23, 49, 68, 74
   introduction of, 50–51
   prohibition of, 136
   of USSR, 69
interdependence, new thinking
   and, 112
intermediate-range nuclear forces
   (INF), 1
   double zero, 52, 55
   deployment of, 30–31, 55
   negotiations on, 20–21, 44, 56,
   204
   zero option, 52
International Civil Aeronautics

Organization (ICAO), 29, 85,
   86n19
international law, new thinking
   and, 113
International Monetary Fund
   (IMF), 139
Inter-Regional Group of People's
   Deputies (MDG), 285–86,
   316–17
"Intervention in Afghanistan and
   the Fall of Détente, The," 163
Iran, 41, 156, 165, 170, 305
   controversy in, 62
   Iran-Iraq War, 175
   Kissinger and, 154
   Nixon and, 154
   Reagan and, 166
Iran-Iraq War, 174, 175
Iraq, 52, 156, 305
   Iran-Iraq War, 174, 175
   Kuwait and, x, 3, 138
   U.S. intervention in, 59, 61
ISKAN, 115
Islamic fundamentalism, 166, 175
Israel, 79–82, 104, 155
   Egypt and, 156–57
   Kissinger and, 154
   Nixon and, 154
   U.S. and, 82, 156
   USSR and, 156, 174–75
Ivanov, Nikolai, 282, 315n12

Jackson-Vanik Amendment, 59,
   136
Jakes, Milos, 196
Japan, 77

Jaruzelski, Wojciech, 19, 75, 202
Jefferson, Thomas, 277
John Paul II (pope), 91
Jones, T. Harding, in Group B, 48

Kadar, Janos, 201, 222
Kadarism, 201
KAL-007
  Gromyko and, 88
  Reagan and, xxii, 87–89
  shooting down of, 29–30, 31, 54,
    84–85, 86n19, 88–90
Kamenski, General, 85
Kant, Immanuel, 115
Karmal, Babrak, 11
Kastrup, Dieter, 247
Kataev, Dmitri, 289
Kazannik, Aleksei, 316n14
KC-135 airplane, 85
Kennedy, John F., 183
  Cuba and, 38
  Khrushchev and, 54
Kennedy, Paul, 47
KGB, 33, 44, 46, 65, 82, 298, 304,
    322
  Afghanistan and, 163, 164
  Andropov and, 72–73
  Angola and, 159
  assessments by, 55
  Reagan and, 34, 34n25
  surprise attack and, 72
Khalq (People's) Party, 162
Khasbulatov, Ruslan, 316n14, 319
Khomeini, Ayatollah, 165
Khrushchev, Nikita, xv, 149
  Cuba and, 114
  Kennedy, John F. and, 54
  at United Nations, 114

Kirienko, Sergei, 322, 323
Kissinger, Henry, xvi, 155, 160, 162
  détente and, 110, 153–54
  on German unification, 235
  Gorbachev and, x, 206, 226
  Israel and, 154
  Middle East and, 154, 157
kitchen cabinet, 48
Kliuchevski, Vasili, 62
Kohl, Helmut, xii, xvi, xix, 214,
    215, 220, 232, 233, 238, 239,
    247, 251
  German unification and, 9, 136,
    237, 239, 240, 246, 248, 251,
    252, 253, 256, 267, 269, 270
  Gorbachev and, 134, 215, 235,
    240, 241, 243, 243n18, 251,
    256–57, 259, 260, 261, 268
  Mitterrand and, 235, 245,
    245n21, 246
  Ten-Point Plan and, 234–35,
    242–44
Komchatov, Vladimir, 289
Kondrashov, Sergei, 159
Konstantinov, Ilia, 292n42
Korea, 183, 188, 305. See also KAL-
    007; North Korea
Korean airliner. See KAL-007
Kornienko, Georgi, 14
Kosygin, Alexei, xx
  foreign policy of, 114
Kovalev, Sergei, 319
Kozyrev, Andrei, 187–88, 325
Krenz, Egon, 223, 231–32, 239n13,
    241, 242
Kriuchkov, Vladimir, 173, 263
Kuwait, Iraq invasion of, x, 3, 138
Kvitsinski, Yuli, 21, 22, 241

Landsbergis, Vytautus, 224
Latin America, 15, 19, 149, 153, 161, 179
  national liberation movements in, 66
  USSR and, 46, 66. *See also* Central America
Latvia, 284, 296, 298
launch-on-warning system, 55
Lebanon, 53, 166
  attack on marine barracks in, 83
  civil war in, 175
  Israeli invasion of, 80
  U.S. troops in, 82–83
Lebed, Aleksandr, 315n13
Legvold, Robert, 181
Lehman, John, 65n2
  in Group B, 48
Lenin, Vladimir, 38, 45, 161, 163, 182
  goals of, 42
Leninism. *See* Marxism
Lévesque, Jacques, 258, 260–61
Lewis, Samuel, 166
Libya, 156
Ligachev, Egor, 262, 263, 278, 309–10, 312n9
linkage, xxi–xxii
  Nixon and, 99
  Reagan and, 16
  rejection of, 99
Lithuania, 224, 233, 284, 296, 298, 323n21
  elections in, 287n31
long-range theater nuclear forces (LRTNF), 21n13
LRTNF. *See* long-range theater nuclear forces

Lubbers, Ruud, 238
Lukianov, Anatoli, 298
Luzhkov, Yuri, 318

Macmillan, Harold, 211
MAD. *See* Mutual Assured Destruction
Madrid Conference, 139
Malta summit, xvii, 2, 136–37, 233–36, 239–40, 243n18, 247, 257, 262, 264, 268, 270–71
  German unification and, 257
  Gorbachev at, 257
Mariam, Mengistu Haile, 158, 173
Marshall Plan, 203
Marxism, 18, 45, 97, 113, 118, 128, 152n2, 158, 185, 186
Matlock, Jack F., Jr., xii, xxii, 40, 45, 48–50, 52–55, 98, 170
  on Reagan, 7–8
McFaul, Michael, xix, 5–6
  commentary on, 305–25
MDG. *See* Inter-Regional Group of People's Deputies
medium-range nuclear forces (MRF, MNF, MRNF), 21n13
Memoirs (Gorbachev), 39
Middle East, 8, 63, 77, 138–39, 156, 166–67
  Andropov on, 83–84
  Arab-Israeli War, 155
  Gorbachev and, 174
  Grinevsky and, 5
  Iran-Iraq War and, 175
  Kissinger and, 154
  Nixon and, 154
  potential war in, 79, 81–83

Middle East (*continued*)
  Reagan and, 166
  USSR and, 78, 177
  wars in, 81. *See also* Afghanistan;
    Egypt; Iran; Iraq; Israel; Leba-
    non; Syria
MIG-21, 157n8
Midgetman missiles, 49
military-industrial complex, 122
  Russian coup and, 298, 304
  in U.S., 64, 71, 122
  in USSR, 114, 132, 143
Mirski, Georgi, xiv, xxiii, 4–5,
    182–89
MIRVed missiles, 22, 51, 53, 67
  of USSR, 68
Missile and Outer Space Problems
    Sector, 72
missiles
  ALCM, 42
  anti-ballistic, 42, 50
  crisis with, 63
  cruise, 67
  FROG, tactical ground rocket,
    156n7
  GLCMs, 21n14, 50, 55
  Midgetman, 49
  MX, 23, 67
  Pioneer, 76, 77
  S-200 (SAM-5), 80
  SA3, 156n7
  SLCM, 49
  SS-4, 76
  SS-5, 76
  SS-16, 51
  SS-18, 68
  SS-19, 68

SS-20, 21, 21n14, 44, 53, 68, 76–
    77, 125
SS-24, 69
SS-25, 69
SSBNs, 49, 67
tactical, 52, 74. *See also* intercon-
    tinental ballistic missiles;
    MIRVed missiles; Pershing II
    missiles
ZSU-23-4, anti-aircraft gun, 156n7
Mitterrand, François, xii–xiii, xvii,
    xix, 204, 211, 212, 248, 250,
    265, 266, 269
  Gorbachev and, 122, 245–46,
    249, 267
  Kohl and, 235, 245, 245n21, 246,
    247, 249
  Thatcher and, 246
MNF. *See* medium-range nuclear
    forces
Modrow, Hans, 232, 239n13, 240,
    241, 242, 245, 250, 251, 252
Moiseev, Mikhail, 121
Montesquieu, Baron de, 115
morality, new thinking and, 113
Moscow City Party Committee,
    310, 311n7, 312, 313
Moscow Initiative Group, 316
Moscow Popular Front, 283–84
Moscow-Berlin axis, 272
Most Favored Nation status
  to Eastern Europe, 206
  to USSR, 136
MPLA, 158
MRF. *See* medium-range nuclear
    forces
MRNF. *See* medium-range nuclear
    forces

mujahedeen, in Afghanistan, 1, 130
Murashev, Arkadi, 286n29, 317–18
Muslim fundamentalists, in Russia, 60
Mutual Assured Destruction (MAD), 23, 95
  deterrence and, 100
  Reagan and, 100, 106–8
  rejection of, 101
Muzykanski, Aleksandr, 289
MX missiles, 23, 67
My Years with Gorbachev and Shevardnadze (Palazhchenko), ix

Namibia, 180, 188
Nasser, Gamal Abdel, 156, 174
National Intelligence Estimate, 199, 221
national liberation movements, 41, 46, 115, 159, 286
  in Africa, 66
  in Baltics, 271
  USSR and, 65–66
National Review, 108
National Security Council, 88, 96, 99, 108, 197, 235
National Security Decision Directive (NSDD)
  NSDD-32, 67, 95–98, 98n12
  NSDD-59, 100
  NSDD-61, 100
  NSDD-75, 96n7, 98–100, 98n11, 98n12, 109, 110
  NSDD-85, 100
nationalism
  dangers of, 137
  in Russia, 61

NATO, 57, 58, 61, 72, 77, 127, 138, 202n23, 204, 222, 235, 238n10, 239, 268–69
  cohesion of, xxiv
  on conventional arms, 137
  expansion of, 61, 272
  Germany in, 6, 135, 230–32, 234, 236, 237, 244, 246, 247, 248, 249, 251, 263–64, 266, 269
  maneuvers by, 74
  Russia in, 295
  Warsaw Pact and, 42, 92, 240
  Yugoslavia and, 52, 59
Nemeth, Miklos, 193, 201, 260
Nemtsov, Boris, 310n6
neutron bomb, 41, 66
new thinking, xi–xiv, 116–28
  achievements of, 128–40
  Cherniaev and, 141–43
  compromise and, 113
  diplomacy and, 258
  economic integration and, 13
  German unification and, 134–36, 138, 258–260, 266–67
  Gorbachev and, 111–148, 167, 183, 209, 211, 216, 225–26, 258, 266, 267
  human rights and, 124–25, 137, 148
  interdependence and, 112
  international law and, 113
  morality and, 113
  nuclear weapons and, 112, 116, 117, 122–23, 142, 219, 220
  origins of, 112–16
  Reagan and, xii–xiii
  Western Europe and, 209, 215

Nicaragua, 166, 173–74
  U.S. and, 186
Nicholson, Arthur, xii
Nitze, Paul, 22, 28, 65n2, 108
  in Group B, 48
Nixon, Richard
  as anti-Communist, 64
  Brezhnev and, 11, 15, 114
  détente and, 110, 152, 153, 207
  Germany and, 227
  Gorbachev and, 122
  Iran and, 154
  Israel and, 154
  linkage and, 99
  USSR and, 67
nomenklatura, 44–45, 280, 286,
    309, 312, 319, 325
  of CPSU, 5, 311n7
  in Eastern Europe, 132–34
  Yeltsin and, 291, 309n4, 311n7,
    312, 312n8, 316–18
nonproliferation, 62
North Korea, 42, 305
NSC-68 report, 108
NSDD. *See* National Security De-
    cision Directive
nuclear freeze movement, 105
nuclear weapons, xxii, 192, 211
  elimination of, 95, 105, 107, 117,
    118
  new thinking and, 112, 116, 117,
    122–23, 142, 219, 220
  proliferation of, 59
  Reagan and, 95, 105, 109
  tactical, 74
  in West Germany, 248
Nudel, Ida, 104

Odom, William, 307n3
Ogarkov, Nikolai, 74, 81, 163
oil, 154, 162, 193
  control of, 77–79
  OPEC and, 43
  rising price of, 61, 156, 193
  in Siberia, 133
Olympics, 11
  Romania and, 208, 225
O'Neill, Thomas, 37n26
OPEC embargo, 43
Organization for European Eco-
    nomic Cooperation, 203
Osipovich, Gennadi, 86
Ostpolitik, 207, 213, 214, 227, 232

pact-building, 151
Pakistan, 129, 170, 171, 177
  in Afghanistan, xv
Palazhchenko, Pavel, ix, 10
Palm, Viktor, 286n29
Palme Commission, xi
Pamiat groups, 282–83
Paris summit (1990), 137
peace movements, 31, 105
  in Europe, 21–22
Pearson, David, 87
Pentecostals, xxi, 2, 27, 103–4
perestroika, 5, 120, 125, 129, 130,
    131, 134, 135, 137, 167, 169,
    171, 172–73, 174, 175, 179,
    218, 219, 221, 222, 259, 264,
    269, 270, 276, 280
  U.S. and, 137, 139
  Yeltsin and, 276
Perle, Richard, 65n2
  in Group B, 48

Pershing II missiles, 21n14, 50, 55, 67–68, 118
 in Germany, 31, 33
Petrov, Nikolai, xix, 7
PHARE. *See* Poland/Hungary Aid for Restructuring of Economies
Pioneer missiles. *See* SS-20 missiles
Pipes, Richard, 65n2, 109
 in Group B, 48
PLO, 156, 174
Poland, 19, 43, 65, 191, 193, 194, 195, 197–200, 202, 207, 209, 215, 218, 226, 248, 270, 277
 Afghanistan and, 76
 communism in, 202, 215, 277, 302
 democracy in, 75
 Gierek and, 207
 investment in, 195–96
 Roundtable Agreement, 194, 202, 215
 Solidarity, 19, 75, 194, 202, 294
 USSR and, 65, 75–76, 194n4, 239
Poland/Hungary Aid for Restructuring of Economies (PHARE), 205
Polianski, Dmitri, 313
Polozkov, Ivan, 315
Poltoranin, Mikhail, 313
Ponomarev, Boris, 151, 162–63
Ponomarev, Lev, 289, 291n38, 303n63
Popov, Gavriil, 286n29, 290, 317
Primakov, Evgeni, 132, 152n2, 157, 167, 170, 171, 309, 322n17, 325
proliferation, of nuclear weapons, 59

propaganda
 about imperialism, 151
 about Yeltsin, 315
 anti-USSR, 73
 Brezhnev and, 169
 of USSR, 32–34
Prunskene, Kazimira, 224
Putin, Vladimir, 45, 58, 147, 318, 322n17
 anti-terrorism and, 61
 Bush, G.W. and, xiv
 disarmament agreements and, xv

rational choice theory, 274
razriadka, 15
Reagan Doctrine, 186
Reagan, In His Own Hand (Skinner, et al.), 109
Reagan, Ronald, xix, 34, 41, 47, 48, 54, 56, 57, 64–66, 69–70, 94–110, 172, 184, 188, 191, 203, 204
 Andropov and, 2, 26–27, 41, 90–91, 105, 220
 as anti-Communist, 90, 172
 Brezhnev and, 41
 Carter and, 13
 Chernenko and, 41
 on communism, 18–19, 97
 Congressional Medal of Honor to, xiii
 democracy and, 59, 97
 détente and, 66, 94, 108
 diplomacy by, 7, 102
 Dobrynin and, xxi, 27, 39, 70
 Gorbachev and, xxiii–xxiv, 38–39, 106, 116, 117, 122–24, 139, 179, 180, 188, 222

Reagan, Ronald (*continued*)
  KAL-007 and, 87–89
  KGB and, 34, 34n25
  landslide victory of, 63
  linkage and, 16, 17
  Middle East and, 77, 166
  military and, 15–16
  negotiations and, 101–5
  new thinking of, xii–xiii
  planning of, 7–8
  realism of, 36
  reelection of, 34n25
  on SALT II, 16, 105
  SDI and, 93, 100
  strategy of, 24–25, 93–102
  third world and, 91, 166
  warmonger, cast as, 34, 155
  zero option by, 52
realism, 36
Reed, Thomas C., 96
refugees, in Hungary, 231
revanchism, in Russia, 61
Reykjavik summit, xxiii–xxiv, 8, 57,
    106, 122–25
  Western Europe and, 204
Rhodesia, 160–61
Rice, Condoleezza, xvi, xix, 3, 4,
    10, 255, 264, 266, 269, 270
*The Rise and Fall of the Great
    Powers* (Kennedy, P.), 47
Rodman, Peter, xxiii, 7
Romania, 134, 195–96, 198, 206,
    209, 231, 239
  in crisis, 242
  Olympics and, 208, 225
Romanov, Grigori, 145, 310, 312n9
Roosevelt, Franklin D., 275

Ross, Dennis, 236, 265
Rostow, Eugene, 65n2, 108–9n36
  in Group B, 48
Roundtable Agreement, 194, 202,
    215
Rowny, Edward, 65n2
  in Group B, 48
RC-135 airplane, 85
Russia
  autonomy of, 292
  China and, 62
  coup in, 138, 276, 296, 298–300,
    299n56, 304, 307, 321
  foreign policy and, 59
  military-industrial complex in,
    296, 298
  Muslim fundamentalists in, 60
  nationalism in, 60, 61
  in NATO, 295
  revanchism in, 61
  secessionism and, 224. *See also*
    Gorbachev, Mikhail; Putin,
    Vladimir; Russian Federation;
    Yeltsin, Boris
Russian Congress of People's Dep-
    uties, 298–99, 301
  elections to, 287–92
  Yeltsin and, 315
Russian Federation, 285, 291
  creation of, 3
  as sovereign state, 292
Rutskoi, Aleksandr, 316n14
RYAN-Nuclear Missile Attack, 72
Ryzhkov, Nicolai, 284, 315–16

Sadat, Anwar, 155, 156–57, 174
Sakharov, Andrei, 19, 172–73, 289,
    301

death of, 318
deportation of, 165
MDG and, 285, 286n29
Yeltsin and, 314
SALT. *See* Strategic Arms Limitation Treaty
SALT I, 1, 13–14, 67
détente and, 40–41
Reagan on, 16
suspension of, 12
verification in, 16–17, 17n6
SALT II, xxi, 16, 17, 19, 105, 108n36
as dead, 50
transparency of, 52
verification in, 52
"SALT II and the Growth of Mistrust," 159
sanctions, against USSR, 1, 12, 28, 28n21, 29
Sandinistas, 165, 173–74
Saudi Arabia, 154, 156, 167
Schifter, Richard, 243n18
Schmidt, Helmut, xx, 207
Scowcroft, Brent, 217n54, 225, 234, 235, 236
perestroika and, 137
SDI. *See* Strategic Defense Initiative
SDI-killers, 56
SDP. *See* Social Democratic Party
Seleznev, Gennadi, 309, 322
self-determination, 237, 238, 247, 256
September 11 attack, 300
Sestanovich, Stephen, 185–86
Shabad, Anatoli, 292n42

Shakhnazarov, Georgi, 143, 145, 178, 199, 221
Sharonin, Viacheslav, 72–73
Shcharansky, Anatoli, 89–90, 102–4
Shelepin, Aleksandr, 313
Shemiaev, Lev, 289
Shevardnadze, Eduard, xix, 120, 121, 168, 173, 175, 296, 227, 243
on Germany, 242n18, 244, 257, 258, 262, 271, 272
Gorbachev and, 144, 263, 265
Hungarian-Austrian border and, 257
resignation of, 296
Soviet press and, vii–viii
short-range nuclear forces (SNF), 211
Shultz, George, xvi, 10, 139
consensus-building by, 34
Gorbachev and, 116, 125–27
Gromyko and, 30, 89–90
KAL-007 and, 86, 88–90
NSDD-75 and, 98, 99n14
as secretary of state, 25, 54, 103–4
Silvanskaia, Marina, 198
Single European Act, 202, 203, 204n26, 206
Title III of, 205
Skinner, Kiron K., xii, xxii
Skuratov, Yuri, 321
SLBMs, 49
of USSR, 69
SLCM missiles, 49
Smirnov, Nikolai, 77–78

SNF. *See* short-range nuclear forces

Sobchak, Anatoli, 285, 286n29, 318

Sobianin, Aleksandr, 319

Social Democratic Party (SDP), 260

socialism, 134, 148, 150, 152n2, 154
   Brezhnev on, 184
   capitalism and, 114, 117
   crumbling of, 177
   dismantling of, 267–68
   eventual victory of, 38
   prestige of, 161
   questioning of, 175–76
   reform of, 5–6
   social-democratic concept of, 143
   third world and, 158, 169, 178

*Socialist Orientation of the Liber-
   ated Countries* (Brutents, et
   al.), 185

Soiuz-83 maneuvers, 74

Solidarity, 19, 75, 194, 202, 294

Solov'ev, Vladimir, 115

SORT. *See* Treaty on Strategic Offensive Reductions

South Yemen, 156, 165

"Soviet Capabilities for Strategic
   Nuclear Conflict, 1982–1992,"
   (CIA Estimate) 68

Soviet Congress of People's Deputies, 281, 285, 299

Soviet Union. *See* USSR

Staar, Richard, 65n2

Stalin, Joseph, xv, 38, 45, 114, 116,
   161, 196, 268, 275

Stankevich, Sergei, 283–85, 286n29,
   290, 317

Star Wars. *See* Strategic Defense
   Initiative

Starovoitova, Galina, 286n29, 317

State Committee for the State of
   Emergency (GKChP), 297–98

State Committee on Foreign Economic Cooperation (GKES),
   46

State Planning Committee, 44

Stepashin, Sergei, 322n17

Stevenson Amendment, 136

The Story of a Treacherous Deal
   (Primakov), 157

Strategic Arms Limitation Treaty
   (SALT), 94, 160. *See also*
   SALT I; SALT II

Strategic Arms Reductions Talks
   (START), x, xv, 1, 44, 52–53,
   53
   negotiations on, 30
   START I, 52–53, 58, 91, 138
   START II, 58, 325
   START III, 58.

Strategic Defense Initiative (SDI),
   1, 23, 44, 55–56, 70–72, 172
   ABM treaty and, 50
   Andropov on, 93, 101
   curtailment of, 53, 57
   Gorbachev and, 119
   MAD and, 100, 106
   non-influence of, 57
   Reagan and, 93, 105–7
   sharing of, 106
   USSR dissolution and, 147–48

Stroev, Egor, 309

Stroganov, Boris, 72

Strougal, Lubomir, 196

submarines, 69
Sudan, 156
Suez Canal, 155
Sumon, Petr, 321
superpowers, 40, 42, 52, 90
    détente of, 1, 180, 224
    Europe between, 191–227
    Middle East and, 154
    moves by, 101
    negotiations by, 94, 105
    nuclear weapons of, xv
    Soviet perspective on, 218–27
    third world and, 149, 162
    U.S. as, 219–20
    USSR as, 71, 114, 219, 271
Suslov, Mikhail, 45
Sverdlovsk Oblast, 278, 314
Syria, 156
    USSR and, 77–84, 174

tactical missiles, 52, 74
Talbott, Strobe, 52
tanks, 46
Taraki, Mohammad, 163, 164
Tarasenko, Sergei, 159
    on Germany, 241n17, 262, 263,
        265, 271
TASS, 88, 97
Teltschik, Horst, 214, 215, 220, 225,
        239, 243n18, 248, 250, 265
Ten-Point Plan, 234–35, 240, 268
    Genscher and, 243–44
    Gorbachev and, 240, 242, 243–4,
        261
    implementation of, 251–52
    Kohl and, 234–35, 242–44

terrorism, 60, 61
    as common enemy, 300
    Haig accusations about, 65–66
    September 11, 61, 300
Thatcher, Margaret, xii, xvi–xvii,
        xix, 2, 184, 204–5, 205n27,
        210, 220
    as anti-Communist, 172
    Bush, G.H.W. and, 9, 246
    Germany and, 210–11, 238, 239,
        246, 248, 249, 265, 266, 269
    Gorbachev and, 111, 132, 226,
        227n7, 267
    Mitterrand and, 246
theater nuclear forces (TNFs),
        21n13
third world, 149–81, 182
    alliances with, xiv
    Andropov and, 79, 178
    crises in, xxiii
    détente and, 155–65
    fatigue with, xiv, 5
    Gorbachev and, 173, 175, 179–
        81, 183
    Reagan and, 91, 188
    socialism and, 158, 169, 178
    superpowers and, 149, 182
    U.S. and, 153–55, 188
    USSR and, 41, 45, 46, 115, 129,
        149–81, 168, 182, 187, 189
Tiutchev, Fedor, 269
TNFs. See theater nuclear forces
Tolstoy, Leo, 115, 306
Topol-M ICBM system, 56
Tocqueville, Alexis de, 17
Treaty of Rome, 203, 247
Treaty on Strategic Offensive Re-
        ductions (SORT), 58, 59, 61

Trident SSBNs, 49, 67
Trident-2 SLBMs, 49
Troianovski, Oleg, 160, 178
Trube, Sergei, 289
Tsar Boris (NTV production), 313
Turkey, 81
Two-plus-Four plan, 232–33, 257, 265

Ugly American, The (movie), 182
Ukraine, 197, 223–24, 299
unification. *See* German unification
unilateral advantage, 15
unilateral military intervention, 61
UNITA rebels, 167
United Nations
    Gorbachev at, 111–112, 127–28, 146, 256
    Khrushchev at, 114
United States (U.S.)
    ABM treaty and, 59
    Afghanistan and, xxi, 186
    Angola and, 186
    Cambodia and, 186
    China and, 184
    containment policy of, 97, 108, 109, 155, 177
    diplomacy by, 155
    Egypt and, 184
    Europe and, 53, 202–3
    imperialism by, 66, 88, 117, 124, 169
    Iran and, 59, 61
    Israel and, 82, 154, 156
    Lebanon and, 82
    Nicaragua and, 186

perestroika and, 137
as superpower, 153–55, 219–20
third world and, 153–55, 182, 183, 188
USSR
    in Afghanistan, 1, 5, 11, 44–46, 52, 65–66, 75, 79, 128–31, 142, 146, 155, 162–65, 167–73, 180, 184–85, 188, 207
    in Africa, 13, 45–46, 66, 142, 152–53, 155, 160–62, 168, 178
    al-Asad and, 80
    China and, ix, 42–43, 62, 159–60, 187
    defense industry in, 42–43
    democracy and, 59, 179
    diplomacy by, 177
    dissolution of, 3, 56–57, 96–97, 109–10, 139–41, 147–48, 295–300, 299
    East Germany and, 75, 127, 138, 231
    Eastern Europe and, 112, 120, 132, 134, 138, 198–200, 221, 226–27
    economy in, 130, 137, 142, 144, 149, 167, 171–72, 177, 179, 184, 187, 193, 196, 219, 223, 263–64, 276
    Egypt and, 156, 156n7, 157n8, 165, 177
    elections in, 280–82, 287–91
    European integration of, 259
    as evil empire, 1, 2, 70, 88, 103, 127, 166, 172, 191, 307
    exports to, 12
    financial aid to, 232

Great Britain and, 132, 220
Grenada and, 32
human rights in, 114
in IMF, 139
in India, 177
Israel and, 174–75
KAL-007 and, 29
Latin America and, 66, 161, 168, 178
national liberation movements and, 65–66
negotiations with, 101–5
Nicaragua and, 173–74
Nixon and, 67
peace offensive, 210
Poland and, 65, 75–76, 194n4, 239
poverty in, 115
propaganda against, 73
propaganda of, 32–34, 169
sanctions against, 1, 12, 28, 28n21, 29
Syria and, 77–84, 174
third world and, 41, 45, 46, 115, 129, 149–82, 187, 189
Western Europe and, 131–32
in World Bank, 139. *See also* Andropov, Yuri; Brezhnev, Leonid; Gorbachev, Mikhail; Khrushchev, Nikita; Russia; Stalin, Joseph
United Workers Front, 282
Ustinov, Dmitri, 20, 66–68, 71–72, 75–76, 79–81
Afghanistan and, 163
KAL-007 and, 87–88
Utkin, Anatoli, xiii

Vance, Cyrus, 94, 160
Varennikov, Valentin, 163
velvet revolutions, 132, 134, 316
verification, of SALT II, 16–17, 17n6, 52, 105
Vietnam, 15, 129, 153, 183, 184
aftermath of, 31–32, 41
USSR and, 42, 52
Vietnam syndrome, 41, 167
Vladivostok Agreement, 16

Walesa, Lech, 277, 302
walk in the woods, 53
Walters, Vernon, 249, 270
Waltz, Kenneth, 274
Wandel durch Annäherung, 232
Wandel durch Kraft, 232, 261
War and Peace (Tolstoy), 306
war of the blind, 63
Warsaw Pact, 6, 204, 208, 222, 223, 224, 226, 239n13, 244, 268
on conventional arms, 137
democracy in, 2
disbanding of, 57, 138, 225, 307
maneuvers by, 74
NATO and, 42, 92
Warsaw Treaty Organization, 218, 221, 225
Watergate, 184
Weinberger, Caspar, 30, 34, 65, 66, 68
in Group B, 48
KAL-007 and, 88
Weingast, Barry, 274
Weizsäcker, Richard von, 134
Wenders, Wim, 269
West Germany, 207, 209, 212–15, 224, 227, 253, 266

West Germany (*continued*)
  eagerness of, 215
  nuclear weapons in, 248
  Thatcher and, 210–11
Western Europe, 192, 202–7
  diplomacy by, 220
  Eastern Europe and, 133, 219
  new thinking and, 131–32, 138,
    209, 213
  Reykjavik summit and, 204.
Wilson, Woodrow, 182
World Bank, 139
World Trade Organization (WTO),
  59
Wörner, Manfred, 268

Yakovlev, Aleksandr, 173, 198, 241,
    244, 258, 263, 271
  IMEMO and, 143–44
Yakunin, Gleb, 289, 291n38,
    303n63
Yalta, 209, 212
Yazov, Dmitri, 121, 173, 263
Yeltsin, Boris, xix, 7, 60, 140, 223,
    224, 242, 273–325
  as accidental rebel, 277–79
  activism of, 323n21
  as anti-Communist, 276–77, 288,
    290–95, 308, 314
  attempted suicide of, 279
  capitalism and, 276, 293–94
  as cold war's end catalyst,
    273–325

communism and, 301, 304,
    306–7, 325
  CPSU and, 277–78, 288n34,
    312–13
  democracy and, 276, 293–94,
    320–23, 325
  Democratic Russia and, 288–91
  elections and, 281–84, 294, 313–
    19, 321–22
  firings by, 311, 311n7
  Gorbachev and, 60, 136, 277–82,
    291, 297, 315, 316, 324
  liberalization under, 5–6
  nomenklatura and, 316
  perestroika and, 276
  propaganda about, 315
  Sakharov and, 314
Yom Kippur War, 38, 155
Yugoslavia, 198, 206
  NATO and, 52, 59

Zakharov, Gennadi, xii
Zaslavski, Ilia, 286n29, 318
Zelikow, Philip, xvi, xix, 4, 235,
    255, 264, 266, 269, 270
zero option, 52
Zhivkov, Todor, 75, 134, 222
Zia-ul-Haq, President, 129
Ziuganov, Gennadi, 319
Zoellick, Robert, 236, 252, 252n35,
    265
Zubok, Vladislav, xiii